The Iron Industry of the Weald

Henry Cleere and David Crossley

WITH CONTRIBUTIONS BY
BERNARD WORSSAM
AND MEMBERS OF THE
WEALDEN IRON RESEARCH GROUP

Leicester University Press 1985

First published in 1985 by Leicester University Press

Designed by Douglas Martin
Phototypeset in Linotron 202 Melior
Printed in Great Britain at The Bath Press, Avon

The publication of this book has been assisted by grants from the
Twenty-Seven Foundation and the Isobel Thornley Bequest Fund, to whom
the authors and the publisher express their thanks

British Library Cataloguing in Publication Data
Cleere, Henry
The iron industry of the Weald.
1. Iron industry and trade – England – Weald
(Kent) – History
I. Title   II. Crossley, D.W.
338.4'7669141'094223   HD9521.7.W4

ISBN 0-7185-1213-8

The Iron Industry of the Weald

This book is dedicated with admiration and affection to Fred Tebbutt, first chairman and current president of the Wealden Iron Research Group and field archaeologist without peer

Contents

Contents

List of illustrations

Abbreviations used in the notes and the Gazetteer

APC	*Acts of the Privy Council* (see Bibliography)
ASH	see ESRO
Bodleian	Bodleian Library, Oxford
BL	British Library (Egerton, Harleian, Lansdowne collections)
BWIRG	*Bulletin of the Wealden Iron Research Group*
DH	see ESRO
Dulwich MSS	Archives of Dulwich College, London
East India Co.	East India Company Records, India Office, London
ESRO	East Sussex Record Office, Lewes; main collections thus: (e.g.) Glynde . . .; those abbreviated are ASH: Ashburnham, and DH: Dyke Hutton
GMR	Surrey Archaeological Society, Muniment Room, Castle Arch, Guildford
Guildhall	Guildhall Library, London
Hereford RO	County Record Office, Hereford
HMC	Royal Commission on Historical Manuscripts, Calendars of MSS collections
KAO	Kent Archives Office, Maidstone
Lambeth Palace	Archives of the Archbishops of Canterbury, Lambeth Palace, London
L & P Henry VIII	*Letters and Papers, Henry VIII* (see Bibliography)
NGR	National Grid Reference (Ordnance Survey)
PRO	Public Record Office, London; followed by class number of document
Sc. Mus.	Science Museum Library, South Kensington, London
SAS	Sussex Archaeological Society MSS: now housed in East Sussex Record Office, Lewes, referred to with prefix ESRO SAS
SM:AM	Scheduled Ancient Monument, with county list number, e.g. SM:AM(Sx) 471
SNQ	*Sussex Notes and Queries*
Staffs RO	County Record Office, Stafford

Surrey RO	Surrey County Record Office, Kingston-on-Thames
SyAS	Surrey Archaeological Society
VCH	Victoria County History
WAM	Archives of the Dean and Chapter of Westminster
WIRG	Wealden Iron Research Group
WSRO	West Sussex Record Office, Chichester
Cal. Lib. Rolls	*Calendar of Liberate Rolls*, vol. II (1930), vols. IV–VI (1959–64)
Cal. Mem. Rolls	*Calendar of Memoranda Rolls (Exchequer), 1326–7* (1968)
Cal. Pat. Rolls, Ed. III	*Calendar of Patent Rolls, Edward III*, XI, 1358–61 (1911)

Introduction
and acknowledgments

During two distinct historical periods, the Weald of Kent and Sussex was the major iron-producing region in Britain. From the end of the first century BC until the end of the Roman occupation, iron was being produced on an industrial scale and traded widely both within the province of Britannia and in adjacent provinces of the Roman Empire. There was a hiatus in the Early Saxon period and only scattered ironmaking before the Norman Conquest. However, during the Middle Ages the industry began to expand again, to judge from the records of large-scale purchases of iron by the Crown.

The second major period of Wealden ironmaking began in the last decade of the fifteenth century, when the blast furnace was introduced from the Low Countries. During the sixteenth century, immigrant ironmasters working for the Crown and other landowners built the industry up until it was technologically the most advanced in Britain, so that by the end of the century the Weald was pre-eminent among the iron-producing regions of Britain. A slow decline set in during the seventeenth century, although the Wealden ironmasters maintained a monopoly of gun-founding. However, with the advent of the coke-fired blast furnace in 1709 the decline was irreversible, and one by one the remaining Wealden ironmasters withdrew, leaving their Midlands and Scottish rivals supreme. Nowadays, the Weald has reverted to agriculture and forestry, and the only surviving evidence of its great industrial past lies in a few great slag heaps from the Roman period and some picturesque hammer ponds. So total was the eclipse of the Wealden iron industry that diligent fieldwork is needed to understand the origins of place-names such as Furnace Field, Forge Farm and Cinder Mead.

The first serious attempt to trace the history and topography of the Wealden iron industry was that of the Reverend Mark Antony Lower, who published a series of papers in the early volumes of the *Sussex Archaeological Collections* in the first half of the nineteenth century. Fieldwork continued, usually on a local basis, and the work of James Rock and Herbert Blackman in the Battle-Brede area is especially worthy of notice. In the present century the first publication on the industry was *The Historical Geography of the Wealden Iron Industry* by Miss M. C. Delany (1923). In the following year Margaret Richards completed a doctoral thesis on the industry, but this received little attention until comparatively recently.

The most revered name in Wealden iron studies is that of Ernest

Straker. By profession a bookbinder, he dedicated many years to an intensive and systematic study of all the remains of the industry, the fruits of his work being published (at his own expense) in a remarkable study in field archaeology, *Wealden Iron* (1931). A sensitive and sympathetic account of this remarkable man at work by the late I. D. Margary, himself a distinguished field archaeologist who had more than a passing interest in the Wealden iron industry and who supported the fledgling Wealden Iron Research Group in every way, was published in *WIRG Bulletin, 3* (1972).

In the mid-1960s, Henry Cleere, who had just begun research on the Roman iron industry in the Weald, and David Crossley, an economic historian with a special interest in sixteenth- and seventeenth-century industry, both of whom were conducting excavations on ironmaking sites in the Weald, began to discuss the possibility of setting up a group to carry out fieldwork, excavations and documentary research. Encouraged by Ivan Margary, they issued a public invitation to archaeologists, local historians and others to attend a meeting at the Royal Pavilion, Brighton, on 20 April 1967. To their surprise, over 80 people responded to the invitation and, after hearing their proposals for an ambitious programme of work that would probably need at least ten years to complete, enthusiastically formed themselves into the Wealden Iron Research Group.

The Group was organized in a number of local teams, of which the Buxted group was initially the most active and imaginative. Organization of the work of the Group was quickly (and thankfully) transferred by the two founders to elected officers and committee, who organized the programme of fieldwork in regular 'forays', as they were christened by the Buxted group, published the twice-yearly *Bulletin*, and arranged regular meetings at which distinguished speakers lectured on different aspects of the Weald and on early ironmaking technology. The Group obtained a grant from the Carnegie (United Kingdom) Trust (through the Council for British Archaeology) in 1968 for the purchase of equipment, and in 1981 gained the BBC *Chronicle* Award for independent archaeological research.

One of the primary objectives of the Group from the outset was to publish a new study of the industry, half a century after the work done by Straker, Richards and Delany. This book was planned during the 1970s, and is essentially a team effort. Henry Cleere and David Crossley have taken responsibility for the chapters on the early and later periods respectively, and Bernard Worssam of the Institute of Geological Sciences, and a founder-member of the Group, has contributed the chapter on the geology of the Weald. The appendices are, respectively, a short account of the history and organization of the Group, which it is believed may be of use to others planning similar projects; the text of a paper which illustrates the working methods of the Buxted team in their study area, reproduced by permission of the Editor of the *Sussex Archaeological Collections*; and tables showing changes in prices in the industry between the sixteenth and the eighteenth centuries. The Gazetteer brings together the results of many hundreds of hours of fieldwork by members of the Group, and the field notes have been compiled by Margaret and Fred Tebbutt and Dot Meades. Joe Pettitt, originally Secretary of the Group, has kindly contributed towards the documentary entries for sites in the west of the Weald. The authors are grateful to many people, within and beyond the Group, for assistance while the book was being written. Many are acknowledged in the text, but particular mention should be made of the help of James Money and Anthony Streeten in making available the results of the Garden Hill excavation in advance of publication, Margaret Tebbutt's compilation of fig. 74, Peter Leach's work on site plans, figs. 28–9, 40, 42, 46, 65, Pam Combes' photographs of Wealden castings and Jeremy Hodgkinson's 'stop press' additions to the gazetteer of bloomeries. Brian Awty, Anthony Fletcher, Jeremy Goring, Dot Meades, Richard Saville and Fred Tebbutt have kindly read sections of the text. Colin Brent supplied numerous helpful references. We are grateful to Mrs M. James for giving access to the notes on John Browne assembled by her father, the late Mr R. M. Towes. To anyone whose assistance we have not specifically mentioned, we apologize. Material in Chapters 7–10 has been gathered during work towards a Ph.D. thesis at Sheffield University.

The present book is in no sense the last word on the Wealden iron industry: every chapter contains questions to which answers are still needed, questions, moreover, that in many cases arise out of work done by the Group in the last 16 years. But the Group continues to flourish, with over 100 members, and it publishes its *Bulletin*, now annually. The authors are fortunate in that this provides a channel in which material within this book may be supplemented and corrected as further research is done.

The 16 years' work that is reported in this book has only been possible as a result of assistance in cash and in kind from many organizations. The grant from the Carnegie (United Kingdom) Trust enabled the Group to provide itself early on with maps and surveying equipment. The excavations carried out by members of the Group were supported by grants from the Department of the Environment, the Iron and Steel Institute, the Carborundum Company, and the Hastings Museum.

Other research and experimental work benefited from the support of the Social Science Research Council, the Nuffield Foundation, the Sussex Archaeological Society (Margary Fund), the Sheffield University Research Fund, British Steel Corporation, the Historical Metallurgy Group, and Johnson Matthey & Co. Ltd. The County Councils of both East Sussex and West Sussex have offered practical help in the production of the Group's Bulletin, and their respective archaeological officers (Mr A. G. Woodcock and Mr F. G. Aldsworth) have been the source of much help and advice, as have the Director (Mr P. L. Drewett) and members of the Sussex Archaeological Field Unit. The staff of the Archives Offices at Lewes, Maidstone and Chichester have been of constant help. In particular we would thank Judith Brent and Christopher Whittick for their advice and encouragement. Finally, none of the work could have been carried out had it not been for the willingness of so many owners and tenants of land to grant permission for exploration and excavation. To all of these the debt of the Wealden Iron Research Group is profound.

HENRY CLEERE   DAVID CROSSLEY
Council for British Archaeology   *University of Sheffield*

June 1983

Chapter 1   The geology of Wealden iron

Bernard Worssam

1 Introduction

The Weald is usually thought of as the tract of country bounded by the Chalk escarpments of the North Downs to the north, the South Downs to the south, and that between Alton and Petersfield to the west. Except for the lower part of the Purbeck Beds, which belongs to the Jurassic, the rocks at surface in the Weald belong to the Cretaceous System (fig.1). They comprise the clays with thin limestones that form the Purbeck Beds, overlain by a thick group of sandstones and clays, the Wealden Beds, overlain in succession by the Lower Greensand, the Gault (clay), the Upper Greensand, and the Chalk. The Purbeck and Wealden Beds were deposited in fresh to brackish water, while the Lower Greensand and succeeding divisions were deposited beneath the sea. The Chalk is a soft white limestone and gives its name (in Latin, *creta*) to the whole system.

The rocks within the Weald have been brought to the surface by a huge upfold or anticline, the Wealden Anticline. Most of the fold has been removed during long-continued denudation, by processes of weathering and erosion, but its original size and shape can be inferred from the attitude of those rocks that remain.

The greater part of the country within the Chalk escarpments is occupied by the outcrop of the Wealden Beds, around which the Lower Greensand, Gault and Upper Greensand form relatively narrow encircling belts (fig.2). From the points of view of its distinctive type of landscape and the history of its settlement, it could be claimed that the Wealden Beds outcrop is the only part of the Weald worthy of the name, and indeed it was so regarded by Ernest Straker. The bulk of the Wealden iron industry was certainly based on this area, which provided its iron ore, but ironworking spread on to the Lower Greensand tract at the western end of the Weald, where streams provided a plentiful source of power for forges and some furnaces (fig.3).

The Wealden Anticline extends under the English Channel into northern France, where its eastern end forms the country inland from Boulogne known as the Boulonnais. The Wealden Beds there are quite thin, but a thicker development (up to 100m) of Wealden Beds is

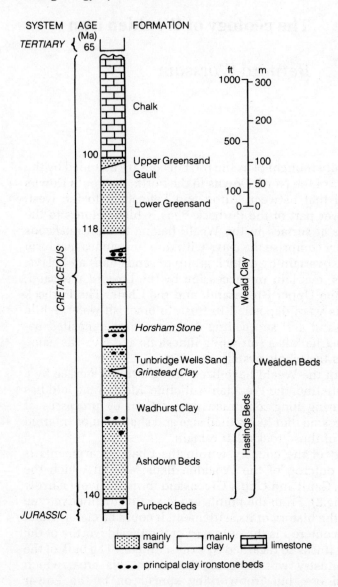

Fig.1 Generalized vertical succession of geological formations at outcrop in and around the Weald.

found farther to the south, in the Pays de Bray, between Dieppe and Beauvais. The extensive Chalk cover of northern France is there breached along an anticline trending north-west to south-east and about 80km long (as opposed to the 190km length of the Wealden

Anticline along the axis from Petersfield to Boulogne). It was Wealden rocks in Bray, fresh- to brackish-water sands and clays (Lorenz 1980: 455, 457), that supplied the iron ore to support an earlier example of the transition from bloomery to blast furnaces.

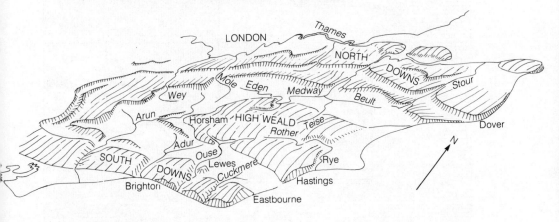

Fig.2   Relief of the Weald.

2   Geological history

The origin of the Wealden iron ore and its present-day distribution are dependent on the environment in which the rocks were formed, over a hundred million years ago (see fig.1), and on the stages by which the structure of the district has come to be expressed in the present-day landscape.

Each of the geological 'formations' shown in fig.1 is a reasonably distinctive group of mainly clay or mainly sand or sandstone beds, and these are the units that are shown on geological maps. During the Cretaceous period the part of the earth's crust that is now the Weald tended continually to subside, so that it was continually either under water or subject to flooding. The total thickness of sediments that accumulated in the central part of the Weald to form the Wealden Beds alone must have been at least 600m.

Throughout the deposition of the Wealden Beds, for the first 20 million years or so of the Cretaceous, the Weald was part of a vast freshwater-to-brackish swamp or lake. P. Allen (1981) has reconstructed its geography. Its northern limit lay somewhere to the north of the line of the present North Downs escarpment, and the London area formed low-lying land. To the south of the Weald the swamp extended across most of what is now the English Channel without

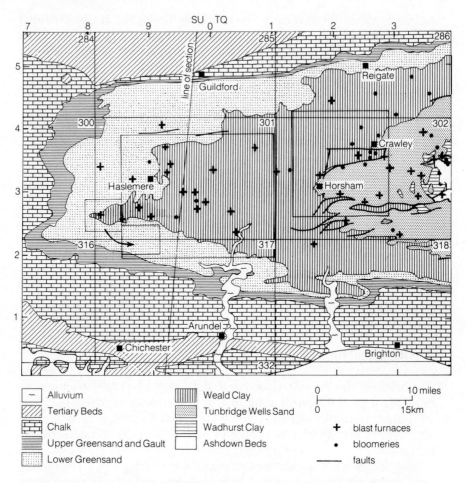

Fig.3   Sites of furnaces in relation to the geology of the western part of the Weald.
Rectangles numbered 284 upwards are Geological Survey 1in./1:50,000 map sheets;
smaller rectangles show areas of figs. 7 and 8.

quite reaching the present Normandy coast west of Le Havre, while an
arm of it extended south-eastwards through the Pays de Bray. Short
rivers drained into the swamp from the London area, a longer one
from Cornwall and Devon, and others from Brittany. They brought in
the deposits of mud, silt and sand that subsequently, compressed
under accumulations of later deposits, became layers of clay, siltstone
and sandstone. At first there was a predominance of silt and sand,
forming the Ashdown Beds, then an extensive lake in which the
Wadhurst Clay accumulated. Sandy deposits built out into the lake

gave the Tunbridge Wells Sand, while finally more prolonged subsidence of the whole area resulted in accumulation of the Weald Clay. The Ashdown Beds, Wadhurst Clay and Tunbridge Wells Sand are grouped together as the Hastings Beds.

The climate of Wealden times was warm. Fossil plant remains indicate that the swamp and its bordering lands supported a vegetation which consisted of primitive plants, namely gymnosperms, ferns and the horsetail, *Equisetum*; flowering plants did not appear until later in the Cretaceous. There may have been well-marked wet and dry seasons. Some of the commonest plant fossils are black, carbonized fern fronds. Harris (1981) has deduced that these are the debris of savannah fires. It was still the age of the dinosaurs. One of the larger ones, *Iguanodon*, was the first dinosaur to be described. Its remains were discovered near Cuckfield in about 1830 by Gideon Mantell, a Lewes doctor who contributed much to the beginnings of geological science.

After deposition of the Wealden Beds, subsidence extended across a wider area of south-east England, the sea broke into the swamp and the beds were buried beneath the marine sands and clays of the Lower Greensand, Gault and Upper Greensand, then in turn, as the sea spread widely across northern Europe during later Cretaceous times, these were overlain by the Chalk which slowly accumulated over 35 million years to attain an eventual thickness of over 300m.

At the end of the Cretaceous period, 65 million years ago, subsidence of the Wealden area gave place to uplift. A tendency to uplift must have prevailed throughout the succeeding Tertiary era, which lasted until a million years or so ago. Uplift has continued through most of the succeeding Quaternary era, the era of the ice ages, in which we live.

The central Weald emerged above sea level early in Tertiary times, for flint pebbles from the Chalk are found in abundance in the early Tertiary deposits of the London Basin. The folding of the Wealden Anticline probably took place principally in mid-Tertiary times, however, as a distant echo of the earth movements that further south in Europe were giving rise to the Alps.

3 Structure and denudation

The structure of the Weald is shown by the amount of inclination, or dip, of its strata. At the time of their deposition the beds must have been practically horizontal, whereas at the present day they dip northwards on the north side of the Weald, westwards at the west end, and southwards on the south side. Within this broad anticlinal structure there are smaller folds, as well as the abrupt breaks in continuity of the strata known as faults.

Using the geological maps of which figs.3 and 4 are simplified versions, and taking known thicknesses of the formations, sections across the Weald can be drawn as in fig.5, showing the structure to a depth of about 300m (1,000ft) below sea level. The Purbeck Beds and the Hastings Beds in the central part of the Weald are much faulted, but the faults do not continue far into the Weald Clay. Because the vertical scale in fig.5 is about ten times the horizontal, the steepness of dips is much exaggerated. In reality the general or regional dip of the northern flank of the Wealden Anticline is only about 1° and that of the southern flank about 3°. These dips would be sufficient, however, to have brought the top of the Chalk to an altitude of some 970m (3,200ft) above OD along the crest of the anticline. The central Wealden summits of the present day are little above 240m above OD, about the same height as the summits of the North and South Downs. This gives some measure of the amount of denudation that the Weald has suffered since the early Tertiary.

The denudation of the Weald has been brought about by its rivers transporting the debris of weathering out to sea, eroding their beds and their banks in so doing, so that deeper and deeper layers of the Wealden structure have been revealed. Nearly all Wealden rivers rise near the central axial line of the Weald and follow short courses northwards or southwards. These are courses that would have been taken by streams draining the flanks of an anticlinal fold such as that of the Weald on its first emergence above the sea. The present day rivers may, therefore, have originated as long ago as the early Tertiary. Whether they are indeed so ancient or whether the sub-aerial denudation of the Weald was interrupted in late Tertiary to early Quaternary times by an incursion of the sea are questions that were raised by the original geological survey work of Topley (1875), received thorough discussion from Wooldridge and Linton (1955), and are still far from being settled (Worssam 1973; Jones 1980). Whatever the detailed course of events, however, it is true enough to say that the general effect of denudation has been gradually to etch out the landscape so that outcrops of harder rock, notably sandstone formations and the Chalk, stand out to form ranges of hills, while the softer clay formations form vales.

In the central Weald the headstreams of most rivers are incised into narrow steep-sided valleys locally termed ghylls. These could well have resulted from intensified stream erosion during the last glacial stage of the Quaternary. Easily dammed, they have helped to provide

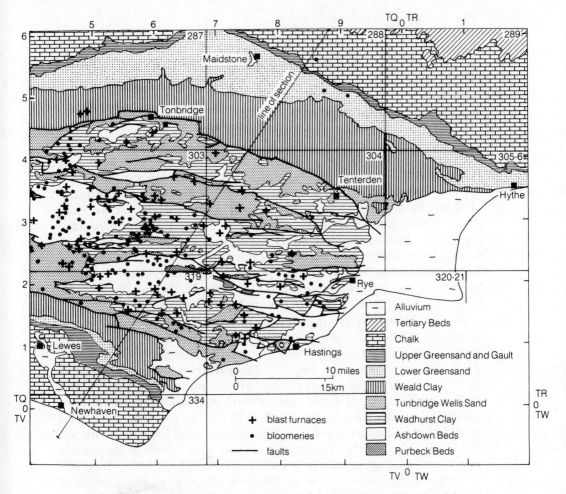

Fig.4   Sites of furnaces in relation to the geology of the central to eastern part of the Weald.

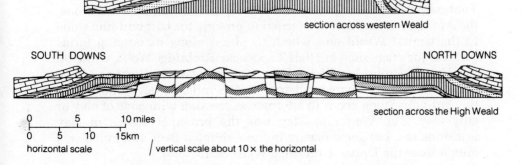

Fig.5   Sections across the western Weald (fig.3) and the High Weald (fig.4).

the water power needed by the iron industry, while the deeply cut stream beds must have aided prospecting for ore.

4   The landscape of the Weald

Fig.2 gives a much generalized bird's-eye view of the Weald, showing its main physical features. The outcrop of the Purbeck Beds and Hastings Beds makes a generally elevated tract of country, the High Weald, bounded on the east by the coast at Hastings, and northwards of there by Romney Marsh; it extends westwards as far as Horsham. The limestones of the Purbeck Beds, in the centre of this tract, were formerly worked for lime-burning and for building stone. Some clay ironstone occurs towards the top of the formation. West of Royal Tunbridge Wells the Tunbridge Wells Sand displays three sub-divisions, from below upwards the Lower Tunbridge Wells Sand, Grinstead Clay, and Upper Tunbridge Wells Sand (fig.1).

Being relatively rigid strata, cramped into the core of the Wealden Anticline when the main movement of compression took place, the Purbeck Beds and Hastings Beds yielded to the stress by undergoing displacement along faults. Most of the faults run east–west. Because of this faulting the outcrops of the various formations, in particular that of the Wadhurst Clay, have a very disjointed appearance on small-scale maps such as figs.3 and 4. In fact, in much of the central Weald the major faults are over 1.5km apart, and between them are tracts of only gently dipping strata, so that given a reasonably large-scale geological map (one inch to a mile or 1:50,000 or larger) it is rarely difficult to follow in the field the run of the geological boundaries.

Each of the formations tends to have a characteristic type of landscape: thus much of the Wadhurst Clay outcrop is covered by pasture or woodland; on the Ashdown Beds south of East Grinstead is the wide area of heathland known as the Ashdown Forest; the Lower Tunbridge Wells Sand includes a development of massive sandstone, the Ardingly Stone, that is quarried to provide the best building stone in the central Weald and which in places along its outcrop forms picturesque crags such as High Rocks near Tunbridge Wells; while on the Upper Tunbridge Wells Sand outcrop east of Horsham is St Leonard's Forest, where sandstone beds similar to but thinner than the Ardingly Stone occur in alternate succession with beds of clay or silty clay. The Wadhurst Clay was the principal source of clay ironstone ore, but some occurs in the Ashdown Beds and much was mined from the Upper Tunbridge Wells Sand.

The outcrop of the Weald Clay is a lowland that can be called the Low Weald. It is broadest in the western part of the Weald, west of Horsham. On the north side of the Weald the lowland is 6–8km wide, extending eastwards to the northern edge of Romney Marsh. On the south side of the Weald the Low Weald is a less well-marked feature of the landscape. As well as clay, the Weald Clay includes thin layers of sandstone and of shelly limestone. The latter, composed largely of the remains of fresh- to brackish-water snail shells, is known geologically as Paludina Limestone and locally by names such as Bethersden Marble and Sussex Marble. The Weald Clay also includes extensive deposits of clay ironstone. A prominently developed hard flaggy sandstone near the base of the Weald Clay in the western part of the Weald is the Horsham Stone. It forms an escarpment at its outcrop, and this is indicated as a V-shaped ridge to the west of Horsham in fig.2. The narrow westernmost prolongation of the Low Weald south of Haslemere (fig.3) is the Vale of Fernhurst.

The Lower Greensand is a varied group and includes a number of distinct formations. Its escarpment reaches its greatest height towards the western end of the Weald, in the summits of Leith Hill, on the west side of the Mole Valley, and Black Down, north of the Vale of Fernhurst (fig.2). On the south side of the Weald the escarpment peters out east of the Adur valley, the Lower Greensand as a whole becoming quite thin between there and the coast at Eastbourne.

Between the Lower Greensand and the Chalk escarpment lies the Gault Clay vale known as the Vale of Holmesdale on the north side of the Weald. The Upper Greensand thickens westward of Reigate and builds a prominent escarpment at Selborne at the western end of the Weald, where it includes the rock types described as 'freestone' and 'malm' by Gilbert White in his *Natural History of Selborne* (1788). The Upper Greensand thins eastwards on the south side of the Weald.

5 Iron ore in the Weald

Rocks potentially of use as iron ore occur both in the 'solid' geological formations of Cretaceous age shown in fig.1 and in the relatively recent Quaternary or 'drift' deposits of the Weald. The ore on which the Wealden blast furnace industry was based was undoubtedly clay ironstone from the Wealden Beds. While most bloomeries also used this, it seems possible that some made use of a concretionary ironstone formed by weathering processes taking place at the present day in the subsoil and known by local names such as shrave or crowstone. A third possible source of ore is ferruginous sandstone occurring in the Lower Greensand. A fourth is ironstone found locally in the Clay-with-flints, a drift deposit on the Chalk of the North Downs.

(A) CLAY IRONSTONE

Clay ironstone generally occurs as nodules, bun-shaped lumps usually about 5 to 25cm in diameter, but it can also form layers, from 2cm or so up to as much as 0.6m thick. It occurs interbedded with the clays, silts and fine-grained sandstones of the Wealden Beds. It is a hard, pale grey, fine-grained rock. Its main constituent is ferrous carbonate, $FeCO_3$, in the form of the mineral siderite. This mineral contains up to 48 per cent by weight of iron (Fe). Because of its high content of iron, the rock is noticeably heavy by comparison with more common sedimentary rocks. The density of siderite, 3.8, is nearly half as much again as that of limestones, i.e. pale grey rocks formed predominantly of calcium carbonate, $CaCO_3$, of density 2.71, and which clay ironstones, at least in the fresh state, superficially resemble.

An alternative name for clay ironstone is siderite mudstone. In these names the term 'clay' or 'mudstone' refers to the grain size of the rock (a majority of particles less than 0.0039mm in diameter), without implying the presence of clay or mud as an essential constituent, though as a result of the mode of origin of the rock it happens that some clay is commonly present as an impurity.

Clay ironstone has a minutely crystalline structure. This shows in thin slices of the rock examined under a microscope as a mosaic of colourless rhomb-shaped crystals. As well as ferrous carbonate (and some clay minerals), clay ironstones can also contain small proportions of calcium carbonate, magnesium carbonate ($MgCO_3$) and manganese carbonate ($MnCO_3$). These substances are important in iron smelting because they can act as fluxes.

Like the clay and the silt with which it is associated, the iron in clay ironstones would have been transported into the Wealden basin of deposition by the rivers of Cretaceous times, and these in turn would have derived their burden of sediment from the weathering and erosion of the lands bordering the basin.

The catchment area of rivers draining into the Wealden Basin would in some parts have been formed of clays of Jurassic age, newly uplifted and exposed to denudation, in others (e.g. the London area) of much older (Devonian) red sandstones. Iron is present in both rock types, in clay minerals and to a minor extent as pyrite (iron sulphide) in the clays, and giving their red colour to the red sandstones. Soil processes acting on these diverse rock types would have made the iron available for transport by converting it to iron oxides within the very fine-grained to amorphous mixtures of hydrated iron and aluminium oxides ('sesquioxides') that occur in almost all soils, or, in waterlogging conditions, removing it in solution in the ferrous state. In accounting for the occurrence of clay ironstone in the Wealden Beds the problem is therefore not so much one of the source of the iron as of the circumstances in which it was transported and then concentrated in the newly formed sediments.

The clay and silt particles would have been carried along in the waters of the streams that entered the Wealden basin of deposition, to fall to the bottom as the currents bearing them along lost their momentum.

The iron had a number of possible methods of transport. As the ferrous ion, Fe^{++}, in solution (an ion is an atom or group of atoms that has lost or gained one or more electrons and as a result is positively or negatively charged), iron can be transported for long distances in solutions that are slightly acidic and reducing. The water of Wealden rivers may well have been of such character, rendered acidic by the decay of vegetation. Precipitation of iron as ferric hydroxide, $Fe(OH)_3$, may then have taken place when the river waters entered an open lake, the resultant oxygenation removing some of the organic matter and so rendering the water less acidic. Alternatively, if the iron were in the form of ferric oxide in suspension as an iron colloid, its transport could have continued in the oxygenated water, until its deposition took place along with that of the clay particles.

As deposits of mud built up. on a lake bottom they may have incorporated some organic matter and would have trapped some of the lake water. Within the mud, carbon dioxide produced by oxidation of organic matter could have reacted with the iron oxide or hydroxide to form iron carbonate. With continual deposition of mud the pressure on its lower layers increased so that, at possibly 1m or less below the lake floor, water began to be expelled upwards from the sediment, the mud began to harden into clay, and iron carbonate solutions, becoming saturated, began to crystallize (see Ho and Coleman 1969).

The crystallization of iron carbonate may have started at widely spaced centres, around scattered tiny shell fragments or the like. Fine laminae of quartz silt can be seen to continue undisturbed through some nodules, giving an indication of the slowness of their growth. Most nodules also contain a little interstitial clay. Growth would have stopped when all the iron carbonate available became used up. This manner of growth explains the ovate form of most nodules, flattened along the vertical axis, which was the direction of greatest pressure. It also explains the sharp contact against the surrounding clay that most nodules show. Ions present in lesser amount in the lake water or exchangeable cations in clay minerals would have contributed the small amounts of such substances as calcium carbonate and magnesium carbonate found in some clay ironstones.

The suggestion that the crystallization of the carbonate took place beneath the surface of the sediment on a lake floor accords with the view expressed by J. H. Taylor (1969: 180) that the stability field for iron carbonate is a limited one and the necessary pH-Eh conditions probably occur more commonly below the sediment-water interface than above it. The same view is taken by Curtis *et al.* (1975). These authors, by separately analysing 11 successive layers within a 4cm thick clay ironstone bed in the Coal Measures of Yorkshire, found that it varied in composition from the centre, where the iron carbonate was relatively rich in manganese, to its top and bottom surfaces, where the carbonates were richer in calcium and magnesium. The formation of the bed may have been long-continued, starting soon after deposition of the mud but with the outermost carbonate layers perhaps only precipitated after burial beneath hundreds of metres of later-deposited sediment. From studies of carbon-isotope ratios Curtis *et al.* (1972) concluded that the principal source of the carbon in siderite nodules is organic matter.

The production of iron carbonate at certain levels in the Wealden Beds can perhaps best be attributed to the particular abundance of organic matter in certain environments, for example in clays on the outer fringes of sandy deltas. Broadly speaking, each major occurrence of clay ironstone does in fact occur in clays in proximity to developments of sandstone, namely in the Wadhurst Clay just above the sandy top Ashdown Beds, in the lower Weald Clay fringing the Horsham Stone, and in the upper Weald Clay of the western Weald in association with a group of thin sandstone beds.

A type of Wealden clay ironstone that appears to form layers of greater than usual lateral extent, perhaps continuous for several kilometres, is essentially a quartz siltstone into which a siderite solution appears to have infiltrated and crystallized between the quartz grains. Rock of this type forms layers from 0.2m up to 0.6m thick. As an ore, it would have been of poorer quality than ironstone occurring as nodules, because of its high content of silica. The analysis of one such layer, from Broadfield Forest near Crawley (Worssam and Gibson-Hill 1976: 78), showed 22.43 per cent SiO_2, compared with an average SiO_2 content around 8 per cent for nodular clay ironstone. In the former most of the SiO_2 would have occurred as quartz grains whereas in the latter most of it would have been combined with the aluminium oxide of the analysis in the form of clay minerals. The disadvantage of poor quality might well, however, have been outweighed by the greater ease of mining such beds, owing to their greater continuity.

Within the Wadhurst Clay are thin layers of limestone composed of closely-packed drifted shells of a small species of bivalve, now referred to the genus *Neomiodon* but formerly known as *Cyrena*, hence the name 'Cyrena' limestone. In some layers near the base of the formation siderite has crystallized in the interstices between the shells; they thus constitute a calcareous shelly ironstone which must have been of value as a flux.

Sweeting (1925) has recorded gypsum (calcium sulphate) as present in cavities and in veins traversing Wadhurst Clay ironstone nodules. Its production must have long postdated the formation of the nodules, and may even be a result of recent weathering. Calcium sulphate has also been recorded in ores used at Panningridge (Tylecote 1972).

Some clay ironstone nodules are formed of sphaerosiderite. The iron carbonate in these, instead of occurring as interlocking crystals, has crystallized as minute spherical aggregates (about 0.2mm in diameter) with a radiating structure, more or less closely scattered in a clay matrix. Nodules of this type can contain 20–40 per cent of clay. They would make ore of very poor quality and there is no evidence that they have been worked. In hand specimen they can, however, superficially resemble normal clay ironstones but have a finely granular or 'sugary' rather than a smooth appearance on broken surfaces. Such nodules occur at a distinct level in the lower part of the Weald Clay near Crawley (Worssam 1972), and sphaerosiderite is common in the 'Fairlight Clays' of the lower part of the Ashdown Beds on the coast near Hastings. The mineral seems to have formed under shallow-water, intermittently emergent conditions of deposition.

(B) SHRAVE

Under the action of weathering, which is effective down to 3m or so below the present-day ground surface, siderite becomes oxidized to limonite (ferric oxide), which looks like and is chemically similar to the rust that forms on iron. Weathering commonly starts on the outside of a nodule of clay ironstone and works towards its centre, forming successive crusts of limonite, that readily break off. When the eighteenth-century ironmaster John Fuller wrote that they reckoned any mine better for having the 'shuck' upon it (Saville 1979), he must have meant this coating of iron oxide.

Where, as is common in the Weald, soils are poorly drained and there is alternate waterlogging and drying-out, iron oxides produced by weathering are mobilized in the presence of acid soil waters in wet periods and precipitated when the soil dries out. The reaction tends to be irreversible and leads to the formation of the iron pan known to farmers as shrave, chevick (in Surrey), crowstone (in Kent), or ragstone or puddingstone (in west Sussex). On clays with only a moderate amount of iron, the shrave may occur as scattered soft patches a centimetre or so in diameter, or be noticeable merely as iron-mottling. On outcrops of ironstone beds, however, where the soil contains abundant limonite fragments, their cementing-together can result in the formation of lumps of iron pan with high iron contents – a sample from an ironstone outcrop near Crawley (Worssam and Gibson-Hill 1976: 78) contained nearly 40 per cent Fe_2O_3. On river terraces in the Weald the greater freedom of water percolation in the gravel than in clay soils allows the formation of large masses of iron pan, attaining 0.6m or so in thickness and 2m or more in length. Where the gravel contains pebbles of limonite high iron contents can result. The erratic nature of the occurrence of iron pan would probably have rendered the material unsuitable as an ore, however, except locally for bloomeries. It seems to have been used in the medieval bloomery at Thundersfield Castle, Horley (Hart and Winbolt 1937). In the case of the iron pan in river gravels, the high content of silica owing to the presence of siltstone and sandstone as well as ironstone pebbles would have been an added disadvantage.

(C) LOWER GREENSAND IRONSTONE

Topley (1875) suggested as possible sources of ore the brown sandy ironstone or 'carstone' that occurs in the Folkestone Beds (a sand formation in the Lower Greensand), and quartzose sands with abundant brown limonite grains that are particularly well developed in the Sandgate Beds (another Lower Greensand formation) near Midhurst in Sussex. The proportion of silica in the form of quartz sand in carstone is very high, but nevertheless it may have been the ore used in a bloomery at Chapel Farm, Lenham Heath, Kent, on the Folkestone Beds outcrop (Miles 1974). The limonite sand near Midhurst was investigated by Lamplugh *et al.* (1920: 228–9) and Hallimond (1925: 84, 112). The former quoted two analyses, one giving iron 23 per cent and 'insoluble matter' (presumably silica) 56.3 per cent, the other, iron 16 per cent and 'insoluble gangue' 70 per cent. There is no evidence that this sand has ever been worked.

(D) IRONSTONE IN THE CLAY-WITH-FLINTS

On the crest of the North Downs between Maidstone and Ashford are patches of sand with, in places, abundant fragments of a soft fine-grained sandy ironstone. Topley (1875) suggested that this could have provided a source of ore, but only recently, with the discovery of bloomery slag on the summit of the Downs above Hollingbourne (Pettitt 1973), has evidence come forward that it may actually have been used.

6 Distribution of iron-ore workings

Depending on the geological horizon of the principal clay-ironstone beds (fig.1), iron-ore workings are clustered in three separate areas of the Weald. These are: 1) the High Weald eastward of West Hoathly, where Ashdown Beds and Wadhurst Clay ore was worked (fig.6); 2) the Horsham-Crawley area at the western end of the High Weald and on adjacent parts of the Weald Clay outcrop, working iron ore from the Upper Tunbridge Wells Sand and the lower part of the Weald Clay (fig.7 and fig.6 (inset)); and 3) the western end of the Weald (fig.8), where the industry utilized clay ironstone from near the top of the Weald Clay.

The location of iron-ore deposits was only one among many factors governing the siting of furnaces, and the clustering of furnaces into three corresponding areas is less clearly marked (figs.3, 4). None the less the course of the industry in a particular area must to a considerable extent have been governed by the quality and availability of local ore supplies. Thus the High Weald eastward of West Hoathly contained the majority of ironworks at all periods; furnace sites are closely spaced, with bloomeries more numerous than blast furnaces. In the Horsham-Crawley area furnace sites are more widely spaced, and blast furnaces and bloomery sites are about equally numerous. Working was well established here in Roman times, but the blast furnace industry did not outlast the seventeenth century. In the western end of the Weald there was very little ironworking before the sixteenth century and bloomeries are consequently few, but some of the blast furnaces persisted until late in the eighteenth century.

7 Minepits and marlpits

So far as evidence from Romano-British sites goes, it seems that ore was then dug from shallow quarries or from bowl-shaped pits. At

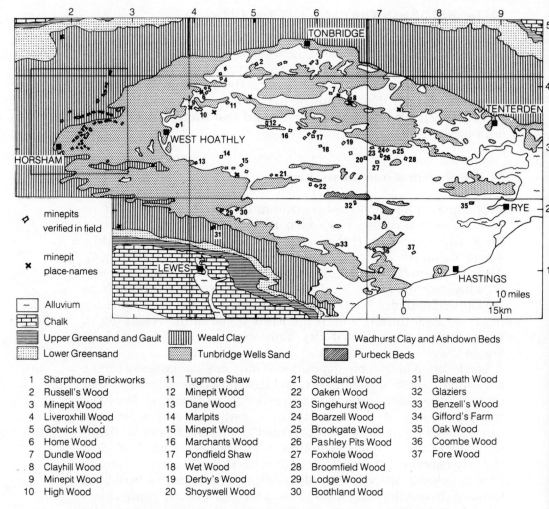

Fig.6 Minepits in the Weald eastward of Horsham. For names in the Horsham–
Crawley area (outlined), see fig.7.

Petley Wood (Lemmon 1951–52; Cleere 1975) iron-ore pits were
discovered, some as large as 15–20m diameter by 15m deep, tapering
towards the bottom.

In the westernmost part of the Weald the principal if not the only
method of obtaining ore was by means of minepits. To judge from the
appearance of worked ground at the surface, and from contemporary
descriptions, these appear to have been vertical shafts, about 1.8–
2.4m in diameter, that were sunk to the seam or layer of ore and there

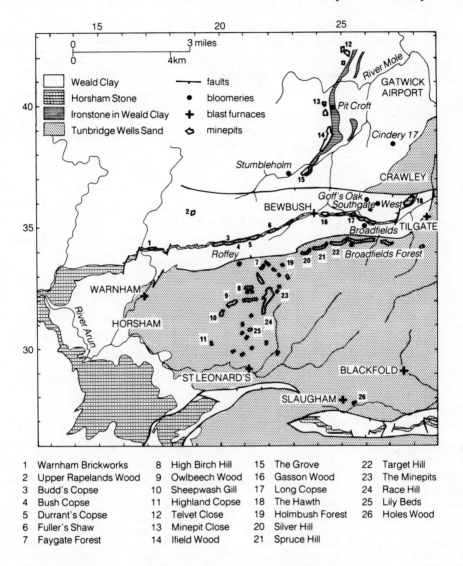

Fig.7 Minepits in the Horsham–Crawley area, based on Worssam 1972: figs.2 and 3 (by kind permission of the Council of the Geologists Association).

1 Warnham Brickworks	8 High Birch Hill	15 The Grove	22 Target Hill
2 Upper Rapelands Wood	9 Owlbeech Wood	16 Gasson Wood	23 The Minepits
3 Budd's Copse	10 Sheepwash Gill	17 Long Copse	24 Race Hill
4 Bush Copse	11 Highland Copse	18 The Hawth	25 Lily Beds
5 Durrant's Copse	12 Telvet Close	19 Holmbush Forest	26 Holes Wood
6 Fuller's Shaw	13 Minepit Close	20 Silver Hill	
7 Faygate Forest	14 Ifield Wood	21 Spruce Hill	

widened out to take as much ore as could safely be got without the sides caving in. The pit would then be filled with the material dug from a new pit a short distance away. They were known as minepits because the local name for iron ore was 'mine'. This method of excavation was in use for coal mining up to the seventeenth century

Fig.8   Minepits in the western Weald, based on Worssam 1964: figs.2 and 3 (by kind permission of the Council of the Geologists Association).

1	Hopkiln Reeds	13	Killinghurst Great Copse	25	Hogs Hill Copse	37	Bullocks Copse
2	Minepit Copse	14	Furnace Moor	26	Dale Copse	38	Quell Wood
3	Hambledon Hurst	15	Bushman's Copse	27	Furnace Wood	39	Windfall Wood
4	Vann Copse	16	Lambels Copse	28	Leazers Wood	40	High Field Row
5	Blunden's Wood	17	Dickhurst Great Copse	29	Willard Copse	41	Lord's Wood
6	Denyards Copse	18	Gospelgreen Copse	30	Turner's Copse	42	Colehook Common
7	Holmen's Grove	19	Boxalland Copse	31	Whitter's Copse	43	Hammond's Wood
8	Pond Copse	20	Jay's Copse	32	Henley Copse	44	Arundel Holt
9	Stroud Wood	21	Newland Copse	33	Verdley Wood	45	Gerrards Rough
10	Fowlshatch Copse	22	Perry Copse	34	Lower Common Wood	46	Westlands Farm
11	Frillinghurst Wood	23	Sopers	35	Copygrove Copse	47	Willets Farm
12	Newhouse Great Copse	24	Bridge Reeds	36	Fulwick Copse		

in the Midlands and north of England. The pits in the coalfields were known as 'bell pits' from their widening-downwards shape.

From consideration of the dip of strata in relation to the width of tracts of worked ground, the depth attained by the deepest minepits can be estimated as about 12m. Because clay ironstone is broken into small fragments disseminated through the clay subsoil for 1m–1.5m or so below the ground surface, there would be little ore worth digging at depths less than say 1.2m. This gives some point to the remark of Ray (1674: 125) referring to iron-working in the Hastings Beds area, that 'The Iron-mine lies sometimes deeper, sometimes shallower in the Earth from 4ft to 40 and upward'.

Although the worked ground may have been reasonably well levelled-off after the pits had been dug and filled, subsequent compaction of the filling would have led to the mined ground presenting its present-day appearance of being pock-marked with saucer-shaped craters, 1.8–2.4m in diameter and up to 0.6m deep. Because the soil is an impermeable clay, the craters hold pools of water in the winter months; in the summer they dry out, but have a characteristic lining of grey, mud-coated dead leaves and twigs. Such ground serves well enough for the coppiced hazel woodland that is still widespread in west Surrey and Sussex. In some woods in the western Weald the craters are closely spaced, with rims but a foot or two apart, and the ground looks as if it has suffered a bombardment – Minepit Copse (SU 950 370) (fig.8), is a particularly striking instance; in other woods the ground is merely slightly uneven, with craters scattered at wide intervals. For arable farming, or for laying down for pasture, further levelling must have been necessary.

The surface evidence for the form of minepits in the western Weald seems reasonably clear, even though it has not been confirmed by actual excavation. As regards the central Weald, Topley (1875: 334) wrote that the 'bell-pits', as he called them, of that area were about 6ft (1.8m) in diameter at the top, rarely more than 20ft (6.1m) deep, and sometimes were connected by levels. Pits of this description, but as much as 15m deep and widened out to 6m across at the bottom, certainly were in operation in the early nineteenth century to obtain limestone from the Purbeck Beds, on the testimony of men who had worked in them (Topley 1875: 384).

Wadhurst Clay minepits were actually seen in section on the 20m-high south face of the Sharpthorne Brickworks in 1983. The face cut cleanly through 12 pits, irregularly spaced along a distance of 120m, and recognizable by their loosely-packed filling of angular clay fragments. They were 3 to 4m wide and vertically sided, not undercut at the bottom. The deepest ones reached about 12m below ground surface. Each intersected a number of thin (3 to 15cm) ironstone seams; a total thickness of 20 to 40cm of ironstone would have been obtained from a 12m deep pit. A piece of timber recovered from one mine-shaft (Swift and Tebbutt 1983) has given a radiocarbon date of AD 1200 ±50 years.

In the Wadhurst Clay tract the economics of ore extraction may have been bound up with those of marl digging. The use of 'marl' as a top-dressing on fields was widespread in many parts of England from the thirteenth century or even earlier (Straker 1931a: 106; Stebbing 1941), until late in the nineteenth century. The practice does not seem to have been adopted uniformly across the Weald. Marlpits and marlpit place-names are not found on the Weald Clay outcrop of west Surrey, though they abound on the geologically similar Weald Clay of Kent. Marl digging was intensive in the central Weald, where pits are found on both the Wadhurst Clay and the Grinstead Clay. Typically, marlpits are wide, open excavations 15m or more in diameter and 2m or more in depth. Many are water-filled and to a casual observer might appear simply as ponds. They are commonly in the corners of fields or just inside woods. One often finds a group of four or more closely set ponds, separated by clay baulks a metre or two wide. These could have resulted from intermittent digging, the earlier pits being already water-logged when digging was resumed. Some marlpits are very large. Straker (1931a: 263) cites records of an excavation in the western side of the angle in the Tunbridge Wells to Crowborough road at Steel Cross (TQ 530 317), fully 12–15 acres in extent, dug for marl in the seventeenth century by a licence which included the right to sell the mine. The site is on the basal Wadhurst Clay (Bristow and Bazley 1972: 68).

The term 'marl' is used nowadays only for clays that are distinctly calcareous, but the marl from Wealden marlpits must have been a material containing little or no calcium, and though hard when freshly dug would have weathered rapidly to a stiff and tenacious clay. Pits sited close to the base of the Wadhurst Clay would encounter most clay ironstone, which must then have proved a valuable by-product.

How seriously marling was taken in the seventeenth century is shown by vol. I of the Royal Society's *Philosophical Transactions* (1665: 91–3), where it is reported that a committee set up to enquire into current practice in agriculture had decided to send out a questionnaire to 'persons Experienced in Husbandry all over England, Scotland and Ireland ...' The first five questions enquired as to kinds of soils, of manure, duration of fallow and so on, while the sixth required answers as to the depth of 'Marl' from the surface, its thickness, colour, time of year for its application, and the number of loads applied to the acre, all as if marling was as much an accepted part of farming practice as is the application of artificial fertilizers today. By Topley's (1875) time of writing, marl was still being dug, though rarely, and only for application to light land; the general opinion was that it was worthless. The application to the light soils on sandstone divisions of the Hastings Beds may have been the chief value of marling in the Weald, for a stiffening of the topsoil by addition of clay probably greatly helped their moisture retention. This might explain the frequent concentration of the pits on the Grinstead Clay (e.g. Bristow and Bazley 1972: 93, 94) and close to the top of the Wadhurst Clay, for carriage on to Tunbridge Wells Sand fields, and near the base of the Wadhurst Clay for spreading on fields of the Ashdown Beds outcrop.

8 Local details

(A) THE HIGH WEALD EASTWARD OF WEST HOATHLY

The minepits shown in fig.6 are in the main those recorded in the explanatory memoirs to geological sheets 287, 303, and 304, notably by Dr C. R. Bristow and Dr R. A. Bazley. Sites given in the *WIRG Bulletin* are also included. It is perhaps because iron ore was a by-product of marlpits that areas of minepitted ground are more thinly scattered than further west. All the minepitted areas shown eastward of West Hoathly are on the Wadhurst Clay except those at Marlpits (4482 2856) and Glaziers (670 210), which are on Ashdown Beds, and minepits on the Weald Clay at Balneath Wood. Additional minepits on Wadhurst Clay, reported by Dr R. W. Gallois, are in Target Shaw (3550 3575), Minepit Wood (363 350), Bird's Eye Wood (357 338), Giffard's Wood (369 339), Sloe Garden Wood (3753 3214 to 3710 3177) and Pains Wood (379 292). Bazley (in Bristow and Bazley 1972: 27, 39) has noted that remains of old bell-pits are a feature of the Purbeck Beds outcrop, and that some of these were dug for clay ironstone, though the vast majority were for limestone.

For an area thought to have had Wadhurst Clay ironstone as its main source of ore, the high proportion of bloomeries on the Ashdown Beds outcrop, some 50 out of a total of 140 or so (figs.3 and 4), is remarkable. Clay ironstone may indeed occur more widely in the Ashdown Beds than the few recorded present-day exposures (Bristow and Bazley 1972: 51, 53, 56, 61, 63) would indicate. It is associated with thin layers of silty clay that occur at wide intervals in the general mass of sandstone. Perhaps the best exposure is in shallow pits (TQ

3980 3304), presumed to be worked for ironstone, near the western edge of Ashdown Forest (*ibid.*, 51). It is worth giving in full, the beds being listed in succession from the surface downwards:

	Thickness (m)
Flaggy orange-brown silty fine-grained sandstone	0.61
Blue-hearted siderite mudstone with dark brown exfoliation weathering	0.41
Interbedded orange-brown silt and silty sandstone	0.30
Evenly-laminated grey silt with included thin beds, 6 to 13mm, of siderite mudstone	1.21
Massive fine-grained greyish-white sandstone, patchily ironstained on irregular upper surfaces, forms floor of quarry	0.30

A clay seam at Nutley has the exceptional thickness of 7.6m. Probably the presence of ironstone in this clay was the reason for the siting of minepits at Marlpits (fig.6) (*ibid.*, 53).

Though there are numerous furnace sites in the southern part of the High Weald (geological sheets 319, 320), as well as extensive outcrops of the Wadhurst Clay, published reports of minepits are few. Dr Bristow has recently reported those at Lodge Wood (4420 1976 to 4460 1982) and in Boothland Wood (4695 2000), as well as the Weald Clay pits at Balneath Wood. White (1926: 20) noted that 'old workings' for iron ore abound in the Hawkhurst Common area north of East Hoathly, and in the woods south of Waldron and between Chiddingly and Horeham Road Station.

An area where records of minepits seem to be completely lacking is in the vicinity of Tenterden. Furnace sites also are lacking there and it may be that the Wadhurst Clay ore dies out towards that north-eastern part of the Weald. Certainly there is much silt and Tilgate Stone (fine-grained calcareous sandstone) in the basal part of the Wadhurst Clay of the Tenterden vicinity (Smart in Shephard-Thorn *et al.* 1966: 54). The silty nature of the Wadhurst Clay could go together with a poor development of clay ironstone, and both could result from proximity to a north-easterly inflow into the great Wealden (Lower Cretaceous) lake (see P. Allen 1981: fig.11).

In more central parts of the Weald, Bristow (in Bristow and Bazley 1972: 113) found that the main 'pay' horizon appears to have been a nodular or tabular bed of clay ironstone some 6–9m above the base of the Wadhurst Clay. A manuscript of the ironfounder John Fuller, lists Wadhurst Clay seams worked near Heathfield in the late seventeenth and early eighteenth centuries. The MS comprises an earlier part, reprinted in the *Victoria County History of Sussex*, II (1907) and by Straker (1931a: 103), and a later part only recently discovered (Saville 1979). Fig.9 shows how the named layers may have looked in the sides of a shaft 5½m deep. The lowest bed, Bottom, is described as being 16–30ft (5–9m) below the surface. Presumably it was the practice to sink minepits no deeper than 9m, at which depth there would have been 5m of clay to dig through before reaching the Eleven Foot. From Fuller's description, Bottom was a 'sort of Limestone' useful as a flux. No limestones more than a few centimetres thick are known in the Wadhurst Clay; perhaps a bed of Tilgate Stone is meant. As described by Sweeting (1925: 413), Tilgate Stone is a pale blue to grey, hard, splintery rock that when examined *in situ* bears a distinct

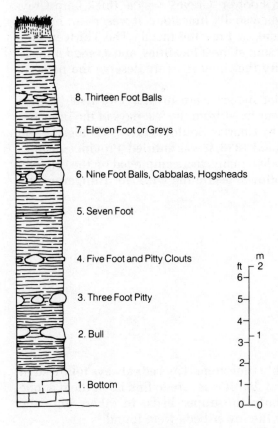

Fig.9   Ironstone layers in the lower part of the Wadhurst Clay, based on Fuller MS.

resemblance to limestone, and even in hand specimens may at first sight be mistaken for limestone; Sweeting gave an analysis showing SiO_2 70.4 per cent, $CaCO_3$ 22.9 per cent. Bull, 1½ft (0.45m), and Three Foot Pitty, 3ft (0.9m) above the Bottom, were presumably layers of nodules. Of the Gray Pitty (a variety occurring at the Three Foot Pitty level) Fuller wrote that it 'works so very hot and fiery in the Furnace ... that it will tear the Firestones to pieces and will very often come through the Furnace unmelted ... However, some of it must be used in all iron serving instead of Limestone'. Dr P. J. Ovenden (in litt.) comments that he would take this to be an ironstone high in calcium and magnesium. The Five Foot was a fine-grained ironstone 2–3in (5–8cm) thick, while Pitty Clouts were larger, coarser-grained nodules at the same level. The Seven Foot was a fine-grained ironstone seldom more than 1–1½in (2.5–4cm) thick. At 9ft (2.7m) above the Bottom, the names Balls, Cabbalas, and Hogsheads were given to nodules of different sizes. The Eleven Foot or 'Grayes' was a 'thick hard Graystone'. This could have been a shelly limestone. It was 'fit for nothing but paving, or to make Lime, or Flux the metal'. The Thirteen Foot Balls were described as present at most localities, and as good mine as any, 'but so few in quantity that they scarcely deserve the name of another stratum'.

Near Ashburnham similar names were in use. Two lists (Topley 1875; Straker 1931a) have survived from the last days of the industry. One of them was acquired by Charles Gould, a Survey geologist, from the Earl of Ashburnham. Dated 1836, it was entitled 'Provincial names of the beds from Thos. Hobday, many years employed on the estate in drawing mine' and is as follows, beginning with No. 1 uppermost:

No. 1   Twelve Foots
    2   Greys
    3   Foxes
    4   Greys
    5   Hazards
    6   Bulls
    7   Cheveliers
    8   White bands
   10   Pitty
   11   Colours

Beds 2 and 4 were probably limestone. The beds always followed in the same order of succession, but it was rare to find all of them at one locality. In some places only the upper beds, in others only the middle, and in others only the lower beds were found.

A mid-nineteenth century attempt to revive iron-ore mining was made at Snape Wood, near Wadhurst, as a result of iron ore being discovered during excavation of the railway cutting. The ironstone was worked in mines consisting of galleries and cross-cuts on both sides of the railway from August 1857 to September 1858, the ore being sent to Staffordshire (Topley 1875, 72, 337). Straker's account (1931, 291) reads as if he had explored the galleries. He noted wrought iron trolley rails still remaining. The ore can be seen in the north face of the railway cutting as a massive seam of silty siderite rock, 0.45m thick (Worssam and Gibson-Hill 1976). Two seams were worked in the mine but were very irregular, dying out suddenly and reappearing at intervals. This and the ore's low iron oxide content (40 per cent) and high silica (26 per cent) no doubt accounted for the failure of the enterprise.

A little clay ironstone occurs in the Tunbridge Wells Sand of the area east of West Hoathly, but nowhere apparently in sufficient quantity to have interested the iron industry.

Nodular clay ironstone occurs in the grey shales of the lower part of the Grinstead Clay. Only two minepit localities have been recorded, both by Dr R. W. Gallois. These are Mill Place Wood (TQ 3665 3508) (which may be on Wadhurst rather than on Grinstead Clay) and north of Paxhill Park (at 3619 2704).

Two or three clay ironstone seams are present in the Weald Clay north-east of Tenterden, of recorded thickness up to 13cm and extensive enough for their outcrops to have been mapped (Sheet 304) near High Halden, Woodchurch and Bethersden (Shephard-Thorn *et al.* 1966: 78–82). These seem to have escaped the notice of the iron industry. Other Weald Clay ironstone beds that appear not to have attracted exploitation occur in the southern Weald between Twineham (240 205) and Wivelsfield Green (360 195) (1:50,000 Geological Sheet 318, 1984).

(B) THE HORSHAM-CRAWLEY AREA

The distribution of minepits in this area is shown in fig.7. Those southwards of grid line 31 were mapped by Dr R. G. Thurrell. Additionally, minepits on Upper Tunbridge Wells Sand, some of them beyond the area included in the diagram, occur at Eastland Hill (2281 2648) and (information supplied by Dr R. W. Gallois) at The Birches (292 384), at Rickmans Green (3005 3885) and east of Haywards Heath at Cripland Court Farm (350 245).

In 1973 a 2.5m deep sewer trench on a building site in Broadfield Forest, south of Crawley New Town, crossed a belt of minepits and revealed at least some of the layers that would have been familiar to the miners. The succession was as follows, spread out along a distance of some 60m (Worssam and Gibson-Hill 1976: 77):

Bed no.		Thickness (m)
8	Weathered light grey silty clay	1.5
7	Silty siderite mudstone	0.08–0.15
6	Dark grey shaly clay, with 3cm layers of fine-grained clay ironstone at 0.02m to 0.3m intervals; a lens of clay ironstone up to 0.2m thick and 1.8m in extent occurs at the top of the bed at one place	1.2
5	Grey, roughly laminated silty clay	0.5
4	Grey, hard, silty sandstone	0.6
3	Medium dark grey, slightly silty, laminated mudstone	0.6
2	Dark grey, laminated siltstone	0.6
1	Medium grey, silty, laminated hard sandstone	0.9

The thickest and most persistent ironstone seam in this section and the one that bulked most largely in debris from the trench was bed 7, and this may have been the chief bed sought in the minepits, though the ironstone layers in bed 6 would also have been useful. It is unlikely that any minepits were carried below bed 5. Bed 7 is a hard, pale grey rock which, weathering to limonite along bedding and joint surfaces, produces dark-brown coated blocks or 'boxstones'. It resembles the Snape Wood (Ashdown Beds) ironstone in appearance and constitution. Analysis of a sample of the grey unweathered rock proved iron oxide 38.6 per cent and silica 22.4 per cent. This is poor for an iron ore, but since the belt of pits along the outcrop of the bed extends virtually uninterrupted for some 4km westwards (as far as Silver Hill in fig.7) its persistence may have made up for its lack of quality.

The Tunbridge Wells Sand of St Leonard's Forest (strictly speaking the Upper Tunbridge Wells Sand because it lies above the Grinstead Clay) consists of sandstone beds, none more than about 4.5m thick, separated by relatively thick sequences, perhaps 12–15m or more, of clays and silts. Bed 1 in the Broadfield Forest trench section represents the top of a sandstone bed.

Ironstone can still be seen in banks of streams in St Leonard's Forest, much as the original prospectors must have seen it. A stream section (TQ 1973 3130) in the wooded valley north of the house named St Leonard's exposes a 15cm thick bed of weathered silty ironstone.

Some of the ironstone in the Upper Tunbridge Wells Sand occurs as layers 15cm or so thick within the sandstone beds, as in an old quarry in Hook's Copse (220 338) (Worssam 1972: 39). However, it is unlikely that such ironstone could have been extracted by means of minepitting. South of Roffey Bloomery, on the Upper Tunbridge Wells Sand, is a wide sandstone outcrop with fragments of sandy ironstone abundant in the soil of ploughed fields. Some are cemented together by iron oxide into hard conglomeratic lumps up to 0.6m across, resembling the 'shrave' of gravels on the Weald Clay. Such material could conceivably have been used as an ore in the bloomery, but Weald Clay ore (at the Horsham Stone level) is not far to the north, and the advantage of a site on the sandstone outcrop may have been the well-drained nature of the ground.

The worked area known as The Minepits is now a Forestry Commission conifer plantation but was photographed by Straker (1931a: 107) when an open oak wood. Here are some very large craters, up to 9m across at the ground surface and 2.5m deep. The pitted ground is on the flat top of a ridge between two deep valleys, where, since the beds are nearly horizontal, the iron ore seam could have been followed underground by workings that maintained a near-constant level.

The iron ore worked in the Weald Clay of the Horsham-Crawley area was a bed or beds within 3m or so of clay immediately below the Horsham Stone. A narrow belt of minepits runs along the outcrop of this sandstone between Warnham Brickworks and Crawley, passing close to the Romano-British bloomery at Broadfields and terminating in The Hawth. North of Ifield, minepits at the same stratigraphical level have been traced northwards to beyond Charlwood. The Horsham Stone has died out there but its ironstone is strongly developed and itself makes a distinct escarpment. The main area of development of the Horsham Stone is from Warnham westwards around the axis of the Wealden Anticline, thence continuing through Denne Hill, south of Horsham, and south-eastwards beyond Cowfold. It forms a prominent though discontinuous, because repeatedly faulted, ridge. There are many diggings for sandstone on the dip-slope surface of the ridge, but others solely for ironstone appear to have been a series of open pits just below the crest of the ridge. In Sparrow Copse (151 294) and High Wood (147 300) some sandstone diggings were carried deeper as 'bell-pits' for the extraction of clay ironstone (Thurrell *et al.* 1970). There is no certain evidence for the thickness of the iron ore below the Horsham Stone, but fragments that have been found are of a very fine-grained and probably quite pure clay ironstone. The best-quality iron ore so far analysed from the Weald is roasted ore found in a bloomery furnace of the Broadfields site, and which could have come from the Horsham Stone horizon. As a result of efficient roasting this ore contained 73.80 per cent of ferric oxide, together with 4.55 per cent of manganese oxide (Mn_3O_4) (Worssam and Gibson-Hill 1976; Gibson-Hill and Worssam 1976).

Intensive prospecting for iron ore in the Horsham-Crawley area is suggested not only by the close spacing of pitted ground along the main ironstone outcrops but also by the existence of two isolated patches of minepits, one in Upper Rapelands Wood and the other in a small copse (2615 3570), in an area now built-over, about midway between Long Copse and The Hawth (fig.7). Both are at Weald Clay horizons well above the Horsham Stone, where clay ironstone would not be likely to persist for any distance. Other isolated workings, in Minepit Wood near Tilehurst Farm, close to Dorking (fig.6) (Dines and Edmunds 1933: 36, 177), would have worked clay ironstone very near the top of the Weald Clay. They may have supplied Ewood furnace.

The Hawth, a copse now within the bounds of Crawley New Town, is a good place in which to see minepits, being a public open space beside a main ring-road (Hawth Avenue). The copse is on the dip-slope of a short but steep escarpment formed by the Horsham Stone. The craters that mark the sites of pits increase in size down the dip-slope, and those along the north-western border of the copse are very large, up to 2.5m deep. The dip here is fairly steep (5° to 10°, north-westwards) so that to follow the ore for any distance under-ground deeper shafts than usual would have been needed. There is a local tradition recorded by the Crawley Local History Society that ore from The Hawth was used in Tilgate furnace, and that it was carried there on sledges for the distance of about a kilometre, mostly down-hill.

(C) THE WESTERN WEALD

In this area the mapping of iron-ore workings is practically complete (fig.8). In addition to those previously recorded (Worssam 1964) the pits between Hammonds Wood and Westlands Farm and those at the far west end of the Vale of Fernhurst have recently been discovered by Dr Bristow.

Evidence of early iron working has been found in the fortified camps of Hascombe and Piper's Copse (Tebbutt 1973), while there is a bloomery site of unknown date at Coombswell (Ovenden 1973). Apart from these sites and from possible late medieval working at the

Lurgashall bloomery, the area seems to have been left untouched by the iron industry until Tudor times, when a number of blast furnaces were established.

Ore for the blast furnaces seems to have been obtained wholly from minepits. The remains of these pits, in woods and copses and occasionally in open fields, form a belt that extends westwards from Vann Copse near Hambledon in Surrey, then southwards following a sinuous course into the Vale of Fernhurst in Sussex, and emerges to tail off eastwards in the workings at Colehook Common. The pits between Hammonds Wood and Willetts Farm seem well placed to have served Pallingham furnace.

The nature of the seam or seams that were worked is not known exactly, but the development of ironstone, partly as nodules and partly as a continuous silty bed 7 to 20cm thick, in a stream section in Fowlshatch Copse (925 349) which may originally have been the side of a minepit (Worssam 1964: 536), is remarkably similar to that in the Broadfield Forest section.

All the areas of pitted ground have definite boundaries, not only in the down-dip direction (where the limit of workings would depend on the increasing depth of the seam) but also laterally, as if definite plots of ground had been marked out for mine-pitting. The eastern boundary of worked ground in Hambledon Hurst, however, is an exception. It shows a ragged edge, as if ore that was dying out was being vainly sought. Eastward of there are only scattered groups of pits in Blunden's Wood and Vann Copse, and then there are no more workings at this level in the Weald Clay certainly as far as the slopes below Leith Hill, 16km to the east. Since workings are absent also throughout the central and eastern part of the area shown in fig.8, those workings shown must have in effect constituted a distinct iron-ore field, serving a fairly clearly defined group of furnaces, which as well as those in fig.8 may have included Vachery, Dedisham and Knepp (fig.3).

References are made to iron-ore mining in the western Weald in an account of Petworth Manor in the seventeenth century (Wyndham 1954). Thus in a lease of Frith furnace in 1641 the lessee, William Yaldwin, was forbidden to dig more than 9m deep for his ore. He was also obliged to fill in the pits. The minepits in Gospelgreen Copse are shown in a 1610 map of Petworth Manor.

The absence of marlpits in the area included in fig.8 gave point to an attempt (Worssam 1964) to calculate the total production of the workings (excluding those near Pallingham and Coombe) and match it to an estimated iron output from the furnaces. On the basis of 12 furnaces with an average life of 50 years each, but each working for only two-thirds of its existence, and producing 220 tons a year, the total amount of cast iron produced during the existence of the industry would have been 88,000 tons. Such an amount could have been produced from clay ironstone yielding 20 per cent of iron on smelting, if the product of each pit had been seams or nodules equivalent to no more than an 8cm layer of ironstone. One of the intriguing problems of the western Weald iron industry that still requires solution is whether the industry really was based on so thin an iron-ore seam as this.

Chapter 2   **The bloomery process**

1   The theory of smelting

Iron ore consists essentially of two components – an iron compound (oxide, carbonate, etc.) and a non-metallic part, known as the gangue, consisting of sands, silts and clays. The process of smelting thus involves two operations: the chemical separation of the iron from its compound and the physical separation of the gangue. This process is carried out in a furnace in which the right conditions can be obtained for these two processes to be carried out simultaneously, the resulting products being metallic iron and refuse in the form of slag.

Although iron ore is much commoner than copper ore, it was copper that was first produced by smelting, probably because it is technologically simpler to reduce the ores of copper than those of iron. It appears likely that iron was first produced as a by-product of copper smelting, since iron ores were used as fluxes in early copper production, to make the slag more fusible (Charles 1980: 165–7). The potential of the white metal found in the refuse from copper smelting was recognized and soon iron ores began to be smelted alone.

This early process is known as direct reduction, since pure metallic iron is produced directly from the ore. The later blast-furnace process is one of indirect reduction, since the product of the process is not pure metallic iron but an iron-carbon alloy, which requires further processing to produce pure iron. The earlier process is known as bloomery ironmaking, from the Old English word *blóma*, the mass of reduced iron resulting from smelting with the direct reduction process.

As Bernard Worssam points out in Chapter 1, the main Wealden ore is clay ironstone, in which the principal constituent is iron carbonate, $FeCO_3$. The first step in the smelting of iron carbonate is the removal of the carbon dioxide, CO_2, that it contains. This is a relatively simple process, requiring only heat, which can be expressed as

$$FeCO_3 + \text{heat} \rightarrow FeO + CO_2$$

The carbon dioxide is driven off in the form of gas, leaving ferrous oxide, FeO. In practice (see p. 35 below), the ferrous oxide usually attracts more oxygen, and is converted to ferric oxide, Fe_2O_3, which forms the raw material for the reduction or smelting process proper.

Iron oxides are very stable compounds and require very high temperatures if heat alone is used for reduction. However, the process of dissociating the iron and oxygen atoms can be carried out in another form, using a reducing agent – that is to say, a material with a high affinity for oxygen which can draw the oxygen atoms away from the iron atoms in the oxide. The reducing agent used in the bloomery process is carbon monoxide, CO, resulting from the combustion of carbon

$$2C + O_2 \rightarrow 2CO.$$

Hot carbon monoxide removes the oxygen from ferric oxide in three stages:

$$3Fe_2O_3 + CO \rightarrow 2Fe_3O_4 + CO_2$$

$$Fe_3O_4 + CO \rightarrow 3FeO + CO_2$$

$$FeO + CO \rightarrow Fe + CO_2$$

The carbon monoxide is converted to carbon dioxide, CO_2, which escapes upwards in the form of gas, and pure metallic iron remains in the furnace.

The second essential operation referred to above is the separation of the gangue, or stony constituent in the ore. The melting points of silica, SiO_2, and alumina, Al_2O_3, which are the principal chemical compounds in sands and clays, are very high indeed, at temperatures much greater than could be achieved by early technologists. However, they can be combined with other minerals to produce an artificial mineral with a much lower melting point, such that it can be led to collect at the base of the furnace and, if necessary, run out in a liquid form. This artificial mineral is known as a slag.

In modern ironmaking practice, limestone; $CaCO_3$, is fed into the blast furnace along with the ore and fuel and combines with the silica and alumina: this is known as a flux. However, the use of lime as a flux was not known to the earliest ironmakers, who had to sacrifice part of the available iron in the ore to produce a fluid slag:

$$2FeO + SiO_2 \rightarrow Fe_2SiO_4.$$

This compound, known as fayalite, melts at 1,150–1,200°C, a temperature easily attainable in early iron-smelting furnaces.

Thus, the bloomery process requires iron ore, a carbon reducing agent and a source of oxygen, and its products are metallic iron (in solid form, since its melting point of over 1,600°C is not attained in the bloomery furnace) and an iron silicate slag.

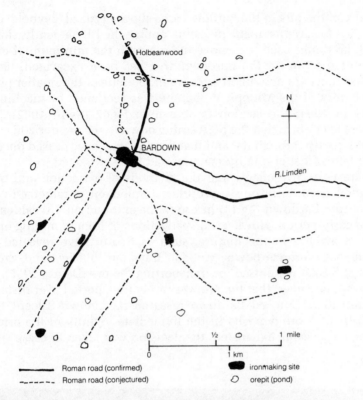

Fig.10   Map of the Bardown area, showing orepits (from Cleere 1976).

2   Raw materials

(A) IRON ORE

The occurrence of the Wealden iron ores is discussed by Bernard Worssam in Chapter 1. It is clear that these ores were mined opencast, usually in large pits but also perhaps in a form of bellpit in the western part of the Weald. Evidence from Bardown (Cleere 1970) suggests that the ore was located by prospecting along the small Wealden rivers and was initially extracted by cutting back from the outcrops revealed as the soft overlying clays were worn away by water action. Once the initial lens of high-quality nodular ore had been exhausted, shafts were probably sunk at intervals, to locate new deposits of this ore, a large pit being dug when it was discovered. The map (fig.10) of the environs of the Bardown settlement (from Cleere 1976: fig.1) shows the density of presumed orepits around this major ironmaking establishment.

Many of the pits in the Bardown area show a typical 'keyhole' plan, the roughly circular main pit being approached by a gently sloping ramp, no doubt used to remove the ore with the minimum of effort. None of the pits in the Bardown area has been excavated, largely because most are now filled with water, but one of the smaller pits in the vicinity of the Minepit Wood site was sectioned by machine by WIRG in 1981; the section is shown in fig.67 (Swift 1982). This appears to confirm that the pit was dug down to the ore horizon – and, indeed, partly through it – and that digging may have ceased once the small lens of better-quality material had been extracted.

There is no evidence about the methods of extraction and trans-portation used: only one appropriate implement, a rather rare iron spade from Bardown (fig.11) has so far been found on a Wealden site of the early period. However, investigations of Roman mining opera-tions elsewhere in the Empire, such as Spain, have revealed that leather bags, bronze bowls, wooden trays and buckets and various types of basket were used for transporting the ore (Davies 1935). It is apparent, however, that the ore was rarely transported over distances of more than 1km. At Bardown research has shown (Cleere 1970; 1976) that, as ore deposits in the immediate vicinity of the original settlement became exhausted, the decision was taken to cease smelt-

Fig.11   Roman iron spade from Bardown, with modern spade for comparison (photograph: H. F. Cleere). (Scale in inches.)

ing at the main settlement and establish smaller workplaces close to the new deposits being exploited (see below, Chapter 4).

In its as-mined state, the siderite nodules were too large for use in the small furnaces employed for smelting. They needed to be broken up into smaller pieces with a larger surface area that would enable the reduction process to be carried out more efficaciously. Moreoover, they tended to contain a good deal of water, which needed to be driven off outside the furnace. This latter fact was exploited by the early ironmakers by roasting the ore in a simple heap or in some cases, as at Bardown, in specially constructed open roasting hearths.

The principle involved was that of the expansion of water when it is heated to its boiling point. The small amounts of water contained in minute fissures and cracks in the ore lumps expanded enormously as the temperature reached 100°C and the forces generated shattered the lumps of ore, often explosively, as experiments with a reconstruction of a Roman roasting furnace (Cleere 1971a) demonstrated. At the same time, the iron carbonate was converted to iron oxide, as described above, with the release of carbon dioxide. The resulting product of the roasting operation was a quantity of irregularly sized lumps of ore, transformed from the grey-green of the original siderite ore to the purple of ferric oxide.

Patches of burnt clay soil, usually round in plan, and associated with scraps of roasted ore, are not uncommon on early Wealden sites. The Bardown settlement provided two examples of a specially constructed hearth that was indisputably used for ore roasting. These were pits approximately 2.50m long by 0.80m wide, dug into the natural soil to a depth of about 0.2m (fig.12). They were lined with stones along the sides, probably originally in about four courses, giving a total depth of 0.4–0.5m, and the walls and base were liberally coated with puddled clay. The furnace was open at one of its narrow ends. The experiments with a reconstruction of one of these hearths suggested that they were filled with alternate layers of ore and charcoal or dry wood; the lowest layer of charcoal was then ignited and the whole mass allowed to burn itself out. Some broken flagon necks found in the debris of one of the Bardown hearths indicated that bellows might have been used to boost the temperature, these having been employed as tuyeres to protect the wooden nozzles of the bellows.

When the roasted ore had cooled it was sieved or screened to remove the smaller particles, of probably under 5mm cube. The evidence for this is incontrovertible: deep beds of roasted ore particles of below this size are common finds on the refuse heaps of the early Wealden sites, and there was a dump of the same material alongside

Fig.12   Ore-roasting furnace II from Bardown (photograph: H. F. Cleere). (Scale in inches.)

one of the Bardown hearths. There was an excellent reason for this treatment: small ore particles would tend to clog up the air passages in the smelting furnace, reducing its permeability and requiring greater blast pressure from the bellows, or in extreme cases making the whole smelting process ineffective because insufficient heat could be generated.

(B) FUEL

The second basic raw material needed for smelting iron ore is a carbon reducing agent. In the modern blast furnace coke is used, but that is a relatively recent innovation, introduced by Abraham Darby I at

Coalbrookdale in 1709. Up to that time, all iron ore was smelted using charcoal.

The very name of the Weald (cp. German *Wald*) implies that this was a region rich in trees. It was not until the late Saxon period that permanent clearance of the ancient woodland was undertaken: during the prehistoric and Roman periods the clays and sands of the Wealden series supported a mature woodland cover of oak, ash, hornbeam, beech, alder, etc., the exact combination of species depending, as Rackham (1980) has recently demonstrated, on local juxtapositions of soils, drainage, aspect and other factors. There was thus an ample – almost inexhaustible – supply of fuel at hand in intimate association with the iron ores of the Weald.

There is no evidence of how the wildwood (to use Rackham's graphic term) was exploited by the early ironmakers. Calculations based on the Bardown settlement (Cleere 1976) have suggested that there was little management of the woodland, trees being felled and lopped to provide material for charcoal burning; however, Rackham (1980: 108–9) has challenged this view, suggesting that a form of coppicing, known from elsewhere in the Roman world, was being implemented in the Weald in the Roman period. Examination of charcoals from the Bardown settlement has indicated that there was little, if any, selection of wood for charcoal burning: the species identified there include oak, ash, beech, hornbeam, birch, hazel, hawthorn and elder, with oak predominating, as might be expected from the relative proportions of these species in the wildwood cover in that region.

There is little evidence for the method of charcoal burning used in the Roman period from the archaeological record, but classical authors indicate that it was of the heap type still in use occasionally in the Weald today. An area of hard-burnt clay nearly 2m in diameter at Bardown was in all probability the base of a charcoal heap; there was no trace in the middle of any holes that would indicate that the cords of wood were stacked round a central flue, as in more recent practice. Nor is there any direct evidence for the size of branches used, though examination of stray finds of charcoal suggest that the diameters varied between 20 and 100mm. There is, however, clear evidence of screening of the charked wood to remove the small-sized materials, as in the case of iron ore: deep layers of charcoal fines alternate with roasted ore fines on refuse tips, and it would seem that material below 5mm cube was discarded. The upper limit is less well attested: lumps of as much as 50mm cube have been found at Bardown and elsewhere.

(c) CLAY

In addition to the two smelting raw materials, ore and charcoal, a third raw material was needed for smelting, namely clay, for building furnaces and hearths. Chapter 3 attests the prevalence of clay in the Weald: the Wadhurst Clay is especially plastic and refractory, which means that it can be used for building furnaces that will withstand the thermal stresses resulting from the high temperatures involved in the smelting without undue distortion or disintegration, whilst the Ashdown Sand contains a high proportion of clay particles and could also have been used for furnace construction (although it seems likely that at Bardown, where the main settlement is built on Ashdown Sand, Wadhurst Clay was brought from the other side of the River Limden for building the furnaces).

Examination of smelting furnace remains at Bardown, Broadfields, Cow Park and elsewhere suggests that the furnaces were durable and could be re-used repeatedly, and this was confirmed by the smelting experiments in a reconstructed Roman furnace (Cleere 1971a). In fact, failure of the furnaces seems generally to have been confined to the front part, and the rear walls were re-utilized when the furnaces were rebuilt.

Stone was occasionally incorporated into the structures of the Wealden bloomery furnaces. At Minepit Wood (Money 1974), for example, the walls of the furnace were strengthened with lumps of sandstone in several courses, and the best preserved furnace at Holbeanwood (Cleere 1970) incorporated a single lump of sandstone to form the top of the tapping arch (see below), but furnaces of the prehistoric and Roman types could be sturdily made using clay alone.

A detailed dissection of three of the Holbeanwood furnaces revealed that grog (small fragments of fired clay) was used as filler. This offered obvious advantages, since the reduced expansion and contraction on heating and cooling from a grogged clay would reduce cracking and increase stability.

3   Smelting furnaces

There is a considerable literature on the classification of bloomery iron-smelting furnaces, e.g. Coghlan (1956), Schubert (1957), Tylecote (1962), Cleere (1972), Martens (1978) and Pelet (1977). These are based on the wide variations in form to be observed among the furnace remains from the archaeological record across Europe and among the bloomery furnaces still to be observed in use by modern primitives in Africa and Asia.

Basically, the furnace is an enclosed combustion chamber equipped with means for supplying an air blast and with or without provision for the molten slag to be tapped off; there must also be an aperture to enable waste gases to escape to the atmosphere. It may be built partly or wholly above ground, and may be free-standing or built into a bank or the side of a pit. Most of the classifications are based on morphological variations in furnace profile, ranging from the cylindrical shaft to the 'beehive' hemispherical type. The only functional distinction that can properly be made is between the furnaces with and furnaces without provision for tapping off the molten slag, although certain broad groups (called 'shaft' and 'domed' furnaces in Cleere's (1972) classification) may be seen as distinct.

The slag-tapping and non-slag-tapping traditions have a distribution that is broadly mutually exclusive in Europe. The two exist side by side in eastern central Europe, e.g. the Burgenland (Austria), Hungary, and Bohemia, but can be seen to diverge during the second half of the first millennium BC. Non-slag-tapping furnaces are distributed throughout modern Poland, Pomerania, Schleswig-Holstein, and Denmark, whilst only furnaces of the slag-tapping type have been found in Germany, France and Britain (until the Middle Saxon period). This distribution is illustrated by Pleiner (1965) in one of the most important surveys of early ironmaking yet published.

During the prehistoric and Roman periods in Britain only slag-tapping furnaces appear to have been in use. A study of the 70-odd early furnaces from the Weald at this time shows that they fall into two groups. The earlier type is the domed slag-tapping furnace (Cleere's 1972 Type B.1.i), illustrated by examples from Cow Park, Pippingford Park, Minepit Wood, and Broadfields. This type was in use from the first century BC until the mid-first century AD – probably continuing in use after the Roman occupation of AD 43. The Romans appear to have introduced the shaft slag-tapping furnace (Cleere's Type B.1.ii), represented by the 12 furnaces at Holbeanwood in the Weald, but widely distributed in Roman Britain at, for example, Ashwicken (Tylecote and Owles 1960), Wakerley (Jackson and Ambrose 1978), Wilderspool (May 1904) and elsewhere. The two types are illustrated in fig.13, which shows the Minepit Wood and Holbeanwood furnaces.

The shaft furnace persisted in the Weald until the end of the Roman period, as the Broadfields site demonstrates. When ironmaking was reintroduced into the Weald in the Middle Saxon period, the non-slag-tapping furnace makes a brief appearance, as represented by the Millbrook furnace (Tebbutt 1982). It is logical, bearing in mind the distribution of this type of furnace (Cleere's 1972 Type A.2), which

a

Fig.13   Roman iron-smelting furnaces from (a) Minepit Wood and (b) Holbeanwood (photographs: J. H. Money; H. F. Cleere). (Scales in inches.)

b

predominates in the Anglo-Saxon homeland of western Schleswig-Holstein (Hingst 1952). With this type of furnace, the molten slag was not tapped (i.e. allowed to drain outside the furnace), but collected in a hollow at the base, to be removed as a solid cake at the end of the smelting or left *in situ*, a new furnace being built for the subsequent smelting operation; the Millbrook furnace shows several relinings, and so the former method was probably in use in the Weald.

(A) THE IRON AGE DOMED FURNACE

The best-preserved example from the Weald is that from Minepit Wood (Money 1974). This had an internal diameter of about 0.6m and stood about 1m high. Its walls, of clay strengthened with stone, were 0.3m thick at the base, and tapered to about 0.2m at the top. There was a tapping aperture in the front, tapering from 250mm on the outside to 150mm on the interior, the height of which was probably originally about 0.3m. There were holes about 25mm in diameter in the wall at three points – facing the tapping aperture and 90° on either side of it – some 250mm above the level of the flat internal hearth. The tapping aperture opened into a deep hollow some 2m long, flanked at the end nearest the furnace with massive sandstone blocks. It is conjectured that the tapping aperture would have contained a further tuyere (a clay nozzle to receive the wooden tube of the bellows), but in this case closer to the hearth level than the other three holes referred to above, which would also have served to accommodate bellows tubes.

A number of furnaces of this type were found in early contexts at Broadfields (Gibson-Hill 1975, 1976), there was one at Pippingford Park (Tebbutt and Cleere 1973), and Cow Park (Tebbutt 1979) produced a further three examples. Both the latter sites, like Minepit Wood, were dated by pottery to the first half of the first century AD.

(B) THE ROMAN SHAFT FURNACE

Furnaces of this type are known from Holbeanwood and from the full Roman period at Broadfields. They consist essentially of clay shafts, about 0.3m in internal diameter and with walls 0.25–0.3m thick at the base. Their original height can only be inferred as at least 1m, by analogy with more complete examples from Ashwicken, Norfolk (Tylecote and Owles 1960). There was an aperture at the base about 200mm wide by 250–300mm high, in front of which was located a shallow depression 300mm in diameter and up to 150mm deep. None of the furnaces excavated has given any evidence of the sidewall apertures that are such a notable feature of the Minepit Wood type.

The Ashwicken furnaces were built into a bank of sand, which would have provided both stability and thermal insulation. Ploughing and water erosion have destroyed most of the features at Holbeanwood, but there is slight evidence that these too were built into banks, in this case of clay. The layout of the Holbeanwood site, one of the 'satellite' workplaces of the Bardown settlement, suggests that the furnaces were built in batteries, with two or three in operation simultaneously: two such batteries, and a possible third, were identified.

The antecedents of this type of furnace are difficult to establish with certainty. The domed type has close parallels on the Rhine and its tributaries, especially the Siegerland (Gilles 1936), dated to the first century BC and later, but comparable data are missing for the shaft furnaces. Examples are known from southern Germany and Austria, but the dearth of information from countries lying within the Roman *limes*, notably France and Belgium, makes it difficult to establish such a clear-cut pedigree. What is incontrovertible, however, is the dating: none of the shaft furnaces so far excavated in Britain is earlier than the second half of the first century AD, and so it is reasonable to infer that this type was a Roman importation into the province.

(C) THE SAXON NON-SLAG-TAPPING FURNACE

This type of furnace, of which that from Millbrook is the only example known from the Weald, consists of a depression about 1m in diameter and about 0.5m deep, which probably originally had a superstructure that was conical or cylindrical in shape made of clay 200–300mm thick and perhaps standing to 1.5m high, by analogy with similar furnaces known from Schleswig-Holstein and Poland. There was no tapping aperture, but one or more tuyeres would have positioned in the wall just above ground level. There is no associated slag-tapping hollow.

Archaeomagnetic testing of the Millbrook furnace gave a date of AD 800–35. Slag cakes from furnaces of this type (known to Continental scholars as *Schlackenklotze*) have been found in Early Saxon contexts at Mucking (M. U. and W. T. Jones, private communication), and there are clear indications of ironmaking using furnaces of this type in Middle Saxon Northampton (Williams, J. H. 1979). At Ramsbury (Haslam *et al.* 1980), it appears that the earliest furnaces, dating from the earlier Middle Saxon period, were of this type, to be superseded by a slag-tapping shaft furnace. The links with furnaces in southern Denmark and Schleswig-Holstein are very clear and support the view that this type of ironmaking furnace was brought to Britain by the

Anglo-Saxon invaders, to be replaced in the ninth or tenth century by a reintroduction of the slag-tapping furnace.

4   The ironmaking process

The process of producing iron in the bloomery furnace requires that the ore be reduced with carbon monoxide formed by the combustion of charcoal. It is possible to reconstruct how this was probably carried out in practice in antiquity as a result of experimental work on reconstructions of early furnaces (e.g. Gilles 1958; Tylecote et al. 1971; Cleere 1972; Bielenin 1973; Adams 1979) and of studies of modern primitive ironmaking practice (e.g. Cleere 1963b; Dr Jean Brown unpublished).

The first step, whichever type of furnace was being used, was to raise the interior of the furnace to a high temperature, of the order of 1,000°C. This was done by kindling a fire in the base, charging the furnace with charcoal, and blowing the fire with bellows, inserted through the tuyeres. Little is known about the bellows used in antiquity, beyond some inadequate representations on, for example, Greek red- and black-figured vessels. Leather, wood and ceramic examples are known from other archaeological contexts, but the exact type in use in the Weald in antiquity remains in doubt.

More is known about the tuyeres, the clay nozzles inserted into the furnaces to protect the wooden blast tubes of the bellows. The simplest type was a clay cone, with an internal diameter of 20–30mm. However, a more elaborate type is known only from the Weald, a double tuyere with twin outlets: fig.14 shows two examples from Bardown, and others have been found at Beauport Park and Chitcombe. These would have been inserted through the blocked-up tapping aperture on the slag-tapping shaft furnace and the jets of air would have spread around the restricted hearth area, creating high turbulence and uniformly high temperatures across the whole combustion zone; they would have been more effective than the single-vent tuyeres, which would have tended to create a single hot zone on the back wall of the furnace facing the blast.

The size of the trumpet opening on the outside of the furnace would have made it possible for two bellows to have been luted on with wet clay; the two bellows, operated alternately, would have maintained a high level of blast into the furnace. However, a strange pottery vessel from the Little Farningham Farm Roman site (fig.15) suggests that a more sophisticated method may have been in use. It is believed that bellows were attached to two of the three holes in the side of the pot,

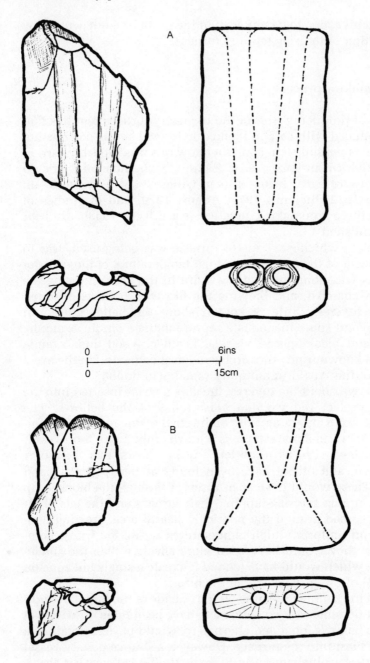

Fig.14   Roman double tuyeres from Bardown (Cleere 1963a).

0   3ins
|—————————————————————|
0   5cm

Fig.15 'Bellows pot' from Little Farningham Farm, (photograph: M. C. Lebon).

and an outlet nozzle to the third; single flapper valves of leather could have been fixed on the inside over the two bellows intakes. In this way a sustained constant blast could have been fed into the furnace with alternating bellows operation.

Once a sufficiently high temperature had been achieved within the furnace – judged by some empirical criterion such as flame luminosity – additions of ore would have begun, probably in relatively small amounts, of, say, 1kg, accompanied by roughly equal amounts of charcoal. The combustion of charcoal with the oxygen from the air supplied by the bellows would produce carbon monoxide, CO, at a high temperature, at which it is highly reducing. As the hot carbon monoxide moved up the furnace it came into contact with the small ore particles, from which oxygen atoms were captured, converting the carbon monoxide into carbon dioxide CO_2 and leaving free iron atoms, which gradually coalesced into discrete metal particles. At the same time, the high temperatures engendered in the furnace brought about fusion between the silica in the gangue and part of the ferrous oxide, forming small particles of liquid fayalite slag, which slowly trickled downwards under the influence of gravitational forces.

Repeated additions of small quantities of ore and charcoal would have been made at intervals over a long period, as a result of which metallic iron would begin to collect at the base of the furnace, together with a steadily increasing pool of liquid slag. In the slag-tapping furnace this would gradually rise to the level of the tuyere, but in the non-slag-tapping furnace it would fill the below-ground cavity. In the former case, part of the sand or loose clay blocks used to fill the tapping parture would be removed from time to time, to allow the liquid slag to flow out and solidify in the shallow depression in front of the tapping aperture. Since the slag would freeze quickly when exposed to air temperatures the solidified cake that built up would tend to consist of an agglomeration of solidified runnels of slag, giving the wrinkled appearance so typical of tap slag. It is even possible that the whole aperture was not blocked up and that a small orifice was left at the base, allowing the molten slag to run continuously from the base: this certainly proved successful in one experimental smelting on a reconstructed Roman furnace (Cleere 1971a). A similar structure would be observable on the *Schlackenklotz* formed in the non-slag-tapping Saxon furnace, but the whole mass would be considerably greater than that formed by periodical tapping into the shallow depression in front of a slag-tapping furnace.

The duration of an individual smelt was determined by the size of the furnace. In the case of the slag-tapping shaft or domed furnace, it was necessary to remove the spongy bloom of reduced iron either through the top or the tapping aperture of the furnace without too much damage to the furnace structure, which would be re-used for further smelts. The determining factor in the case of the non-slag-tapping furnace was the capacity of the below-ground cavity: once this was filled with slag it would be impossible to reduce any more ore without contaminating the bloom with slag. It is difficult to be precise about the exact production capacity of the different types of furnace. Experiments with the Roman shaft furnace reconstruction (Cleere 1971a) produced 10kg of iron in a relatively short shift, and Gilles (1960) assumed a daily output of 15kg from his reconstructed domed furnaces. However, it would seem reasonable to assume that the skilled Roman ironmaker was capable of producing at least double this quantity of iron in a day. By analogy with the large furnaces of the non-slag-tapping type operated on an experimental basis in the Holy Cross Mountains of southern Poland (Bielenin 1974), a daily production of perhaps 25kg might be expected from the Millbrook Saxon furnace.

5 The product

The primary end-product of bloomery smelting was a spongy mass of iron, its interstices filled with slag, known as an unworked bloom. Before being worked into tools, weapons, or implements, unworked blooms needed to be consolidated into a coherent metal block and to have the entrapped slag removed. This was done by repeated heating and hammering. It will be remembered that fayalite slag is fluid at a temperature of 1,150–1,200°C. Iron can be forge-welded at about 1,200°C, which means that the two processes can be carried out simultaneously.

The unworked bloom was heated up with bellows in a small open forging hearth, remains of which are very common on Wealden ironmaking sites. All that remains of them is a hard-burnt patch of clay 0.3–0.6m in diameter and usually slightly concave in section. The bloom would have been heaped up with charcoal and blown hard with bellows, probably protected by a clay tuyere, until it was white-hot, which meant that a temperature of around 1,200°C had been attained. It would then have been removed from the hearth with tongs, placed on an anvil of stone or iron (or even wood), and hammered vigorously until its colour showed that the heat had been lost. This would have the effect of expelling the entrapped slag, which would have been literally squirted out, solidifying as it went into characteristic thin platelets of slag, and of welding the discrete metallic components together. Heat would have been lost rapidly during this process, and the whole cycle of heating and hammering would have to be repeated on several occasions. During the heating process, some of the entrapped slag would doubtless have run out naturally and dropped into the forging hearth, there to mingle with small fragments of iron that became detached and with pieces of the oxide scale that formed on the outside of the bloom while it was being heated and which were doubtless knocked off by the ironmaker as he withdrew the bloom from the fire. In this way thick clinkery deposits, known as cinder or 'furnace bottom' (as they are conventionally described), would build up within the forging hearth, for subsequent removal.

For the Wealden ironmakers in the prehistoric and Roman periods the final product was most probably not an artefact but a worked bloom, of the type found at Little Farningham Farm (fig.16). In

Fig.16 Bloom from Little Farningham Farm: (a) before cleaning, (b) after cleaning, (c) section (photographs: (a) and (b) Ancient Monuments Laboratory, (c) G. T. Brown).

modern terminology this was a semi-finished product, used for distribution to finishing establishments, there to be fashioned into tools, weapons and the myriad other iron artefacts in use in Roman Britain, such as nails, general domestic ironwork and boat fittings. Worked blooms are rare finds in Britain, but the handful that are known from the Roman period are all roughly comparable to the Little Farningham Farm example: they are about 200mm long and weigh around 2kg. So far no semi-finished products have been found that can be dated to the prehistoric period, but it is not unlikely that these took the form of the currency bars (D. F. Allen 1967) that are so common on Iron Age sites in Britain and Gaul in the first centuries BC and AD.

6   Waste products

Wealden ironmaking sites are generally identified by the waste products of ironmaking. These fall into four categories – ore refuse, charcoal refuse, slag, and furnace debris. The first two of these have been dealt with already – the beds of screened-out fine roasted ore particles and charcoal dust, which are instantly recognizable and distinct from the other forms of refuse.

One very characteristic find associated with ore preparation is the shelly *Cyrena* limestone that occurs in close association with the ore of the Wadhurst Clay. This is composed almost entirely of the shells, rarely more than 5mm across, of the lamellibranch *Neomiodon* [*Cyrena*], stained reddish-brown by iron oxide. Although the appearance of this material suggests that it is ferruginous, the iron content is less than 3 per cent and so it is worthless as a source of metal. This appears to have been recognized by the Roman ironmakers, who rejected it, although paradoxically they might have improved the yield of iron from their ore by charging it to the furnaces, since the lime, CaO, of which it is mainly composed would have assisted in the fluxing off of the silica gangue and reduced the amount of iron oxide that was sacrificed. Occasional finds of a glassy black slag, as at Minepit Wood, for example (Money 1974), may indicate that shelly limestone was being charged to some furnaces, since this type of slag is high in lime.

Slags and cinders arise in two components of the process – the smelting furnace and the forging hearth. Smelting furnace residues comprise tap slags, described above, and cinders, together with the large slag agglomerations (*Schlackenklotze*) from the non-slag-tapping furnaces. Tap slags may be complete cakes, reproducing the configurations of the depressions into which they were tapped, or fragments, varying considerably in size. It has been suggested that the larger fragments represent slag cakes that have been broken up mechanically, using hammers, and the smaller fragments those cakes that were shattered by being doused with water when very hot. Cinders are the clinkery accretions of slag mixed with ore fragments and charcoal which collected in the bottom of the bloomery furnace during the early stages of the smelting and which would have been raked out at the end of the operation.

The furnace bottoms resulting from the reheating and working of blooms have already been described. Some of these are full of voids, very similar in appearance to the cinders resulting from the smelting process, but others, as a result of prolonged heating at very high temperatures, have remelted and are very dense.

Schlackenklotze have a very characteristic gradation from a cinder-like structure full of voids and with much included ore and charcoal at the base through to the dense wrinkled structure of tap slag. The slag block itself reproduces the dimensions and contours of the pit into which it ran during the smelting process.

Furnace debris consists of broken pieces of baked clay which formed the superstructure of furnaces that have collapsed or have been dismantled at the end of a smelting campaign. Some of these may be very large, giving a clear indication of the curvature of the furnace wall, but most are quite small. Furnace interiors can be identified because of the concretion of slag on them; in the hotter zones (i.e. the lower part of the furnace) the slag can be seen to have penetrated deeply into cracks in the clay lining, but higher up it forms a skin adhering to the surface. The location on the furnace of individual fragments can also be identified by the degree of firing of the clay, the hottest zones being characterized by the grey colour on the interior surface.

Roughly shaped lumps of clay, often showing finger marks and glazing on one surface, have been found on a number of sites. It has been postulated that these formed part of the blocking of the tapping aperture, the glazing (usually green) resulting from contact with the highly alkaline wood ash on the inside of the furnace. Tuyere fragments are often found: they can be recognized by the grooves or holes that survive, usually with adherent slag on one end.

An examination of several Wealden refuse heaps and an analysis of the deposition of the different types of refuse has suggested that operations at some of these establishments worked on an annual cycle (Cleere 1971a). A well-known illustration from Straker (1931a: 331) shows a section through the great slag bank at Beauport Park while it was being quarried away for road metalling in the nineteenth century (fig.22). The layered structure had also been observed at Bardown and at Holbeanwood, and a close analysis of one of the dumps at the latter site showed that there was a repeated sequence of charcoal fines, ore fines, slag, and furnace debris. It has been postulated from this that all the efforts of the workforce were concentrated on one phase of the overall operation in turn. Thus, during the winter and early spring wood would have been cut, charked, screened, and stocked, the fines being discarded on to the refuse bank, until an adequate stock had been built up. Then in the early summer the emphasis would have been switched to ore mining and preparation, the ore being dug, transported to the working site, roasted, and stocked, the fines being once again discarded. Once an appropriate stock of roasted and screened ore had been built up, smelting could begin, and would continue until all the ore and charcoal stocks had been exhausted: this would be an appropriate operation for the late summer and autumn. Slag would regularly be dumped on the refuse heap. Finally, when all the ore and charcoal stocks had been used up, the furnaces would be cleaned out and rebuilt, discarded furnace lining and other debris being dumped on the bank, overlying the slag from the previous phase. Bearing in mind the colours of the materials produced in each of these phases, a regular layering of the type shown in the engraving might well be the result of regular annual cycles of the type described.

Chapter 3   Prehistoric ironmaking in the Weald

1 Continental origins

The most recent account of the development of ironmaking in antiquity (Wertime and Muhly 1980) contains a valuable summary by Pleiner of what is known of early iron metallurgy in Europe (Pleiner 1980), which shows the knowledge of iron smelting reaching north-western Europe in the second half of the first millennium BC. The chronological bar chart (Pleiner 1980: fig.11.3) shows the full Iron Age, with iron smelting, starting around 300 BC and what the author describes as the 'full and fledged [sic] civilization of iron' about 200 years later. The map showing the spread of iron in Europe (Pleiner 1980: fig.11.2) shows knowledge of iron technology coming into Britain from the Rhineland.

This is something of an oversimplification. Tylecote (1962: 175–216) collected most of the evidence available at that time, and this survey is still largely representative: only a handful of sites have been discovered since then. His table 70 lists 28 sites where evidence of ironmaking has been recorded, widely distributed, from Shetland down to Somerset and Sussex. Furnaces are only reported on four sites: Kestor, Devon (Fox 1954), Chelm's Combe, Somerset, Rudh' an Dunain, Skye (Scott 1933–4), and Rowberrow Warren, Somerset (H. Taylor 1922–3). All these sites contained 'bowl' furnaces – that is to say, non-slag-tapping furnaces of a simple type (Cleere 1972: Type A.1). To these must be added the group of Wealden domed slag-tapping furnaces of pre-Roman (or very early Roman) date: Broadfields, Cow Park, Minepit Wood and Pippingford Park. It will be seen that there is a clear distinction between the distributions of the two types of furnace: the A.1 furnaces are all on the western side of the British Isles and the B.1.ii furnaces are concentrated in the Weald. Moreover, there is a spread of dating for the former from 400 to 100 BC for the A.1 furnaces, whilst the B.1.ii furnaces are all dated to the early first century AD.

This seems to indicate two separate traditions of ironmaking coming into Britain. The earlier, based on a non-slag-tapping furnace, appears to have been introduced in the earlier part of the pre-Roman Iron Age and to have a westerly distribution, implying an origin in north-western Gaul, or even further south. The later group, utilizing a domed slag-tapping furnace, dates from the century preceding the Roman invasion and may be assumed to have close affinities with the Rhineland. In archaeological terms, this would relate the earlier group to the Iron Age B communities and the later to the Belgic invaders of the first century BC. Unfortunately, owing to the sparseness of archaeological information from the putative homelands of these two cultural groups, at least so far as ironmaking technology is concerned, the only clear link that can be established is between the Wealden domed furnaces and those from the Siegerland (Gilles 1936).

2 Prehistoric sites in the Weald

Fig.17 shows that evidence of pre-Roman ironmaking in the Weald is concentrated in two areas, on the northern and southern fringes respectively. There appears to have been no ironmaking in the High Weald in the prehistoric period.

So far as the northern group is concerned, there appears to have been a movement into the Weald from the Chalk and Greensand some time towards the end of the first century BC. It is possible that this was the result of political pressure, although the old concept of Belgic

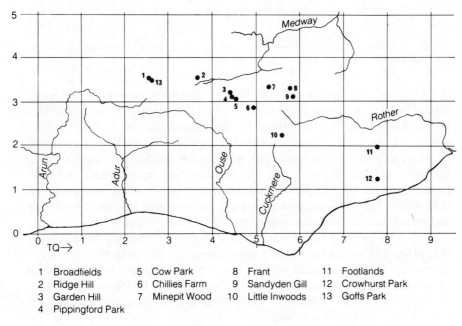

1	Broadfields	5	Cow Park	8	Frant	11	Footlands
2	Ridge Hill	6	Chillies Farm	9	Sandyden Gill	12	Crowhurst Park
3	Garden Hill	7	Minepit Wood	10	Little Inwoods	13	Goffs Park
4	Pippingford Park						

Fig.17 Distribution map showing prehistoric ironmaking sites in the Weald.

expansionism seems to have been discarded in recent years by Iron Age scholars. It is more likely that this movement was the result of a deliberate decision to exploit the rich iron ores of the northernmost ridge of the Wadhurst Clay. Defended enclosures such as Saxonbury (Winbolt 1930) and Garden Hill (J. H. Money, personal communication) appear to have been established at this time, largely based on ironmaking.

The small workplaces in the vicinity of Garden Hill, such as Pippingford Park and Cow Park (fig.18), appear to have been related to

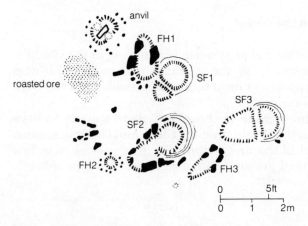

Fig.18   Layout of smelting furnaces (S F) and forging hearths (F H) at Cow Park (based on Tebbutt 1979; fig.1).

the Garden Hill settlement. Neither of the two excavated has produced any evidence of habitation, and so the presumption is that the ironmakers lived in the defended enclosure and set up their workplaces where ore was close at hand. However, the picture is clouded to some extent by the existence within the settlement itself of two furnaces of the domed type: the explanation must await the full publication of this important excavation, but it seems not unlikely that these furnaces represent a very early stage in the life of the settlement, when ore was being exploited from close at hand.

Little can be said about the relationship of Saxonbury to ironmaking, since no workplaces have been found in its vicinity. The early history of the Broadfields settlement is also far from clear: certainly there was no defended enclosure of the Garden Hill/Saxonbury type in the area. However, all three have factors in common which allows them to be treated as a group.

The second prehistoric ironmaking concentration is on the south-

ernmost Wadhurst Clay Ridge, above Hastings. Here the interpretation
is more complicated, since there have been no major excavations on
any of the sites and, moreover, continuous exploitation into the
Roman period has tended to obliterate traces of prehistoric working.
The evidence comes from three sites: Footlands and Crowhurst Park,
both of which have produced pottery, like that from the northern
group of sites, securely identified as being of Cunliffe's Southern
Atrebatic type, and Beauport Park, where traces of a round house of
Iron Age type have been found in the vicinity of the second century
Roman bath-house. No furnaces datable to this period have been
found: all the later ones are clearly of the Roman shaft type.

In all probability this was an initiative quite independent of the
incursion into the Weald from the north. It has been suggested (Cleere
1975) that this venture may have orginated with the Regni further
along the coast to the west. The well-known Cogidubnus inscription
from Chichester (*RIB*, I: 91) may perhaps have been prepared by a
guild of smiths (*collegium fabrorum*) that was established before the
Roman conquest by a group of local entrepreneurs, who had recognized the potential of the iron-ore deposits in this area, shipping
ingots out by sea both to other parts of the Belgic south-east and even
across the Channel to Gaul.

Thus, by the time the Romans arrived in Britain in AD 43 there was
a vigorous and technologically well advanced ironmaking industry in
existence on the fringes of a region that was rich in iron ore and
woodland, the two essential raw materials for this industry that was
recognized by the Romans as a key one in their economy.

3 The economic basis

Britain can be said to have entered the full Iron Age around the
mid-first century BC with the advent of the Belgae from the lower
Rhineland. They brought with them the iron-based economy of
central Europe, with a great growth in the use of iron for a wide range
of uses. Caesar, who visited Britain in 55 and 54 BC, records that there
was iron production in the maritime region of Britain, but that it was
small in output (*De Bello Gallico*: v.12). However, the Greek geog-
rapher, Strabo, writing half a century later, in the famous passage
referring to exports from Britain (iv.99), includes iron along with
slaves and hunting dogs. Clearly, this reflects the great impetus given
to iron production during this half-century. The exploitation of the
Wealden iron ores in this period must surely be a manifestation of this
major development.

The two Wealden areas were well placed to supply iron, doubtless in the form of semi-finished products, for trading within Britain and elsewhere. Products from the northern group could easily be transported overland to the small tributaries of the Thames, and thence downstream to the Essex region, where excavations in Colchester over the past 50 years have revealed the material richness of the Trinovantes and their extensive trade links with Europe. Products from the southern group could be shipped from small estuarine ports on the Rother and Brede coastwise either to the Chichester-Fishbourne area or to Kent. It is not inconceivable that the ironmasters responsible for these enterprises were themselves refugees from the Romans in Gaul and the Rhine estuary, who brought with them advanced technological knowledge on ironmaking and retained close connections with their fellow-tribesmen who had remained in Romanized Gaul.

It is unfortunate that so little excavation has been carried out on the ironmaking sites in the Battle-Sedlescombe area. Their magnitude in the Roman period is manifested by the enormous refuse heaps that either remain or which are recorded as having been quarried for road metalling in the nineteenth century. The exiguous evidence from Beauport Park, Crowhurst Park and Footlands gives rise to speculation that there may be substantial evidence on these and other sites in this region of considerable ironmaking activity in the prehistoric period. This would seem to be implicit in the fact that the ironmaking establishments in this region were 'nationalized' by the Romans very soon after the invasion of AD 43 (see Chapter 4). Had there not been a sizeable industry in this region when the Romans arrived it is arguable that they would not have taken it into public control so promptly: the potential must surely have been obvious.

It is not entirely unjustifiable to suggest that the existence of this industry was one of the main reasons for the Roman invasion. Classical authors imply that the British operation was solely political, in that Rome needed to secure its northern frontier against the Celtic tribes in Britain who were giving support and comfort to their rebellious cousins on the other side of the Channel. However, the importance of a major iron-producing industry had been recognized by the Roman power on at least one earlier occasion, when the great industry of Noricum (Styria in modern Austria) was added to the Empire by the Emperor Tiberius. The existence of a substantial industry in the Weald by the first century AD may well have been an important factor in deciding the Emperor Claudius that extension of the Roman Empire to Britain was desirable.

Chapter 4   Roman ironmaking in the Weald

1   The extent of the industry

Schubert (1957: 36–7), following Straker (1931), but with some characteristic looseness of interpretation, lists no fewer than 18 sites of the Roman period from the Weald. Some of these were only tentatively identified by Straker as Roman, using phrases such as 'slag of a Roman type was found'. In other cases, the presence of a bloomery was assumed from the presence of slag metalling on a Roman road, but this does not necessarily imply the existence of an iron-smelting site in the immediate vicinity. In a paper prepared over ten years ago (Cleere 1975), one of the present authors discussed 36 sites which have been proved by excavation or by finds of pottery or coins to be Roman. Since that time, work by the Wealden Iron Research Group has increased that number to about 60, and there is a strong presumption that a proportion of the other bloomery sites listed in Gazetteer A are Roman in origin. These sites are shown on fig.19. Many of the stretches of Roman road near them are metalled with iron slag, where as yet undiscovered sites may be postulated: this is particularly the case along Margary's Route 130, in the St Michaels-Rolvenden area.

Geographically these sites may be said to fall into two main groups: (a) the coastal sites, such as Beauport Park, Chitcombe, Crowhurst Park, Footlands, Icklesham, Oaklands Park, etc., and (b) the High Weald sites, such as Bardown, Great Cansiron, Knowle Farm, Minepit Wood, Oldlands, Ridge Hill, etc., with an extreme westerly outlier at Broadfields. The former group is concentrated in a relatively small area measuring some 16 × 10km, whilst the remainder are spread across some 50km of the High Weald.

Fig.20 (from Cleere 1975) is a chronological chart covering the 36 sites discussed in that paper. It shows that, by the end of the first century AD, ironmaking was in progress at most of the coastal sites and at the High Weald sites of Broadfields, Oldlands, Ridge Hill and Walesbeech, and in all probability at Great Cansiron as well. By the mid-second century, operations had started at a number of other sites in both areas, including Bardown, Chitcombe, Petley Wood, etc.

Fifty years later, at the beginning of the third century, the picture is beginning to change. Operations at the main Bardown settlement had ceased, although the site was still occupied, but the satellite site at Holbeanwood, about 2km away, had started working, and other

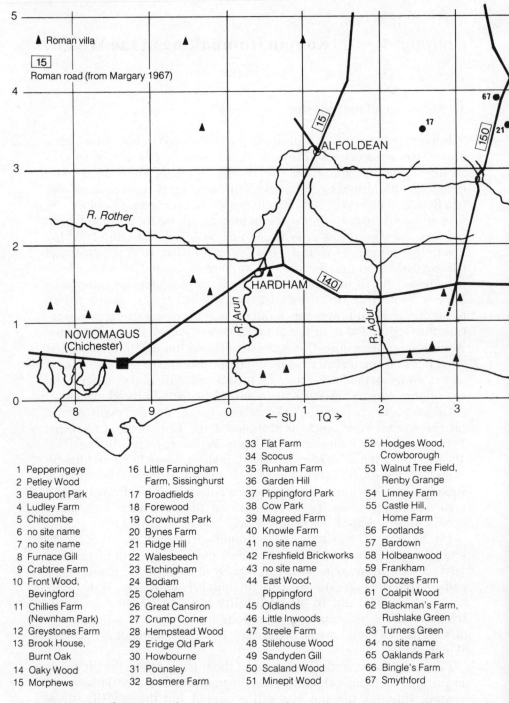

Fig.19 Distribution map showing Roman ironmaking sites in the Weald. For full identification of sites, see Gazetteer B.

1 Pepperingeye
2 Petley Wood
3 Beauport Park
4 Ludley Farm
5 Chitcombe
6 no site name
7 no site name
8 Furnace Gill
9 Crabtree Farm
10 Front Wood, Bevingford
11 Chillies Farm (Newnham Park)
12 Greystones Farm
13 Brook House, Burnt Oak
14 Oaky Wood
15 Morphews

16 Little Farningham Farm, Sissinghurst
17 Broadfields
18 Forewood
19 Crowhurst Park
20 Bynes Farm
21 Ridge Hill
22 Walesbeech
23 Etchingham
24 Bodiam
25 Coleham
26 Great Cansiron
27 Crump Corner
28 Hempstead Wood
29 Eridge Old Park
30 Howbourne
31 Pounsley
32 Bosmere Farm

33 Flat Farm
34 Scocus
35 Runham Farm
36 Garden Hill
37 Pippingford Park
38 Cow Park
39 Magreed Farm
40 Knowle Farm
41 no site name
42 Freshfield Brickworks
43 no site name
44 East Wood, Pippingford
45 Oldlands
46 Little Inwoods
47 Streele Farm
48 Stilehouse Wood
49 Sandyden Gill
50 Scaland Wood
51 Minepit Wood

52 Hodges Wood, Crowborough
53 Walnut Tree Field, Renby Grange
54 Limney Farm
55 Castle Hill, Home Farm
56 Footlands
57 Bardown
58 Holbeanwood
59 Frankham
60 Doozes Farm
61 Coalpit Wood
62 Blackman's Farm, Rushlake Green
63 Turners Green
64 no site name
65 Oaklands Park
66 Bingle's Farm
67 Smythford

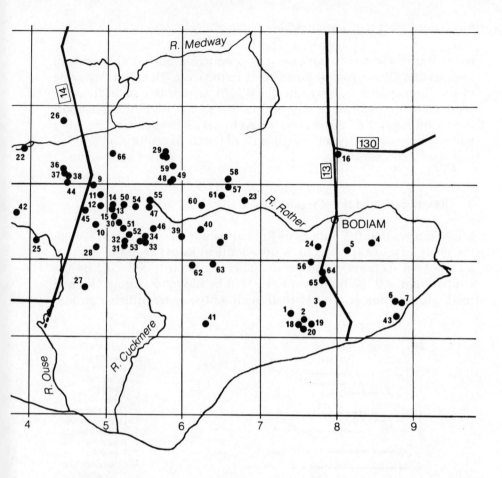

satellites, such as Coalpit Wood and Shoyswell Wood, were also probably operating at this time. Holbeanwood is the only one of the Bardown satellite sites to have been excavated, but there are several similar sites, at roughly the same distance from the Bardown settlement and linked to it by rough slag-metalled tracks, where iron was made. A similar situation may well have obtained at Crowhurst Park, where the main settlement seems to be ringed by subsidiary sites such as Bynes Farm, Forewood, and Pepperingeye; there are also indications that Oaklands Park and Beauport Park may have had satellite working places as well.

The next important stage comes in the mid-third century. Operations had certainly ceased at the Bardown complex, and there are strong indications that ironmaking ceased at many other sites around the same time – Chitcombe, the Crowhurst Park group, Knowle Farm, Oaklands Park, Ridge Hill and Walesbeech, for example, have produced no late third- or fourth-century material. By the end of the third century iron appears to have been in production only at Footlands in the east and Oldlands and Broadfields in the west. The great flowering of the Roman iron industry in the Weald, which left such dramatic remains as the enormous slag and refuse tips at Bardown, Beauport Park, Chitcombe and elsewhere, seems to have been between the latter part of the first century and the middle of the third century, a period of less than 200 years.

2   Classification of the Roman sites

Fig.20 shows that the pattern of Roman penetration into and through the great forest of the Weald is not identical as between the western and eastern sections of the region. This is primarily reflected by the road system. All the Roman sites lie within 3.5km of a known Roman road, either a major arterial road such as the London-Brighton and

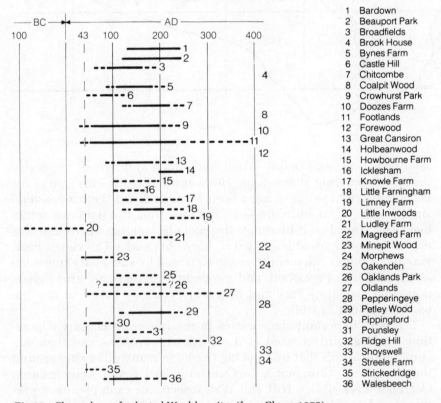

1   Bardown
2   Beauport Park
3   Broadfields
4   Brook House
5   Bynes Farm
6   Castle Hill
7   Chitcombe
8   Coalpit Wood
9   Crowhurst Park
10   Doozes Farm
11   Footlands
12   Forewood
13   Great Cansiron
14   Holbeanwood
15   Howbourne Farm
16   Icklesham
17   Knowle Farm
18   Little Farningham
19   Limney Farm
20   Little Inwoods
21   Ludley Farm
22   Magreed Farm
23   Minepit Wood
24   Morphews
25   Oakenden
26   Oaklands Park
27   Oldlands
28   Pepperingeye
29   Petley Wood
30   Pippingford
31   Pounsley
32   Ridge Hill
33   Shoyswell
34   Streele Farm
35   Strickedridge
36   Walesbeech

Fig.20   Chronology of selected Wealden sites (from Cleere 1975).

London-Lewes highways or one of the minor roads and ridgeways. For example, the Ridge Hill/Walesbeech group lie close to the London-Brighton road (Margary's Route 150); Broadfields is near Margary's Track VI (Margary 1965) and equidistant from Stane Street (Route 15) and the London-Brighton road (Route 150); Oldlands and Great Cansiron lie on the London-Lewes road (Route 14); Bardown and Holbeanwood straddle Margary's Track V (the Mark Cross-Sandhurst ridgeway); Magreed Farm and Knowle Farm are on his track IV (the Heathfield-Hurst Green ridgeway); and the coastal group lie near or on the complex of minor roads in the south-east corner of Sussex, linked to Watling Street at Rochester by Route 13. This suggests an alternative classification of the sites, based on their relationship to their communications by both land and sea and on their possible markets.

This alternative classification, which is more representative of the organization of the industry, distinguishes two groups of sites: the western group, orientated on the major highways running north-south, and the eastern group, with a primary outlet by sea from the estuaries of the small rivers Rother and Brede.

It is postulated that the western group of sites, such as Broadfields, Great Cansiron, Oldlands, and Ridge Hill, may have been set up to exploit ore bodies discovered during road-building operations. Of this group of sites, only that at Ridge Hill had been excavated until recently (Straker 1928). Straker suggested that this, the farthest north of the Roman sites that he had found, probably had its market outlet in London. This comment probably provides the key to this group of sites. Routes 15 and 150 connected the prosperous and densely populated agricultural areas of the South Downs, with their fine villas and centuriation, to the mercantile centre of the province; they were roads along which goods of great value would have passed. Both ends of the roads would be potential markets for iron in large quantities. During the first and second centuries, and well into the third, there were hardly any military establishments in the south and only the Cripplegate fort in London, and so it can be safely assumed that this was essentially a civilian operation. It is not inconceivable that the large works, such as Great Cansiron and Oldlands, with their relatively long periods of operation, were set up by entrepreneurs, either individuals or corporate groups similar to the *collegium fabrorum* of Chichester. Limited companies or guilds of this type could have ensured a steady revenue from relatively modest ironmaking activities along the main highways, supplying markets at their two ends. There is a strong presumption, therefore, that the operations of this western group of sites were in the hands of civilians and based on land transport of their products. Serving as they did markets in the most settled part of the province, they were not exposed to military or economic pressures, and probably continued to operate well into the fourth century.

In the eastern group the earliest sites are those in the Battle-Sedlescombe area: Beauport Park, Chitcombe, Crowhurst Park, Footlands and Oaklands Park; Footlands and Crowhurst Park may well have been in existence at the time of the conquest in AD 43. The later sites, which seem to have started up in the first half of the second century – Bardown, Knowle Farm, Little Farningham Farm, Magreed Farm – lie further north, in the High Weald. There appears to have been a northward shift some time between AD 120 and 140, and at the same time satellite sites, such as Bynes Farm, Forewood and Pepperingeye, may have been set up around Crowhurst Park. Such evidence as there is implies that a number of the early sites in the eastern group began producing on a very large scale in the mid-first century. There is no evidence as to who was responsible for the operation of these works. The apparent increase in the degree of organization bespeaks a government-administered undertaking rather than a native industry. This was essentially a sea-based operation, at least at the beginning. Margary claimed a relatively early date for his Route 13, though not so early as for the major arterial Routes 14 and 150. He does, however, imply that Routes 130 and 131 are later, largely because of the imperfection of their alignments. One should not, therefore, see these roads as the primary outlets for the products of the eastern group sites, at least in their earlier phase.

The important roads for this early period are those which appear to wander somewhat purposelessly around the Hastings-Battle-Sedlescombe-Staplecross-Udimore area. If these are studied carefully, it will be seen that they link the five early sites quite efficiently. Margary (1947) proposed three stages of development in this area. In the first, products from the works were shipped by sea from the south coast in the Hastings area and the Brede estuary. Later, the iron-making activity moved further inland, local roadways and ridgeways being built to serve the new settlements. These led to ports on the Brede and Rother estuaries for shipment out to sea. Finally, in the third stage road communications were established with East Kent and with London via Rochester.

During the first stage, which Margary suggests lasted from the conquest to AD 140–50, material could have been moved from Beauport Park along Track III through Ore to a possible harbour near Fairlight. This is an attractive proposition in view of Peacock's recent identification of the Fairlight Clays as the source of CL BR stamped tiles found on Wealden sites (Peacock 1977). However, as yet no Roman settlement has been found in this area, and Fairlight would in fact not have been a very secure haven. One is tempted therefore to conceive of iron being moved north-east to the more sheltered Brede estuary near Sedlescombe. The Oaklands Park site lies on the edge of Sedlescombe, and foundation digging in the Pestalozzi Village located there has revealed a slag-metalled road surface of Roman date. Footlands is only a short distance from Sedlescombe and is linked with it by a well-proved Roman road. Chitcombe is situated to the north of the Brede estuary, but it is connected by road to Cripps Corner, only a couple of miles from Sedlescombe. The nodal point of all these communications would therefore appear to be the head of the Brede estuary, and it would seem to be justifiable to postulate a port installation somewhere in that area.

In Margary's second period, which from evidence at Bardown and Little Farningham Farm seems to have begun around AD 140, or perhaps a decade before, there was a drive into the High Weald. The focal point of the new road system also appears to have shifted north. The Bardown-Holbeanwood complex is served by a road running directly along the Limden valley to join Track IV near Hurst Green; it appears to disregard Track V (the Mark Cross-Sandhurst ridgeway, claimed as pre-Roman by Margary), which is crossed by the track joining Bardown and Holbeanwood. The contour road to Hurst Green is clearly marked and has been observed from the air by one of the present authors.

The Magreed Farm and Knowle Farm sites lie along Track IV, which joins Route 13 at Sandhurst. Little Farningham Farm is just to the east of Route 13 itself, about 8km north of Sandhurst. From here, Route 13 continues southwards to cross what would have at that time been the mouth of the Rother estuary at Bodiam.

It is suggested that Bodiam superseded the hypothetical Brede estuary port some time in the mid-second century. The site lying on the south bank of the river (Lemmon and Hill 1966) showed occupation from the first century, but its main occupation levels certainly date from the second century and go through to the early third century.* Until the Brede estuary port can be located and excavated so as to give more precise dating evidence for the first stage, it is not permissible to assume that it was replaced by Bodiam; it is quite

---

* The discovery in March 1977 by the Field Group of the Robertsbridge and District Archaeological Society of a bloomery site with Roman pottery about 400m from the main site reinforces the connection between the hypothetical Bodiam port and the iron industry.

conceivable that both ports continued in operation. However, it will be seen from fig.19 that the Rother estuary port was located at a point virtually equidistant from all the main centres of iron production. It was, moreover, connected by road with both Sandhurst road junction and that in the neighbourhood of Cripps Corner. Silting has been proceeding steadily on this part of the coast for many centuries, and so it is conceivable that this process led to the transfer of the main port from the Brede estuary to that of the Rother.

Margary's third stage, which is not easy to date accurately but which may have begun in the early third century, involves the construction of the two major roads, Route 13 to Rochester and Route 130 to Canterbury. These roads must have been built before the industry in this part of the Weald had virtually ceased in the mid-third century, otherwise they would have served no apparent purpose, there being no settlements other than ironworks in the region. The excavations at Bodiam show a marked decline at the beginning of the third century, and so the date for the construction of Route 13 from Sissinghurst northwards and Route 130 from St Michael's eastwards may be set some time in the second or third decade of the third century.

Why was it necessary for these roads to be built? There are two possible reasons, which are not necessarily mutually exclusive. First, it is likely that, as has been suggested above, the estuaries were silting up rapidly, and that navigation across what is now Romney Marsh was becoming increasingly hazardous, so that it became desirable to switch from seaborne to landborne transportation. Second, it is possible that a change in ownership led to the need to open up new markets. By about AD 250 most of the major sites were no longer functioning; however, Footlands continued into the fourth century and could clearly have benefited from these new roads.

Another possible explanation that might be considered concerns the relative vulnerability of the sea lanes to attack by pirates and raiders, especially from the beginning of the third century onwards. Road transport would doubtless have been somewhat safer and would have prevented heavy losses of a valuable raw material, with obvious military potential. However, the whole subject of the situation in the Channel in the years preceding the establishment of the Saxon Shore forts is one in which reliable data are conspicuously missing, and so this can only be offered very tentatively to explain the construction of Routes 13 and 130.

Brodribb (1969) has catalogued all the finds of stamped tiles of the *Classis Britannica* known up to the end of 1968: 'the presence of stamped tiles in quantity is likely to reflect naval activity' (Cunliffe

1968: 257). The idea of tiles being manufactured by contractors for the fleet stamped with the CL BR emblem is possible, but it cannot be paralleled elsewhere. A direct connection may be assumed between the fleet and the sites that have so far produced specimens of these tiles. So far, stamped tiles have been found at the following sites associated with the Roman iron industry: Bardown (28 examples), Beauport Park (over 1,600) and Little Farningham (over 50). They have also appeared in a late second-century context at Bodiam. Of the Bardown tiles, all the stratified examples were found in a late second-early third-century context. The Little Farningham Farm specimens all come from a late second-century context. Those from Beauport Park come preponderantly from the roof and floors of a bath-house that was probably built in the mid-second century and was rebuilt and enlarged at least twice before its final abandonment in the mid-third century. It can, therefore, be claimed incontrovertibly that the *Classis Britannica* was controlling these sites and the port at Bodiam in the period between the mid-second century and the early third century.

Of this group of sites, only Bardown has been excavated in any detail (the bath-house alone at Beauport Park has been fully excavated). It is clear from Bardown that there is no break between the 'pre-stamped-tile' occupation and the unquestionable fleet control period. Little Farningham Farm, like Bardown, appears to have been set up in the mid-second century and also exhibits a 'pre-stamped-tile' phase, but again without any discontinuity of occupation, and the same is true of Bodiam, where occupation began in the first century. In default of any evidence to suggest a change of ownership during the latter half of the second century, one is inclined therefore to accept Cunliffe's view that the practice of stamping tiles was not introduced by the *Classis Britannica* until the end of the second century.

This evidence leads to the assumption that the second phase of the eastern group of Wealden ironmaking sites was operated under the direct control of the *Classis Britannica*. At present there is no evidence of a positive nature to confirm fleet control during the first phase, when the large works in the Battle-Sedlescombe area were in operation and sending their products out through the hypothetical port in the Brede estuary. However, the large scale of operations at this time, combined with the continuity of such sites as Beauport Park, makes centralized control seem most probable. A pre-Roman industry existed, but on only a very limited scale and lacking the resources that would permit it to expand to meet the requirements of the army. It would seem logical, therefore, for the fleet to have taken over.

3   Organization of the Roman industry

It is generally accepted that the state owned the mineral rights in all
provinces during the early Empire; in practice this meant that they
were vested in the Imperial *patrimonium* or private estate and thereby
made an important contribution to the *fiscus* or 'Privy Purse'. Davies
(1935: 3) summarizes the position as follows: 'In the provinces ... the
Roman state usually took over those mines which had been crown-
property at the time of the conquest, and perhaps all others known to
exist, so that *de facto* it was normally the precarious as well as the
absolute owner of minerals.' However, this is nowhere explicitly
stated, and a study of the development of mining administration in
the more important provinces from the point of view of mineral
resources, such as Spain, Noricum (modern Austria) and Dalmatia,
suggests that imperial assertion of mineral rights was more of a
convention that evolved piecemeal than an established and legitimate
prerogative. However, the importance to the *fiscus* of firm control over
mineral resources was obvious, although it was not until the reign of
Vespasian that this policy was confirmed by the establishment of an
extensive network of Imperial estates, which included the major
metal-producing regions, and of powerful bureaucratic machinery
(Rostovtzeff 1957: 110).

Generally speaking, the state – viz. the *patrimonium* – was the
largest direct owner and exploiter of mines; however, a varied pattern
developed, based partly on the circumstances of the accession of
individual provinces to the Empire and on the relative importance of
the mineral resources. This pattern was modified for political and/or
economic reasons, during the first two centuries of Imperial control.
Most Roman provinces exhibit several phenomena in common, so far
as their respective iron industries are concerned:

1   Massive increases in mining and ironmaking activities following
    absorption into the Roman Empire.
2   The assertion of nominal State control over mineral resources,
    which manifests itself in the earliest period in the form of direct
    exploitation of gold and the larger silver deposits and the
    granting of franchises for other types of mining.
3   A period of exploitation by rich entrepreneurs, lasting until the
    end of the first century in Spain, the mid second century in
    Noricum, and the end of the second century or the early third
    century in Gaul and Dalmatia.
4   Assumption of direct responsibility for mining and ironmaking
    operations by Imperial officials (*procuratores ferrariarum*), most

probably working through small concessionnaires (*coloni*) or managers (*vilici*).

5 The establishment of Imperial estates with no citizenship rights, a low level of urbanization, but considerable social protection for the inhabitants.

It appears, furthermore, that 4 and 5 above were probably contemporaneous, although the outlines of the Imperial estates may have been laid down at an earlier stage. The process of absorption wholly into the *patrimonium* represented by these steps does not seem to have occurred simultaneously throughout the Empire. In Spain, for example, it was part of the Flavian reforms, which established the model for the application of this process, possibly under military pressure, in the Antonine period in Noricum and the Severan in Gaul and Dalmatia.

This supports the view of Rostovtzeff (1957: 340–3) that the general trend was towards the elimination of large capitalists and concentration of the exploitation of mineral resources into the hands of Imperial officials. He further points out that a policy developed from the time of Hadrian of giving preference to small contractors. He goes on to claim that this system later gave way to direct exploitation by the use of criminals (*damnati in metallum*) or slaves under military supervision. However, there is little evidence (with the exception of gold mining, always a special case) of this practice, and none in the iron industry, at least before the fifth century, and so this development – the general application of which is open to challenge – will be disregarded in the present study.

There is no direct evidence for the existence of Imperial estates in Britain. However, the existence of such estates in the settled southern part of the province has been postulated in the past: their existence has been deduced primarily from the non-territorial organization implicit in the settlement pattern in certain areas. A large tract of country with no early villas and at some distance from any large towns or *civitas* capitals has been taken to imply the existence of a different form of land ownership from the normal, and Imperial estates have suggested themselves. The best-known examples are probably those of Cranborne Chase and the Fenland, where the criteria laid down above seem to be complied with (Rivet 1964: 102–3, 117; Frere 1974: 312–13).

A study of the Ordnance Survey *Map of Roman Britain* reveals another possible Imperial estate in the Weald of Sussex and Kent. The traditional interpretation of the sparse Roman occupation of this region has always been based on the impenetrable nature of the forest cover on the wet claylands of the Weald which, it is argued, prevented its being deforested and ploughed until the advent of the Saxons with their improved ploughs and cultivation techniques (e.g. Brandon 1974: 71; Wilson 1976: 7). However, the most recent account of Anglo-Saxon agricultural methods challenges the widely held view that the Anglo-Saxons introduced the heavy plough, and suggests that this implement was already in use during the Roman period (Fowler 1976: 27–8). Moreover, the traditional view of the impenetrable Wealden forest has been seriously challenged by recent intensive fieldwork on Ashdown Forest (Tebbutt 1974), which has revealed very widespread penetration and settlement from the Mesolithic period onwards.

It would therefore seem permissible to seek another explanation for this lack of Roman urban or villa settlement in the Weald. The clue would seem to lie in the pre-Roman ironworking in the Hastings area and the reference in Caesar to iron production in the maritime region of Britain (*nascitur ibi ... in maritimis regionibus ferrum: De Bello Gallico*, v.12). This would seem to indicate a pre-existing iron-mining region which was absorbed into the Imperial *patrimonium* at the conquest; the parallels with Dalmatia and Noricum would make the foundation of an Imperial estate likely. The possibility of acquisition by inheritance, as occurred in Noricum, should not be overlooked. It has been suggested (Cleere 1975) that the Chichester inscription referring to a *collegium fabrorum* (*RIB* I: 91) might represent a link with the iron-mining in the Hastings area. If so, it is conceivable that this would have been under licence from the king, and that the Wealden iron industry did not come under direct Roman rule until the death of Cogidubnus around AD 80–90 (Cunliffe 1971: 14; see also Cunliffe 1973: 124).

If the Weald did become an Imperial estate towards the end of the first century, it appears to have been exploited in two ways – direct state working (by the *Classis Britannica*) in the eastern part, and leasing – perhaps to *conductores* or *collegii*, although no epigraphic evidence has survived – in the western half.

The involvement of the *Classis Britannica* in the iron industry of the Weald is amply attested by inscriptions from four sites connected with ironmaking (Brodribb 1969; Cleere 1975: 186–90). The most recent survey of the *Classis Britannica* (Cleere 1977) links the expansion of the fleet from its invasion base at Richborough to Dover and the iron-mining area with the erection of the Great Foundation at Richborough c.AD 85; the earliest stamped tiles from ironmaking establishments appear at the beginning of the second century. This may lend support to the hypothesis advanced above, that the

Weald remained part of Cogidubnus's *patrimonium* as client-king until it was bequeathed to the Emperor on his death. However, this may be purely coincidental; the creation of the suggested Imperial estate may be more properly linked with the reforms begun by Vespasian.

The case for the existence of an Imperial estate based on the ironworks of the Weald appears to be a strong one. There is evidence of direct state participation (at least until the mid-third century) in the eastern region, there are no towns within the Weald itself, and villa settlement is confined to the peripheral Greensand and Chalk. The differences in road pattern between the eastern and western parts of the Weald, referred to above, tend to confirm the existence of different modes of exploitation. A conservative view might be to consider the putative Imperial estate to be confined to the eastern region. However, it is clear that 'free miners' were operating on Imperial estates in other provinces; and more thorough exploration of mining areas in Noricum and Spain, in particular, might produce parallels for the 'mixed economy' postulated for the Weald.

There is one further link between the *Classis Britannica* and the Imperial administration that should be taken into account. Under Antoninus Pius, M. Maenius Agrippa L. Tusidius combined the posts of *praefectus Classis Britannicae* and *procurator provinciae Britan-niae* (*Corpus Inscriptionum Latinarum*, XI, 5632; Pflaum 1960–1: no. 120). At this time the fleet was well established as responsible for iron production in the eastern Weald, a major source of iron for Britain and also, perhaps, for the north-western provinces (Cleere 1975: 189; Cleere 1977). There would seem to be some logic in the combination of the command of the fleet with the provincial procuratorship. Support for this view comes from the unpublished Beauport Park inscription; this so far undated dedication (which is hardly likely to have been much later than the end of the third century) relates to the rebuilding of the bath-house under the supervision of a *vilicus*, named as Bassus or Bassianus. This is suggestively reminiscent of the series of dedications by the *procurator ferrariarum* and his *vilicus officinae ferrariae* from the Briševo-Ljubija region of Dalmatia (Wilkes 1969: 267–8). The pluralism implied in the Maenius Agrippa inscrip-tion may have been reproduced at the ironworks: i.e., whilst control of the mining operations was vested in a civilian (the *vilicus*), support services, especially transport and matériel (including tiles), were the responsibility of the fleet and its personnel. This might help to explain the apparent heavy involvement of a military unit in indust-rial operation, which has no parallels in other fleets of the Roman world.

4   The ironmaking settlements

Too few ironmaking sites in the Weald have been excavated to enable what follows to be more than a hypothetical analysis. However, when the excavation data are studied in association with the more general information available on the location and probable organization of the industry, certain broad categories emerge.

So far as size of site is concerned, the variation is enormous, ranging from the possible 8–10ha of Beauport Park through smaller establishments such as Bardown which cover some 3ha to the small satellites such as Holbeanwood covering perhaps 1,000m^2 and the even smaller workplaces like Minepit Wood or Pippingford Park, where a single furnace and a small slag heap represent a very small-scale operation.

There would seem to be a strong case for regarding Beauport Park as some kind of headquarters. In addition to a fine six-room military-style bath-house (fig.21), there is considerable surface evidence in an area that is not accessible for excavation of substantial buildings with tiled roofs and possibly stone wall-footings. There is clear demarcation between what appears to have been the industrial area, where considerable furnace remains were discovered in the early 1970s when a golf course was constructed, and which lies on the hillside above the immense slag heap, now largely quarried away (fig.22), and the living area, on slightly higher ground to the east of the settlement.

This pattern is repeated at Bardown, another fleet settlement, which was excavated during the 1960s. Fig.23 shows the general layout of the site. The large slag and refuse dump lies on the south bank of the little river Limden, and further to the south at a higher level, considerable evidence of ironmaking was revealed in the form of roasting hearths, forges, a charcoal-burning hearth, etc. A major slag-metalled road running north-south bisects the site, separating the working area from the substantial timber-framed barrack block discovered in the final season of excavations. The working area had gone out of use by about AD 200, and part of it lying just to the west of the central roadway had been used for dumping rubbish, which was almost exclusively non-industrial in character.

These are the only sites where excavation and surface fieldwork have enabled such a clear picture to be built up. It is especially regrettable that the piecemeal nature of the excavations at Broadfields, a consequence of the rescue context in which the work was carried out, made it impossible to derive a clear impression of the general layout of what appears to have been an operation on the scale of Beauport Park or Bardown.

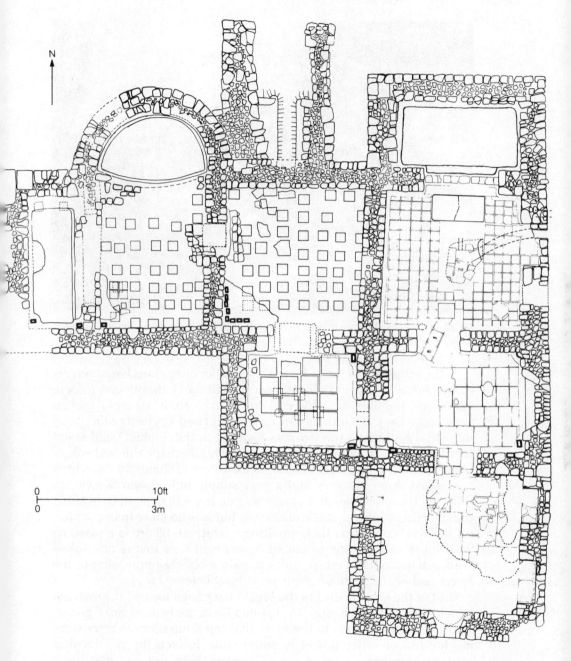

Fig.21   Plan of bath-house at Beauport Park.

Fig.22   Engraving showing Roman slag heap in Beauport Park during removal for road metalling in the nineteenth century (from Straker 1931a: 331).

At the other end of the scale are the smaller operations based on one or two furnaces. The satellites, represented by Holbeanwood (Cleere 1970) and possibly also Bynes Farm (Lucas 1950–3), are a special case, since they are unlikely to have comprised anything other than industrial buildings, the workers residing in the 'mother' settlement (Bardown and Crowhurst Park respectively). Perhaps the best example of the small settlement is that at Cow Park (Tebbutt 1979), which comprised three furnaces and a very simple hut. However, even in this case it can be argued that this was no more than an outlier of the Garden Hill establishment and that the hut was no more than a shelter for the workers during their smelting operations. There is a pressing need for the excavation of one of these small sites that is not linked with a major settlement, in order to gain a clearer impression of the lower end of the scale of ironmaking establishments.

Most of the Roman sites in the Weald have been located through the remains of their slag heaps. These often lie in the beds of small rivers, and this has given rise to the view that the Roman ironmakers were making use of water power in some form. In fact, the relationship between slag heaps and streams depends upon the fact that these small streams often follow geological faults between the Ashdown Sand and the ore-bearing Wadhurst Clay. They cut down through the

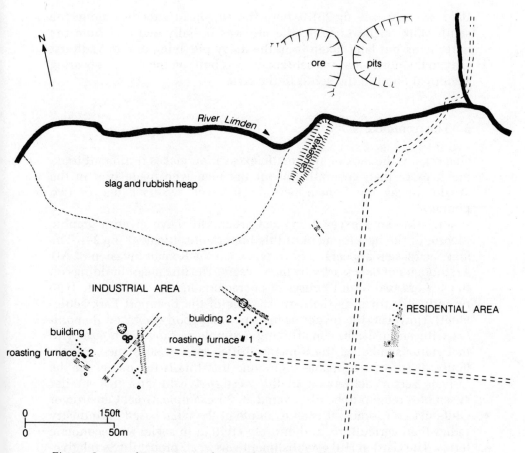

Fig.23 Layout of Roman ironmaking settlement at Bardown.

soft overlying clays in the latter to the harder ironstone deposits, which then outcrop in the sides of the steep little valleys ('gills') that are so common, especially in the High Weald.

When a slag heap has been identified, it is necessary to explore the surroundings for the possible working area and also the source of iron ore. The former can confidently be predicted as lying higher up the slope from the slag: it is impracticable to dump refuse *above* a working and/or living area. The ore source may be in the stream itself or along its banks, but if the operation is of any significance it is likely that the ore body first located will have been exhausted, and that other pits will be revealed in the vicinity. These three components – slag-heap, working area and ore source – may be considered as constant features of every site. They are well illustrated by the

Bardown site (see fig.23), where the slag-heap stretches along the south bank of the Limden, the ore was initially quarried from the north bank but later taken from the many pits lying in the Wadhurst Clay to the north, and the settlement was built on the non-ore-bearing Ashdown Sand to the south of the river.

5   The ironmakers

Once again, the lack of systematic excavation makes it difficult to do much more than generalize about the men who made iron in the Weald during the Roman period. However, we have one or two pointers.

James Money's excavations at Garden Hill have given a graphic picture of the development of this important settlement (fig.24). The first occupation appears to have preceded the Roman invasion of AD 43, though not necessarily by many years. The first major buildings on the site are two round houses of characteristic Iron Age type (a type recently identified as the earliest stage of the Beauport Park settlement). However, the owner or his successor soon embraced *Romanitas* with enthusiasm, constructing a simple rectangular house with that status symbol of the Romano-British man of substance, a bath-house. It seems reasonable to assume that this is the model for the 'private sector' settlement in the western Weald, and that similar ensembles remain to be discovered at, for example, Great Cansiron or Oldlands. In essence, it is an example of the villa, based on industry rather than agriculture, and entirely civilian in social and economic terms. The Garden Hill establishment was in all probability a relatively modest one, where ironmaking was abandoned when some of the larger settlements were established; at the latter it would not be unreasonable to expect to find villas more nearly comparable with those on the Downs.

Bardown represents the military ironworks admirably. The only substantial building on the site was a sturdy timber-framed barrack block of standard type which would have housed some 40 men. Discovery of a number of fragments of flue-tiles on the site suggests that there may have been another, more substantial building in the settlement – perhaps a bath-house or a separate dwelling for the detachment commander.

The origins of the ironmakers themselves are difficult to discern. The building and pottery styles, together with the type of smelting furnace used, that are identified with the earliest ironmakers in the northern part of the Weald (Garden Hill, Pippingford Park etc.) point to an ultimate source in Gallia Belgica, and a similar Continental origin may also be attributed to the pre-Roman ironmakers at Crowhurst Park and Footlands. However, the military takeover in the eastern Weald and the introduction of the shaft furnace overlaid and obliterated the earlier evidence in that area, and there is no indication of the specific geographic or ethnic origin of the imperial ironmakers. It is possible that in the first instance these were imported from other provinces with long-established ironmaking traditions, such as Noricum, but it is equally arguable that the bulk of the workforce was recruited within Britain. It is important to repeat what has been said earlier: there is no evidence for the use of slaves in the iron industry of the Weald. The ironmakers were certainly freemen, but it is not clear whether those working in the fleet establishments were naval personnel or civilian craftsmen employed by the Imperial procurator.

It is instructive to consider the likely number of ironmakers working in the Weald during the Roman period. Experiments by one of the present authors on a reconstruction of a furnace of the B.1.i type (Cleere 1971), which were designed more to study the operating conditions for Roman ironmakers than to investigate the technology involved, combined with observations of a similar type of furnace operated by primitive Indian ironmakers (Cleere 1963b), produced information on which it is possible to base some calculations regarding the likely manning requirements of Roman furnaces, and thereby the industry as a whole during the Roman period.

It became clear from the experiments that the process could be operated without undue fatigue by a team of three at the most: two would be responsible for alternating between operating the bellows for blast and preparing the charges of ore and charcoal, whilst the third would be needed as foreman or charge-hand, supervising the additions to the furnace of charge materials, checking slag evolution, etc. This was the pattern with the Indian furnaces, where one worker was responsible for the arduous work of pumping the double foot-bellows and adding the charge to the furnace for a shift of about two hours, while his colleague prepared more stocks of burden material, removed slag, and generally tidied up the site. The supervisor (an elderly woman) was clearly the master ironmaker and checked all activity around the furnace. It is possible, of course, that a charge-hand of this kind could supervise the work of several furnaces operating at the same time: at Holbeanwood, for example, where it appears that groups of three furnaces were operating simultaneously, probably only one supervisor would be needed for each group.

Examination of slag and refuse dumps at Bardown, Holbeanwood and Beauport Park suggest that the ironmaking process was a cyclical

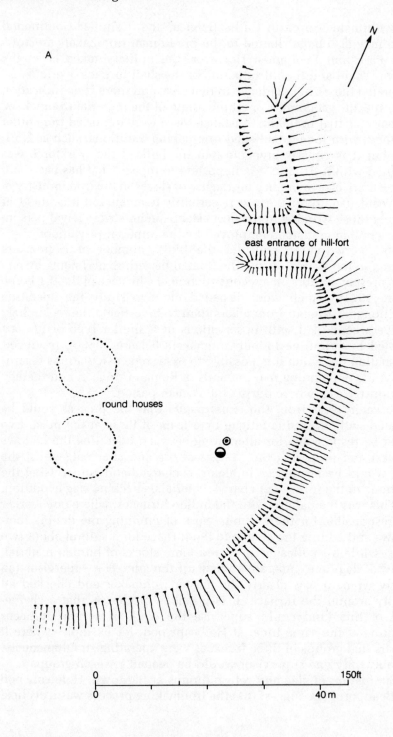

A

east entrance of hill-fort

round houses

0   150ft

0   40 m

B

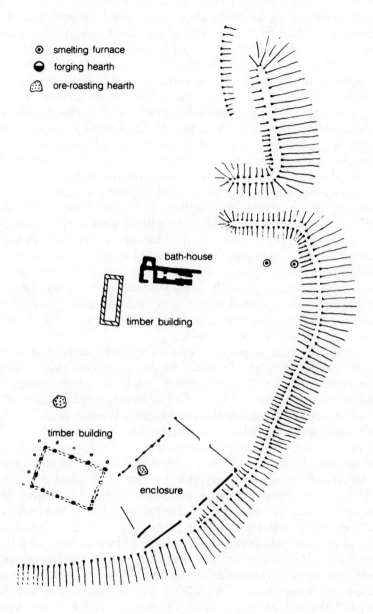

- ⊙ smelting furnace
- ◕ forging hearth
- ⬡ ore-roasting hearth

bath-house

timber building

timber building

enclosure

Fig.24   Sketch showing Iron Age (A) and Romano-British (B) features at Garden Hill (based on information kindly provided by the excavator, J. H. Money).

one (Cleere 1971b). Successive layers of distinctive materials – charcoal and roasted ore fines, tap slag, and furnace structural debris – were observed on all these sites. These are interpreted as signifying that the operations of ore-mining and treatment, timber felling and charcoal burning, smelting, forging and furnace reconstruction were not carried on simultaneously at a major settlement but were performed consecutively on an annual cycle. This would result in characteristic refuse material being dumped in succession.

This hypothesis was applied quantitatively to the Bardown settlement, where it was calculated that seven or eight furnaces would have been in operation in any year in order to produce the 40–5 tonnes of iron annually that is calculated to have been the output from the size of the slag dump (Cleere 1976). It was calculated that some 13–15ha of woodland would need to be cleared to produce sufficient charcoal to sustain this output of iron (although in a personal communication since the paper was published Dr Oliver Rackham has suggested to the author that coppicing may well have been practised in the Roman period and so the area to be cleared would have been smaller: nevertheless, the amount of wood that had to be cut and charked remained the same at nearly 6,000 tonnes). This is a very large amount of timber indeed, and it seems very unlikely that a unit of some 25 men (assuming three workers per furnace plus a manager) could have cut and charked this in a season.

Similarly, a large quantity of iron ore had to be dug to feed the furnaces for this production. Bielenin (1974: 265) indicates an ore/iron ratio of 6:1 for bloomery smelting, which means that the Bardown annual iron output of 40–5 tonnes required 240–90 tonnes of ore a year. At Bardown the good quality Wadhurst Clay nodular ore lies some distance below the surface, and so a considerable quantity of overburden – weighing perhaps three times the ore extracted – had to be moved. Here, therefore, there was a further requirement for 1,000–1,200 tonnes of material to be moved by hand in a year.

Thus, to prepare the charge materials for smelting it was necessary for some 7,000 tonnes of material to be dug and cut and transported. If it is assumed that each worker could deal with 2 tonnes of material per day, some 140 days would be needed by a 25-man unit to dig the ore and cut the timber. The smelting itself, assuming that seven furnaces were in operation continuously, and that the average daily make per furnace was 30kg (Cleere 1976: 236), would have taken at least 200 days. It is possible, of course, that a larger number of furnaces was in operation, which would obviously shorten the smelting phase of the cycle; however, calculations based on the Holbeanwood satellite workplace, which was almost completely excavated and where the total number of furnaces and approximately the total slag production are known, indicate that the smelting phase was indeed of the order of 200 days.

A smelting phase of 200 days and a combined ore-mining and timber-cutting phase of 140 days leaves only two weeks in a year for ore preparation and charcoal burning, which is manifestly too short a period for these lengthy processes. The evidence of the slag dumps, however, does not suggest that they were concurrent operations; it looks, therefore, as though the time for ore-mining and timber cutting and hauling was considerably shorter. To reduce these periods more personnel must therefore be postulated. If the number of workers per furnace is increased to five, giving a total workforce at Bardown of 41 (assuming eight furnaces to be available), the time needed for this operation would be some 15 days to dig the ore and 75 days for the timber cutting, which leaves 75 days for the charge preparation stage. This seems a more realistic organization, and so it will be assumed that a minimum of five workers was needed for each furnace.

With an average daily make of 30kg of iron and a smelting phase of 200 days, the annual output of a shaft furnace of the B.1.i type was around 6 tonnes. Taking iron production from the Weald as varying between 150 and 750 tonnes per year (see next section), it will be seen that the minimum workforce would consequently have varied from a little over 100 to over 600. It should be emphasized that this was the basic process personnel total, and that it needs to be doubled to take account of administrative and transport personnel, and that the total population resident in the area, including families and those supplying goods and services, might well have been three times higher again, giving total populations between 600 and 4,000.

6 The economics of the industry

The data from which any attempt to evaluate total production and consumption figures must be based are twofold: *slag dumps* give an idea of the total production during the life of a site, and *associated finds* (pottery, coins, etc.) enable that life to be quantified in years. In theory, at any rate, it should be possible to calculate from the slag volume remaining the iron production that was required to produce it as refuse and from this to estimate an average annual tonnage output during the lifetime of the site. However, there is a considerable degree of uncertainty in making such calculations, which are set out in a paper by one of the present authors (Cleere 1976).

Slag production can be equated directly with iron production. Work

on reconstructed furnaces and calculations based on furnace remains
(e.g. Bielenin 1974; Cleere 1976; Gilles 1961; Tylecote *et al.* 1971)
indicate a 3:1 slag:metal ratio: that is, 3 tonnes of slag were produced
for every 1 tonne of iron. The weight of slag in a dump can be
calculated from the volume measured by assuming a specific gravity
of 3.0: thus, a *slag volume* of 100m³ is equivalent to a *slag weight* of
300 tonnes, which represents an *iron production* of 100 tonnes, which
can be simplified to the equation:

$$\text{slag volume (m}^3) = \text{iron production (t)}$$

Cleere (1976: table 1, 238) has estimated the equivalent iron
production at the six major eastern Weald sites as follows:

Site	Slag volume (m³)	Slag weight (tonnes)	Iron production (tonnes) Total	Annual
Bardown	4,500	13,500	4,500	40
Beauport	30,000	100,000	30,000	210
Chitcombe	10,000	30,000	10,000	70
Crowhurst	10,000	30,000	10,000	50
Footlands	15,000	45,000	15,000	40
Oaklands	20,000	60,000	20,000	140

The production figures are broken down into an average annual
production based on the scanty dating evidence for most of these
sites. To the total of 550 t/a (tons per year) for these six major sites
should probably be added a further 50 t/a for the other eastern Weald
sites.

Three sites in the western Weald are worthy of consideration in the
same way – Broadfields, Great Cansiron and Oldlands. The area of the
slag dump at Great Cansiron seems to be at least 1.5ha; its depth is not
known, but it may be assumed to average 1m, giving a volume of
15,000m³. However, this is not solid slag and a correction factor of 0.5
needs to be applied, to account for voids, domestic rubbish, etc.,
which gives a slag volume of 7,500m³, equivalent to a total iron
production of 7,500 tonnes. Finds suggest a late first to late second-
century date: if this is interpreted as a 150-year life, iron production
was 50 t/a. No data are available on Oldlands, since most of it has
disappeared, but it was apparently comparable in size with Great
Cansiron, and so a similar annual production rate may reasonably be
inferred. At Broadfields, by contrast, the extent of the slag dump is
unknown, but many furnaces have been discovered, and so here again
a production of 50 t/a may be assumed. To these three sites should be

added the other western Weald sites, whose production may also be represented as 50 t/a, giving an annual production for the western Weald of 200 tonnes.

The eastern Weald settlements, which appear to have been under state control, were in operation from just before AD 100 until the mid-third century, whilst the western settlements had a longer life – until at least the mid-fourth century in most cases. This gives total estimated production figures as follows:

Date	Production (t/a)
43–100	150
100–150	700
150–200	750
200–250	750
250–300	200
300–350	200
350–400	50

If the calculations of iron production are based on slender evidence, calculations of consumption are pure speculation. Nevertheless, it is desirable to attempt an assessment of the general trends and indications of consumption in order to put the production figures into some kind of perspective.

As a starting point, a classification of broad categories of iron usage in the Roman period is essential. The following may be identified:

1 Tools and implements (knives, chisels, scythes, hammers, ploughshares, etc.)
2 Weapons (swords, javelins, etc.)
3 Constructional ironwork (nails, hinges, window fittings, locks, etc.)
4 Miscellaneous uses (boat and cart fittings, horseshoes, barrel hoops, furniture and cabinet-making fittings, etc.)

Tools and implements may be assumed to have had a relatively long life: a carpenter, for example, would collect a set of tools – chisels, hammers, saws, augers, planes etc. – at the outset of his career and would care for these, replacing them only when they were worn out or irreparably broken.

Similar considerations apply to iron weapons. A well-made sword or *pilum* was a personal weapon whose owner would have taken a professional pride in it and kept it clean and sharp. There would have been an irreducible wastage due to breakage or loss in the field, and projectile weapons such as javelins or ballista bolts were not always recoverable. However, it is not unreasonable to assume that a Roman soldier would not have replaced his entire weight of weaponry more than twice during his career, representing say 30kg in total.

An accurate estimate of the usage of iron in domestic building construction is well-nigh impossible. No quantitative survey has ever been made of the total weight of iron in any Roman building. Such a survey should be theoretically possible: whilst stone and tile robbing or re-use was common, the likelihood of nails being re-used is not great, since most would have corroded, once removed from their timber, very quickly to a point where re-use was impracticable. Careful recording of all nails in the excavation of a Roman building should give a picture that is accurate to within 10 per cent of the total use of nails in that building before demolition or decay. The amount of iron used would, of course, have varied according to the type of construction: a timber building would have contained a greater weight of iron in relation to its cubic capacity than a stone-built one (although iron nails and holdfasts would have accounted for a considerable weight of metal in a villa, from the roof timbers, the *tegulae*, the box-flue system, and the door and window fittings).

Finally, there are two categories of 'miscellaneous' use which must have been substantial consumers of iron. Horseshoes were used to reduce abrasion of hooves, and therefore by definition they were subject to extreme wear; there must consequently have been a steady demand for replacements. However, since even less is known of the equine population of Roman Britain than is known of the human population, it is impossible to quantify this demand in any way. Boat building was another heavy consumer of iron: nails were used both in construction and to hold in caulking, as one of the London boats reveals (Marsden 1974). It would appear not unlikely that the larger Roman boats could have contained at least 50kg of iron, and possibly even more, if iron anchors were used. Again, however, the shipbuilding industry of Roman Britain is totally unknown, and so this consumer sector must be disregarded – somewhat reluctantly, in view of the connection demonstrated between the *Classis Britannica* and the iron industry of the eastern Weald.

It is a mistake to assume that all the above materials were produced in their finished form and shipped out direct from the Roman ironworks of the Weald to the consumers. Finds of iron objects are relatively rare on Wealden sites, with the exception of the omnipresent corroded iron nails. It is much more probable that the output of the Wealden ironworks was being transported out in the form of what are today known as 'semi-finished products'. In the Roman period this was represented by the iron bloom, of the type discovered during excavations at Little Farningham Farm (fig.16) and known from a number of sites in Britain (Brown 1964). These were easily transportable and could have been used for the manufacture of a large variety of artefacts by military and civil smiths, working close to their ultimate customers. There is a strong presumption that the hoard of one million iron nails (7 tonnes) from the Agricolan legionary fortress at Inchtuthil, Perthshire (Angus *et al.* 1962) was forged by military smiths from iron made in the military ironworks of the eastern Weald. Semi-finished products from the 'private sector' of the western Weald most probably made their way by road to London, where they were worked up into finished products for much of the settled south-east of the province, then being distributed by road into East Anglia and the Home Counties and by water along the east coast, up the Thames valley, and across the North Sea to the Rhine provinces. Chichester would act as a secondary distribution centre by road and/or sea to the south-west.

Production from the military ironworks of the eastern Weald is estimated to have been of the order of 600 t/a. With a military presence of 63,000 in the second century (Frere 1974: 296–7), this represents a per capita production of nearly 10kg per annum. It is inconceivable that the army could have maintained a rate of iron usage at this level for some 150 years, especially at a time of relative political stability and one when, moreover, most of the military establishments had been rebuilt in stone. Either this iron was released on to the civilian market or it was shipped across the Channel to the army on the Rhine *limes*. The latter would seem to be the more likely, in view of the lack of major iron-producing regions between the mouth of the Rhine and Noricum.

The military 'market' was dictated by strategic considerations. For most of the Roman period there were three legions in Britain, based at Caerleon, Chester and York, *auxilia* in a series of forts in Wales and in the northern military district, and the garrisons of the northern frontier works. As discussed in a recent paper on harbours (Cleere 1978), military port installations are to be identified, albeit exiguously, at all three legionary fortresses, the coastal forts in Wales such as Carmarthen and Segontium, and at South Shields and Maryport at opposite ends of the northern frontier defences. Iron from the eastern Weald sites would have been taken by road (and perhaps also by river down the Rother) from the ironworks to the port at Bodiam, whence it would be shipped by sea across the shallows of modern Romney Marsh to the main *Classis Britannica* base at Dover. From Dover it could be distributed by sea up the east coast to York and South

Shields and westwards to Wales, Chester and Maryport. It seems reasonable to suggest, moreover, in view of the surplus referred to above, that from about AD 120 until AD 250 some 400 tonnes of iron was being exported annually to the army on the Rhine *limes*. This would have been transported on the short sea crossing from Dover to Boulogne (that is, between the two main bases of the *Classis Britannica*), and thence taken by water coastwise to the mouth of the Rhine for distribution by barge – possibly by the *Classis Germanica* – to the legionary fortresses and other military installations on the frontier.

The securing of supplies of this important military matériel by the army for its own use was obviously a sound strategic step, and it becomes more important when it is seen as covering several provinces from a single base. It is tempting to see the original decision as having been made by Hadrian when he initiated his programme of frontier works. Initial state involvement in the iron industry of the eastern Weald, perhaps on the initiative of Agricola, was expanded considerably at the start of the second century, when large quantities of iron would have been needed on the northern frontier of Britain (this seems to be borne out by the expansion of the more southerly sites such as Beauport Park and the extension into the High Weald represented by the establishment of Bardown). Once the initial demand for iron for the Wall had been met, there was obviously a surplus available; instead of dismantling the successful and productive industry of the eastern Weald, the military high command made arrangements for the surplus to be shipped across to the garrison of the Rhine frontier, which had in all probability been dependent hitherto for its supplies of iron on the industry of distant Noricum or on the local small-scale operations.

7　The end of the Roman iron industry

Two stages can be recognized in the decline of the Roman iron industry in the Weald. The first came in the first half of the third century, when some time between AD 220 and 240 the settlements under fleet control in the eastern Weald, such as Bardown and Beauport Park, were closed down. The reason for this is not known. The *Classis Britannica* itself disappears from the record around this time, along with other provincial Roman fleets (Cleere 1977), and the great headquarters at Dover was also dismantled (Philp 1981). However, the need for iron on the part of the army cannot have diminished significantly, and so it can only be surmised that the Weald – which was wide open to attack from Channel pirates and where the river estuaries were silting up seriously – was abandoned in favour of another iron-producing area that was more secure, such as the Forest of Dean. Of the known settlements in this region, only Footlands seems to have continued to produce iron, perhaps under private management.

The second stage coincided with the decline of Roman social and economic life in the province during the fourth century. By the end of the third century, only Oldlands and Broadfields in the western group and Footlands in the eastern were still functioning, and little later fourth-century material is known from any of these settlements. The last furnaces were quenched by the end of the century and the last settlers moved out, and the wildwood moved back to the clearings to reclaim its own.

There is no incontrovertible evidence of permanent occupation of the Weald during the sub-Roman period. The general picture is one of desertion, the Wealden forest being the resort of fugitives and hunters. It was not until the seventh century at the earliest that the seasonal swine pastures of the Downland Anglo-Saxon settlers began to be occupied permanently, and the earliest records date to the middle of the eighth century (Brandon 1974: 78). Everything points to this settlement having been predominantly agricultural. The potential of the iron-ore resources appears to have been unrecognized, or perhaps ignored. The main area of iron production in the Anglo-Saxon period seems to have been in the Midlands, and in particular in the Forest of Rockingham (Schubert 1957), one of the areas of primary Anglo-Saxon settlement through the rivers of eastern England, and where an iron industry existed throughout the Roman period.

The only ironmaking site in the Weald so far known that can securely be dated to the Saxon period is that at Millbrook (Tebbutt 1982; see also Chapter 2 above). This is of great interest, since the furnace type and technology seem to have close affinities with the 'non-slag-tapping furnace' tradition of the Anglo-Saxon European homeland.

Unfortunately, only the furnace was excavated in a rescue excavation, and nothing is known of the associated settlement. It is impossible to establish whether this was part of a settlement devoted solely to ironmaking or whether it was an ancillary activity on an agricultural settlement. Moreover, no other bloomeries have been securely dated to the Anglo-Saxon period. However, there are many bloomeries listed in the Gazetteer (Section A) that cannot be attributed to either the Roman period or the Middle Ages. Although the indications as a result of sampling by members of the Wealden Iron Research Group and by the relative distributions of Roman and undated sites are that the majority of the latter are almost certainly Roman, the possibility of a small number dating from the Anglo-Saxon period cannot be ruled out.

Chapter 5   Iron in the Weald in the Middle Ages

Fifty years after Ernest Straker wrote *Wealden Iron*, many aspects of the medieval industry remain tantalizingly obscure. There were no great centres of smelting, as characterize the Roman industry, no prominent earthworks, as have attracted attention to post-medieval activity. Nor do documentary sources throw more than occasional light on the actions or products of the medieval smelter or smith. There are useful references to purchases of iron by the Crown, but these give little topographical guidance. Local sources are not plentiful, although enough is now known to indicate the districts where the industry was most active. These classes of document may be placed alongside fieldwork on a relatively modest scale to provide the basis for a fresh synthesis. It is also useful to notice technological developments that took place elsewhere, notably the adoption of water power in the later Middle Ages. These suggest a framework for changes in the Weald.

This chapter sets out to explore three main problems, the likely form and chronology of the development of the industry, its location, and the methods in use.

1   The form and chronology of the medieval industry

There are no medieval sources which provide either a deliberate survey or an incidental overview of the industry. The references are occasional: to purchases of iron, to mining ore, to bloomery smelting, and to smiths. A point to stress at the outset is that references are concentrated in the thirteenth and fourteenth centuries, but it has never been conclusively established that this represents the true pattern of activity. The most obvious problem is how far iron was smelted in the Weald in the Saxon period. Until recently there were only two references. The first was to a late-seventh century charter in which Oswy, king of Kent, granted an iron mine at Lyminge, north of Hythe, to the Abbot of St Peter's Canterbury in 689. Although sparse ores do occur in the Greensand in this area, the grant might well relate to dependent lands on the Weald clays (Birch 1885: I, 107). At the end of the period a *ferraria* is mentioned near East Grinstead in the Domesday survey of 1085 (Darby and Campbell 1962: 473). A significant addition is the recent excavation of the bloomery at Millbrook, on Ashdown Forest, which is radiocarbon-dated to the ninth century (Tebbutt 1982). Even so, the scale of Saxon production of iron in south-east England remains a problem and requires thorough research.

At the end of the period, also, much remains to be done, for the years between the end of the fourteenth century and the introduction of the blast furnace at the end of the fifteenth have yielded little information.

(A) THE EVIDENCE OF TRADE

Between 1250 and 1370 the Crown made sporadic purchases of iron objects in the Weald, on occasion involving considerable quantities. Some of these were noted and discussed by Straker and Schubert, and need only be mentioned in outline here. Certain purchases of iron were for the construction or repair of royal buildings. For example, in 1253 the sheriff of Sussex was to provide 12,000 nails from his bailiwick, to be taken to the king's house at Freemantle near Kingsclere, Hampshire, for the completion of the roof. Two years later the sheriff was to buy two cartloads of local iron, to be passed to the Keeper of the King's Works at Guildford. A later case was the purchase in 1370 of nails and bars by the clerk of works at Leeds Castle, Kent, for windows and spikes and for repairing cogwheels in the mill.[1]

On a larger scale, purchases were made for military needs. The following cases relate with fair certainty to Wealden iron, although as a good deal of imported iron was available in south-east England the whole quantities need not be from local sources. The earliest known case was in 1242, when the keepers of the estates of the Archbishop of Canterbury were required to make 5,000 horseshoes and 10,000 nails for delivery at Portsmouth. A month later the archbishop's officials received funds for a larger consignment, 8,000 horseshoes and 20,000 nails, conveyed to Portsmouth from Maidstone and Otford. As suggested below, it is possible that the latter totals included the first order. From this time the Wealden industry was equal to providing for the large and irregular needs of armies. The largest known purchase was of 30,000 horseshoes and 60,000 nails by purveyance in 1254. Other examples comprised the 30,000 horseshoes and 29,000 nails obtained in 1320, and 3,000 and 80,000 respectively in 1327.[2] Further iron goods whose purchase is recorded are 406 iron wedges or pegs bought in the Weald in 1275, and 343 wedges made in the Weald three years later, one of a series of purchases of a variety of iron objects in the area. The Crown also bought blooms, to be worked by its own smiths, as illustrated by the carriage of 32 blooms from Newenden to Dover Castle in 1326.[3]

Rather more specialized were the arrows purchased in the Weald. In some cases it is uncertain whether their points were of iron, and references may merely be to the supply of wooden shafts. For example the 300 sheaves to be sent by the sheriffs of Sussex and Surrey to the king at Kenilworth in 1266 were to be 'well prepared', but the materials are not described.[4] Such doubts attach to the 6,000 arrows bought at Horsham in 1338, which were to be of good dry wood, the heads well sharpened. Horsham was a centre of the trade in arrows. It provided part of a batch collected by the Sheriff of Kent in 1342, and 150 of 266 sheaves supplied in London in 1346.[5] Nevertheless, iron and steel arrowheads were certainly made in the Weald, for in 1359 Thomas atte Leghe, 'fletcher', was instructed to employ Kent and Sussex smiths to forge 500 steel heads for arrows purveyed for the King's use.[6] Also significant is the inclusion of iron-tipped arrows in rents. This was the practice at Rotherfield early in the fourteenth century, and was recorded in the accounts of the Duchy of Lancaster manor of Maresfield over the late fourteenth and much of the fifteenth century.[7]

Apart from the Crown trade, inevitably irregular and related to war, there was a commercial traffic in and beyond the south-eastern counties. London took Wealden iron, although merchants there also bought from other sources, English and foreign. Much Spanish and Baltic iron of high quality reached the Thames. The Forest of Dean was also a regular supplier, the high yielding ores producing an excellent product at a relatively low cost of extraction. The most quoted example of the Wealden trade with the capital is that in strakes for cart wheels. In 1300 London ironmongers complained that these were being sold in lengths shorter than usual, and that future deliveries should be checked against a standard rod. To this can be added a case in the Court of the Lord Mayor of London in the following year, in which a London ironmonger was presented for going outside the City to Southwark to do business with merchants and smiths bringing horseshoes and nails from the Weald.[8]

Of the local trade there is no doubt, for several estate records show the purchase of blooms or bar iron in the fourteenth century. In some cases blooms were brought to be worked by estate smiths, as at Boxley Abbey, Maidstone, where seven blooms of 'Wealden' iron were bought in 1334, and Penshurst, where purchased blooms were used in 1346 to repair carts. There are many cases of bar iron being bought, for example by the manor of Rotherfield in 1325 for the repair of ploughs,

for the same purpose at Petworth in 1349–53 and at Robertsbridge
Abbey for carts in 1360. Estates also required ready-made iron objects:
the Rotherfield record of 1325 also shows that plough-wheels and
horseshoes were being bought.[9]

These examples indicate that the industry could produce supplies
of iron on some scale in the period 1250–1400. Can orders such as
those of the Crown tell us anything of the scale of activity in particular
localities? Most place the source of supply only in the most general
terms. One assumes a westerly collecting area for the deliveries to
Freemantle or Guildford, and that the blooms sent to Dover would
come from somewhere close to the eastern Rother. The fourteenth-
century material points to sources near Horsham and Crawley, but
the iron bought in this district could have been delivered from a
wide area of the central Weald.[10]

There is, however, one thirteenth-century transaction which is
more specific. As outlined above, on 17 April 1242 the Archbishop of
Canterbury was requested to have 5,000 horseshoes and 10,000 nails
at Portsmouth eight days from the close of Easter, 4 May. The order
would be made up of 3,000–3,500lb of iron; thus, assuming a
bloom-weight of 30lb, we see that the archbishop's smiths would need
at least 100 blooms within 18 days.[11] As all the equipment had to
reach Portsmouth within this period the rate of production would in
fact have to be rather greater. It has been estimated, as a result of
modern trial smelts, that small bloomeries can operate on an approximate 24-hour cycle. So it is tempting to suggest that the archbishop's
smiths would require no less than six furnaces to produce sufficient
iron for forging. However, there is no means of knowing how many
blooms or finished items would be held in stock on the estate or
available from other sources. Nevertheless, this reference is an important indication that the archbishop's lands, stretching southwards
from Maidstone and Otford into Sussex, were seen by the Crown as a
reliable source of iron.

(B) ORGANIZATION AND DEVELOPMENT OF THE WEALDEN IRON INDUSTRY

The documentary references mentioned above are concentrated in the
thirteenth and fourteenth centuries. As will be seen in section 2 of this
chapter, there is a good deal of local confirmation of activity at this
time. The problem which faced Straker, and still puzzles us, is
whether the concentration of documentary references on these two
centuries is an accurate reflection.

Little progress has been made in filling the blank in the record between the *ferraria* mentioned in the Domesday survey of 1085 and the first of the thirteenth-century references. The *ferraria* is assumed to be an ironworks, and there is no reason to challenge this. It was located near East Grinstead, formerly an outlying part of Ditchling, relatively close to the ninth-century bloomery recently excavated at Millbrook on Ashdown Forest. Whether the industry was neglected by the compilers of Domesday must remain a matter for speculation perhaps only to be resolved by the excavation of firmly dated eleventh-century material. The only hint of twelfth-century working comes from pottery found with slags at Chandler's Farm, Hartfield. This lies, perhaps significantly, between Ashdown Forest and East Grinstead, but the site cannot be conclusively dated to the twelfth century rather than the beginning of the thirteenth.[12]

At the beginning of the thirteenth century the information is inconclusive. On the one hand there were smiths in the south-east Weald around Robertsbridge: there are rentals of Robertsbridge Abbey which, although undated, are ascribed to the period 1220–30 and refer to 'Peter the smith' and the heirs of 'Philip the smith' at Robertsbridge, and 'Ralph the smith' of Werthe (now Worge), between Brightling and Burwash. Whatever the position in the east, in the west of Sussex iron was either not easily obtained or of poor quality; in 1225 the bishop of Chichester was advised by his steward to obtain his supplies from Gloucester.[13]

It is not surprising that the industry developed during the thirteenth century to the point where it could meet demands on the scale posed by the wars of Henry III and his successors. This was a period when local requirements for iron fostered the growth of smelting, for at this time land clearance for new cultivation flourished. New farms were taken in from the woodlands as the Wealden clearings expanded, and in consequence the smiths met a need for wrought-iron goods, whether for agricultural equipment or for building. Agrarian expansion proceeded hand-in-hand with population growth, and by the end of the thirteenth century the regional economy had developed to a significant extent, with the products of a more populous countryside marketed through the growing towns and small ports of Sussex and Kent. Such links themselves fostered the trade in iron, with bar traded to London as well as being used for the construction of carts and ships.

The Weald was a favourable region for the growth of forest industries. Although expansion of settlement certainly took place, in certain districts it was an arduous and slow undertaking, yielding, on completion, small fields on cold clays or, in the High Weald, on stretches of sandy soil whose yields were meagre. For many, the attractions of woodland occupations would be as great as those of farming, leading men to combine their agricultural pursuits with wood-cutting, charcoal-burning, ore-mining and roasting and, for the skilled minority, smelting and smithing.

We know a little of the bloomeries in which such men worked from those documented examples which were run as part of landed estates. The best known is Tudeley, near Tonbridge, operating on the South-frith lands of the Clares in the fourteenth century. Here, over the space of 40 years, there were several changes in the way the works were run. When the surviving accounts begin, in 1329, the bloomeries were in hand, but in 1334 they were leased to Thomas Springet. By 1346 he was in arrears with his rent and smelting had ceased. In 1350 the works were rebuilt, and now Thomas Springet re-appears, this time as manager for the estate, remaining in charge until 1354 when a new lease was made. This time the tenant was Richard Colepepper, who appears to have continued operations for the rest of the decade, obtaining a renewal in 1359. He was in arrears in 1362 and is not heard of subsequently. It is likely that Colepepper was a small landowner or yeoman farmer, for in 1362 it appears that he had lost his own sub-tenant and a workman in the epidemic of the previous year.[14] Another landowner whose estate contained an ironworks was John de Lynleghe. He was an opponent of Edward II, and after the suppression of such 'contrariants' in 1320 there is a reference to his lands at Withyham, his forge and its stock, although there are no details of how it was operated. There is one earlier reference, but this is only to an iron mine, in a dispute in 1263 between Agnes Malameins and Isabel de Aldham. The mine, at or near East Grinstead, had been on the lands of Isabel's first husband Ralf de la Haye, but since his death had produced no profit. There is no reference here to the smelting of the ore.[15]

Even from sources such as these we can only gain occasional glimpses of those who worked in the forest or at a forge. The most prominent of the Tudeley tenants, Thomas Springet and Richard Colepepper, seem unlikely themselves to have been ironworkers. Robert Springet, who, in 1340, leased another Southfrith bloomery, Newfrith-juxta-Bournemelne, was perhaps of similar status. Thomas Henry, who rented two Southfrith bloomeries in 1350 is not otherwise known, but a possible ironworker is John Coppyng, who purchased ore from the estate in 1339. Unnamed, however, are the blowers who worked the bellows at Tudeley in 1329. Wood was cut in the forest of Southfrith and outside the estate; it was made into charcoal and was also used to roast the ore. Those involved on these pursuits are neither enumerated nor named, but would comprise a larger group than the workers at the bloomery itself. A source which does refer to men working in the industry is a dispute over the digging of ore at Horley in 1372. The steward of the Surrey manor of Banstead, of which Horley was an outlier, licensed John Neal to dig 200 loads of ore in the waste, but in doing so, Neal damaged a road regarded as a public highway, for which he was fined, together with others whom we may assume to be miners also.[16]

That we have no more information on the peasant worker in the industry in the thirteenth and fourteenth centuries is a consequence of the particularly poor survival of manorial documents in the Weald. Where they exist, references to the leasing of land give little information about the livelihood extracted by tenants from their holdings. This contrasts with iron-bearing areas where manorial control was strict and well documented. In Yorkshire, for example, the court rolls of the manor of Wakefield show how lucrative a closely regulated iron industry could be in the fourteenth century, for there mining, wood-cutting and smelting were carried out on short leases under tight control (Faull and Moorhouse 1981: 780–3).

It is usual to regard the industry in this central period of the Middle Ages as essentially rural, with the production of blooms taking place within the forest and secondary working being carried out in villages and towns. Tudeley and its neighbours, and the excavated fourteenth-century bloomery at Minepit Wood, Withyham (Money 1971), correspond with such a pattern. However, it should not be taken for granted that the tasks of smelter and smith were always spatially separated. At Alsted, an excavated manorial ironworks on the North Downs, smelt-ing and smithing were done in adjacent hearths during the thirteenth century (Ketteringham 1976: 17–31), so perhaps the smiths in villages or even small towns also produced blooms if ore and charcoal were conveniently obtainable. This is suggested by the results of excava-tions at Godmanchester, Huntingdonshire. Here, in a smithy access-ibly sited by the main highway, there were not only forging hearths but the bases of bloomery furnaces (Webster and Cherry 1975). So smiths such as those at Robertsbridge, Lindfield or Crawley may not only have purchased blooms from woodland smelters, but also have produced their own.

The period of greatest activity in the Weald was interrupted and perhaps curtailed in the longer term by the Black Death, the great bubonic plague of 1349. The effect of mortality was immediate, for prices of iron increased as production fell and wages in the industry rose. The shortage is illustrated by an entry in the accounts of the Manor of Petworth in 1349–50: 'and for iron bought for maintaining the ironwork of the ploughs this year 8ˢ 4ᵈ, and so much because iron is dear by reason of the mortality'. The immediate effect on the prices of many goods is well known. Foodstuffs were expensive in the months after the plague owing to disruption of harvests and markets, despite the reduction in the numbers of consumers. With iron the effects were longer-lasting, even permanent. The Petworth accounts contain a further comment on the high price of iron in 1352–3, relating to purchases at Duncton and Heyshott. In 1355 the problem was recognized nationally by legislation prohibiting the export of iron, among other commodities, from the ports of the south-east.[17] In the still longer term the increase in wages paid to those working in estate establishments was permanent, and at Tudeley labour costs remained 50 per cent above their pre-Black Death level.

There are two reasons for the continuation of high costs and prices in iron production. First, the available labour force was curtailed in part by mortality, a factor not restricted to 1349, but extended into subsequent decades by new outbreaks of disease. The epidemic of 1360–1 was severe in the Weald, and its effects were noted in the Tudeley accounts. Second, there was some mobility of workers in the forests at this time. Farms fell vacant, and some would be attractive enough for those in woodland occupations to take up such tenancies. There would thus have been fewer men pursuing those supplementary occupations which provided ironworks with their materials. By contrast, much of the market for iron would remain. The campaigns of the Hundred Years' War continued intermittently. As we have seen, the Crown required arrows in 1359, and smiths from Sussex and Kent were employed to make steel arrow-heads. In addition the general rural demand for iron would not decline at the same rate as the loss in population: vacant farms were hard to lease, and over England as a whole there is a picture of estates carrying out improvements in building and equipment in order to attract tenants.

It is not known in any detail how these factors balanced out in the Weald; indeed, remarkably little is known about the local industry between 1370 and 1500. The Tudeley ironworks ceased to be leased or worked before 1370, but whether owing to general or particular factors is not known.

There are four references to iron-working sites in the fifteenth century. In 1433, at Croucheland, Ticehurst, a pond and a place for a forge were granted to Richard Burdon of Hadlow. In the following year a forge was recorded as newly built at Derefoldgate, Burwash, and references to this establishment continue in subsequent Ashburnham accounts. There is a mention of a second new forge at Burwash, in 1477. Finally, the last fifteenth-century reference before the Newbridge blast furnace of 1496, is to 'the ierne founders of Buxted' of 1490. The technical implications of this are considered below; we must assume that a bloomery, or some development of it, was in operation at Buxted late in the century.[18]

2   The location of the industry

The documentary and field evidence so far available suggests that the medieval industry was more concentrated in the northern and central parts of the Weald than was the case either in the Roman period or after 1550. This impression is carried right through from the sparse signs of Saxo-Norman activity until the fifteenth century. The documented thirteenth-century locations include the iron mine at East Grinstead (1263) and Crawley, with the references to smiths in court rolls of 1265–6 (A. J. Taylor 1939: 18, 22), while, on the ground, Hartfield and Alsted lie in and just beyond this northern area. The latter, indeed, outside the Weald, probably drew its ore from the northernmost deposits in the Weald.

The fourteenth century provides a similar distribution, notably in the Withyham area, with John de Lynleghe's ironworks and the furnace excavated at Minepit Wood; near Tonbridge, with four bloomeries near Tudeley in the forest of Southfrith; and around the border between Surrey and Sussex, with the iron mine at Horley, the ore-roasting site at Thundersfield (Hart and Winbolt 1937), smiths at Crawley and Horsham, and the supply of horseshoes from Roffey.[19]

In the fifteenth century there are fewer references, and the balance is altered by the appearance of works at Burwash and Ticehurst. Activity was maintained to the north of Ashdown Forest: field-walking at Upper Parrock, Hartfield, has shown numerous bloomery sites around an outlier of the Wadhurst clay. Five of these have produced late medieval pottery, and an adjacent abandoned settlement has been shown to have been occupied until about 1500 (Tebbutt 1975).

If this northern emphasis is more than the accident of the survival of documents and the discovery of a small sample of sites in the field, it needs some explanation. The answer could in part lie in the availability of suitable ores near the surface. Wealden ores vary both in appearance and in quality, as John Fuller was to emphasize in the eighteenth century. Just as certain beds were favoured for the blast furnace, so the Wealden bloomsmith may have operated more successfully with certain 'orestones'. More certain is the effect of the market. As well as the local trades noted above, London required the cheap qualities of iron which Wealden ores appear to have produced. Nevertheless, in the fourteenth century the needs of the Hundred Years' War could upset any such pattern, and it is known that consignments from the Horsham area were carried to Shoreham for shipment (Pelham 1931: 172).

Field and documentary information about smelting sites provides the essential basis for establishing the pattern of location of the industry. However, there is a network of less precise references which should be added, though with reservations. These largely comprise instances of occupational names and references to smiths. Until the early fourteenth century occupational surnames had considerable fluidity, and can be used with some assurance as indicating the trade of an individual. At varying times, in different areas, the relationship becomes less firm, the occupational element merely remaining in a family name. Thus Sayer 'the blower', in the Sussex eyre roll of 1291, and Gilbert 'le blowere' of Crawley, who appears in the subsidy roll for 1296, are more convincing as ironworkers (blower: bellows-man) than is John Blower of Warbleton in 1436. Similarly, personal names such as 'faber' or 'smith' at Robertsbridge or Werthe (Brightling) in the early thirteenth century should be taken more seriously than John Ferro(ner) of Mayfield in 1427. Yet when a family maintained an occupation over several generations, surnames could still relate to their trade. Thus in 1346 'Stephen the smith' appears in a Penshurst account as selling iron to the estate for the repair of carts, and in 1370 'Solomon the smith' sold nails and bars for work at Leeds Castle, Kent.[20]

Rents of iron or iron objects may be subject to similar reservations when recorded in the later Middle Ages. In documents of the 1380s iron-tipped arrows appear as rents at Maresfield and survive in rentals through the fifteenth century. At Framfield an iron fork was paid as rent in the 1420s and 1430s.[21] These symbolized local ironworking, but whether they indicate that it was still continuing is another matter.

3   The archaeology and technology of the unpowered bloomery in the Middle Ages

(A) FIELD STUDIES

When, half a century ago, Straker (1931a) surveyed the medieval industry, he had virtually no field material to aid him. Despite his assiduous work in the Weald, none of the bloomeries he located could be said with any certainty to be medieval, and for those where he did consider such a claim the evidence now seems unconvincing. For example, he found cinder deposits near Tonbridge which he related to the fourteenth-century Tudeley documents, but this could not be proved (p.220). His other examples were as doubtful. Cinder at Newefrith was speculatively linked with a second bloomery mentioned in the Tudeley documents (p.220). Colliers Green, Ewhurst, was only thought medieval because of the resemblance of slags to those at the Tonbridge sites (p.319). At Roffey, near Horsham, cinder was assumed but not proved to relate to the documented sales of iron in the fourteenth century (p.442). A site at Herrings, Dallington, produced pottery of 'late medieval' date, but its relationship to slags and cinder is unknown; further, pottery was also found there which Straker regarded as Iron Age in origin (p.361). A site north of Horley was thought to correspond with the dispute over mining of 1371, but excavations in 1927 on land known as Cinderfield produced no result (p.456). Two place-names noted by Straker have not lived up to his hopes. Hammerden, near Ticehurst, has been explored for slags, but what was found could not be dated, and no documentary references to a forge have been found (p.297). 'Hammerwyse', a field name at Potmans, has proved inconclusive (p.354).

The picture was slow to change. The first definite medieval site was discovered in 1936, when excavations at Thundersfield, to the east of Horley, located an ore-roasting hearth associated with thirteenth-to-fifteenth-century pottery. It was thought at the time to be the base of a smelting hearth, but its size (3m diameter) makes roasting likely. Unfortunately Schubert confused this site with Cinderfield, referred to above.[22]

Since 1965 there has been a growth of interest in the smelting operations of the period, and the work of the last 15 years can now be brought together. Field survey both over the Weald as a whole and in certain areas selected for intensive search has made it evident how many bloomeries have operated at one time or another. The problem of dating is, however, immense, and resources have not been sufficient for a programme of sampling for archaeomagnetic or radiocarbon dating. In a search area to the east of Ashdown Forest, 182km^2 were covered, in which 261 bloomery sites were found. It cannot be known what proportion this figure represents of the total actually existing in the area, for the search was necessarily governed by ground-cover, by accessibility, and by dispersal of cinder due to ploughing. Twenty-nine sites were checked for dateable material, largely by trial cuttings through cinder deposits, and four of these were found to be medieval. Thus about 35 medieval sites could have been present among the 246 recorded (see Appendix 2 and Tebbutt 1981).

Fieldwalking in other areas has resulted in medieval pottery being found among cinder scatters. Chandler's Farm, Hartfield, is the earliest, with twelfth- or thirteenth-century pottery found amongst bloomery slag where a stream cuts the deposit. Thirteenth-century pottery was found among slag at Spaulines, near Buxted, fourteenth- and fifteenth-century ware at Hodges Wood, Crowborough, and fifteenth-century pottery at Piping Wood, Buxted.[23] It is important that only those sites where the association between pottery and slag is certain should be taken as medieval. In two cases, Maynards Gate and Felbridge, first examination of surface scatters suggested medieval activity, but excavation has not proved this. At Maynards Gate medieval pottery was found immediately above the base of a smelting hearth, but magnetic dating suggested that the latter was in fact Roman. At Felbridge, impressions gained during fieldwalking were shown to be incorrect, and smelting here is also more likely to have been Roman than medieval. As there was no sign, in either case, of nearby medieval habitation it seems likely that domestic rubbish was being spread on the fields.[24]

(B) THE USE OF TRADITIONAL BLOOMERY METHODS IN THE WEALD

The results of fieldwalking give an impression of widespread use of the Wealden ores, but naturally stop short of showing how medieval bloomeries were operated. The core of such information must come from excavated and documented examples. The former comprise Minepit Wood and Alsted, while the main documentary source is the series of accounts for Tudeley, near Tonbridge, in which four bloomeries are mentioned. Slight information also comes from brief references to the works of John de Lynleghe at Withyham. At Alsted the smelting hearths date to the mid-thirteenth century, while the rest of the sources relate to operations in the fourteenth century.

(C) ORE SUPPLIES

The details of medieval mining practice in the Weald are concealed by our inability to assign a date to surviving earthworks. Much of what can still be seen disturbing the ground in woods and shaws relates to post-medieval mining, to judge by the frequent proximity of blast furnaces of sixteenth- to eighteenth-century date. References to mining in the thirteenth and fourteenth century create the impression that much ore came from shallow workings at the outcrop. At Tudeley, there is no hint of any mine of any size; ore was dug 'in *fodicione petrarum de orston*'; there are no references to any special equipment with which to do so. Similarly, the ore dug near Horley in 1372 apparently came from an open working. There is a hint of a longer-term source in the Lynleghe case of 1322, which mentions a mine of iron. However, while tools for smelting are noted, mining equipment is not. The thirteenth-century 'mine' near East Grinstead, however, does seem to have been used for some time. It is referred to as an entity, making a profit, or not, over several years. Yet these indications do not conclusively point to single workings from which ore could be extracted over a long period: the term could be used, loosely, to cover an area which was worked over with shallow excavations.

There are firm signs that ore was roasted prior to smelting. This practice removed moisture and impurities and made the ore more porous and easily broken to the best size for the furnace. A hammer for breaking ore appears in the Tudeley documents for 1350–1. A roasting hearth was excavated at Minepit Wood, and the outline of stones formed a kerb remarkably similar to those illustrated by Georgius Agricola in *De Re Metallica* in the sixteenth century (1556; 1950 edn: 275). The practice is confirmed in the Tudeley accounts by frequent references to the burning of ore. Here *petris combustis* or *petris ardendis* appear in most years' accounts, and the roasting operation is quite distinct from smelting. It is worth emphasizing this evidence for roasting; by contrast, in the early years of the operation of blast furnaces in the sixteenth century there are few signs that the practice was used.

(D) CHARCOAL

The management of the medieval woodlands of Sussex to provide the smelters' fuel is known from thirteenth-century sources. On the Archbishop of Canterbury's manor of South Malling, which stretched north from Lewes to Kent, underwood was cut on 10- or 12-year rotations to provide wood for fuel and for woodland crafts. Most references are merely to cutting, in the case of Tudeley in the lord's forest. The charcoal was supplied in 'tens' or 'dozens'. The latter have been estimated as being about 3m³ in settled volume, as delivered. The labour intensity of charcoal production is emphasized by the doubling of its price after the Black Death, caused by a shortage of forest workers.

As well as charcoal, 'eling wood', probably the wood used in roasting, was supplied from the forest. But even with this require-ment, the total area of woodland required for iron production would seem small by comparison with the forest cover of the Weald. It has been suggested that a bloomery required about 2 acres of wood annually for each ton of iron produced. An output of four tons in a season, and cutting on a 12-year cycle suggests that 100 acres of well-managed wood could supply a small bloomery of the size of Tudeley, indicating that 300–400 acres might be set aside on the Southfrith estate for the bloomeries referred to in the surviving accounts (Brandon 1974: 103; Hammersley 1972: 32).

(E) THE BLOOMERY

The documentary sources cast no light upon the design of the furnace itself. The only excavated example within the Weald is the base of a furnace found at Minepit Wood (fig.25). Here the interior of the hearth was approximately 30cm in diameter, with a surviving tuyere aperture. There was no clue as to the height of the furnace, a problem which has beset the interpretation of all medieval bloomery sites so far excavated in Britain. Thus it is not possible to suggest whether the Wealden smith used a shaft furnace or a lower structure, a development of the bowl furnace.

The efficiency of the Wealden furnace, in terms of ore consumption, cannot be assessed. The only potential source is the Tudeley account, which unfortunately sets out and values the ore used by the amount of iron it would make, rather than giving actual quantities. Charcoal consumption, however, can be established, being fairly steady at just over 2 loads (1 load = 120lb) per bloom. The weight of the bloom is not stated; a standard of 30lb has been suggested, but not proven, being produced after approximately a day's work.

Examination of medieval Wealden sites shows that the slag was generally tapped from the furnaces. The black tap-slag with its typical appearance of viscous flow is usually found; a case where this was definitely not so was at Alsted, on the North Downs (fig.26), where the mid-thirteenth-century hearth was set below the ground surface, preventing the tapping of slag.

Apart from the furnace or hearth, the smelter's equipment is referred to in the Tudeley accounts. Both here and in the Lynleghe case bellows are mentioned, with several references at Tudeley to the leather used for repairs. In the latter source there are also references to tuyeres. These were of iron, and in 1353 damaged (perforated) tuyeres were repaired. The bellows were operated by as many as four blowers at Tudeley, but it is not stated whether they worked with their hands or their feet. As tuyeres are usually referred to in pairs, two blowers would work at a time, taking turns with the third and fourth men. A variety of tongs, shovels, and less identifiable tools were used at

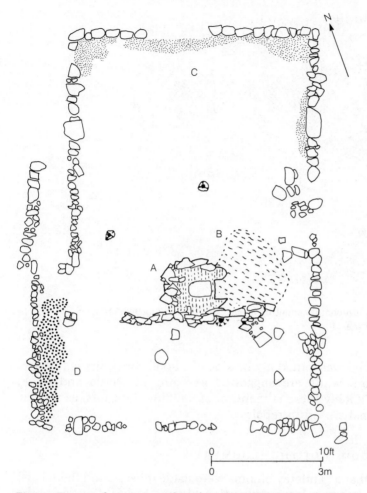

Fig.25   Fourteenth-century smelting furnace at Minepit Wood, Withyham (TQ
523338) (after Money 1971: opp.96). Charcoal (C) and roasted ore (D) were stored
within the enclosure. The furnace (A) had its tuyere on the south side, and cinders and
slags (B) had been raked eastwards.

Tudeley, where there was also an axe for cleaving the blooms into
small pieces of iron for forging.

   Both the Minepit Wood excavation and the Tudeley accounts have
shown that smelting took place in a wooden building. At Tudeley
considerable repairs were undertaken in 1343 and 1350, and the
footings and post-holes at Minepit Wood have demonstrated the kind
of cover building that was used. Here it has been suggested that an
enclosure surrounded the storage space for charcoal and ore, and that

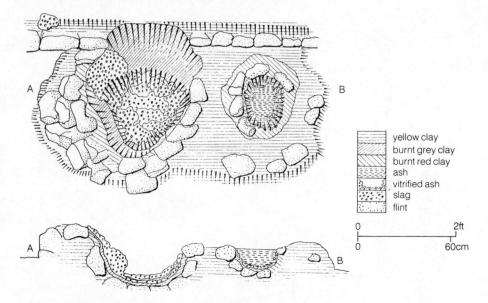

	yellow clay
	burnt grey clay
	burnt red clay
	ash
	vitrified ash
	slag
	flint

Fig.26   Thirteenth-century smelting furnaces at Alsted (TQ 293558) (after Ketteringham 1976: 20).

a working shed was joined to one side of a hood covering the furnace. The enclosure walls are suggested as being of wattle and daub; indeed, at Tudeley there is mention of daubing the walls, as well as boards and nails used in repairs.

(F) THE PRODUCT OF THE BLOOMERY

It is certain that at Tudeley blooms were made for sale, and there is no sign of any hammer-forge converting blooms to bar. Similarly, the excavated area at Minepit Wood bore no indication of forging. By contrast, Alsted was a site where both smelting and forging took place in the thirteenth century, although by the beginning of the fourteenth smelting had ceased. Nevertheless, Alsted is important in dispelling certain preconceptions about the iron trade. In the first place, it lies beyond the scarp of the North Downs and, although amply wooded, is likely to have depended for its ore on sources in the Weald, not less than 12 miles distant. Indeed, Alsted was held by a family (De Passele, later Pashley) who had estates in the Weald. Early in the fourteenth century, when forging was the sole activity, blooms rather than ore would have been brought to Alsted. It is possible that after 1362 the smelting may have taken place at Charlwood, for by then a Pashley had married into the Arundel family, lessees of ore-rights at Charl-wood. Thus, it has been suggested not only that blooms but also ore could be carried some distance. Further, it has been confirmed that smelting and forging at times took place in one establishment, in this case in a location where smelting was unexpected. This leads us to treat references to smiths and to 'smith' personal names as relevant to the smelting side of the industry, and not necessarily to be dismissed as blacksmiths, only producing artefacts from blooms or bar.

Assuming a bloom weight of 30lb, the annual output of a Wealden bloomery might amount to about 3 or 4 tons. But the Tudeley accounts show how widely output could vary from year to year: in one period of direct estate management, from 1329 to 1334, annual production ranged between 112 and 231 blooms. From 1350 to 1354 totals varied even more, between 39 and 252. This variation was because the bloomery was essentially a discontinuous process, producing one bloom in a day's smelt. There was no pressure to keep the furnace in production, as was to be seen in later periods with the blast furnace, which was run on a continuous basis, its costs tied closely to the length of time for which operation could be prolonged. Thus the bloomery reflected local market opportunities. A further problem is the weight of the bloom. This cannot be stated with any certainty, and the estimate noted in this chapter is derived from documented bloom weights of the period, which do not necessarily reflect Wealden practice.

The quality of the iron produced in the Weald in the Middle Ages has been suggested as poor, limited by ores which were difficult to smelt and high in phosphorus. Indeed, one writer has emphasized the limitations in the markets of London and the south-east of England in the face of competition from other sources (Hammersley 1972: 34).

There is little question of the superior reputation of certain im-ported irons. Those from Spain and the Baltic were shipped into south-east England and the high prices they commanded enabled suppliers to meet the costs of transport. Typical are consignments brought into Sandwich in 1299. Peter de Sancto Petro of Bayonne imported 60 thousandweight of Spanish iron, and Gilbert la Bast likewise paid duty on 23 thousandweight. In London at this period stocks of Spanish iron are recorded, in the hands of Spanish mer-chants (Salzman 1931: 409–10).

A quality advantage was also possessed by iron from the Forest of Dean. This was made from low-phosphorus hematite ores, and was regularly traded to London, where it commanded a higher price than iron from the Weald. Dean iron was competitive not only in London but also in the south. In addition to the instance of the Bishop of

Chichester being advised by his steward to buy iron from Gloucester in 1225, work at the king's house at Freemantle in 1253 used iron from Gloucester as well as from the Weald. In general the Weald provided for the trade in iron for making plain items such as nails, horseshoes, wedges and bars. This is seen in the larger military orders of the period, in which horseshoes and nails predominated. When a mixture of irons was required, the Wealden contribution was of simple items. For example, when siege-machines were being built in 1278–9, less than 2 per cent of the iron came from the Weald, and this was made up of wedges and nails.[25]

Yet this impression is perhaps too simple. In the first place, Wealden ores vary considerably in their composition. In the south, some deposits are relatively high in sulphur, in a form which is difficult to remove by roasting. Smelting here would produce an iron suitable for the nail maker, but unsatisfactory for the more demanding applications. Some ores have high phosphorus contents, making the iron difficult to harden. Yet there are ores, not least some of those in the northern Weald, which appear suitable for a useful range of applications. For example, ore from Sharpthorne, south of East Grinstead, has been used in recent experimental smelts. It contains phosphorus, but in a quantity which allows a small but useful degree of hardening to be given to the bloom during forging.

This perhaps explains the case we have noted in 1359 when Thomas atte Legh, 'fletcher', was requested to employ Kent and Sussex smiths to forge 500 steel arrow-heads for the king. Using the ores referred to, it would have been possible for these smiths to use local blooms, cut, forged and hardened, as satisfactory heads.

Unfortunately no programme of analysis of iron objects from medieval Wealden contexts has been carried out. Despite the difficulty of proving local origin, such an investigation could well give a firmer base to speculation about the quality of iron made in the region.

4   The water-powered bloomery forge

Over the whole of Europe the bloomery underwent a remarkable evolution in the later Middle Ages, which could increase annual production several times over. The key to this change was the use of water-wheels to power the hammers and bellows. The water-powered bloomery characterizes a chapter in the iron industry, in the Weald as elsewhere, which lasts well beyond the end of the Middle Ages, into the period normally associated with the blast furnace.

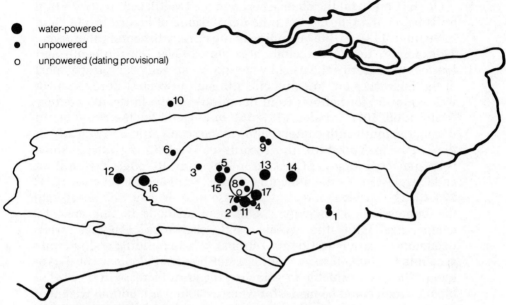

Fig.27 Medieval bloomeries.

Un-powered bloomeries

No.	Parish: site name	NGR	Published reference
1	Brede	TQ 887128	
		888149	
2	Buxted	494232	BWIRG 6, 21
		498225	SNQ 17, 167–8
3	Forest Row: Brambletye	415351	BWIRG 6, 18
		416351	BWIRG 6, 18
4	Hadlow Down	519225	
5	Hartfield	452341	Tebbutt 1975
		471387	SNQ 17, 167–8
6	Horley: Thundersfield	300426	Hart and Winbolt 1937
			BWIRG 4, 28
7	Rotherfield: Piping Wood	509277	BWIRG 13, 7–9
	Minepit Wood	523338	Money 1971: 86–119
8	Hodges Wood	526324	BWIRG 15, 3
	(Maynards Gate	538297	BWIRG 12, 4–7 – dating inconclusive)
9	Tonbridge: Tudeley	620447	BWIRG 15, 8
10	Merstham: Alsted	293558	Ketteringham 1976

Probable water-powered bloomeries or medieval water-powered hammer forges

11	Buxted: Little Forge	513260	below p. 341
12	Ewhurst: Coneyhurst Gill	083404	below p. 323
13	Frant: Brookland	618349	below p. 319
14	Goudhurst: Chingley	682335	below p. 322
15	Hartfield: Newbridge	456325	below p. 346
16	Horsham: Roffey	206335	Straker 1931a: 422
17	Mayfield: Woolbridge	571265	below p. 367

On the Continent the change began in the twelfth century, with iron mills being first referred to in the Berry region of France in 1116 and in Spain in 1138: by the beginning of the thirteenth century there were 14 examples in the Barcelona area alone. Over the thirteenth and fourteenth centuries the use of water power spread over Europe: most of the references are to hammers, although in central Europe power was also used for bellows from the middle of the thirteenth century (Duby 1968: 107; Crossley 1981: 35). In England the transition began during the fourteenth century, and can be seen particularly clearly in the north. In Yorkshire, the records of West Riding estates show water-powered forges at Creskeld in 1395, and at Tong, Clayton West and Crigglestone in the fifteenth century (Faull and Moorhouse 1981: 775–6). The survival and study of these records may well exaggerate the impression of development of new methods in this area, by comparison with the Weald and elsewhere. Another well-documented case is in County Durham, where building and working accounts for 1408–9 survive for a water-powered bloomery at Byrke-knott. These are valuable for showing the great increase in the size of bloom which could be made, for whereas 30lb was a normal weight of iron made in a manually blown hearth, at Byrkeknott the figure approached 200lb (Lapsley 1899: 509–21; Tylecote 1962: 451–8). The development came at a time when wages were high and labour was short, after the demographic reversal of the mid-fourteenth century, and it allowed an important reduction in costs. Comparison of the Tudeley and the Byrkeknott accounts shows charges for labour at the forge little if at all greater for a bloom estimated at six times the weight.

In the Weald there are no bloomeries for which information about water power is so explicit. The only excavation directed towards this problem has been the work undertaken on the lowest levels at Chingley Forge. Here a mid-fourteenth century timber mill-race was found, containing a fragment of a water wheel approximately 2.45m in diameter. The upper members of the frame of the race formed a massive foundation alongside the wheel emplacement, whose purpose was not entirely certain. There were three possibilities: the structure could have been for corn-milling, for fulling, or for iron-working. There were no mill-stone fragments, although there were parts of a gearwheel which would not have been out of place in a mill. There was no indication at all of fulling stocks, although stocks and trough might well have been moved when the site was abandoned. But, again, there was no direct evidence of iron working, in the shape of hearths, hammer, or an anvil base.

What led to the suggestion that a forge had operated at Chingley was the charcoal and the slag found near the race. The charcoal would have been necessary for a string-hearth on which blooms were reheated during forging, even if the actual bloom-hearth had been elsewhere. The latter possibility was suggested by the small quantities of tap-slag. The amount was slight enough to be the result of scatter, perhaps from carts at times used for carrying slag, but here employed for bringing blooms to the forge. There is also some documentary indication of smelting at Chingley, which lay on the estate of Boxley Abbey. In an undated account considered to be of about 1310 blooms are referred to, although in other fourteenth-century accounts iron appears to be purchased for repairs to carts. One possibility is that unpowered bloomeries similar to the Minepit Wood example were operating in the woodlands around the valley of the Bewl, and that their products were forged at Chingley. Unfortunately, the most likely position for an anvil base had been cut away by the seventeenth-century forge anvil pit, making proof of this hypothesis virtually impossible.[26]

No other excavations have taken place on water-powered medieval ironworking sites in the Weald, and the study of this topic is made difficult by lack of specific documentary references and by the difficulty of identifying examples in the field. Nevertheless, there is sufficient information to suggest a pattern within which future work might be placed. The fifteenth-century references to forges comprise Burwash, Ticehurst and perhaps Buxted, to which Newbridge can be added as a result of field studies. In 1434 rent was paid on a forge newly built near Burwash, at 'Derefoldgate'. This has not been located, and the type of forge is not made clear. The second new forge at Burwash appears in a rental of 1477, built 'near the church'.[27] It is not known which, if either, of these was the forge rented by David Harvy in 1525 and taken over by John Collins in 1526. It is, indeed, still supposition that either of the fifteenth-century entries in the rental relate to water-powered forges. The 1477 case is the less likely, for the nearest suitable water to Burwash church, the River Dudwell, lies at least 800m from the church, at Dudwell Mill. At Ticehurst, the forge was mentioned in 1433 at 'Croucheland'. This, also, has not been found, but in addition to a building, a pond is referred to; unfortunately, there is no continuity through to any documented sixteenth-century forge. The third possible case is at Buxted where, in 1490, 'founders' produced metal mentioned in accounts of the Archbishop of Canterbury. The technical aspects of this reference will be discussed in the next chapter, but it is likely that some form of bloomery was in use. Fieldwork has suggested Little Forge, Buxted, as a possible location, for although this is best known as the site of a post-medieval finery forge, bloomery tap-slag has been recorded in a section cut by the stream. This deposit lay beneath the cinder from the finery. Newbridge is also considered likely to have had a bloomery, for in addition to the slag associated with the blast furnace built in 1496, bloomery tap-slag has also been found.[28]

The subject of the water-powered bloomery does not end with the close of the Middle Ages. Even though the blast furnace reached the Weald at the end of the fifteenth century, the spread of the new method took several decades, during which bloomery iron continued to be made. The shift from one form of production to the other can be seen in more detail elsewhere in Britain, later in the sixteenth century and in some districts in the seventeenth, and patterns of overlap between bloomery and blast furnace form a model for the Weald. For example, in the West Midlands blast furnaces were built throughout the second half of the sixteenth century; in Derbyshire and Yorkshire they appear in the half-century after 1580, as bloomeries gradually passed out of use. In north Lancashire, indeed, bloomeries were in operation over the whole of the seventeenth century, with eventual replacement in the eighteenth. It can be suggested that the contraction of the bloomery sector in the Weald occurred during the first half of the sixteenth century, although there is a dearth of definite information.

The major difficulty is to find out what the works described as 'forges' in the years before 1550 actually produced, as the term could be used for a bloomery or for a finery converting pig iron to bar. Also, the bloomery was both laid out and equipped in ways which made rebuilding as a finery forge possible. Each required a water-driven hammer and two hearths with water-powered bellows. The bloom-hearth could be replaced with a finery, and the string-hearth where the bloom was reheated had its counterpart in the chafery. A number of examples have been recorded in the Weald where bloomery tap-slag has been found on sites best known as fineries. Little Forge, Buxted, is indeed one of these, with finery cinder overlying the bloomery slag referred to above. Brookland, near Frant, has similar deposits. A third case is at Woolbridge, Mayfield: here there is a bay, with tap-slag appearing on the downstream side, yet there is also a small amount of furnace-bottom cinder which resembles that from a finery. There are no sixteenth-century references which can be attributed with any certainty to Woolbridge, although 'Hammer Wood' is adjacent, a name whose earliest appearance has not been established.[29]

Written sources also indicate a period when the processes used at forges were changing. Burwash forge has already been referred to as a late bloomery, and it is suggested that here the end of bloomery working came in 1525–6. David Harvy, the tenant until 1525–6, is not otherwise known, certainly not in connection with any blast furnace. John Collins, on the other hand, is, for he operated Socknersh furnace by the 1530s. Indeed, as he was recorded as employing eight French workers in 1525, this date is a likely one for the operation of the indirect process. Near Frant there were two forges: Brookland and Verredge. These were sold by Humphrey Lewknor to John Barham in 1521. It is most unlikely that conversion of pig iron to wrought-iron bar would be taking place in this part of the Weald before that date, for the nearest existing blast furnaces lay 10 miles and more to the west. Indeed, Barham is not known to have leased a blast furnace until 1547, so his forges may not have been adapted for some time. Nearby is Bayham forge, leased by William Wybarne from Bayham Abbey in 1525. Here, too, there is no known link with an early blast furnace, and adaptation would best correspond with the growth of local pig iron production after about 1540. Finally, in Ashdown Forest certain forges were in operation at and beyond the time of the introduction of blast furnaces. Hartfield Forge was referred to in the will of Thomas Wildgoose in 1496, the Steel Forge was built in the Forest between 1503 and 1509, and Parrock was referred to as a forge alone until 1513, thereafter being worked with a blast furnace. However, each of these raises technical problems which suggest that they may have been exceptional cases, and they will be considered in detail in the context of the blast furnace, to which we turn in Chapter 6.

In the light of these examples it is necessary to examine all the early finery forges for bloomery slags as a guide to the size of the industry at the end of the Middle Ages.

NOTES

1. *Cal. Lib. Rolls*, IV, 122; VI, 203; PRO E101/544/23.
2. *Cal. Lib. Rolls*, II, 118, 132; IV, 162; PRO E101/378/4.
3. PRO E101/467/7/3, 7; *Cal. Mem. Rolls(Exch.)*, 240.
4. *Cal. Lib. Rolls*, V, 232.
5. PRO C62/115, Pipe Roll 16 Ed, III; E101/528/17.
6. *Cal. Pat. Rolls, Ed. III*, XI, 222.
7. PRO SC6/1148/13; PRO DL29/441/7082.
8. Sharpe 1899: Bk C, 88–9; Salzman 1931: 78
9. PRO SC6/886/6; KAO U1475/M62; PRO SC6/1148/13; Salzman 1955; 47; ESRO A1475.
10. PRO E101/378/4.
11. Dr I. H. Goodall and Mr J. M. Lewis have kindly advised on the likely weights of horseshoes. Mr Lewis has weighed the least-corroded thirteenth century example from Dyserth Castle (Nat. Mus. Wales 21.24/57) – 212.2g. Bloom weights are estimated in Schubert 1957: 139–40.

12. *BWIRG*, 6 (1973), 20.
13. ESRO A1745; KAO U1475/M242; *Royal and Hist. Letters* (Rolls ser.), I, 278.
14. PRO E101/485/11; PRO SC6/890/22ff.
15. PRO SC6/1146/2; PRO JUST 1/912a, m. 17d.
16. PRO KB 27/443.
17. Salzman 1955: 47, 67, 81, 88; Statute 28 Ed. III, c.5; see Mott 1961: 152, for a discussion of costs.
18. ESRO Dunn 2/9; ESRO ASH 200a; Lambeth Palace, Roll 1352 (Receivers' Accounts).
19. Straker 1931a: 442.
20. PRO JUST 1/924 m. 45; Hudson 1909: 47; Courthope and Fermoy 1931: 141; Lambeth Palace, Mayfield, 700; KAO U1475/M62, 700; PRO E101/544/23.
21. Lambeth Palace, ED 456–9.
22. At Roffey ploughing exposed a large area of bloomery slag in 1982. For Thundersfield, see Hart and Winbolt 1937: 147–8.
23. *BWIRG*, 8, 8–9; 15, 3; 13, 7–9.
24. *BWIRG*, 12, 4–7; 2, 5, forthcoming.
25. PRO E101/467/7/3, 7.
26. Crossley 1975b; particularly PRO SC6/1251/2. Recent field-walking at Roffey has suggested that a water-powered site may relate to the scatters of bloomery waste: see n.22 above.
27. ESRO ASH 200a.
28. *BWIRG*, 8, 26.
29. See Gazetter for Brookland, Little Forge, Verredge, Woolbridge.

Chapter 6   The introduction of the blast furnace

The years between 1490 and 1540 were of particular significance in the history of ironmaking in the Weald, for it was during this time that the change took place from the bloomery to the blast furnace and finery forge. This was the period of immigration of French workers and of the growth of the Weald as a supplier both of iron armaments to the Crown and wrought iron to the expanding markets of London and south-east England.

These developments firmly established the Continental technology of iron production in England, providing the base not only for growth in the Weald in the middle of the century and beyond, but also for the change from bloomery to blast furnace over the rest of the country.

1   Ashdown Forest: the nucleus of change

(A) THE ESTABLISHMENT OF NEWBRIDGE IRONWORKS, 1496

One of the best-known events in the history of the Wealden industry is the establishment of the furnace and forge at Newbridge (fig.28). In

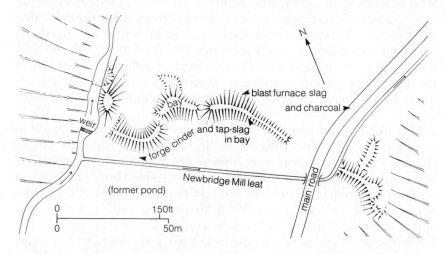

Fig.28   Newbridge ironworks (TQ 456325). The first English blast furnace, built on Duchy of Lancaster land in Ashdown Forest in 1496. Bloomery tap-slag, present in the bay, is assumed to be from an earlier use of the site.

December 1496, Henry Fyner, goldsmith of Southwark, was instructed to set up a works in Ashdown Forest to produce iron for the king's artillery on its Scottish campaign.[1] The lands of the Duchy of Lancaster in the forest provided ample supplies of wood and ore: the valleys of the streams flowing off the high sandy ground were, and indeed still are, well covered with trees. Ore outcrops in the surrounding claylands, and at Upper Hartfield there are woods with large areas disturbed by mining. The place chosen for the building of the works lay on the stream which flows north-eastwards from Pippingford through Newbridge to join the Medway beyond Withyham. The stream is dammed just to the south of Newbridge, and slags show this to have been where the works were placed. There is a possibility that the chosen site took advantage of earlier operations, for bloomery tap-slags have also been found close to the dam, suggesting that water power had been used there for the older process.

There was no delay in construction or in starting production, for payments were made for the first batches of iron in the early months of 1497, and in April carriage was charged for iron shot taken to the Tower of London. Although many of the payments were made to Fyner, the works were in fact leased to a French worker, Peter Roberts (Grand, or Graunt, Pierre). His rent was at an annual rate of £20, or six tons of iron, with an entitlement to cut wood and dig ore in the forest and an obligation to maintain the buildings and equipment. Although the lease was for eight years, it was altered after only nine months to a joint tenancy with Fyner, who handled the iron in London. After the sole tenancy ended there appears to have been trouble over debts due to Fyner, and Roberts found himself imprisoned for his failure to pay. At the end of 1498 another Frenchman, Pauncelett Symart, became tenant, on a seven-year lease.[2] Symart also had difficulty in keeping to his rent payments, falling into arrears virtually from the start; indeed, his debts appeared in Duchy of Lancaster accounts for the next 30 years.

Why Roberts and Symart found the terms of the tenancy difficult to meet cannot be determined from the rentals and accounts which survive. Even if their costs were higher or their output lower than they had envisaged, they were certainly able to produce both pig iron and wrought-iron objects. There is no doubt that from the start they were operating the indirect process, for in January 1497 payment was authorized 'upon fining and forging certain iron for the ordnance'.[3] Nevertheless, there is confusion in the early accounts in the terms used, in particular for pig iron, which was named 'rough iron'. There are references both to this rough iron and to 'rough iron fined'. It might be expected that the latter was pig iron which had been put through the first melting in the finery hearth, to form a bloom, but both varieties commanded the same price, £2 13s 4d a ton. Further, both were sent to a founder, Simon Ballard, for casting into shot, which in the case of the fined iron would cause problems, due to its higher melting temperature. Thus it does seem likely that there was some misunderstanding on the part of the book-keeper, but this does not obscure the certainty of a two-stage process, using furnace and forge, rather than a powered bloomery. This conclusion is reinforced by the listing of equipment in an inventory taken in 1509. In this the tools and bellows are listed under three heads, the furnace, the finery and the hammer. This shows that in addition to the blast furnace there were two further hearths, one for refining, the other for reheating the iron during forging under the hammer. This was the typical 'walloon' system, customary in the Netherlands and to be used in Britain for almost three centuries.[4]

The wrought-iron products of Newbridge are thoroughly recorded in the early accounts; the original instructions to Henry Fyner listed parts for gun-carriages, namely strake-bars for axle-trees, cross-bars, forelocks, bolts, bolsters, nails 'with other things as shall be necessary for the binding of the stock and wheels of the ordnance'. It is made clear that these objects were made 'of iron wrought by the water hammer', and the price, £4 6s 8d a ton, contrasts with that of the 'rough iron'.

(B) CONTEMPORARY IRONWORKS IN ASHDOWN FOREST

It has been assumed, but never conclusively established, that the Newbridge ironworks was a case of a completely alien technology transplanted into a district where no evolution of old methods of smelting had taken place. As shown in the last chapter, our know-ledge of medieval Wealden furnace design is slight, and of the use of water power in local bloomeries scarcely less fleeting. Nevertheless, there are signs both before and after 1496 of an interesting diversity of methods, with a wider involvement of immigrants than at Newbridge alone.

There are three signs of change before 1496. Firstly, the arrival of French immigrant ironworkers from the Pays de Bray had begun some years earlier. The first known arrival was that of John Stiele in 1491, while another two are known to have come to Sussex by 1496 (Awty 1981). These figures are no doubt only a fraction of the actual arrivals, for they comprise only those who survived to have their dates of migration recorded in the denization rolls of 1541 and 1544. That many more had come to England in the early years and had since died is suggested by the pattern of arrivals early in the sixteenth century. At this time there were many children among the immigrants, and it has been shown by Brian Awty that it was common practice for families to travel some years after the adult men had established themselves. The late-fifteenth-century immigrants could have occupied themselves in a number of ways. They brought knowledge of Continental processes and could have helped in some evolution of the English bloomery towards the high shaft furnace. On the other hand they may have worked in or around traditional bloomery forges, whether as ironworkers or as ore-miners, wood-cutters, or charcoal-burners.

There is a second significant record which does indeed suggest that changes were already under way by 1496. Rhys Jenkins commented many years ago on the entry in a Canterbury Cathedral receivers' account of a payment to 'iernefounders of Bukstede' in 1490.[5] No early works are otherwise documented at Buxted, on the south-eastern fringe of the forest, nor is it known whether Frenchmen worked there. The term 'founders' suggests that some method existed for producing liquid iron, and in view of the arrival of Continental workers there is reason to take the possibility of a high furnace seriously. A high shaft bloomery, charged with a greater proportion of charcoal than normal, could produce liquid iron, owing to the quantity of carbon lowering the melting point of the charge. Schubert (1952: 108) also accepted the possibility of some form of blast furnace at Buxted, but favoured the idea that wrought iron from a bloomery was being melted with the aid of a flux such as antimony or tin, a method which he indicated was known on the Continent at the time.

Finally, by 1496, one of the French immigrants was at work at Hartfield forge. In the will of Thomas Wildgoose, who died in that year, John Stiele, who had come from France in 1491, was shown as occupier of the forge (Straker 1931a: 245).

Before tracing the development of iron production in the locality after 1496, we should take notice of the production of cast ammunition in the forest in the year that work began at Newbridge. References to the operations of Simon Ballard appear to be of considerable potential interest, although his methods are not known. As noted above, 'rough iron' and 'rough iron fyned' were recorded as delivered to Ballard, who certainly cast 'rough iron' into shot, although it is less clear what he did with metal described as 'fyned'. The pig iron, to be cast, would be re-melted, but there are no contemporary descriptions of the kind of furnace Ballard would employ. The most likely would be a form of finery hearth, in which the metal would be heated to a temperature sufficient to be run into moulds, although in less oxidizing conditions than in a normal finery. If Ballard really did use fined iron for gunstones, he would probably have needed a flux to melt such metal, with its low carbon content. Ballard does not appear to have done his casting at Newbridge itself. Iron was delivered to him in the forest, but no location is given. But his foundry cannot have been far away, for the gunstones were taken by carriers to the Tower from Newbridge, rather than from any other point in the forest. A water-powered establishment would be likely, comparable in its needs with a finery, and a point on the river running through Newbridge would be the most convenient.[6]

The two decades after construction at Newbridge show other facets of innovation in the district. An important variation in smelting methods came in the years between 1503 and 1509, when the Steel Forge was set up in Ashdown Forest. In 1503 Claude Rombosson, cutler, and Vincent Breke, steelmaker, both of London, agreed with the Crown to lease six acres of land of their choice in Ashdown Forest, on the stream flowing to the King's forge. There they were to build 'mills and forges, a great hammer and wheels' to make steel and also plates for harness. The lease was for ten years, and under its terms timber could be cut for building, ore could be mined, and alder, birch and willow cut for charcoal.[7] These new works were to give their name to the river which flows from Pippingford to Newbridge, and the Steel Forge pond is marked on a map of 1692, close to the place where Pippingford blast furnace was to be built in or just before 1696.[8] The Steel Forge had been built by 1509, when it was described as *novo edificat*, and it is henceforth mentioned regularly under various lessees in Duchy of Lancaster accounts until after 1550.[9] The key to the method of production that was used lies in the reference to ore in the lease. This shows that the forge neither decarburized pig iron nor subjected wrought iron to cementation in order to reach the carbon content of steel. The process used must have been a variant of the bloomery, in which the ratio of charcoal to ore would be sufficient to produce a high-carbon bloom. The carbon content had to be sufficient to make bar that could be hardened by heat treatment, in other words a steel. The kind of product envisaged is shown by the involvement of a cutler, and by the stated intention of making harness plates, meaning body armour. Recently, experimental smelts have been carried out in a small shaft furnace using ore from Sharpthorne, five miles to the west of the Steel Forge, and it has been found possible to produce a steely bloom which can be forged and hardened.[10]

Such a development of bloomery methods, taken further, leads to the production of iron so high in carbon that its melting-point is low enough for casting to take place. In the second decade of the sixteenth century there are signs that ironworkers in the district were moving in this direction. In 1512 Clays Harms was named as a gunstone maker of Ashdown Forest. In that year he made 300 round shot, 315 cross-barred shot and 100 shot with pikes for the king's ships. Richard Sackfield, probably Sackville of Withyham, was also casting shot. Finally, at Parrock forge, probably owned by John Warner, Robert Scorer was a maker of gunstones in 1509 and 1513.[11] Five years later, however, this site was known as Parrock *furnace*, a significant change which shows that, although the forge could contain hearths capable of casting liquid iron, it had remained distinguishable from a blast furnace (Straker 1931a: 241–2). In none of these cases is there evidence that the gunstone makers were merely obtaining pig iron from New-bridge furnace for re-melting.

(C) THE FIRST IRON GUNS IN THE WEALD

After Pauncelett and Lambert Symart established themselves at New-bridge, they expanded the range of objects which they cast, for they began to produce parts for ordnance. This is indicated by a Duchy of Lancaster account for 1509, which shows that a John Nicholas had owed money for iron and for '*vibrellis et cam'is*'. In an inventory of 1509 these terms were used for guns and chambers, listing such objects in stock and setting out their weights. It may be that the iron had been delivered before the gun parts, but the arrears arose in the years 1501–6, so the gun parts seem to date from before 1506.[12]

The two-part cast cannon indicated by these terms was characteristic of the early stages of the change from the wrought-iron gun typical of the fifteenth century to the one-piece iron casting. The former type was made up of hoops and bars of iron and was deficient in strength and in accuracy of finish, so in the fifteenth century such pieces began to be replaced by guns cast in bronze and iron. The high cost of bronze guns gave considerable incentive to perfect cast-iron substitutes, but founders appear to have had difficulty in producing such castings in one piece. The two-part guns were, however, unsatisfactory in that it was hard to form a seal between the barrel and the chamber. Indeed, the wrought-iron guns, with all their deficiencies, remained in use for some time, as has been shown by the presence of such pieces on the Mary Rose, which sank off Portsmouth in 1545.

There are no details of how these early guns were cast: there are no references to moulds, and none to any pit or vault in which, in later Wealden practice, moulds were set vertically to receive the liquid metal. The calibre and length of the barrels are not set out, but their weights, 721lb and 860lb, suggest that moulds would be of a size to require some form of pit. In addition, these weights show the amounts of liquid metal that would have to be held in the furnace hearth for a cast. It is not possible to tell how the barrels were finished, for there is no reference to a boring mill at Newbridge (for boring mills, see Chapter 10, pp. 260–2).

Newbridge works were said to be in a poor state in 1509, and a commission was appointed to enquire into their decay and whether they were suitable for re-letting. This was the occasion on which the inventory was drawn up. In the end, Pauncelett Symart vacated the tenancy in 1512; in that year he was sold top wood and underwood sufficient for charcoal for making iron left at the furnace.[13] This must have been the last of his stock of pig iron, and it appears that the ordnance venture had ended by this time. In 1512 Symart was succeeded by Humphrey Walker, the king's founder, who paid an annual rent of £14 13s 4d, compared with the £20 previously charged. There is no sign that Walker manufactured ordnance, but rather that he made bullets for the king's bronze guns. He appears to have died within the next four years, and although his rent is noted from 1516 until 1519 it is not clear who was paying it, or even whether Newbridge was still at work. Indeed, there was a call for a check of stock and equipment in 1519, suggesting that, as in 1509, the works were in disarray; if any inventory were made, it has not been found.[14]

2   The growth of the industry to 1548

Between 1520 and 1548 the Wealden industry underwent a period of radical change. In 1520 there were only two recorded blast furnaces, one (Newbridge) being out of use, and an unknown number of bloomeries. In 1548, however, petitioners from the coastal towns of Sussex claimed that in the county there were 53 furnaces and 'iron-mills', under which term we must include both finery forges and any remaining bloomeries.[15] In accounting for such growth there are three important and interacting topics: the market for iron, the skills required for its production, and the involvement of landowners whose estates provided ore, charcoal and water power.

(A) THE MILITARY AND CIVIL MARKETS FOR IRON

The early developments in Ashdown Forest owed their impetus to the military needs of the crown. Towards 1520 these had relaxed, partly owing to a reduced level of campaigning, partly, one suspects, because the annexation of the town of Tournai under Henry VIII brought a new source of arms of high quality. After 1520, however, Crown military commitments were frequently prodigious, with French and Scottish campaigns which called for high spending on arms, and projects as grandiose as the artillery fortifications of the south coast of England. The Crown over-extended its resources on such matters, particularly in the last years of the reign, bringing increasingly frequent taxation and the accelerating debasement of the currency. In such circumstances the Wealden industry offered a convenient, cheap and secure source of iron, as the renewal and successful development of gun-founding in 1543 illustrates.

Just as significant was the growth of the regional economy under the impetus of the needs of London. The capital was a magnet for the trade of the kingdom, and even at the beginning of the century the comments of foreign observers showed London as a city on the scale of Continental capitals. In the three decades from 1520 the major export trades were largely concentrated there at the expense of the outports, and the booms in cloth shipments between 1530 and 1550 brought prosperity to many trades and an acceleration of migration to man the services and crafts which were their accompaniment. The iron industry of the south-east benefited in two ways from this growth. The direct trade to London was fostered by building, as suburbs began to expand, particularly on the riverside. It also grew with requirements for shipping and the innumerable kinds of equipment of which a developing port has need. Just as the suppliers of materials such as iron and timber found growing sales in London, they also benefited indirectly from the effect of the needs of the capital for food supplies. South-east England enjoyed a widening prosperity at this time, as the growing population of the capital led to specialization in agriculture over the home counties. At the beginning of the century London relied upon the nearer parts of Essex, Kent, and the Thames valley for grain, with coastwise trade routes providing supplements when prices were high. Over the first half of the century the radius of supply grew to encompass virtually all of the south-east, and the prosperity of landowners and farmers was reflected in their expenditure on equipment and on building. The rural smiths, buying their bar iron in the Weald, provided the parts for ploughs, harrows, waggons, and for the improved houses and barns characteristic of the rebuilding which came at this time.

It is significant that change in the scale of the market for iron, sufficient to absorb the output of blast furnaces and finery forges, appeared in the south-east 30 years before the Midlands, where the first blast furnaces were not built until between 1560 and 1570.

(B) THE GROWTH OF IRON-MAKING SKILLS

Attention has already been drawn to the presence in the Weald of workers from the iron-making districts of northern France at the beginning of the sixteenth century. It is known that the maximum movement occurred between about 1506–10 and 1530, with particular peaks in the 1520s. The sources on which estimates are based are the two surviving denization rolls of 1541 and 1544, with confirmation from returns of tax-payers for the subsidies of 1524 and 1525 and of 1543, 1549 and 1550.[16] It has been seen that the rate of migration is harder to assess the further back we go from the date of compilation of the denization returns, due to intervening mortality, so the figures for the 1520s, and particularly the 1530s, will be more reliable than those for the earlier years.Thus the peaks of migration around 1524 and 1529 may well have been even greater by comparison with the 1530s than the following table showing immigration of French ironworkers into the Weald between 1490 and 1540 (after B. G. Awty) indicates:

1491–1495	4
1496–1500	1
1501–1505	1
1506–1510	11
1511–1515	14
1516–1520	15
1521–1525	39
1526–1530	30
1531–1535	11
1536–1540	11

The risks of estimating the numbers and dates of immigration lie in the nature of the records. The denization rolls are the result of attempts by the English government to ensure the loyalty of aliens in time of war, by having them take out letters of denization. Unfortunately, many do not seem to have done so, for certain aliens, known for example from the accounts of Sir William Sidney's ironworks at Robertsbridge and Panningridge, do not appear in the records. Those who were not, at the time, in regular employment were even less likely to be named, for the format of the returns suggests that the initiative in applying for letters of denization was particularly that of landowner employers. Also the extent of mobility was considerable. This is clear from sources after 1544, and there is no reason why it should not have been equally so before, with individuals moving between contract and self-employment in different forest and mining occupations. Nevertheless, the returns are a valuable source, particularly the 1544 list, which includes districts of birth and year of arrival in England. The subsidy rolls are also an insecure basis for estimating numbers of immigrants. In these, aliens can be identified by the distinctive way in which they were taxed, for they paid double the rate levied on Englishmen, based on a valuation of goods or wages. If neither possessions nor pay could be assessed, the foreigner paid a poll tax. However, only aliens in regular employment appear, so someone working on his own account in some woodland occupation, or even a skilled ironworker temporarily out of work, might well not be recorded. These two main sources can be supplemented by records relating to particular localities. The muster rolls of men liable for military service are occasionally useful for the identification of aliens, and Straker noted a reference to 49 Frenchmen in the roll for Netherfield Hundred in 1539.[17] At Rotherfield there survives the parish register for 1538, in which aliens can be identified. There are, finally, certain sources specific to particular ironworks which amplify the record, of which the Robertsbridge and Sheffield accounts are the most important.[18]

The area whence the French workers came is now firmly defined by the use of statements of origin in the 1544 denization return. The Pays de Bray, stretching south-east from the French coast at Dieppe towards Beauvais, had a medieval tradition of iron-smelting. This was strengthened in the mid-fifteenth century by the arrival of workers from the Liège area, who brought the skills of using the blast furnace and finery forge, which had been developed in the southern Netherlands. The Bray is geologically reminiscent of the Weald, and is indeed an interesting area for the field worker, with place-names relating to iron-smelting, together with physical survivals such as slags and cinders, water-courses and dams. Although the industry was prosperous at the end of the fifteenth century, for the next 40 years it faced problems which explain why many workers were prepared to leave, particularly as the opportunities for employment grew in England. The acceleration of migration came in the 1520s, when harvests were poor and food prices were high in Normandy and Picardy. Further, the woodlands of this part of France were under pressure from other users, whose demands for firewood must have made long-rotation coppicing more profitable than the frequent cutting which met the needs of the charcoal-burners. The developing food trades around the valley of the Seine also played their part in the decline of the iron industry, for not only were woodlands cleared for agriculture, but the sites of water-powered ironworks could also more profitably be used for corn-mills. Also, the growth of the local textile industry provided alternative employment, as well as a further use for water power, that of the fulling mill.

Thus an unfavourable environment in the Pays de Bray made migration an attractive course for those employed in forestry and iron-smelting. Of the regions to which they could move, a few did choose the forest parts of the borderlands between France and Flanders, but conditions in England offered greater incentives, resulting in a movement to the Weald which, by 1600, may have totalled between 500 and 600 male immigrants (Awty 1981).

(c) THE SPREAD OF INNOVATION, 1520–1530

The pattern of immigration shows that the wooded areas of the Weald were offering employment beyond the needs of the local population, which would itself have been recovering from the low levels of the fifteenth century. Yet it is hard to be precise about where the growth in Wealden ironmaking was taking place in 1520 and which landowners were undertaking investment in the new methods. We saw in the last chapter that a few water-powered bloomeries can be located with confidence. But as their numbers are small, further examples should be sought among later finery forges which had originated as bloomeries. The stocking and operation of such bloomeries would provide some employment, but it is at the blast furnaces and finery forges with their larger scale of operation that we should seek the major employment of French workers.

The two blast furnaces which clearly were extant in 1520, at Newbridge and Parrock, had varying fortunes at this time. Newbridge was out of use in 1519, and was not re-let until 1525, when Sir Thomas Boleyn leased the works at a rent of £4. This was perhaps a concession to a courtier, for it was far lower than paid in earlier agreements. Boleyn appears to have sub-let, for in 1534 the tenant was Simon Forneres, the king's gunstone maker. In 1539, a year in which a survey of the works was made, they were held by William Nysell.[19] The Boleyn tenancy is important, for the new lessee was well aware of the potential of the industry, even if Newbridge itself had been bringing little return to the Crown. Sir Thomas was a frequent visitor to Paris around the year 1520: he could well have travelled through the iron-smelting districts of Normandy, but more significant is his acquaintance with Nicholas Bourbon, son of an ironmaster from Champagne. In 1517 Bourbon wrote *Ferraria*, a verse description of smelting and forging by the new processes, which is convincing by its accuracy. Boleyn was also involved in the English occupation of Tournai, a centre of the arms trade.[20] Parrock furnace also went through changes of tenancy in this period. Its owner in 1525 was Richard Warner, possibly son of the John Warner referred to in 1513.

Robert Scorer had been the tenant in 1513, supplying gunstones to the Crown. He was replaced by John Caryll in 1518, after the adaptation of the works to a fully-fledged blast furnace and forge. Caryll's tenancy was the first known involvement in the industry of a family who were to become prominent among Sussex ironmasters over the sixteenth century (Straker 1931: 241–2).

Besides Newbridge and Parrock, the Steel Forge was still in use in the 1520s, but of other early works in Ashdown Forest no more is heard. The independent founders of ammunition had disappeared, and Hartfield forge, which has never been satisfactorily identified on the ground, receives no further mention. Nevertheless, despite the apparently hesitant change to the new technology, Hartfield parish contained numerous aliens: the subsidy returns of 1524 and 1525 listed no less than 36, the largest concentration in the Weald (Cornwall 1956: 130–1).

The new methods were also associated with the presence of immigrants at Socknersh and Burwash. John Collins of Socknersh took over the tenancy of Burwash forge in 1526, and by the time of his will of 1536 had built Socknersh furnace. However, before either of these references it is learned from the 1524 subsidy rolls that Collins had seven Frenchmen in his employment, with eight recorded in 1525. This poses the possibility that Collins built his furnace early in the 1520s, and took Burwash forge for the refining of his pig iron.[21]

The other concentrations of aliens in 1524 and 1525 are less easily associated with ironworks. Nevertheless, there are groupings which appear significant in the light of later references. Principal among these are the 11 aliens, mostly described as Frenchmen, set at the end of the 1524 subsidy returns for Shoyswell hundred, under Pashley. There is of course a risk that the names were thus placed only for clerical convenience, and should have been scattered over the hundred, but there are grounds for taking the connection with Pashley seriously. Sir James Boleyn, brother of Sir Thomas, owned land there, and in 1543 he was to sell the manor, which included an iron furnace, to Thomas May. The presence of Frenchmen in 1524 suggests that the family acquaintance with the potential of the industry had led to the construction of an ironworks in the early 1520s. Even so, there are other possibilities, if less convincing: Etchingham forge was in operation in 1540, and is perhaps close enough to Pashley for workers to be listed there. Darfold furnace,[22] which lies between Etchingham and Pashley, is, however, a less likely place, for it can be argued with some conviction (see p. 328) that the furnace which supplied Etchingham forge was Darvell, in Mountfield parish.

Elsewhere in the south-eastern part of the Weald many of the aliens

listed in 1524–5 are too scattered for clear relationships with ironworks to emerge, for small numbers of French workers could have
been occupied in forestry without being directly connected with
smelting. Nevertheless, where they were recorded, and where ironworks are also found at the beginning of the 1540s, the possibility of
early construction should be noted. In Hawksborough hundred, for
example, there were, apart from John Collins' employees, ten aliens in
1524. Warbleton is within this district: here the origins of ironworking
are obscure, but in 1548 there were said to be four ironworks, of which
the most likely identifications are Markly and Warbleton Priory
furnaces and Steel and Woodmans forges. There is no means of telling
which, if any, of these were in existence 20 years before.[23] Stream
furnace or forge, Chiddingly, might also be added to this group as a
possible early employer in the area. In Netherfield and Battle hundreds 17 aliens appear, with a further 4 in Robertsbridge hundred.
There are individual names also at Framfield and Wadhurst. However, apart from the possibility of Darvell, none of the ironworks extant
in these areas in the decade after 1540 can be proved to have been
built before that date.

(D) RAPID GROWTH: TO 1548

By mid-century, the Wealden industry had grown to a remarkable
extent. This is shown by the proceedings of the commission
appointed to investigate complaints made in 1548 by the coastal ports
of Sussex about the shortage of wood. To the question of how many
ironworks then existed in Sussex, a jury from Rye, Winchelsea, and
Hastings gave an answer of 50 upwards, while the Lewes and
Pevensey juries agreed on a total of 53. The restriction of the count to
Sussex is hardly important, for production in Kent and Surrey is
unlikely to have been significant. In addition to these totals, specific
reference was made to ironworks which lay within ten miles of the sea
or six miles of the South Downs. It is not yet possible to list the 53
works from available information; indeed, the total is hard to extend
beyond 40. However, the Gazetteer shows that there remain sites of
furnaces and forges for which little or no documentary material is yet
known, some of which might be expected to fit into this period. The
material included in the affairs of the 1548–9 commission is complemented by the names of those employing aliens mentioned in the
subsidies and, in particular, the denization returns earlier in the
decade. In very few cases, however, are their works located, and
certain ironmasters' activities are not yet fully identified. What
emerges is that a wide cross-section of Sussex landowners, from the

greatest magnates to those of modest means, were taking advantage of
their resources of ore and timber by the middle 1540s. Some operated
their new works directly, as parts of their estate demesnes, others
leased to tenants. Some of the tenants, indeed, were themselves
landowners, while others were of yeoman-farmer origin, or men with
experience as skilled workers in the industry.

At the head of this pattern of interests comes the renewed involvement of the Crown in the iron industry. Although Newbridge and the
Steel Forge in Ashdown Forest were still leased out, a new furnace
was built in 1534 at the east end of the forest, at the 'Stumblet' (fig.29)

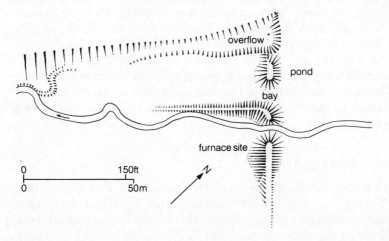

Fig.29   Stumbletts furnace (T Q 399306): plan of bay and site of blast furnace.

(Straker 1936–7). This was at first managed by John Levett, of Little
Horsted, who has been tentatively suggested as being of immigrant
stock. After his death in 1535, the furnace was operated by Levett's
brother, William, who was Receiver of the Royal Revenues in
Sussex.[24] He was referred to as the king's gunstone maker in 1541, and
at some time in the next eight years he extended his interests to
Buxted. Here in 1543 he arranged the casting of the first cannon made
in the Weald since the early attempts at Newbridge. It is assumed that
the Buxted guns were of the one-piece type, for the casting was
supervised by Peter Baude, from the Houndsditch foundry in London,
where bronze guns of one-piece design were made. Baude was
succeeded by Ralph Hogge, who supervised work for Levett until he
himself took over Levett's position as official supplier of gunstones to
the Crown. He indeed was to supply the Crown with ordnance and
ammunition for the next 40 years. Levett's activities were of the

greatest importance in the growth of the industry and the encouragement of its skills, so it is a pity that so little is known about the timing
and location of his early work (Schubert 1957: 171). He was a supplier
of gunstones to the Crown in 1540, but it is uncertain whether these
would come from the Stumbletts furnace or from Buxted. Certainly
his interests in the Hartfield area continued, for aliens employed by
him lived there in 1543. Buxted may, of course, have been constructed
as an ordnance establishment, but there is no means of telling, for we
rely on the bald statements of sixteenth-century observers who
recounted only what was to them the vital aspect, the casting of
ordnance. Nor indeed is it certain where the works lay, for although
Levett owned lands at Oldlands, there is no proof of a furnace there.[25]

Cast-iron guns were particularly needed by the government at this
time. Building was still taking place at the coastal artillery forts, and
iron guns were well suited to these static positions. They were
cheaper than bronze pieces, and on land their weight, which harmed
the stability of ships, was of little consequence. There are many
references to Levett's deliveries of guns and shot to the Crown in the
1540s. In 1546 he was paid £300 for making iron guns, and typical of
his trade in ammunition is an order of 1545 for 300 shot for cannon,
200 for culverin and 300 for falcons, to be sent to Portsmouth. This
was a year in which an unfavourable report on the fortified defences
of the Isle of Wight recommended that pieces should be obtained from
Levett for their improvement. The development of gun-founding at
Buxted was followed in 1546 by the construction of a double furnace
at Worth, on the lands of the Duke of Norfolk, after their confiscation
by the Crown. A double furnace embodied two furnaces in the same
structure, made necessary by the need to cast pieces such as culverins,
beyond the capacity of a single hearth of the time. In the early 1540s
the Duke of Norfolk had a furnace and a forge at Sheffield, and here he
is recorded as employing aliens. Ordnance was not produced there,
and before 1546 the Worth lands were used only for wood. The
development of the Norfolk estates by the Crown was managed by
Levett, and accounts exist for the years 1546 to 1549.[26]

Demands of the Crown also fostered the trade in bar iron. The
accounts of Sir William Sidney for Robertsbridge forge show bar as
well as cast iron supplied for works at Camber castle in 1542–3.[27]
Indeed, Sir William, as a courtier, must have been particularly aware
of the potential of the industry at a time of high spending on arms,
whether or not he had any intention of producing ordnance. The
establishment of the Sidney works does indeed reflect considerable
confidence, for not only were a forge and furnace built at Robertsbridge in 1541–2, but a second furnace was also put up on rented

ground at Panningridge, eight miles to the south-west. In the event, two furnaces were not justified, for that of Robertsbridge was blown out in 1546, and the forge was supplied entirely from Panningridge. Sir William's plans for ironworking on his Robertsbridge estate, the lands of the dissolved Cistercian Abbey which he acquired in 1539, may well have been influenced by contacts with another landowning family, the Lunsfords, who had ironworking interests in the far south of the Weald. The details of their activities are something of a mystery. 'Mr Lunsford' employed aliens in 1544, appearing in the denization return. The family had acquired lands near Crowhurst late in the fifteenth century and there is a place-name, 'Lunsford's Cross', north-west of Bexhill. A near-contemporary reference appears in the Panningridge furnace account for 1547, in which a man named Lunsford borrowed charcoal from the Sidney works. Panningridge is five miles from Lunsford's Cross, which is itself a mile west of Catsfield furnace, undocumented apart from a reference of 1569 in Bexhill manor rolls. The Sidney association goes back well before the construction of Panningridge in 1542. A John Lunsford of East Hoathly had died in 1529, and although his will made no reference to ironworks it does mention individuals later active in the industry. In particular, certain lands were left to Sir William Sidney, in default of Lunsford's heirs. Further, some significant names appear among those appointed to hold parts of Lunsford's estates on behalf of his heirs. They include John Levett, Thomas Oxenbridge, whose relation Robert owned Darvel furnace in 1539, and Thomas Darrell, the next generation of whose family were to be much involved in iron production.[28]

A number of other landowners of substance were involved in iron-smelting by the early part of the 1540s. In each case much remains to be discovered of the details of their activities, but the pointers are significant. Although the Nevills, Lords Abergavenny, are not referred to as employers of aliens in 1544 or in any of the subsidies of the decade, the Rotherfield parish registers include numerous aliens whose most likely employment would be in connection with Eridge furnace on the Abergavenny lands. The absence of the Abergavennys from the records of the 1540s could well arise from their works being leased to a tenant whose name has not been associated with Eridge. Although not of comparable wealth or status, Sir William Barrentyne had substantial lands at Horsted Keynes. He appears as an employer of aliens in Danehill Horsted in the 1543 subsidy, which suggests that Horsted Keynes furnace was in operation. Also of some standing were the Tyrwhitts and the Pelhams. Sir Robert Tyrwhitt owned Etchingham forge in 1542; as has been noted, this lay in an area where iron was smelted in 1524–5. However, Tyrwhitt's involvement before 1542 is yet to be proven, as are early origins for his works. Problems also surround the Pelhams, who later operated Waldron furnace and Bibleham and Brightling forges. Nicholas Pelham had just one alien servant in Hoathly and Waldron in the 1543 subsidy, but is shown as a more substantial employer in the denization return of the following year. There are no specific references to Waldron furnace until 1560, but the employment of aliens must lead to a search for a much earlier origin (Awty 1979).

Of the smaller ironmasters referred to in 1544, some had long been connected with the industry. John Barham's ownership of Brookland and Verredge forges went back over 20 years, and it is likely that in the interim he would have converted them from bloomeries into fineries. William Wybarne had leased Bayham Abbey forge in 1525, and he also remained an employer of aliens in 1544, although it is not known where he was working at this time.[29] The Bowyers remained active at Hartfield, Mrs Bowyer employing ten aliens in 1543, most probably at Parrock.[30]

The nature of the sources for this period concentrates attention on individuals rather than places, sometimes with the latter remaining unrecognized. However, the reverse is on occasion the case. For example, in the early 1540s aliens were being employed at Isenhurst, now hardly a hamlet, south of Mayfield. John Baker employed three aliens there in 1543, and William Woddy was named there in the same subsidy. At some time the small stream which flows through Isenhurst has been much used for ironworking, for Old Mill was formerly a furnace, and Moat Mill once a forge. However, it is not possible to be certain whether these were in use in 1543. The Mountfield and Battle area is also of interest, for here, too, the location of working is uncertain. The striking point here is that in 1539 there were no less than 49 Frenchmen in Netherfield Hundred, which adds weight to the case for an early start for Darvel furnace. Mountfield furnace is not known to have worked as early as this, but Richard Wekes, who operated there in the 1560s and was, incidentally a partner of Woddy, does appear in the subsidy as employing aliens.

The sources also fail to show how far to the north the industry had spread by the middle of the century. No ironworks can be located with any certainty in Kent before 1550: Vauxhall furnace was 'newly built' in 1553, having been leased to David Willard in 1552.[31] Nevertheless, in the 1543 subsidy return for West Barnfield hundred, Kent, Thomas May had a servant, Bartholomew Jeffrey, and an alien in his employment. Thomas May had purchased Pashley furnace in the preceding year, and Bartholomew Jeffrey was later to be a significant tenant ironmaster in Sussex, leasing Panningridge furnace in 1563. Thus there is a possibility of an earlier ironworks in Kent, owned by May and run by Jeffrey.[32] In Surrey the Nevills were active at Ewood in 1553, when they sold a standing furnace to the Darrells. There is as yet no known reference to when this works was built.

In the subsequent 25 years, however, the industry was to spread into these districts, and by 1574 was to occupy a far larger area, both to the west and north of the area developed in the early sixteenth century. It is to the causes and effects of this great expansion that we turn in the following chapter.

NOTES

1. PRO C66/579 m.23r.
2. PRO DL42/21, f.184.
3. PRO E36/8, 59.
4. The term was occasionally used for pig iron later in the sixteenth century, e.g. (1595) 'raw or rough iron in sows' (PRO REQ2/228/13); DL29/455/7331.
5. Jenkins 1938–9: 37, citing Lambeth Palace Roll 1352.
6. PRO E36/8, 75, 96, 97.
7. PRO DL42/21, f.185.
8. ESRO SAS Acc 1398.
9. PRO DL29/455/7331; 445/7153 sq.
10. BWIRG, 15 (1979), 12.
11. PRO E101/55/29; L & P Henry VIII, I pt.i 1463, vi. The reference to a Sackville interest in gun-founding is an important sign of early landowner involvement in the industry. He is variously spelt Richard and Robert in State Papers.
12. PRO DL29/455/7330, 7331.
13. PRO DL42/95, f.11. Lambert Symart was paid for a consignment of guns in 1511 (E101/55/29) 2 Sep 3H8.
14. PRO DL29/455/7336–7, 445/7155.
15. HMC Salisbury MSS, XIII, 19, repr. in Tawney and Power 1924: I, 231–8.
16. These sources are listed and discussed in Awty 1981; 524–39.
17. PRO E36/50.
18. KAO U1475; Giuseppi 1912: 276–311.
19. PRO DL29/445/7160 records the date of the 21-year lease to Boleyn: successive accounts note his rent long after his death, while still referring to the works as unoccupied. 455/7342–456/7354 are more realistic, showing the Boleyn rent up to 1539, and the payment of a similar annual sum by William Nysell after a year's break (7357). For Simon Forneres see DL 29/456/7352 and 446/7167–8.
20. Rathery 1856: 22. Brian Awty has kindly supplied this reference and has been of constant help over matters concerning French workers in the Weald.
21. ESRO ASH 200a; PRO PROB13/11/41; Cornwall 1956: 148.
22. *Ibid.*, 144; PRO C78/1/57.
23. Cornwall 1956: 146–9.
24. PRO DL29/446/7168.
25. PRO E179/190/191; Holinshed 1586: II, 960, remains the earliest certain source, for there is no evidence that the brief reference in BL Egerton 2642, f.150, predates it.
26. L & P Henry VIII, XXI pt.i, 845; XX/1, 1244; XX/2, 520; Giuseppi 1912: 298–311.
27. KAO U1475/B2/3.
28. KAO U1475/B10/1; Awty 1979: 6, from WAM 12261; PRO PROB11/24/7.

29. KAO U840/T109; PRO SC12/18/60, f.92v. Brian Awty has drawn attention to a reference to Lambert 'Semer of Baham' supplying 'bill helves' (not iron) in 1513 (*L & P Henry VIII*, 1 pt. 2, 3613 (340)).
30. PRO E179/190/191.
31. PRO RE Q2/285/39.
32. Awty 1981: 527 n.16.

Chapter 7   The mature industry

The third quarter of the sixteenth century is a suitable period in which to consider aspects of the operation of the iron industry in the Weald. The written and archaeological sources range widely across the area and cover a great variety of owners and lessees of ironworks; they are sufficient to identify a high proportion of the forges and furnaces and their owners. Further, global estimates of the numbers of works are possible in 1548 and 1574, encapsulating a period of growth and consolidation in which the industry approached, if not reached, its maximum size.

In most respects the innovatory stage of the Wealden industry was past. Skills were being dispersed, for the French nucleus was no longer the sole source of expertise. Immigration had virtually ended by the middle of the century, so continued expansion depended on the spread of experience in founding and forging among the local population as well as on the French families. Growth was also based on the certainty of returns from ironworking: yields were now predictable, and were capable of improvement only as details of operation were refined. Over and above such matters was the ability to sell bar iron in south-east England, in particular in London, whose growth continued through the sixteenth century. This general market became the dominant outlet after mid-century, although the need for arms persisted, if in a changing form. Crown requirements were supplemented by the needs of merchant shipping, in which defensive ordnance was increasingly used, as trade routes spread beyond the ports of north-west Europe.

1   The expansion of the industry in the second half of the sixteenth century

From the total of 53 ironworks of all kinds estimated in 1548, the Wealden industry more than doubled in size in the next 25 years. A key source is the list made in 1574, which survives in seven versions in the State Papers and in the British Library. From these there can be shown to have been 52 furnaces and 58 forges in use or available. The exact numbers may vary slightly according to interpretation of some ambiguous entries, but the order of magnitude is not in doubt. Whereas the 1548 estimate does not differentiate between furnaces and forges, the latter possibly still including bloomeries, the 1574 list is more precise. The survey from which it derived was carried out because of fears that Wealden ordnance was being exported to the Continent, and that this side of the industry was developing in a dangerous manner. Ralph Hogge, who held the monopoly of casting iron ammunition for the Crown, raised the matter in 1573, listing the ironmasters who had lately begun to cast ordnance. The survey ordered by the Privy Council did, in the event, go far beyond this aspect. It recorded not only all furnaces in the Weald, whatever their product, but covered the forges as well. Most owners and tenants were recorded, and although some locations are obscure, the whole undertaking provided a record unique in the industrial history of Tudor England (Cattell 1979).

These figures are the basis for estimating the growth of output over the quarter-century. With them should be placed the figures for production of the best-documented furnace, Panningridge, casting about 240 tons in typical years between the mid-1540s and 1563. Assuming that there were about 25 furnaces in 1548 and 52 in 1574, an optimistic estimate for pig output in the Weald would be 6,000 tons at the beginning of the period, rising to over 12,000 by 1574. At the rates of conversion accepted at Robertsbridge forge in the 1550s these would make 4,000 and 8,000 tons of bar respectively. In fact, bar iron production would be somewhat less than this, for in 1573 Ralph Hogge claimed that seven furnaces were casting ordnance. In 1548 there were probably three. Had their entire production been in this form, about 700 tons in 1548 and 1,700 tons in 1574 would have been denied the forges; however, seventeenth- and particularly eighteenth-century sources show that gun furnaces commonly made pig iron at the start of a campaign while the metal was brought to the best quality. Given the short runs of which some sixteenth-century furnaces were capable, as much as one-third of their product could be of pig rather than castings. But these amount to small adjustments, leaving Wealden bar production rising from perhaps 3,700 tons to 7,500 tons.

Another view would produce lower absolute figures, particularly for the start of the period, when the 1548 total could possibly contain a few surviving bloomeries. Also some allowance has to be made for furnaces which could only run short campaigns or for any which produced on as small a scale as Newbridge, which had cast only about 160 tons in 1539. This latter point, the survival of less effective furnaces, would apply to a lesser extent in 1574. A worst-case assumption for output of pig in 1548 could be about 4,000 tons and, if we assume that all forges achieved conversion figures comparable with Robertsbridge, this would make 2,600 tons of bar. For 1574, if the worst assumptions are also made about campaign lengths, with annual average outputs of 200 tons all cast iron output would be about 10,400 tons, pig iron about 9,500 tons, and bar 6,400 tons. A guideline comes from Dr Hammersley's work on the Port Books, which shows that at least 2,900 tons of bar left south-eastern ports for all destinations in 1579–80, with defective records leading this author to estimate that 4,000 tons were actually shipped (Hammersley 1972: 51–2). Local consumption is unknown, as is the amount carried overland to London. From this evidence, a total tonnage of 6,400 seems feasible.

Besides the growth in output, a noticeable feature of the industry in this period is its geographical extension. In the north-east, the woodlands of Wealden Kent were increasingly employed for smelting. Landowners such as the Darrells and Dykes built furnaces in the Lamberhurst and Horsmonden areas, while further advances took place as far as Biddenden, Hawkhurst and Tonbridge. These works, set up further from the south coast, disposed of their products into Kent and to London by way of Maidstone and the Medway towns. The central northern part of Susex was also a favourable area. The northern fringe of the Weald yielded ample supplies of ore and was well wooded. Sizeable works were developed in St Leonards Forest, expansion continued around Worth, and into Surrey. It was in the west, both in Sussex and Surrey, that some of the most important new developments took place. The Arun and Wey basins were untouched by the industry before 1550, yet a quarter of a century later the stretch of country north of Petworth contained an important group of furnaces, despite the demand on woodlands from the makers of glass, a traditional industry which was strengthened in the years after 1567 by the arrival of numerous immigrant workers. This was an area where, as Kenyon has indicated, profitable uses were being sought for woodlands, and the earls of Northumberland, chronically short of money, provided an example to their neighbours in their search for greater income from their Petworth estates (Kenyon 1952: 235–41).

Despite the extension of the industry by landowners on the fringes, the greater part of the quarter-century's growth still took place within the eastern and central Weald. Even here there were resources for expansion in 1574 and beyond and, in the far south-east of the Weald, construction was to continue into the 1580s.

(A) THE BASIS OF EXPANSION

Expansion in the Weald arose out of an ability to supply a growing market with competitively priced bar iron in the medium and lower quality ranges, as well as relatively small quantities of cast iron. This capability arose out of the nature of the Weald itself, whose terrain and soils presented resources enabling every level of the community to mingle industry with an agriculture which was beset by natural obstacles. It is important to emphasize these resources as the basis of the growth and profitability of the iron industry in the later sixteenth century.

Woodlands

The Wealden woodlands were as essential a source of livelihood to local communities as agriculture. In much of inland Sussex, notably in the High Weald, farms were small and scattered. Heavy, poorly draining clays were difficult to work, while on some of the high sandy ground intensive rotations were impossible to sustain. It was difficult to operate compact high-yielding home farms for estates, yet land could not sustain high rents when leased out. Further, arable produce was not easily conveyed to urban markets, so Wealden farmers found it hard to compete in the supply of grain and livestock to London. In such circumstances there was much to be said for maintaining rather than clearing woods, regarding them as a positive resource rather than as residual waste.

Coppicing was the key to the profitable use of woodland: the important point to grasp is that deciduous trees are a renewable resource, several shoots growing up from the stump after felling. Different occupations required wood of differing sizes, so that particular woodlands and species of trees could be coppiced at the most suitable ages for their users. In addition, the larger trees, once cut, could be divided, branches of differing thicknesses being selected for different buyers. The 'small woods' used for charcoal were either young coppice cut after 7–12 years, or 'top and lop', branches cut from larger trees. In the blast furnace it was a definite disadvantage to be supplied with charcoal made with wood more than about 5–6cm in diameter, for the larger the size, the more likely the charcoal was to reduce to dust, either in transit or when subject to the weight of the charge in the furnace. Such charcoal commanded a low price or was discarded, as is shown by the case of Thomas Blackwell, who complained in 1569 that the charcoal he took over with Burningfold Forge was too dusty to use.[1] Wood of longer growth could be used for hurdles, for poles, for firewood billets, for turning, carpentry, building, or the dockyards; and really fine trees, a century and more old, might go into structures as large as windmills. Regenerative coppicing was well understood, and John Norden, the surveyor, writing at the end of the sixteenth century, makes this clear. There are many documented Wealden examples, of which two will suffice. Robert Welshe's will of 1562 requested that his woods should be coppiced and preserved, while Robert Relfe, in his will of 1609, requested that his woods should be felled and corded, and then coppiced for seven years before being cut again.[2] Even where coppicing is not mentioned as such, descriptions of woodlands show that the practice was in operation. For example, surveys of the manor of Robertsbridge allocated certain woods to the ironworks in the long term, and at both Robertsbridge and Panningridge the same grounds appear in accounts as sources of wood for charcoal over lengthy periods.[3]

Division of woods into different growths of trees can be seen. In some cases timber trees were reserved for the owner, as in the will of Thomas Glydd of Ewhurst (1590), in which the beneficiaries were instructed to sell 1,000 cords of wood from the manor of Dixter 'or so much there be without spoil of timber'. Christopher Darrell leased to Thomas Dyke only tops, lops and underwoods on lands in Frant in 1573.[4] So, if carefully set out, the woodland lease could be an important and long-term source of income for landowners. Conversely, most of the Wealden ironmasters of whom we have record found it vital to make use of leased woods. When, for example, John Garraway rented the manor and ironworks at Parrock from Lord Buckhurst in 1571, the availability of wood was an essential part of the agreement: if the woods on the manor failed to provide 160 cords each year, the tenant was entitled to withdraw.[5]

Thus the development of the iron industry and the growing sophistication of the woodland side of estate management went hand in hand. When woods were measured, the outlets were clearly in the surveyor's mind. This was the case at Framfield, where woods were listed in about 1560, with a note of ironworks within a three-mile (4.8km) radius. Also attempts were made to estimate the amount of wood which an area could produce. The difficulty of doing so is shown by an escape clause in an agreement of c.1564 between Lord Abergavenny and Nicholas Fowle in which woods were sold sufficient to produce 6,000 cords for five years, but if this amount could not be found, Fowle was permitted to go outside the agreed ground. The Abergavenny estate entered into an even larger-scale agreement when the site for Cowford furnace was leased to William Relfe and Bartholomew Jeffrey, with whom there was an arrangement to cut 12,000 cords annually for ten years. Precision would certainly be difficult to achieve with so physically variable a commodity, not least because the cord – the stack of wood – had differing conventional dimensions. Lord Abergavenny, Relfe and Jeffrey agreed in 1569 on a cord 8ft long, 4ft high, and 4ft broad (128ft³). Yet 30 years later

Henry Needler of Horley was arguing with Thomas Whitfield, who operated ironworks at Worth, whether 'high' cords 4ft high by 7ft by 6ft ($168ft^3$) were the subject of their agreement, or whether the reckoning should be in cords stacked a foot lower ($126ft^3$).[6]

In most areas it seems that the management of woodlands developed as the iron industry grew, and that for much of the century charcoal, if rising in price, was generally sufficient in quantity. Confirmation comes from estimating the acreage of coppiced woodland an ironworks, or indeed the whole industry, might be expected to require to function in perpetuity. Dr Hammersley has calculated that 13,000 acres of coppice would be sufficient to provide a blast furnace and forge with charcoal. However, his estimate is calculated in respect of large furnaces in the Forest of Dean, producing 700–750 tons of pig iron annually. The Wealden furnaces had smaller hearths and never remotely approached that figure. In a good year, with adequate water supply, a good choice of refractory stone for the hearth, and a buoyant market, a blast furnace in Sussex would run for long enough to produce about 250 tons of pig. Thus 2,500 acres of coppice would satisfy such a furnace, with a further 1,500–1,600 acres being required for its forge. The 4,000 acres needed for such a combination would be found within a three-mile radius if one-quarter of the land were under coppice. Looked at in regional terms, such estimates seem of about the right order of magnitude. The Wealden iron area is difficult to define exactly, but the land bounded by the furthest-flung ironworks amounts to about 900,000 acres. A reasonable estimate for the number of furnaces and forges in 1574 is 52 and 58 respectively, so even allowing for a high level of activity, the 220,000 acres of coppice required would cover about one-quarter of the surface of the area. It is significant that in 1667 John Evelyn was to estimate that there were 200,000 acres of coppice in the Weald (Hammersley 1973: 606; Evelyn 1664, II: 160).

Contemporary sources provide the impression that considerable areas of the Weald were wooded to this extent, although the few local sixteenth-century estate surveys are sufficiently precise. In the Forest of Dean, in 1641, the area of woods reached 55 per cent of the total, a proportion which could apply to some parts of the Weald, and in the south-east, around Battle, Dallington and Brightling, would fit the density of furnaces and forges. The relationship had to be a close one, for the distance over which charcoal could be carried was normally limited by its friability to 5–6km, although the prosecution of Thomas May, in 1600, for carrying charcoal the nine miles (14.5km) from Cotchford Bridge to Mayfield shows that the distance could be exceeded, no doubt with considerable wastage.[7]

The iron industry was not the sole outlet for wood. There were many other customers, needing trees cut at differing ages. The demands of one group of users, expressed in the price they were willing to pay, could affect the rotations in coppices, leaving others short of supplies or forced to pay higher prices. Such conflicts between users are indeed found at quite an early stage. The complaint of the urban users of firewood in 1548 is a case in point, and the returns to the enquiry of that year contain the specific example of the cutting down of woodland by Alexander Collins for the newly built forge at Hoathly, near Lamberhurst. No doubt the felling of established woods would alarm his neighbours, but there is no reason to think that an experienced ironmaster such as Collins would be engaged in one-for-all clearance. His aim would be the reverse, to fell timber to the stub and to re-establish woods as coppice, giving a high yield, but not necessarily producing the variety of wood traditionally available. Particular opposition came when rights of collection or cutting were threatened. For example, in 1564 David Willard was taking more wood near Tonbridge than he was entitled to cut. Here particular harm was done to tenants allowed manorial timber for repairs to their houses.[8] It is thus understandable that when legislation was attempted for the regulation of wood supply, it included leaving minimum numbers of timber trees. It also prohibited the use of large wood for ironworks, a practice which the prudent ironmaster would only adopt as a last resort.

Legislation against wood cutting barely affected the Weald. The Act of 1558 prohibiting the use for iron of wood more than 1ft² (30cm²) at the stub exempted the Weald, apart from the Surrey fringe, and the Act of 1581 did likewise. Only in 1585 was legislation enacted which seems likely to have had much effect.[9] Nevertheless, by the 1570s and 1580s the signs are that in the south-eastern part of the Weald the pressures were considerable. In 1578 the shortage of wood in the Rye area was blamed on new works erected at Brede while in 1587 concern was expressed in Hastings at the construction of Conster forge, Beckley. Significantly, it was mentioned that the new works were only two miles (3.2km) from Brede furnace and three miles (4.8km) from Westfield forge, implying that contemporaries thought the supply areas would overlap.[10]

Changes in wood prices indicate competition for supplies, particularly in the eastern Weald. Tenpence and 12d was a common price for a cord of wood suitable for the charcoal burner from the middle of the century until the late 1570s. Thereafter higher figures appear, rising to 24d and 30d by 1591, with a remarkable 60d paid at Crowhurst in 1597. Unfortunately there are insufficient runs of ironworks accounts at this time to be sure how typical such figures were, but they contrast strongly with the prices for bought-in wood at Robertsbridge between 1558 and 1568, which rarely exceeded 14–15d.[11]

A corresponding increase can also be seen in the price of charcoal, which rose by a factor of four between 1540 and 1600. Yet output of iron was not only maintained but increased, showing that ironmasters were able to pay the higher prices. Woodlands were thus a buoyant asset, their products rising in value faster than those of agriculture, and with increases of this order the rival wood-using trades must have been hard-pressed.

It would oversimplify the situation to suggest that ironworks always led to a maximum and rational exploitation of woodlands. There do appear to have been occasions when drastic over-cutting took place. When regeneration failed to occur, opposition was aroused and the whole industry gained a bad name. Ashdown Forest, for example, appears to have lost much of the tree cover from its fringes at this time: this could be explained in part by the extent of cutting for furnaces such as those run by Ralph Hogge between Buxted and Maresfield, to the south of the Forest, but failure to regenerate the wood may well have been due to grazing of young shoots on the common lands of the Forest. St Leonards Forest, also, appears to have lost its tree cover after cutting which took place at the end of the sixteenth century, conceivably for the same reason. Nevertheless, the impression of a stable woodland area is a strong one over much of the Weald, particularly when the comments of seventeenth- and eighteenth-century writers are taken into account. Had the dilapidations of the woods been as great in the sixteenth century as some contemporaries made out, the wooded appearance of the Weald in Defoe's day would be hard to explain.

Ore

Contemporary sources are less explicit about the extent of ore digging than about woodland management. Mining made its mark in many parts of the Weald, although the digging of marl can leave similar traces. Many landowners, large and small, who did not themselves exploit their ores, leased mining rights to others. An early example was Ninian Burrell, who let lands at Penhurst to Sir Nicholas Pelham in the years around 1550. Pelham then sub-let to Thomas Glazier, and the ores mined were used at Penhurst furnace. Sometimes ore-bearing lands were included in a furnace lease. For example at Panningridge in 1542 the furnace site was leased from the parson of Penhurst, in whose lands the tenants could mine ore. In this case the ore seems not to have proved adequate for long-term supply, and in the next 20 years a variety of sources were used; some were on the estates of large landowners, but often rights were rented from much smaller men. For example, in 1549 John Cressye's wood appears in the accounts as a source of ore, yet Cressye also figures as a carrier for the ironworks. Here, it seems, was a farmer at Mountfield supplementing his income by carting and by allowing mining on land for which this was the most immediately profitable use.[12] Such a farmer could well have been a tenant, for it was customary on some Wealden manors – Bibleham being a case in point – for copyholders to be allowed to take ore from their lands with the lord's licence. On occasion supplies came from some distance, as in 1560–2, when correspondence between Sir Richard Sackville and Sir Edward Gage shows that Sackville, then operating Sheffield furnace, was interested in ore from Forest Row six miles (9.6km) to the north.[13] Cases of this kind may not have been simply due to exhaustion of nearby deposits, for quality was also important; Wealden ores were of differing types, as the seventeenth-century observations of Hope and Ray and the eighteenth-century Fuller letters show, with yields which could vary between 12 and 41 per cent (Schubert 1957: 244).

One problem of which little is known is that of restoration of the ground after mining. From such silence, it is assumed that ore was most frequently dug in woodland areas where filling and levelling was less important than on agricultural ground. However, if woods were mined, their continued use as coppices had to be safeguarded, and a recent survey at Upper Hartfield has suggested how this was done. The minepits, from which tracks lead towards Parrock furnace, were dug leaving strips of undisturbed ground on which trees grow noticeably better than on the backfill. It would have been simpler to mine in large open-cast diggings, but it is assumed that the miners were restricted to a pattern of excavation which preserved at least some of the potential of the woodland.

Water

The third important resource employed by the iron industry was water. Although possessing an average rainfall lower than much of northern and western Britain, the Weald is dissected by many narrow and often deep valleys or ghylls: if the surrounding catchment areas were well-wooded, water was released steadily into streams, and these could provide adequate power for the lengthening periods for which sixteenth-century technology allowed furnaces to remain in blast. Rights over the flow and impounding of water were, therefore, of the greatest importance to the ironworks and indeed to other users of streams. This was not lost upon owners of such water, who on occasion leased rights to take leats across their land. Bugsell forge, for example, was served by a watercourse across the lands of Haremere manor, over which a dispute resulted in the interruption of supply. Several cases involved the overflowing of land by ironworks ponds. For example, at Benhall forge, in 1574, the height of the bay had to be limited to ensure that the pond would not be increased in size, while in 1598 the area of the pond at Chingley forge had to be redefined. A particularly contentious case involved the pond for Thomas Collins's Socknersh furnace. The water overflowed on to adjoining land, and in 1593 it was claimed that on account of this the neighbours had cut a ditch to drain the pond, at a time when stocks of ore and charcoal had been built up and the furnace campaign was in full swing.[14] Water could cause damage to property rights in many ways. The road between Biddenden and Cranbrook was cut in 1583 when the flood-gates in the bay of Sir Richard Baker's forge were opened, causing damage to a bridge. Effects on neighbouring mills are mentioned in areas where sites lay close together on one stream. In 1587 Beckley furnace was said to threaten the supply to a corn mill, and five years later Bramshott forge interrupted the water supplies to the local millers. Not that ironworks were always the culprits. In 1564 the lease of Freshfield corn mill contained clauses intended to safeguard the water supply to the neighbouring forge.[15] On occasion problems could arise between adjacent ironworks. For example, it is still possible to see how close the end of the furnace pond at Ashburnham lay to the Panningridge furnace tail-race (fig.30) and to appreciate why the latter was clogged by silt deposited by the sluggish flow from the furnace wheel.

Labour supply: the availability of skills in iron-smelting and related occupations

In the last chapter, emphasis was given to the part played by French immigrants in the initial expansion of the Wealden industry. Although the middle of the century saw the end of the influx of alien workers, French families remained prominent in the operation of the ironworks. Some, such as the Tylers, passed a tradition of skilled work from generation to generation, founders of that name working at Fletching in 1556, Ashburnham in 1594 and Framfield in 1628. Nevertheless, local men were skilled in up-to-date methods. Indeed, as the number of works reached their maximum towards the end of the century, a considerable proportion must have relied on the

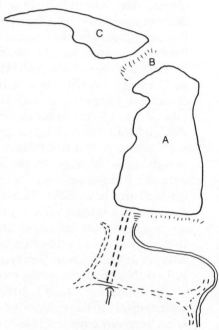

Fig.30   Ashburnham furnace (TQ 686171) and Panningridge furnace (TQ 687174). This view shows the close proximity of these furnaces. In the foreground lies Ashburnham, its drained pond (A) in the centre of the photograph. Panningridge furnace bay can be seen (B), marked by the line of trees on its crest, in the upper centre of the photograph. It will be seen that the Ashburnham pond meadow reaches virtually to the ground where Panningridge furnace stood. Panningridge pond (C) occupied the field upstream (Cambridge University Collection: Crown Copyright reserved).

abilities of English founders, finers and hammermen. A useful indication of such dissemination of skills is given by the identities of eight witnesses to a suit of 1583, in which the finers, James Bewsall, Bartholomew Bonncote and Richard Larbye, have French family names, whereas David Hatcher, founder, William Barden and John Coppin, hammermen, and the finers John Preddam and David Trayford are not considered to have been of immigrant descent.[16]

The widening spread of skills is reflected in the narrowing of the differentials in wages between specialist and other workers. In the 1540s a founder received 8s for a six-day founday and a furnace filler

6s, while labourers' wages were commonly 6–8d for a day's work, half those of a skilled ironworker. The best figures we have are for Robertsbridge and Panningridge, and these show that in the third quarter of the century skilled rates changed little; at Robertsbridge the hammermen and the finer received, between them, 13s 4d per ton of bar iron in 1546; the figure was the same in 1560 and in 1572. The founder and filler gained only an insignificant increase, sharing 14s for a six-day period in 1547 and 14s 8d in 1562. By contrast, other wages rose appreciably. In most cases these are only available as piecework rates, which are difficult to use, owing to variations in working conditions, such as depths from which ore had to be drawn. Charcoal-burning was perhaps least affected by such problems, allowing rates of pay to be considered without adjustment. The rate of 13½d a load paid in the mid-1540s rose to 15d in the early 1550s, to a remarkable 24d in the Robertsbridge woods in 1563, settling and staying at 20d for the next decade.[17]

Erosion of differentials emphasizes that the scarcity value of the skilled ironworker was in relative decline, even though the number of works increased. Founders' and finers' assistants learned their trade and went on to take charge at new works. The original skills brought from France were spread among the Wealden population who, after all, had a long tradition of ironworking by the bloomery method. This process of diffusion can be illustrated in detail at Panningridge where in 1549 and 1550 Charles (Jarrett), a noted French founder, came to repair the furnace wall, hearth, and bellows; he also came in the latter year to spend nine days 'amending of the phurnis wheele'. At this time a man named Peter was the regular founder.[18] In several years Charles was paid a retainer to be available at Panningridge, and it was by such supervision that his experience was transmitted. There is insufficient information about the pay of specialist ironworkers to establish whether varying reputations for skill led to differences in the pay individuals could command. On the Panningridge evidence this seems not necessarily to have been so, for Charles Jarrett, when occupied at the furnace, received 12d a day, the same rate as Peter, the man he appears to have been helping. Certainly some men had doubtful reputations for skill. According to a case of 1585, when Thomas Chatterton offered his services as a founder to John Wilgose, he was taken on only as a labourer, despite a recommendation from Thomas May.[19]

The French workers were not confined to the specialized operations at furnace or forge. Their names also appear amongst miners and charcoal burners. There may at first have been some special skill in preparing charcoal suitable for the blast furnace, but it is hard to believe that this would not soon have been common knowledge in the local woodland communities.

It is often asked how many workers would be taken on at a blast furnace or forge of typical Wealden size. The Sidney accounts show a clerk of works in overall charge, a founder and a filler at the furnace and, at the forge, a finer for each hearth and a hammerman. The clerk received an annual salary, the furnace workers were paid on a time basis, and the forgemen by the ton of bar produced. The outworkers greatly expand the total, but there were great variations in the proportion of the year for which individuals were employed. In the 1540s, in particular, there were many amongst the woodcutters whose names appear in the accounts on only a few occasions in each season. At Panningridge and Robertsbridge this changes, until by about 1560 the tail of occasional workers accounted for only a small proportion of the wood cut. Charcoal-burning and mining exhibit a similar change.

In some occupations there were marked seasonal patterns of employment. In wood cutting, most work was done in the winter, tailing off through the spring, with very few payments made between June and October. Charcoal burners show a less marked pattern, and by the mid-1550s worked over much of the year. Mining was a summer occupation, no doubt because winter rain made pits unworkable; for example, between May and September 1555, Philpott, John Margo and John Cressye's sons dug sufficient ore to operate Panningridge furnace over the winter. The differences in seasonal patterns show that the woodcutters would be able to take more harvest work than their counterparts in the other occupations. It may well be that they had farms of their own which they could leave during the winter for forest occupations.

Such a pattern of casual and seasonal work is also indicated by the fragmentary accounts for Ralph Hogge's works, 1576–81. In these, many names appear only occasionally, not only in wood cutting but in mining and in carriage. Indeed, in certain years five times as many individuals are named cutting wood as burning charcoal, and here also the payments were largely in the autumn and winter, beginning after the harvest period. At Sheffield and Worth the practice was rather different, for although at Sheffield in particular the skilled ironworkers were listed separately in an inventory of 1549, the document totals 23 employees there, and 33 at Worth, with the implication that forest workers were regularly paid, even if on piecework.[20]

One category of work which employed many occasional workers was cartage. The movement of charcoal, ore and pig iron, as well as timber and stone for repairs, must have been a useful source of extra income for men such as those who provided carts for Panningridge furnace. From here as much as 240 tons of pig iron, one ton to the load, had to be carried over hilly ground eight miles (12.8km) to Robertsbridge forge. At Marshalls and Buxted ore and charcoal had to be taken to the furnaces from the southern part of Ashdown Forest and, rather later, the early seventeenth-century Sussex Quarter Sessions records contain many instances of summonses for carriage of iron or material without repairing the damage caused by the carts. There were many farmers who were prepared to take on such work, for in addition to the regular names, fresh individuals appear in the Sidney accounts when, for example, stone, clay or cinder was needed to repair a damaged bay, as at Panningridge in 1555. In addition to road transport the river carriage of iron created employment. In the Robertsbridge accounts up to six lightermen appear in a year. One example was John Biddenden, who was contracted to carry 18 tons of iron from 'The Oke' above Bodiam Bridge to Rye in 1542–3. In the 1560s, during the Robertsbridge steelworks venture, cast-iron plates, shipped to Rye from Cardiff, were also carried by lighter, up the Rother to Bodiam.[21]

2   The ironmasters and their operations

In the middle of the sixteenth century numerous estates took up direct operation of ironworks, fostering the use of woods, ores and streams which had previously been under-exploited or ignored. Of those involved at this time, very few have left even fragmentary accounts. By far the most comprehensive are those of Sir William and Sir Henry Sidney for Robertsbridge and Panningridge, which survive for the years 1541–72. There is nothing comparable in detail or range, although it is worth looking also at the estimate of consumption made at Newbridge in 1539 and at the accounts of the confiscated Norfolk works at Sheffield and Worth for 1546–9. For the later decades the only other accounts are the fragments relating to Ralph Hogge's furnaces in the Maresfield and Buxted areas.

(A) DOCUMENTED WEALDEN IRONWORKS

The Robertsbridge works[22]

Sir William Sidney was an early case of a substantial landowner taking up the production of iron, and his operations were on a sizeable scale from the start. Not only did he have a furnace and a forge built at Robertsbridge in 1541–2, but he also sought further capacity by taking over the lease of Panningridge, where a furnace was projected by William Spycer of Dallington. Spycer had leased 6 acres in the valley of Giffords Gill from the vicar of Penhurst in 1541: the valley was well wooded, ore outcrops were close at hand, and the stream had a good catchment area along the south side of the high ground between Dallington and Brightling. It is not known what considerations led to the transfer of the lease, but once this was done construction of the bay and the furnace was completed during 1542–3. Until 1546 the two furnaces were used, but in that year the first, at Robertsbridge, disappears from the record, not to be put in blast for another 28 years. It had not been trouble-free, and in 1542 the bay was breached by a flood and the furnace considerably damaged. However, the accounts do not explain why it should have fallen out of use: in 1543, for example, it provided pig iron sufficient to make 140 tons of bar at the forge, suggesting that the furnace could cast about 210 tons of pig in a year. In the years 1544–6 both furnaces fed the forge, and it is hard to separate their output. One possible reason for putting Robertsbridge furnace out of blast may have been an over-estimate either of the amount the forge could convert or, perhaps, of the local market. A further question is why the more distant furnace should have been kept in operation. The extra cost of transporting pig iron to the forge varied from year to year around a typical figure of £20–25. The Panningridge rent was more, £33, but this included woodlands, whose coppices can be seen from the accounts to have had considerable long-term potential. It was perhaps the low rent of these woods which tilted the balance towards retaining rather than disposing of the Panningridge lease, thus leaving the Robertsbridge woods for the forge.

By the late 1540s this combination of leased and estate-owned works was regularly producing 160 tons of bar iron from 240 tons of pig each year, and continued to do so until 1563 when the Panning-ridge lease expired. For the following ten years Robertsbridge forge converted bought-in pig on much the same scale, and it was only in 1574 that the estate withdrew from direct operation. In that year the forge and furnace were let to Michael Weston, who rebuilt Roberts-bridge furnace and operated the works using woodlands leased as part of his deal with Sir Henry Sidney.

Comprehensive though the accounts appear, they leave some doubt as to how profitable these ironworks were and what advantages direct operation conferred, by comparison with leasing the buildings and woods to a tenant ironmaster. Methods of calculating profitability have changed as business accounting methods have developed, and we should not expect too much of sixteenth-century records. The annual accounts drawn up for the Sidneys end in every case with figures of 'clear gain', and it is these which were important at the time. In the 1550s these totals cluster in the range £300–350 a year, a useful contribution to estate revenue. It may be anachronistic to fault the calculations behind these figures, but analysis of the accounts does expose important problems. One concerns fuel: until after 1560 the costs of wood were underestimated, for stocks were valued at 3d or 4d a cord, which was the cost of cutting rather than the figure for which they could have been sold. In the early 1560s the practice changed, for increasing amounts were being bought, both growing and cut, and valuations of 14d a cord in 1563 give a better idea of the cost of wood on the open market. Another difficulty is the practice of the Sidneys' officials of calculating their gains on the basis of the iron produced and of the increase or decrease in stocks of wood, charcoal, ore or pig during the year. Thus large stocks of unsold iron would indicate apparent success, obscuring any difficulty in selling the iron.

It is possible, although far from simple, to calculate the actual profit from iron production at Robertsbridge. For example, in 1548 the cost of producing a ton of bar iron can be suggested as approaching £4 5s 0d, compared with a valuation in the stock account of £7. It is also possible to assess the contribution of each stage of the process. For example, it can be seen that in the 1550s the cost of smelting was at times very close to the value put on the pig iron. In 1558, indeed, the cost of smelting, £1 11s 4d a ton, was little less than the valuation, £1 13s 4d. This, however, was the worst case, in a year when prices were particularly low. At the forge, by contrast, bar iron could always be sold well above cost, despite the increasing need to purchase wood outside the estate.

Estate officials would be aware of some of these problems, and the change of policy at Robertsbridge in 1563 may reflect them. Sir Henry Sidney is of particular importance for his attempts to diversify his mineral interests in the decade after the end of the lease of Panning-ridge furnace. Two ventures appear in the accounts for the years 1564–8; one was the smelting of iron on lands in Glamorgan, where Sir Henry was joint lessee of a furnace and forge with Edmund Roberts. Here was a district where competition for wood was less severe, and the Bristol Channel area presented an attractive market for bar iron. There was indeed a unique aspect to this venture: some of the furnace charges included lime; from these were cast 'plates', which were shipped by way of Cardiff and Rye to be converted into steel by partial decarburization at Robertsbridge forge and at a new works at Boxhurst, Kent. For the steelworks venture there are accounts surviving for the years 1565–8, which show how the two forges were equipped and run by German workers. The venture was initially successful, with steel sold in 1566 at prices lower than those of imports. It not only reached London, but went as far as York, Wales and Ireland. However, merchants from Germany in turn undercut the English steel, whose sales and prices fell steadily between 1566 and 1571. The estate receiver's account for 1571 shows sales at hardly more than one-tenth of the level of 1566.

Robertsbridge can be used as an example of another change, withdrawal from iron production altogether in favour of leasing. To justify this, it would be necessary to compare profits from the forge in the decade before 1574 with the rent and receipts from timber after that date. The clear gain figures varied greatly from year to year, that for 1572–3 being significantly low, at £113 9s 6½d. The rent fixed with Weston was £200, an improvement over the returns of 1572–3, but hardly justifiable in the longer term. If there were any advantage it may have been seen in potential sales of wood. However, the 1574 rental and an estate valuation of 1575 both name the ironworks with 'the woods on the demeanes' as worth £200, and the receiver's accounts show no wood sales to Weston or anyone else. There must be a suspicion that other considerations affected the decision, but it is not obvious what these were.

Newbridge, Sheffield and Buxted

There are unfortunately no comparable runs of accounts with which to assess whether the responses of the Sidneys and their officials were typical. Nevertheless, other fragments which are available are useful in particular ways.

The Newbridge memorandum[23] appears to date from two years before the Robertsbridge works were set up, and shows a profit of £1 for each ton of bar sold. However, the output was stated to be a mere 80 tons of bar even under favourable conditions, suggesting that the furnace and forge were very small, perhaps little changed from when they were originally built in 1496. The figures in the memorandum are hard to interpret, as consumption and costs at the furnace are stated in terms of the bar eventually produced. Straker's interpretation was that a conversion rate of two tons of pig per ton of bar was achieved, but this can only be a very rough figure. By comparison, the rate at Robertsbridge was 30–33cwt of pig per ton of bar. Newbridge thus offers a baseline of what could be done at an out-of-date works.

Fig.31 Sheffield Park furnace (T Q 416257): the furnace lay beyond the centre of the bay. It was built by 1546 and had gone out of use by 1571. The furnace was replaced by a corn mill, whose building is hidden by the trees along the bay (photograph: J. S. Hodgkinson).

Closer to Robertsbridge in scale were the ironworks of the Duke of Norfolk. There is a set of accounts for the furnace and forge at Sheffield, Sussex (fig.31), for the years 1546–9, after the confiscation of the duke's estates.[24] He had been employing French workers in 1543–4, but it is not known how long before then that the works had been built, nor how their design would compare with Robertsbridge. Together with the Sheffield records are those for Worth, where a double furnace produced ordnance and pig iron, the latter being converted at the forge. The double furnace was built soon after December 1546 and shows that for culverins, the largest guns made at Worth, a single hearth was not yet sufficiently large. The accounts give clear gain figures for tithe purposes, so it need occasion no surprise that these seemed low: £30 for Sheffield and £40 for Worth are far below those for Robertsbridge, yet the accounts indicate a scale of working comparable with that of the Sidneys. For example, in the period from 31 October 1546 to 17 January 1549, 297 tons of bar were made at Sheffield forge. The furnace seems to have been capable of an output of the same order of magnitude as Panningridge, though the figures are necessarily approximate. It was in blast for 541 days, spread over ten campaigns, indicating a hearth-life rather shorter than at Panningridge in this decade. To produce the bar made at the forge would require 450–500 tons of pig, but the furnace appears to have been unable to achieve this, for 92 tons were bought in. If 350–400 tons were made at Sheffield furnace, this implies a daily output of 13–14cwt a day, which is at the lower end of the range seen in the Panningridge accounts, where output in the 1550s was standardized at 15cwt a day. The Sheffield figures have to be taken with caution, as it is not known whether stocks of pig iron were depleted or enhanced during the two years under consideration. At Worth, 152 tons of bar were made between 24 December 1546 and 17 January 1549, which implies that about 230 tons of pig iron were converted. If this amount had been cast during this accounting period the furnaces would have produced 338 tons, including the recorded 108 tons of guns and shot. A total of 529 days were worked, but it is dangerous to derive a daily output from these figures. We are not told how frequently both hearths of the double furnace were used. The 56 tons of ordnance cast were of different sizes, so the second hearth could have been used for as little as a single campaign. If, for example, only 28–30 tons were of large guns, requiring the second hearth, 308 from the other hearth, in 529 days, would amount to about 12cwt each day. Given the need for slow tapping, or indeed ladling, of iron for shot, and the care needed lifting gun-moulds and casting into them, this figure is not unexpectedly low.

The Hogge papers come from the end of the period, dating from the years 1576–81.[25] They are exceptional in that Ralph Hogge falls outside the pattern of landowner or tenant ironmaster typical of the sixteenth-century Weald. His involvement had begun in 1543, as assistant to Peter Bawde and William Levett in the production of ordnance at Buxted. From the mid-1540s he had managed the furnace, and in 1559 was granted Levett's post of maker of iron shot for the Office of Ordnance. Thereafter his position was of major supplier of shot and guns to the Crown, which set him apart from his contemporaries. By the time of the accounts, Hogge operated four furnaces, Hendall, Langleys, Marshalls, and a furnace near Buxted, of which Iron Plat is the most likely. The records are incomplete, and they do not permit any assessment of production or profit, or comparisons with the performance of others. They give impressions of the wide stretches of woodlands whence Hogge's wood and charcoal came, the large number whom he paid, regularly or occasionally, for work in the woods or in mining, and something of the traffic in guns through Lewes.

(B) THE WIDER PICTURE OF LANDOWNER INVOLVEMENT

These scattered and uneven documents are nevertheless sufficient to explain the attractions of iron production for the Wealden landowner in the middle of the century. From this basis we can survey the involvement of men who have left fewer written records and, in particular, the variety of forms which their involvement could take.

In the middle of the century the emphasis was upon direct operations, as seen in the Sidney accounts. Several of the larger Wealden landowners became involved, notably Lord Abergavenny, Lord Montague, the Sackvilles and the Pelhams. They doubtless perceived the success of those whose involvement dated back to the phase of consolidation of the industry. That certain men were prepared to go further, leasing lands beyond their own estates, speaks of the current enthusiasm. Not only did the Sidneys do this; Sir John Gage in 1554 took on the Crown ironworks in Ashdown Forest, in addition to his operations at Maresfield and Hedgecourt.[26] Among lesser landowners the Darrells owned and rented lands in south-east Surrey and along the Kent-Sussex border; by the 1560s they operated a furnace at Ewood, Surrey, and a forge at Leigh nearby, as well as a group of works in the Lamberhurst district. More compact were the operations of the Culpeppers, again in south-west Kent, working at Bedgebury and Hawkhurst. The Bakers worked ores on the northern fringe of the area, around Hawkhurst and Sissinghurst. These are examples from a large group who played a major part in developing the industry in the central decades of the century.

What is apt to differentiate the various social levels is the length of direct involvement to the running of ironworks. There was a tendency for the great landowners to lease out their operations in the third quarter of the century, whether to the smaller gentry or to tenants of yeoman or skilled craftsman origin. The best-known example is again that of the Sidneys who, as we have seen, abandoned first their furnace and then their forge. The Abergavenny interest also appears to have changed its character at this time. The little that is known about their furnace at Eridge (fig.47) suggests that it remained under direct management in 1574, but the second furnace on the Abergavenny lands, Cowford, was built about 1563 by tenants, William Relfe and Bartholomew Jeffrey, with a controversial time-sharing agreement with the landowner.[27] Under this, the tenants built the furnace, and they and the landowner were to take turns in preparing the furnace hearth; Abergavenny's servants were to operate the first 30 days of one campaign in each year. The Buckhurst interests were also mixed. Sheffield furnace was run direct in the 1560s, after acquisition from the Norfolk family after their possessions had been restored in 1553. However, the other sites with which the Buckhursts are associated – Parrock forge and furnace, Maynard's Gate furnace, Fletching forge, and perhaps a furnace in Heathfield – were all leased out by 1574. Such a mixture of direct working and leasing can also be seen as late as the 1590s in the will of Lord Montague, but in general it can be said that direct ironworks operations become less significant in the economies of the great Wealden estates as the century progressed.[28]

On the smaller estates landowners could take an active interest, as they were less likely to be separated from the practical side of operations by hierarchies of servants, by absences on official business, or by visits to other branches of their estates. In this social stratum was John Ashburnham. He had begun to operate Ashburnham furnace at least by the early 1550s, and it is assumed that his two forges were developed either then or soon afterwards. Certainly John Ashburnham was supplying bar iron to a London ironmonger by 1572 and is recorded as having the Upper Forge in hand in 1574.[29] His operations extended beyond his own lands, for the 1574 lists show his tenure of Panningridge furnace, upstream from his own. The Bakers, likewise, had a lengthy involvement, as did the Culpeppers and the Darrells. Leasing at this level was occasional and for fairly short periods, as in the case of the Darrells with Chingley and Horsmonden furnaces. Some small landowners who had their own ironworks leased further furnaces or forges and conducted most of their operations as tenants. One such was John French, a yeoman farmer at Chiddingly, who appears to have owned Stream, working it as a forge about 1560 and as a furnace by 1574. He had extended his interests in 1567, when in partnership with John Fawkner he took a short lease on the furnace at Hedgecourt in the parish of Worth. The French interest moved westwards: in the 1570s Stephen French leased the eastern half of St Leonard's Forest, jointly with Arthur and John Middleton, who were ironmasters around Horsham.[30] Another family, the Dykes, later prominent in the industry, were described as yeomen of Tonbridge in the late sixteenth century. Thomas Dyke is recorded in 1573 leasing Dundle forge and woodlands in the parish of Frant from the Darrells, from whom he rented Horsmonden and Chingley furnaces in 1579.[31]

How significant a contribution did involvement in the iron industry make to the wealth of Wealden landowners? Amongst the greater families it could form a useful increment to income from rents and farming. In the case of the Sidneys, clear gain figures in the range £300–£350 compare with rents of about £700–£900 from their local lands in the early 1570s.[32] For the smaller landowner the returns could be important, even if the risks grew with their reliance on the industry for their income. Mousley's evidence (1955: 223–4) suggests that at the middling level the Bowyers, Eversfields and Mays could be regarded as significantly dependent on income from iron. In one or two cases an impression of the concentration of a landowner on his industrial activities can come from the proximity of his house. For example, in 1591 Nicholas Fowle built his home at Riverhall close to his ironworks (Straker 1931: 276).

There are few cases where ironworks are known to have led landowners into financial difficulties, for while indebtedness undoubtedly occurred, it is hard to prove that the business venture was the cause. John Ashburnham, for instance, was in difficulties in the years about 1580, and it was a London ironmonger, Giles Garton, who took harsh measures to recover debts from him. His, however, was a case where general spending above his means lay at the root of his troubles.[33] Nor is it certain that the development by Wealden ironmasters of interests in other areas was often due to difficulties they encountered at home. It seems more to have been a positive response to developing markets elsewhere. The Sidney involvement in Glamorgan, outlined above, at first complemented rather than represented a retreat from Wealden activities. Such opportunities attracted William Relfe, with William Darrell, to join a partnership in South Wales. However, the case of Anthony Morley, who took on the Relfe interest after William's death, seems different. Within four years he was the object of a commission in bankruptcy, and as his debts were more to Sussex men than in Glamorgan, it may well be that his diversion to Wales arose out of problems with his Wealden operations. With Thomas Dyke, however, there is no such suggestion. When he bought works near Ripon in 1590 he argued that his experience in the industry fitted him to take on the concern, and the long-standing and successful involvement of his family in the Weald bears him out.[34]

(C) TENANT IRONMASTERS AND THEIR PROBLEMS

Those who rented ironworks ranged from members of sizeable partnerships, commanding experience and skill, to individual lessees whose operations were precarious.

At the top of the scale one of the largest groupings was the association between David Willard, Michael Weston and Robert Woddy. They came together to build Brede furnace in the 1570s: Willard and Weston operated Birchden forge, which Weston bought in 1579, while Weston operated one of the Cowden furnaces (1574), Cansiron forge (1574), and leased Robertsbridge furnace and forge in

1574 when Sir Henry Sidney gave up direct operation. Willard had individual interests in the Tonbridge area, leasing Southfrith furnace and allegedly building two other works and renting two more whose whereabouts are uncertain.[35] Robert Woddy is a more shadowy figure; there had certainly been a Woddy involved in the industry as far back as 1544, when a man of that name employed alien workers:[36] in 1574 he worked Benhall forge, near Frant. This loose association covered a remarkably large area, and was supplemented by the tenure of woodlands. Here is an early example of the kind of partnership formed by ironmasters in the Midlands and the north in the seventeenth century.

The backgrounds of the tenant ironmasters were widespread. Of Willard, Weston and Woddy we can say surprisingly little, but certainly others appear to have come from the iron trades. Bartholomew Jeffrey is described as a Battle ironmonger, but a man of that name had been mentioned in Kent in 1543 as a servant of Thomas May, perhaps at an ironworks as yet unidentified. He was later in partnership with William Relfe, the two men taking on Panningridge furnace after Sir Henry Sidney's lease ended in 1563. They built Cowford furnace at about the same time, but soon seem to have separated, Relfe operating Crowhurst furnace in 1574 and Jeffrey being involved at Buckholt furnace.[37] An ironmonger in an altogether different sphere of trade was Edmund Roberts, who entered the Sidney steel making partnership at Robertsbridge and in Glamorgan. Roberts, described as a gentleman of Hawkhurst, was in fact a London ironmonger, but apart from the Robertsbridge venture seems to have had no other direct involvement, although he was a frequent buyer of bar from the Sidney ironworks.[38] From the industry itself there came a few tenants, although it is more difficult to piece together humble backgrounds than those of more prominent yeomen. Lambert, of immigrant stock, lessee of Vachery forge in Surrey, was described as a forgeman, and was probably related to those Lamberts recorded as aliens at Hartfield and Wadhurst in 1543.[39] Better known is the partnership between Henry Westall and Charles Jarrett, who worked together in the Battle area in the early 1550s. Henry Westall had been clerk to the Robertsbridge ironworks through the 1540s, one of the more complex Wealden operations, comprising a forge and, for a while, two furnaces. Charles Jarrett was a noted founder, a French immigrant. It is not certain where they worked, but in 1551, immediately after Westall had ceased to appear as clerk in the Robertsbridge accounts, he and Charles (Jarrett) appear, with Draper, an ironmonger, supplying pig iron to Robertsbridge forge. Nothing more is heard of an interesting combination of management and technical skills, seemingly backed with capital from an ironmonger who bought quantities of bar iron from Robertsbridge.[40]

Our information about the operations of the smaller tenant ironmasters suggests that they were exposed to risks greater than those faced by landowners. Their sources of income were more restricted, particularly if they operated few or only one works: there was no landed income to tide them over technical or business problems. Further, their commercial expertise seems often to have been limited, lacking the advice of experienced estate officials. The details which support this view are scattered, and admittedly show the worst cases of what could happen, rather than what necessarily occurred. Men at this level have left no accounts or correspondence. Indeed, it is doubtful how far they would ever have kept accounts.

The operational risks

At the technical level there seem to have been accepted standards of performance, of which Appendix 3 presents certain examples. Such standards were not always reached, and disagreements could arise as to the consumption of raw materials or the rate of output at furnace or forge. For example, during Thomas Glydd's tenancy of Panningridge furnace in the 1580s one witness stated that 7 tons could be cast in six days, using 30 loads of ore, another 6 tons, using 24 loads. Estimates of the prices a ton of iron would fetch could also vary. This was not necessarily due to a fluctuating market; it was as likely to result from differing quality, for pig iron was valued according to how well it would convert to bar. Pig offered to Ninian Challenor of Cuckfield, claimed to be worth £3 3s 6d per ton, was found to be so poor that it was said to be worth no more than £1 16s 10d. The sows made by William and Neville Cheeseman at Gosden furnace in the 1590s were said to be 'the worst sows in all Sussex'.[41]

Many problems could lie behind such difficulties. Competition for the best workmen, notably those of French immigrant families, would not favour the small operator. Ore sources were variable, although no firm indications are available of how yields varied with the type of ore charged. The standard of equipment and water supply were also important variables, and particular difficulties could occur if leases were short. It would, for example, hardly be worth the Cheesemans doing much to improve Gosden furnace in 1595 when their tenure was only for three years. The question of how durably to build must have faced Relfe and Jeffrey when they leased the site of Cowford furnace from Lord Abergavenny for ten years in 1563, or Thomas Glydd and Simon Colman when they leased Batsford from Lord Dacre in 1571 for nine years.⁴² An estate works, by contrast, might be designed for a much longer life with less risk of expensive break-downs and repairs.

The business risks

As no accounts have been left by the smaller ironmasters, it is impossible to say how profitable their operations were. Contemporaries' comments can be interesting, if only to show how observers could vary in their estimates. Thomas Illman was the lessee of ironworks at Ifield, comprising a furnace and, less clearly, a forge. In a case of 1573 involving the mortgaging of the works to Roger Gratwick witnesses estimated the net income from the works, varying from Roger's son Richard, who put the furnace as worth £5 a year, to the estimate of an interested party on the other side of the case, Thomas Illman's brother, Richard, who valued the whole works at £25 13s 4d. Two local farmers, whose affinities are not known, suggested £20–5, again probably for the furnace and the forge.

It was in trading operations that the smallest ironmasters were most at risk. As the evidence often comes from legal disputes the dismal impression was not necessarily typical. Nevertheless, what is striking from cases in the Courts of Chancery and Requests is the extent to which business contracts were actually or apparently misunderstood. This was common in a wide range of rural business transactions in the sixteenth century, as Professor Everitt has shown in relation to contracts between farmers and food merchants.⁴³

One type of case which frequently occurs concerns the use and abuse of bonds as sureties for debt. There were instances in the iron trade in which third parties agreed to bind themselves and then became liable for sums greater than those actually in dispute. Ninian Challenor, for example, stood surety in a sum of £200 that iron to be sent by a neighbour to a London merchant would be of quality adequate to fetch £215. It was found to be poor and only realized £105. Nevertheless Challenor was sued for the full £200 rather than the £110 outstanding. Disputes over weights or tallies of materials also occurred, as when in 1590 Thomas Bettesworth of Trotton and Henry Campion of Bramshott Forge disagreed over the weight of sows supplied, the dispute centring on the accuracy of Bettesworth's weighing beam. Problems of reckoning quantities could easily occur over wood, charcoal, ore or sows when works changed hands. For example in 1569 Thomas Melershe of Wonersh sold Burningfold forge to Thomas Blackwell, and they could agree on neither the quantity nor quality of charcoal at the works nor the wood cut in the surrounding area.[44] These problems were also apparent in sales of iron, particularly when the buyers were distant: ironmongers in London and beyond demanded bonds from those standing surety for delivery, and accidents during transit could result in actions being pressed. Distant customers could avoid payment, and the small ironmaster was faced with cumbersome and expensive remedies.

All such cases put the small man at a disadvantage, particularly when through illiteracy or inexperience contracts or procedures could not be understood. While large landowners and their officials could take such matters in their stride, others, like Thomas Glydd, could not. Glydd confessed that he could not keep accounts, while his partner at Panningridge furnace and Kitchenham Forge, Thomas Hayes, was 'crafty and subtle', as Glydd was to find to his cost over their arrangement to share expenses and profits; he ended up in Hastings gaol over debts allegedly due to Hayes, but, according to Glydd due to misappropriation of iron by Hayes abetted by a corrupt employee. Despite his questionable business competence, Glydd had considerable interests in the industry, being involved at Etchingham and Kitchenham forges and Darvell, Panningridge and Batsford furnaces, which formed a compact group well supplied with wood from the district around Brightling and Dallington.[45]

Entanglements over ironworks leases have their counterparts in many landed property transactions. What tends to mark ironworks cases out from others are the encumbrances involving stocks, buildings and repairs, and the provision of rent both in money and in iron. William Waters, for example, leased Buckholt forge and furnace from the executors of Bartholomew Jeffrey in 1575, obtaining from the woods sufficient for 550 loads of charcoal each year, and delivering to the lessors ten tons of iron at an agreed price of £8 per ton. If the woods were insufficient to produce the charcoal he could cut more, paying 8s for each load of charcoal made. The executors disagreed among themselves about these complexities, after Waters had taken the works over, leading to disputes which beset his tenancy. Such complications were made all the worse when the details were not written down. A verbal agreement was at the root of the dispute between Walter Covert and Roger Gratwick in 1583 over a complex arrangement made six years earlier. In this, Gratwick leased Covert's furnace and a half-share of his forge at Cuckfield, woods, ore and equipment. By 1583 Gratwick had forgotten the details, and Covert admitted he had been too trusting over a verbal agreement to which there had been insufficient witnesses.[46]

Matters were made worse when leases were assigned during the course of a tenancy. Misunderstandings could then arise, and the new tenant find himself at loggerheads with the landowner. This happened when John Baker took over Nicholas Fowle's lease of woods belonging to Lord Abergavenny in Waterdown forest in the mid-1560s, for he found his men harassed and the wood he had cut carried away. There could even be cases where transfers were made without the landowner's knowledge. One such concerned Batsford furnace, leased by Thomas Glydd and Simon Colman from Lord Dacre in 1571, yet transferred by Simon Colman to Herbert Pelham in 1577. Dacre brought a case later in that year to stop Pelham's men cutting wood; he had found out about the transfer after it happened and would have objected had he known of the plan beforehand.[47]

At the root of many difficulties was lack of capital. Leases involving transfers in kind, and problems over promptness of payments, all point to the lack of reserves from which many smaller ironmasters suffered. The weakness, by comparison with works on large estates, was that other activities could not subsidize smelting or forging during hard times, when water failed or market prices were depressed. This was an industry where large amounts of money had to be tied up in stocks: it was necessary to accumulate a sizeable proportion of the materials before furnaces could be put in blast, for although a forge could be operated on a hand-to-mouth charcoal supply, a blast furnace certainly could not. As an example of the cost of stocks, Panningridge furnace used charcoal and ore valued at £307 in 1558, enough for 32–35 weeks operation. The actual cost of cutting, coaling and mining was less than this valuation, so the ironmaster with woods in hand would not be faced with expenditure of this order, particularly as he could choose to spread the period of wood cutting over the year. The small man, however, was the most likely to have to rely on the open market, having to buy in advance at outside prices. As the century went on, the trend to leasing accelerated, bringing a greater proportion of ironworks into the hands of the vulnerable, and perhaps explaining the rapid contraction of the industry in the seventeenth century, after wood prices had risen significantly.

3   The market for iron

The successes and the problems of ironmasters large and small derived not only from their command of materials but, at the other end of their operations, from their contacts with the market. This is an aspect of the industry which has had to be pieced together, for there are few coherent sources. The market can be divided roughly into three: the ordnance trade, the largest ironmongers (often from London), and smiths in the locality.

(A) THE ORDNANCE TRADE

After the 1540s there is a period when little information is available about the supply of Wealden guns to the Crown, in particular about the Buxted and Worth furnaces. In particular, it is not known whether ordnance continued to be cast at Worth. In 1550, while still in Crown hands, this works had been leased for 21 years to Clement Throckmorton, who could pay his rent in the form of guns (Giuseppi 1912: 289). But it is uncertain whether this agreement survived the resumption by the Duke of Norfolk. Unfortunately the 1574 survey comes three years after the tenancy would have expired; by this time the occupant was Nicholas Eversfield, and there is no reference to him as a gun producer in Ralph Hogge's complaint of the previous year.

It is from Hogge's petition[48] that the most comprehensive information about gun founding comes. He drew the attention of the Crown to the dangers of exported guns reaching potential enemies, implicitly defending his own position as the major supplier to the Crown by casting doubt on the activities of some of his competitors. Two founders are named, beside Hogge himself, as making only for the Crown. These were Robert Hudson at Pounsley and Arthur Middleton who operated Maynards Gate and Huggetts furnaces. No details of working are available for Pounsley between 1548, when it appears in the list of Sussex furnaces, and 1573, but Middleton's involvement has been confirmed by the excavation of a casting pit at Maynards Gate. Four ironmasters had, according to Hogge, begun to make ordnance in the six or seven years before his petition. One was Sir Thomas Gresham, whom we know from the 1574 list used Mayfield furnace (fig.32), and who was licensed to export guns to Denmark in that year.[49] Michael Weston made guns at Cowden, Nicholas Fowle at Riverhall, and Alexander Fermor at Hamsell. The last two were named as being involved in selling pieces through Lewes into the English Channel gun trade.

Hogge, as the accounts mentioned above show, was a most significant figure in the trade over the whole period. In 1567 he added to his Crown monopoly of shot-supply that of exporting cast-iron ordnance and shot not required by the Office of Ordnance, hence his objection to the activities of Fermor and Fowle. He was developing his complex of works over this period, having two furnaces in use in 1566. These were Marshalls and one of the Buxted furnaces. Unfortunately the details of supply to the Crown are missing, for only

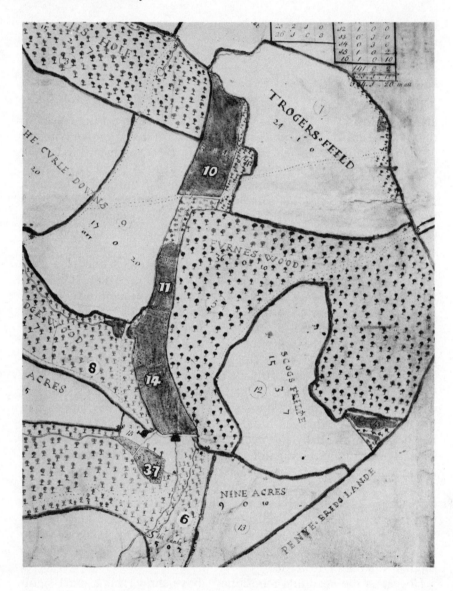

Fig.32   Mayfield: the sites of the furnace and the boring mill (see also fig.65) (ESRO SAS 5831). The furnace lies below the bay at the downstream (east) end of the main pond (parcel 14). Pen ponds can be seen (11 and 10) on the main stream, and also on the tributary stream flowing through Lodge Wood (8). The boring mill probably lay below the bay of the pen pond (37) on the southerly tributary. The forge is assumed from surviving cinder to have been in 'the banks' (6) (photograph: East Sussex Record Office, Lewes).

amounts and values of guns, rather than the names of suppliers, appear in the papers of the Masters and Lieutenants of the Ordnance. These do, however, confirm the position of Ralph Hogge's brother Brian as Clerk of Deliveries at the Tower.[50]

(B) THE BAR MARKET

The market for bar iron may be clearly divided into the large consignments carried out of the Weald, and sales of smaller quantities to smiths in local towns and villages. The distinction is very clear in the case of Robertsbridge forge. Here most of the output was sold in large amounts, between 20 and 80 tons in a year to particular purchasers. In the 1540s there were two major buyers: Webb, who took some of his iron at Southampton, and Draper, who was described as a London man. In 1548 and 1553 respectively these names disappear, although a Mr Webb was buying iron delivered in London from Ifield forge in about 1568. In the 1550s the main purchasers from Robertsbridge were men named Bacon, Golston, Hickeby and Roberts. Throughout the 1560s the last-named was the major buyer, although Bacon bought occasionally. He was also mentioned in connection with the iron from Ifield. In 1570 Draper reappears in the Roberts-bridge accounts. Of this group, the best known was Edmund Roberts. He helped to finance Sir Henry Sidney's steel project, and although he is described as a Hawkhurst man, he did much business in London. He was not only involved in the Wealden trade, but invested in the Muscovy Company of 1555, showing that he had an interest in the Baltic trade, in which the importation of iron and steel played a significant part.[51]

Further information about the bulk trade emerges from lawsuits. John Ashburnham provided Giles Garton, a London ironmonger, with bar, and became indebted to him. Garton also bought from the Morleys and the Alfreys.[52] Other cases show how the iron reached London. From the south-east Weald most went by sea. The more fortunate producers could use river transport to the port of Rye, or to Pevensey Sluice where a warehouse for iron was built about 1580. In the years 1542–74 Robertsbridge iron only had to go by cart as far as Bodiam bridge, whence it was carried by barge down the Rother, to be trans-shipped or sometimes stored at Rye before continuing to London. Bodiam bridge was a collecting point for iron from elsewhere: in 1575 two Winchelsea merchants, Thomas Grene and John Love, were in dispute over iron that the former owned. His excuse for non-delivery was the state of roads which prevented carriage of the iron to Bodiam.[53] Rye and Newhaven were regular ports for the loading of

a

b

Fig.33   (a) The Pevensey gun: a Wealden demi-culverin: (late sixteenth century). The cannon is at Pevensey castle, mounted on a modern reproduction carriage (photograph: J. G. Coad); (b) The cipher of Elizabeth cast on the reinforce of the Pevensey gun.

iron, as is shown by the Port Books. From the central Weald a good deal was carried to London by road, difficult and costly though this could be. In 1605 it cost 12–13s per ton to carry bar from Worth to London, and there are many references to the failure of ironmasters to dump slag on muddy roads.[54] It is not clear what route the early Kentish ironmasters took for their products: in the seventeenth century the Medway was used, but as the improvement of the river south of Maidstone did not take place until after 1630 land carriage would have been necessary to the county town from furnaces such as Bedgebury, Hawkhurst, or those around Tonbridge.

When iron reached London it appears often to have been stored, prior to sale, in the yards adjacent to inns. Christopher Darrell, for example, had much of his iron lodged at the Christopher Inn, Southwark. He thought it safe, although William Skydmore, a London ironmonger, claimed not to have received some iron said to have been delivered there. By contrast another ironmonger, Robert Est, found Alice Norton, keeper of the Christopher, trustworthy and suggested that many Sussex ironmasters found the inn a convenient storage place. The White Hart was another Southwark inn thus used: iron from the works at Sheffield and Worth was placed there in 1549.[55]

Some consignments went far beyond London. The Collinses of Socknersh traded as far north as Stamford and Newark, and Thomas Isted had customers in Nottingham. The cases in which these sales appear show the difficulties of such distant trades. Isted found it hard to recover debts from a customer, Thomas Cadman, and the Collinses had recourse to agents such as John Barton, an ironmonger in Thames Street, London, and, nearer to the customer, Robert Greene of Market Orton, Rutland.[56] What we do not know is what quantity of Wealden iron was sold in such distant places nor how many transactions proceeded without such difficulties.

Local sales accounted for a small proportion of production at Robertsbridge, due no doubt to a situation which favoured bulk shipment by river. Forges less favourably placed may be expected to have been more dependent on the market in their localities. Sussex towns had their ironmongers, and indeed iron was handled by traders in other lines of business such as William Cleggatt of Lewes, haberdasher, or William Cartwright of Brighton, mercer. Some were also exporters; for example, Snelling of Lewes was active in shipping bar and cast iron.[57] In the villages, smiths bought small quantities for their forges: the Robertsbridge Forge Books show petty-cash sales to blacksmiths from places such as Brede, Ewhurst and Northiam, in the locality, and sometimes from more distant parts of Kent such as Ashford and Farningham. Occasionally the accounts show that a smith had some special skill, and in turn provided finished goods for the ironworks. Such were Philpott, a French immigrant, who was a nailmaker, and an unnamed Dallington smith, who repaired bellows and tuyeres for Panningridge furnace (Crossley 1975a: 26).

(C) PIG IRON

Our picture of the market would not be complete without reference to the trade in pig iron which went on between works. While a great quantity of pig was converted into bar in forges run by the furnace master, even these integrated concerns appear on occasion to have found their operations out of balance. The accounts for the Norfolk works show pig being bought for Sheffield forge from three suppliers, Relfe, Jeffrey, and Mychell. The last-named operated Chittingly furnace, whence the iron, amounting to 65 tons, had to be collected. The other two, though well known as a partnership after 1560, are referred to separately in the Sheffield account. They both delivered pig to the forge, but in neither case is the source named. Jeffrey is elsewhere referred to as an ironmonger, which strengthens the impression that here his role was that of a pig iron dealer. Such trading is hinted at in a case of 1569, when pig cast by Thomas Illman of Ifield and sold to Thomas Blackwell for his forge, probably Burningfold, was diverted by Blackwell to a Mr Darrell. This was George Darrell, who by that time was operating a forge at Leigh and, by implication, needed pigs to supplement the output of his furnace at Ewood.[58]

Many ironmasters concentrated on one stage, most commonly the forge, and were thus constantly involved in the pig iron market. Some forgemasters bought and carried pig over considerable distances; for example, in or about 1582, 109 tons were taken more than 30km from Cuckfield furnace to Burningfold forge, which was also supplied with pig from Shillinglee, only 5km away, and with what were termed 'shift' sows from an unspecified furnace in Ashdown, even more distant than Cuckfield.[59]

Such reliance on the market was not necessarily the expedient of the operator unable to afford the capital and rental costs of an integrated pair of sites. The Sidneys moved away from integration when they relinquished Panningridge furnace in 1563, after several years when increasing quantities of pig had been bought in. For the next five years they used pig from several furnaces within ten miles of the forge, buying 30–60 tons in a year from each. Then in 1568 a more permanent arrangement was made in which Richard Wekes, whose furnace was at Mountfield, supplied 210 tons of pig each year. He took in return 70 tons of bar, which, at the conversion rate normal at

Robertsbridge, was half the product of his pig iron. On the basis of pig and bar iron prices in 1566–7 the scheme suited both parties. It also gave the forge an incentive to improve its yield, for it had to provide Wekes with a fixed quantity rather than a proportion of the bar produced from his pig, and could have kept any extra it produced. In fact, yields did not change, and independent variations in pig and bar prices went against Sir Henry Sidney's interest.[60]

(D) PRICES

The arrangement between Richard Wekes and Sir Henry Sidney is a fitting point to comment briefly on prices, for it shows how important short-term changes could be. Not only did temporary shifts in market conditions affect prices: as shown above, variations were also the result of quality differences, a problem which has been insufficiently appreciated. Also, it is not always possible to detect price differences resulting from the inclusion or omission of transport costs. A complex pattern of costs which may include all these factors can be seen at Sheffield forge. Here, in 1546–9 pig iron was bought in: some, delivered by Relfe, cost £1 13s 4d a ton; Jeffrey's delivered price was £1 16s 8d. Yet Mychell charged £1 13s 4d and £2 for lots which had to be collected from his furnace, thought to be Chittingly.

Despite such uncertainties, the movements in charcoal and iron prices are clear. Charcoal quadrupled in price between 1540 and 1600 and, indeed, continued to rise, being eight times the price of 1540 and in the 1630s. This was a far more severe increase even than in foodstuffs, and the consequence for other users of coppice-wood have been indicated earlier in this chapter.

The prices of pig and bar iron did not, however, rise at this rate, growing between two and threefold between 1540 and the end of the century. This was due to the slower rise in other costs: that of ore is extremely difficult to reckon, for quality differences, costs of extraction and of cartage made for great variations: there are too few figures from the end of the sixteenth century for there to be anything more than an impression that prices approximately doubled. Skilled workers' wages, discussed above, rose by even less.

In the sixteenth century the price of Wealden bar iron did not rise to an extent which jeopardized sales, for there was as yet no substantial competition from imports, as was to appear in the seventeenth century. The rise was not indeed exceptional among manufactured goods, and, for many buyers in the agrarian and trading communities, it in fact represented a decrease, in terms of their rising incomes.

It is this factor as much as any other which accounts for the prosperity of the industry in the third quarter of the sixteenth century. The cheapness of its products in real terms, extending the use of iron as a replacement for wood, was to last through the seventeenth century; but as we shall see in the next two chapters it was the ironmasters of the Midlands and of Sweden who were to ally low prices with a quality of product which the Weald could not match.

NOTES

1. PRO REQ2/177/32.
2. PRO PROB11/45/27; ESRO W/A12/329.
3. KAO U1475 E20/2; B8, 10.
4. PRO PROB11/77/1; ESRO DH603.
5. ESRO Searle 7/3.
6. *Ibid.* 13/1; PRO C3/26/77; PRO STAC5/A2/25; PRO REQ2/414/148.
7. Cal. Assize Records, Elizabeth 1, Sussex, no.1934.
8. Tawney and Power 1924, I: 237–8; PRO REQ2/285/39.
9. 1 Eliz. 1, c.15; 23 Eliz. 1, c.5; 27 Eliz.1, c.19. For fuel for the glass industry see Godfrey 1975: 40–50.
10. APC, X (1577–8), 265; ESRO Rye/1/5/109.
11. Brent 1974: 145; BL Add.MSS 33142; KAO U1475/B3/9–10.
12. PRO C3/73/58; KAO U1475/E59; B10/3, 11.
13. ESRO Glynde 1120; Dulwich MSS; ESRO SAS G6/50.
14. PRO C3/13/103; ESRO DH 69, 70; *ibid.* 712; PRO STAC5/C25/10.
15. KAO U38/P28/26/2; ESRO Rye 1/5/109; PRO REQ 2/186/6; ESRO Glynde 2046.
16. Brent 1974: 151; PRO REQ2/125/14.
17. KAO U1475/B1/4, 3/10, 10/1.
18. *Ibid.* B10/3, 11.
19. PRO STAC5/W/2/1, 67/13, F/26/14.
20. KAO U1475/B10/8; Dulwich MSS; Ellis 1861: 127–31.
21. KAO U1475/B2/2, B4/1.
22. KAO U1475 *passim*; see Crossley 1975a.
23. PRO E32/197.
24. Giuseppi 1912: 276–311, drawing upon PRO E163/12/13; E101/483/19, 501/3; see also Ellis 1861: 127–31, reproducing PRO SP10/6/4.
25. Dulwich MSS.
26. ESRO SAS G19/6. For an excellent survey of Wealden ironmasters and their backgrounds see Goring 1978: 204–27.
27. PRO STAC5/A2/25.
28. PRO PROB11/81/22.
29. John Ashburnham employed aliens as early as 1549, PRO E179/190/233; WSRO Lavington 830–1.
30. ESRO SAS G13/97, ESRO Add. MSS 1980, 1982.
31. ESRO DH602–7.
32. HMC, De L'Isle I (1925), 243–7.
33. WSRO, Lavington 830–1; BL Harleian 703, f.12; PRO STAC5/08/36.
34. PRO STAC5/G14/27; Bevan 1965–7; Llewellin 1863; for a review of Sussex ironmasters' activities in South Wales see Hammersley 1972: 123–4.
35. ESRO Rye/1/4/285; PRO C142/243/39; KAO U1475/E5; PRO REQ2/285/39; KAO U38/M1.
36. PRO E179/190/191.

37. PRO C3/172/70; E179/124/268; KAO U1475/B3/10; PRO STAC5/A2/25. The Relfe at Crowhurst is not certainly William, for the lessee (perhaps a relation) in 1588–90 (BL Add. MSS 33142) was Gregory Relfe.
38. See n.57 below.
39. Surrey RO 85/13/205; Awty 1979: 6.
40. KAO U1475/B8/4; see Crossley 1975a: 102 n.18.
41. WSRO EpI I/5/3; PRO C3/206/84; PRO REQ2/186/35.
42. PRO STAC5/A2/25; BL Add.Ch. 30187.
43. PRO REQ2/226/4; Thirsk 1967: 565–6.
44. PRO C3/206/84; REQ2/165/34, 177/32, 244/45.
45. PRO STAC5/G4/28.
46. PRO REQ2/80/18, 84/37; C3/207/25.
47. PRO C3/26/77; REQ2/34/49.
48. PRO SP 12/95/15, 16.
49. *Ibid.* 95/62.
50. PRO E351/2604–29.
51. Crossley 1975a: 25–6, 32–4: Willan 1953: 119–20.
52. WSRO Lavington 830–3, 235.
53. PRO REQ2/211/19. For the use of the marshland channels to Pevensey, see C. Whittick in Bedwin 1980: 95.
54. PRO REQ2/414/148; ESRO Rye/47/27/10, 22.
55. PRO REQ2/31/33; Giuseppi 1912: 284.
56. PRO C3/236/57,243/7.
57. PRO REQ2/129/54, 32/67.
58. PRO E101/483/19; REQ2/244/45; 115/2.
59. REQ2/125/14.
60. KAO U1475/B3/10.

Chapter 8   **The beginnings of decline: from 1574 to the First Dutch War**

1   The industry and its resources

Eighty years were to elapse after the survey of 1574 until the Wealden ironworks were again listed. In 1653, 36 furnaces and 45 forges were said to be extant, figures contained in a record which was probably compiled in 1667 (Parsons 1882: 21–3). The absolute decline from the 52 furnaces and 58 forges in 1574 is clear enough, but it masks a more complex pattern. Within the period some new works were in fact built, even though a greater number disappeared; others were abandoned and later revived; while still more operated infrequently or seasonally, below their nominal capacity. Further, there are indications that at times the pattern of output changed: as some furnaces made more castings and less pig iron, so the activities of their forges were reduced.

After about 1580 it was only in the westerly parts of the Weald that significant new building continued. Barkfold forge appears in 1584, and its furnace in 1602, Pallingham in 1586–7, Ebernoe by 1594, and Thursley by 1608, while Sir William Goring's forge at Burton was first mentioned as late as 1635 (Wickham Legg 1936: 38): and Fernhurst furnace (fig.34) in 1653. Only four new works appeared in the eastern Weald after 1580. Here Beckley forge was one of the last to be put up, built in 1587 and having a furnace added in the first half of the seventeenth century.[1] Equally exceptional, Ardingly furnace was built by Francis Chalenor near the centre of the Weald in about 1597 (Holgate 1927: 31). In Kent a few new works were developed soon after 1574. Comparison can be made between the list of that year and the enquiry of 1588, for which only the Kentish returns survive. This shows that Chingley forge was built on the Bewl close to Chingley furnace and, on the boundary with Sussex, Scarlets and Lower Cowden furnaces appear by 1588–90. Further into the country, Hawkhurst Mill forge was joined by a furnace before 1644.[2]

The net decrease of 13 in the number of forges between 1574 and 1653 is hard to compare with impressions of the bar iron trade over this time. Precise estimates of total output of bar are impossible to make, due to the intermittent operation of forges, and the local trade and the overland sales to London are impossible to quantify. The coastal trade to London was probably maintained into the seventeenth

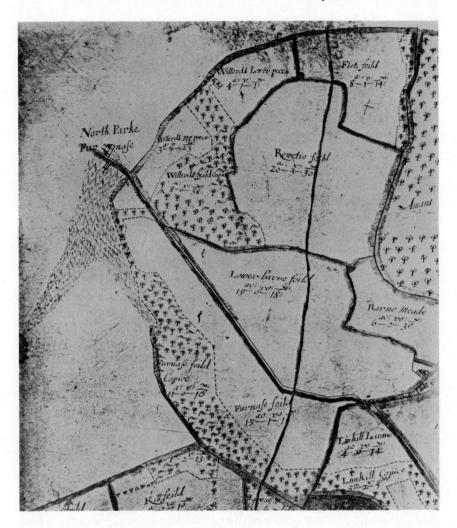

Fig.34   Fernhurst (North Park) furnace in 1660 (West Sussex County Record Office, Chichester, Cowdray M S S 1640; by courtesy of Lord Cowdray).

century, for Hammersley has shown that in 1615 2146 tons of bar came coastwise from the Weald, compared with 2178 tons in 1579–80. Willan has suggested that thereafter there was a rapid decline in shipments, halving between 1615 and 1633, although Hammersley has considered that this may not be a typical year (Hammersley 1972: 51–2, citing Willan 1938: 71).

The total Wealden iron trade to London is further confused by those ironmasters who had built in the western areas late in the sixteenth century, whose route to London was by road. Also, the improvement of the Medway to Yalding in the 1630s attracted traffic from the Kent-Sussex border areas, which could have had some effect on coastwise shipments from Lewes and Rye.

The number of furnaces declined by a proportion similar to that of forges, but there are added complexities. At certain times ordnance and shot were produced in quantity, and the ability to do this suggests that the skills of mould-making and founding developed over the period. The civil castings trade (cp. fig.35) is very difficult to measure but by the second half of the seventeenth century many furnaces had a part in it, so that although pig output may have been reduced in step with forge closures, production of castings could have afforded some compensation. This would have encouraged those skills so necessary for the arms trade, for no less than 17 furnaces made ordnance or shot in the Second Dutch War.

The end of expansion in the east and the continuation of building in the west may in part be explained by the passing of legislation in 1585 which sought to restrict building in the east of Sussex and in Kent to sites where ironworks had previously existed or where the owner could supply sufficient wood from his own lands.[3] However, whatever deterrent this may have been, ironworks and their fuel supplies were probably in equilibrium by this time, their maintenance being assured by, and in turn encouraging, the development of coppicing. If there were difficulties, these were likely to be felt by other users of coppice wood, those in industries and trades which sought billets for firewood, cut at a greater age than for charcoal. Complaints about the building of Beckley forge in 1587 reflect this concern, as do those of the textile workers of Cranbrook in 1637, anxious about supplies of firewood for heating their vats of dye.[4] Despite such cases, the picture is not one of universal alarm about wood supplies; there is little sign of desire on the part of ironmasters to move out of the area: the only late-sixteenth-century case was the ill-fated attempt of Herbert Pelham and George Goring to set up an ironworks on Sir Walter Raleigh's lands in Munster in 1596.[5] Nor did the informed outsider show serious concern: that usually reliable observer John Norden, despite overstating the total of furnaces and forges as 140 in 1607, and noting that some woodlands had indeed been cleared, did not see the industry as an excessive consumer of wood (Norden 1610: 176). Some rival users disappeared: in the west glassmaking ceased in the second decade of the seventeenth century with the enforcement of the use of coal in the industry. Also, the needs of London for fuel were at least alleviated by the remarkable growth in the shipment of coal from the north-east to the Thames.

It would be wrong not to accept that there were certain spectacular reductions in woods, noticeable perhaps because of their exceptional nature. Ashdown Forest, for example, continued to be denuded; by 1632 little great wood was left, by 1658 none. Even the coppices there were slight by 1632, worth only £16 13s 4d, and they were much affected by illicit cutting (Brandon 1963: 119–20). In St Leonards Forest, Crown officials failed to supervise the activities of lessees and others, so that by 1625 no timber trees were standing and the value of all the woods was put at a mere £32. Bewbush furnace, indeed, was said to have gone out of use in about 1642 for lack of wood.[6] But in contrast with such examples of poor control of woodland or of clearance for agriculture, there are well-documented cases of careful coppicing, particularly in those parts of the eastern Weald upon which the industry was increasingly concentrated as it contracted during the seventeenth century. The Pelhams coppiced for Waldron furnace and Bibleham and Brightling forges; the woods around Robertsbridge were well maintained; and when Ashburnham was re-acquired by the Ashburnham family in 1678–80 its 4,000 acres of wood were not only in good order, but included new coppices made during the various ownerships through which the estate had passed.[7] In certain parts of the Weald coppices were extended over once-cleared land, on former assarts in Framfield, Buxted and Mayfield, and on land once used for grain on Waldron Down.[8] The Penkhursts are an excellent example of a family who up to 1660 maximized their income from woods, over and above their own involvement in the iron industry. When their lands were leased in Mayfield, as in 1634 and 1642, wood rights were retained, and there is a series of records of sales of varying kinds of wood, of timber to John Holland of Deptford in 1652–3 and to William Light, joiner of Goudhurst, and of under-wood and tops to the Hammonds of Waldron and Robert Checke of London.[9]

The results of such care are recorded by observers after the middle of the century: John Evelyn referred (1664, II:150) to 200,000 acres of Wealden coppice, an area more than adequate for the works in use during the Second Dutch war, and Andrew Yarranton, writing of England as a whole, saw ironworks as an influence for the preservation rather than the destruction of woods (Yarranton 1677: 60). The decline in the number of ironworks in the first half of the seventeenth century would have provided opportunities for other users, whose requirements maintained the attractions of coppice and timber management for the Wealden landowner.

2   The production and disposal of ordnance

(A) THE CROWN AND THE IRONMASTERS, 1588–1600

The information about iron production in Kent in 1588, mentioned above, provides an introduction to the topic of gun founding, which was to become increasingly important during the seventeenth century. 1588, the year of the Armada, was an obvious time for the reappearance of concern that exported Wealden ordnance was reaching enemy hands. At this time those involved in the arms trade were subject to incentives to take part in illicit business, of the kind faced by Richard Tomson in Flanders in 1593, when he was offered an advance payment of 20,000 crowns to deliver ordnance in Hamburg, Rotterdam or Calais.[10] Suspicions about exports came to a head in October 1588, fuelled by reports that large numbers of guns had recently been sent abroad, and in particular of clandestine shipments from the Thames, through Battersea and Lambeth.[11] Such a trade strengthened the case for an enquiry with objectives similar to those of 1574.

The first step was to request Sir Robert Constable, Lieutenant of the Ordnance, to take bonds from London merchants to ensure that guns were only sold according to regulations with which they were issued. Also, the Lords Lieutenant of the three Wealden counties were given instructions to prevent guns being cast without special licence from the Privy Council.[12] As in the enquiry of 14 years before, a check was to be made of the number of furnaces and each Lord Lieutenant was provided with a list of where these were likely to be found. Texts of two letters have survived, to Lord Howard, for Surrey, and Lord Cobham, for Kent; the accompanying lists have caused confusion, for earlier writers concluded that they indicated the state of the industry in 1588 or not long before. It has, however, been shown by Charles Cattell (1971) that the information the county officers received was taken from the returns of 1574.[13] Only in the case of Kent is the result known: during the summer of 1589 Lord Cobham obtained a return of works in operation in the previous November.[14]

From the autumn of 1588 there was confusion in the industry as a result of the government's interest. In November 1588 Arthur Middleton, who operated Bewbush, Huggetts and Maynards Gate furnaces, complained to Lord Buckhurst, Lord Lieutenant of Sussex, that he was under contract to deliver 20 tons of iron shot to a shipmaster at Shoreham, but was under the impression that he now required a Privy Council licence to do so. John Johnson and Ephraim Arnold found themselves caught in mid-contract in their dealings with London merchants, and petitioned for a licence to cast 120 tons of ordnance.[15]

By early in 1589 the Privy Council was aware that their measures could exceed their aims, and might bring the industry to a standstill. In April Lord Buckhurst and Lord Cobham were instructed to see that a balance was struck between steps to prevent unauthorized exports and ensuring that the makers of guns did not abandon their skills and their equipment.[16] The pressures were maintained for several years: in the summer of 1589 Lord Buckhurst wrote to Walter Covert and others, relaying the concern of the Privy Council over the neglect of a request that each furnace supply returns of its output and customers. A year later new bonds were required from tenants and owners of furnaces, undertaking that no guns or shot of larger than minion size be made without licence.[17] Even as late as 1595 no less a person than Thomas Johnson, the king's gun founder, was affected by the uncertainties still generated by regulation, for in that year he found other ironmasters wary of accepting sub-contracts when his own furnace was fully occupied.[18]

It is clear that the system of bonds did not prevent illicit export. The most difficult cases to detect were those involving founders who held licences to export, yet secretly exceeded the numbers of pieces permitted. John Phillips, of Barden and Ashurst furnaces, seems to have been such a man. In 1588 he held a warrant to cast 12 best demi-culverins of 25cwt for Michael de Decher for the defence of Middleburg, but was accused of illicitly exporting further guns.[19] Another problem was that ironmasters who had not been making guns at the time of the enquiry had not been subject to regulation. Some later began to cast ordnance, and were referred to in a Privy Council letter of October 1590. In Kent, Ballard, Culpepper and Darrell were added to those originally listed.[20] During the 1590s action was also taken against exporters by officials of the customs. In 1591, John Yonge, customer of Chichester, was instructed by the Privy Council not only to check the amount, destination, and prices of guns exported from Sussex and Kent, but also the quantity and dimensions of all guns cast contrary to regulation.[21]

The Wealden ironmasters thus found themselves caught up in a complex of issues. Important aims of Crown policy were to ensure the supply of arms to the States-General of the Netherlands, yet to prevent guns reaching the Spanish Netherlands. Permissions were granted for substantial exports to the Queen's allies, notably Count Maurice of Nassau, and the States of Holland and Zealand, who in 1592 received licensed shipments of 200 pieces, half from London and half from Sussex.[22] The States-General continued to receive licensed exports until the end of the decade.[23]

In these years official regulation of the trade became intermingled with another important matter, that of patents of monopoly. In the absence of sufficient paid officials there was a case for placing regulation in the hands of individuals who, out of a levy on goods, paid a proportion to the Crown and kept the rest. The export of ordnance was subject to grants of this kind. In the early 1590s a patent for the export of certain smaller types of gun was held by a syndicate which included Robert Sackville and a merchant stranger, Giles de Vischer. In 1595 Sackville ousted all members of the group except Henry Nevill, and these two operated until 1601, although de Vischer appears to have been involved in the trade again three years later.[24] Specifically aimed at the illegal trade was a commission to Sir Edward Hoby in 1597 to seek those infringing ordnance export regulations, in return for a grant of half the value of items forfeited. Grants of this kind, as well as customs operations, though serving the interests of the Crown, could be difficult to operate in line with diplomatic policy. For example, when guns were being shipped to the States-General from Rochester in 1598 instructions had to be given to customs officials there to permit export free of payments normally due to patentees.[25]

(B) THE BROWNE ERA: THE ACHIEVEMENTS OF THE ROYAL GUN FOUNDERS

Thomas Browne

Thomas and John Browne, father and son, dominated the production of English iron ordnance for half a century and more. In 1596 Thomas Browne took on the office of Crown gun founder on the death of Thomas Johnson. The latter had held the title since 1585 but his affairs are known only in outline. He had worked at Arthur Middleton's furnace at Maynard's Gate in 1574, and is later described as a Hartfield gun founder and tenant of Horsmonden furnace. He delivered considerable quantities of ordnance to the Crown, payments to his widow continuing after his death.[26]

When Thomas Browne acquired this office, he had been operating Bough Beech furnace, Hever, since before 1589. This he rented and subsequently bought from Thomas Willoughbie, and cast guns for the export trade, notably for the patentees active in the Dutch market. By 1604 his operations expanded to include Ashurst and Horsmonden furnaces, and he was then entering into commitments of some magnitude, military and mercantile. An enquiry of 1609 established that he delivered 463 tons of ordnance to merchants and patentees between 1591 and 1598 and 898 tons after 1604.[27] At the local level he sold through men such as Richard Snelling of Lewes, and more widely through Robert Sackville and Sir John Fearne, the latter the lessee of the privileges of ordnance export regulation between 1604 and 1609.[28] One of his most ambitious commitments was his undertaking in 1600 to deliver 400 tons of iron guns to Thomas Sackville, who himself had considerable interests in the Sussex industry. This was at a time when Browne was having to borrow on some scale in London, and the Sackville deal seems to have stretched his credit to or beyond its limit. In 1600, for example, he had borrowed from Thomas Hodilow, a salter, and the case which followed Browne's failure to deliver the Sackville guns on time illustrates the problems of financing stocks for a long run at a furnace.[29] In 1606 Browne was still indebted in London to an uncomfortable extent, and his troubles were made worse in subsequent years by the difficulties of dealing with the Office of Ordnance. The Lieutenant of the Ordnance, Sir Roger Dallison, was notorious for his debts, accumulated while in office, and for making irregular payments to the founders (Prestwich 1966: 218).

The merchant and export trades

After the end of the war with Spain it is no surprise to see a dwindling in Crown orders for iron ordnance. As a result in 1609 there were reported to be only five gun founders: one in Kent, three in Sussex, and a fifth in Glamorgan.[30] These relied on the needs of merchants and the export trade, the merchants providing the most consistent demand. With the shift towards long-distance trading, and the post-war incidence of piracy, the need for defensive weapons was clearly felt in the Atlantic, Mediterranean and eastern trades as well as in the English Channel. The East India Company, for example, armed most of its fleet, and it was from Thomas Browne that guns were obtained for large ships such as the *Trade's Increase*, fitted out in 1609. Indeed, Company gunners were sent to Kent to prove the pieces.[31] Yet despite the end of the Spanish War there was still concern over where guns sold to merchants might eventually find their way. There were numerous debates in the Commons throughout the reign of James I in which the issues of ordnance export and its monopoly regulation were inextricably mixed.[32] The rights of search for illicitly exported guns remained the subject of patents, which were sources of profit to their holders and to the Crown. It was probably to assuage the concern of the Commons that the enquiry was set up in 1609, whose proceedings give a good deal of information about the output of Browne and his contemporaries, and about their export trade.

An interesting illustration of the illicit export business is the case of Stephen Aynscombe of Mayfield. In 1614 he was involved in two actions over illegal export of guns, one in company with William Gulder of Meeching, the other with George Bynles of Lewes, a man with scant scruple over the niceties of licensing. Just two years later, Aynscombe was in trouble again, for he failed to produce a certificate that he and William Gulder had exported guns.[33] He remained in the trade, however, for in 1619 he leased Pounsley furnace, but soon afterwards was involved in a bizarre attempt to export ordnance to Spain on a counterfeit warrant. This warrant was made using the Privy Seal, which was spirited from London to Lewes. It was used to authenticate a document which purported to show that Aynscombe was entitled to dispatch guns under a scheme whereby the Spanish ambassador had permission to export. In this case Aynscombe bought guns from John Browne, rather than having them all cast at his own furnace. Aynscombe then fled abroad and the Privy Council ordered that Pounsley furnace should be blown out and that the guns found there should be confiscated. The pieces were sold off at the merchant-gun market at Tower Hill, but Aynscombe eventually received a pardon in 1621. Persistent to the last, he is heard of sending ordnance to Scotland three years later, when an order was made for his guns to be seized.[34]

The interest of a case such as Aynscombe's, at the illicit end of the trade, should not divert attention from the profitability of regular sales to merchants. These were not merely a peace-time stopgap for founders such as Thomas and John Browne, but sufficiently attractive for the monopoly of manufacture, and supply of merchant guns, to be well worth seeking. That this became a privilege of some notoriety was due to its outspoken holder, Sackville Crowe, who was awarded the patent in 1620 and kept it for 12 years. Crowe had married into the Sackville family, who had ironworks at Maresfield, Brede, Fletching and Parrock; they, of course, had also been involved in export patents. Sackville Crowe himself had experience of the industry, for his father, William Crowe, had taken a partnership with David Middleton at Freshfield Forge in 1602 and then at Maresfield furnace in 1614, the latter joined by Sackville Crowe in 1617. The relationship with Middleton was a stormy one, and a Chancery case of 1619 gives an impression of the Crowes' business methods. Middleton claimed that he had contributed to the construction of Marshalls furnace in 1617–18, but had then found himself eased out of the business, the furnace being operated by the Crowes as their own.[35] From this inauspicious start Crowe was to be embroiled in wider controversies. His monopoly of the merchant trade was a major irritant to other founders, primarily John Browne, who sought such an outlet to tide him over years when Crown business was poor. Those who saw

Crowe as the epitome of the abusive courtier-monopolist lost no opportunity to feed any controversy in which he became involved. One was the suspicion that in 1619 he had been party to the illegal export of guns, for in that year warrants were issued for the arrest of Crowe and of Walter Lucas, his founder at Maresfield. On this occasion it was ordered by the Privy Council that an inventory should be made of all guns at Sussex furnaces: had this survived it would be an invaluable record of the industry. Crowe's reputation was also harmed by the widely held belief that he was involved in an alleged attempt to entice skilled gun founders to France in 1620 or 1621. Crowe had to face an alliance made up of the opponents of monopolies in general and of founders who resented his assured peace-time outlet for ordnance. This, the Tower Hill market, which Crowe was obliged under the terms of his patent to supply, took about 300 tons each year. Nevertheless, this was an uneasy alliance, for John Browne himself was a patentee, on the military side of the market, and Crowe's hold on the merchant monopoly, fragile as it became after the death of Buckingham in 1628, survived until 1632.[36]

John Browne

John Browne had succeeded his father as ironfounder for the ordnance of the Tower and as the king's gunstone maker in 1615. His activities over the next 25 years are well documented, and a picture emerges of a technical innovator with grasp of the tactical problems of his trade. He came into the business after years when Crown requirements had generally been high, if irregular. For example, in 1613 Thomas Browne had been asked to produce even more shot than normal government funding could cover, and in 1613 and 1614 exports had been held up to ensure that enough pieces remained in England to meet the needs of the Crown.[37]

Such demands did not last, and the prime concern of John Browne, as of his father Thomas, was to secure sales which would permit furnaces to be run regularly at full capacity. We have noted that one means to this end, the supply of the merchant trade, was threatened by the Crowe monopoly. Whatever the risks of the merchant market, where trade recessions would inevitably affect the need for ship's guns, they were as nothing compared with the irregularity of orders and payments from the Ordnance Office. Crown financial problems led to few guns being purchased in years of peace: an enquiry of 1619 showed concern at the poor preparedness of the Navy after a period when no replacements had been made, and in 1622 the captains of Sandown, Deal and Walmer castles drew attention to the poor state of their ordnance. Yet in time of war orders came suddenly, and the Brownes were hard pressed to meet them.[38]

When the Crown required guns, its methods of payment gave the Brownes cause for complaint. Payment in advance was hard to secure, and pressure was required even to secure money for completed orders. Further, it was at times difficult to persuade the Ordnance to take guns which had been ordered during hostilities, after a war had ended. The problems of 1626 illustrated this: in the previous year 300 guns had been ordered in some haste, but when the need was past the outstanding pieces were not required and many were of sizes which were hard to sell on the open market. John Browne fought such practices as far as he was able. To the problems of redundant orders he had no answer, but in time of war he had more bargaining power. When payments were inadequate to maintain stocks of materials he could withhold delivery, as in 1625, when he claimed that £1,000 was needed in order to complete a contract. Later that year he had been paid so little for his current contracts that he transferred his men to work on other orders. Ten years later he did the same, ceasing to transport guns until the Ordnance Office paid what was due.[39]

There were several ways in which John Browne attempted to place his castings business on a more regular footing, both in his dealings with the Crown and with other customers. In the mid-1620s he attempted to produce lightweight castings, for in 1626 the Master of the Ordnance was instructed to test Browne's claim that he had made six pieces of the dimensions and quality of standard guns, yet of one-third less weight.[40] There were sound reasons for such experiments, for the naval market for iron as opposed to bronze guns was limited by the problem of mounting heavy pieces well above ships' water-lines. Large iron cannon were therefore still used more in land-forts than in ships, and even the lighter, longer types were used in merchant vessels more often than by the Navy. Browne attempted to extend the use of his iron guns in ships by two methods, perhaps in combination. One was to use less metal, in what he called 'turned' pieces, by which he probably meant the turning of the exterior on a lathe set up as an adjunct to the boring mill.[41] These lightweight pieces also differed internally: they had a 'drake' bore, a tapered barrel, spreading towards the muzzle. This was in contrast with the parallel 'home-bore' of the conventional gun. It is questionable how accurately a taper could be bored with the equipment of the time, but the intentions are clear enough. The principle was to have minimum clearance between the bore and the shot at the chamber end of the gun, permitting the charge to give maximum initial impetus to the shot. The expanding bore minimized the chance of the shot binding on the uneven walls. There was also the benefit of a reduced internal pressure towards the muzzle, where many pieces were weak. This principle of taper boring was not altogether new, for some early seventeenth-century Continental pieces were finished in this way.

The second innovation appears to have been in the composition of the iron itself, for there were references to guns cast in 'refined metal'. This term never seems to have been explained, and it is only surmise that an alteration to the furnace charge produced a grey cast iron of strength sufficient for guns to be turned to a thinner wall.

The new guns had a good measure of success at proof. In 1626 Browne was rewarded with a sum of £200 for casting iron guns which were even lighter than bronze pieces. His achievement was confirmed by the attempts of Pitt, the Houndsditch founder, to reduce the weight of his bronze guns well below those of the new 'drakes'.[42] Not only small guns were made by the new methods, for in May 1627 4 demi-cannon, 16 culverins, and 120 demi-culverins were to be made, all specified as cast-iron drakes in fine metal. It may be that at times the reduction in weight was overdone, for in June 1628 a warrant to Browne for drakes specified that they were to be 'better fortified in the breech and not less than 600[wt] apiece'. The popularity of the drakes was not affected by suggestions that they were inaccurate – 'so light that the shot was uncertainly delivered'. At the end of the 1620s merchants were purchasing in such quantities that the Crown feared that fine lightweight guns would find their way into the wrong hands abroad.[43]

John Browne next extended his activities by starting to cast bronze ordnance. His efforts to make lightweight iron pieces had not displaced non-ferrous guns, most of which still retained a weight advantage sufficient, in the eyes of the Navy, to offset the great difference in price, ten times that of a traditional iron cannon, and about four times that of drakes in 'refined metal'. In 1634 there was a proposal that John Browne should take over the Houndsditch foundry, but in fact he set up to cast bronze at Horsmonden, where he produced ordnance for several years, receiving old guns from the Tower and from Chatham for melting down. In 1638 his facilities were extended with the building of a new foundry at Brenchley, for in January of that year the Office of Ordnance received an estimate of £1,000 for its construction, and in the summer ordnance was being cast there to equip the *Sovereign of the Seas* and the *Royal Sovereign*.[44]

Throughout the years of the Brownes' command of the Crown market they made attempts to take part in the legitimate export business.

From time to time rights were granted, often to agents of foreign governments, to organize supplies to particular countries. The Brownes had every reason to welcome these arrangements, for they helped to keep furnaces in profitable operation at times when government orders were lacking or when the merchant market was in the hands of a monopolist. In the second decade of the seventeenth century one such scheme concerned the supply of guns to the Netherlands. In 1613 Thomas Browne had been approached by Elias Trippe on behalf of the United Provinces, for 200 iron guns. Trippe obtained Privy Council agreement, having stated that he regarded Browne as the only founder capable of fulfilling the order. The arrangement continued, with Sir Noel Caron as intermediary, but by 1617 was coming under criticism, culminating in government termination of permission to export in 1618. In the final year of trading, export was only allowed in return for loans to the Crown from alien merchants in London, and a final stop was placed on the traffic in 1619 when it was feared that stocks of guns in England had been reduced to a dangerous level.[45] The result of the prohibition was to open the Dutch market to Browne's overseas competitors. The guns made in the Liège district were growing in reputation and found a ready sale in the Netherlands and the emergent Swedish ordnance industry gained an important foothold in the Continental market.

The growth of Swedish competition influenced John Browne's dealings with the government. Irregular Crown ordnance contracts, as well as short-lived and unpredictable concessions to trade overseas, jeopardized his ability to survive the Swedish threat. In 1623 the Privy Council came to the conclusion that the four Swedish ordnance furnaces then in use could not match English quality, but Browne suspected otherwise. He made the most of his fears, supported by a report of that year to Secretary Conway which admitted that, although Swedish pieces had broken in proof, they were much improved. By the early 1630s the Swedes were well entrenched, assisted, according to John Browne, by privileges granted by their own government. Browne's case attracted support in some official quarters, if far too late: in 1635 the Lords of the Admiralty supported a petition by Browne to the king, that his works should be assisted by the prohibition of the import of Swedish cast-iron items, whose low prices had already driven many English goods from Continental markets.[46]

When the prohibition of exports to the Netherlands restricted Browne's opportunities, a new outlet opened in Spain. In 1618 the Crown granted an export licence for ordnance to the Spanish ambassador, Gondomar. Given the previous history of Anglo-Spanish relations this was bound to cause concern, but despite parliamentary protest the Privy Council allowed Gondomar to continue exporting guns made at the Browne furnaces, although merchants and shipmasters were reluctant to handle his products for fear of interception by the Dutch. 1621 saw the end of the affair, although Sackville Crowe, John Browne's long-term adversary, lost no opportunity of referring to the latter's involvement when England again went to war with Spain in 1625.[47]

The third such case arose late in 1623, when the Crown licensed two merchants, Peter Burlamachi and Philip Jacobson, to control the export of guns. This was extended by an export patent in 1626, in force until 1632, but shipments under its protection were intermittent, due in particular to English military needs. When these lessened Burlamachi was encouraged by the Crown to find outlets for English guns, and in 1629 he was instructed to sell 4,000 tons of ordnance in the United Provinces within two years. This was part of an arrangement to secure revenue to pay those foreign debts for which royal jewels had been pledged as security. The Privy Council ordered the Office of Ordnance to find unwanted guns and to deliver them to Burlamachi, and Browne was instructed to produce prodigious quantities for the project. The market became saturated, Burlamachi withdrew, and John Browne himself attempted to run the scheme, failing to obtain satisfactory prices. The result was an increasing indebtedness, which dogged Browne's operations until the middle of the decade. In 1634 he was forced to appeal for help from the Crown in dealing with his creditors, basing his case on his indispensability as a supplier of the military needs of the government.[48] It was indeed to encourage such a view that he began to cast bronze guns in 1634.

Much of what the Brownes, father and son, did and said was directed at an even production of ordnance, year by year, for it was rightly feared that under-employed moulders would leave and that there would be difficulty in assembling a skilled work-force when an upswing in orders arrived. It was not uncommon for the skilled men to move from one furnace to another, and from time to time there were scares that they were being enticed overseas. In 1627 John Browne's skilled workers were thought to have been the objects of a French attempt when Michell Donnevide was arrested in Kent. On questioning, Donnevide was found to have visited Sackville Crowe's ironworks at Maresfield with similar intentions. In the following year a number of workmen left Browne's employment, persuaded to go to Scotland to cast ordnance. They were ordered to return, but Browne was also instructed to provide work for them, failing which they might indeed go. The implication here is clear: Browne's men were as dissatisfied as their employer with irregular working, and were open to offers.[49]

John Browne did attempt to keep his works busy by making other castings. As holder of the office of Crown gunstone maker he produced ammunition in quantity and variety. Ordinary shot, cross-barred shot for mortars, and cases for grenades of various kinds were cast from the furnace fore-hearth, the metal ladled into moulds which were themselves of cast iron. But although such objects could use metal produced early in a campaign and regarded as unfit for guns, sales took much the same pattern as for ordnance. So it was to other kinds of products that Browne had to turn in time of peace. Little is known of how many of the traditional cast-iron objects he made: it is to be expected that fire-backs, grave-slabs, forge-hearth plates, rollers and pipes would have been made when the gun trade was slack, but the quantities would hardly be large enough to occupy a furnace such as Horsmonden. An attempt to expand his production for the civil market can be perceived in 1635, when John Browne gained a patent to cast articles 'in the French fashion.'[50]

3   The traditional iron trade

The operations of the gun founders inevitably overshadow the production of pig and bar iron. Men such as John Browne would, of course, enter this part of the industry from time to time, when ordnance orders were short or when a furnace was being brought to a condition in which iron for guns could be cast. In Browne's case the production of pig cannot have been sufficiently regular or important to justify the operation of a finery, for he does not appear to have had a forge in regular use.

The 40 years before the Civil War saw a decline in the Wealden industry at large, for a significant number of furnaces and forges in use at the end of the sixteenth century passed from the record by 1653. Indeed the list of works operating in that year is likely to underestimate earlier closures, for the needs for iron at the time of the First Dutch War may have led to some being reinstated. It is amongst those which are recorded as going out of use between 1653 and 1664 that such temporary revivals might be sought.

Trends in local sales of Wealden bar iron are hard to estimate, and the extent of competition from iron produced abroad or elsewhere in England must have varied according to the distances from water transport. In the seventeenth century the Forest of Dean industry grew at a remarkable rate, and its high-quality iron was carried long

distances by water and even by land. Imports of bar increased, from
Spain and from the Baltic, consignments into London trebling between 1588 and 1634, an increase of 800 tons. The London market
would have been the most affected by these trades, which grew at a
time of new building in the expanding capital. Elsewhere in the
south-east the period was one of prosperity, deriving from the needs
of London for agricultural goods. Imported iron would have been
available near the ports, but inland, farm building and equipment
would still have provided a market for the Wealden forge-master and
ironmonger.

Reduction in the numbers of works and doubts about the buoyancy
of the market are only one side of the story, for there are signs that the
more favourably situated furnaces and forges remained attractive to
landowners and investors alike. Ashburnham, for example, changed
hands in 1634 and 1641 without periods of vacancy; Robertsbridge
appears to have been successfully let throughout the period, while at
Scarlets Oliver Knight was anxious to enforce his right of inheritance
in 1631.[51] For the outside investor, even some inland sites still had
their attractions: Cotchford forge was sold to a London buyer in 1627,
and Horsted Keynes furnace was mortgaged to Giles Dobbins, a
London ironmonger, in 1646. The works which were active at
mid-century were those most favourably endowed, whether with
convenient coppices or access to coastal or river transport. An
excellent example is the growth of the Farnden works. In 1627 Peter
and Richard Farnden leased the manor of Crowhurst from Sir Thomas
Pelham, then sub-let the manor house and set the ironworks in
operation, developing the woodlands on the estate in conjunction
with their own at Sedlescombe. The position, within six miles of
Hastings, was excellent for the shipment of iron, and the works were
operated by the Farndens for half a century. [52]

Among the ironmasters there are signs that the tenant, so prominent
at the end of the sixteenth century, became less able to profit in the
industry. Not that there are many recorded failures, for Thomas Lucke
of Rotherfield, in 1645, is the only documented bankruptcy. Where
tenants were still obviously successful, their relationships with landowners were important. Peter Farnden, for example, found Sir John
Sackville a valuable associate for his woodlands, and John Fuller
benefited from the partnership with Sir Thomas Dyke after 1650.
Similarly, it has been shown by Anthony Fletcher that the smaller
landowner made no great profit from the industry at this time; indeed,
only two who could be thus categorized and who ran ironworks,
Stephen Penkhurst and Stephen French, were included among the
higher assessments for forced loans to the Crown. Penkhurst, indeed,

profited from his association with a larger landowner, Thomas Sackville, with whom he was to be in partnership at Coushoplea furnace in 1651.[53]

The most fully documented ironworks in this period are those on the Pelham estates. There are accounts running from 1628 to 1657 in the case of Waldron furnace, and from 1638 to 1679 for Brightling and Bibleham forges. A further set, for the years 1690–1716, is referred to in Chapter 9. The accounts are unsatisfactory in that they provide insufficient information for precise reckonings of profit and loss, although it is clear that their contribution to the total income of the Pelham forges; so much of the pig iron from Waldron was sold location of the works; Waldron was distant from Lewes and from the Medway route to the Thames; it was also six miles from each of the Pelham forges, so much of the pig iron from Waldron was sold outside, rather than converted on the estate. Similarly the forges, which were both small, refined pig bought from outside furnaces as well as that carried from Waldron. Nor indeed was all the wood used in the Pelhams' works grown in their own coppices, for both wood and charcoal were bought in when appropriate, just as wood from the more distant Pelham lands was sold to outsiders. Ore was also bought in, as was usually more convenient when supplying Waldron. This extensive contact with the market made for realistic accounting, for the estate saw the full costs of supplying the ironworks, taking into account market values of materials, rather than merely the labour-costs of cutting, charcoal burning or mining, as were often reckoned, if supply were self-contained within an estate.[54]

4   The Wealden iron industry during the Civil War and the Commonwealth

The effects of the Civil War on the industry cannot at present be set out with any certainty. There are two significant questions: to which side Wealden iron was supplied during the war, and whether ironworks were destroyed during the campaigns.

Few of the Wealden ironmasters can be firmly labelled as committed long-term suppliers to one side or the other. For many, such an attribution may be irrelevant, in that their bar iron habitually went to wholesale ironmongers. So it may be wrong to assume that even those with openly expressed sympathies for one side or the other actually supplied the belligerent forces direct. Nevertheless, certain individuals were in a position to do so. On the Parliamentary side Colonel Herbert Morley, owner of Hawksden forge, could well have supplied his regiment. Sir Thomas Pelham's ironworks accounts do not confirm that he was a direct supplier, though his connection with the county militia was strong. Thomas Middleton is an uncertain case, for although a Parliamentary supporter, he is seen as moderate, even lukewarm and although a sequestrator of Royalist property, his own lands and works were in turn confiscated in 1649 for his alleged part in anti-Parliamentary disturbances in Horsham. On the Royalist side the connections are even less clear; the Sackvilles' interest in the industry was indirect, their works being leased out, and this was the period when the Ashburnham ironworks were still in other hands, following the sale of the estates in 1611.[55]

John Browne, as in so many ways, was a unique case. As a supplier to the Office of Ordnance he naturally furnished the Royalist side in the early stages of the war, as his examination by Parliament in 1645 showed. In 1640 he made 120 guns of fine metal for the king's ships, and instructions were given for the release of any of his employees pressed for military service, to allow orders to be fulfilled.[56] In the following year Browne was given the use of the royal ironworks in the Forest of Dean, although by July 1642 he had failed to gain access to them, owing to the persistence of the former tenant, Sir John Winter, and so re-assigned his lease. Browne, further, was accused of having provided workmen to aid the Royalist scheme to cast guns at Oxford.[57] Given his need for continuity of production it would hardly have been surprising if Browne had supplied both sides during the more fluid periods of the war. However, he was too valuable a source of ordnance for the Parliamentary side to take any severe steps against him. The great activity of his works is well portrayed in the account of Barden in 1645 by Sir James Hope in his diary, and his capacity was extended by his use of Richard Tichborne's furnace at Cowden.[58]

Little destruction of ironworks took place during the Civil War. The only known instances are those put out of action by Waller in St Leonards Forest, yet the nearby Tilgate furnace, despite its reputation for having cast ordnance for the Crown, appears to have escaped. In any case, apart from the campaigns of 1642 and 1643, which were largely fought near the coast, there was little military activity in Sussex.

In the years after the end of the Civil War the shape of the Wealden industry is illuminated by the list of furnaces and forges in use in 1653. This has survived as an adjunct to the better-known record of 1667, which is discussed in the following chapter. The origins of the 1653 list are not known, for it is uncertain whether it was compiled from memory in 1667 to demonstrate the contraction of the industry during the intervening decade, or whether it had been made in unknown circumstances in the year to which it relates (Lower 1866; Parsons 1882; see also Cattell 1973: 190ff.). Some of the works in this list were mentioned in a record of August 1653, when six Wealden ironmasters were named as supplying shot to the government. This was a memorandum of Thomas Newberry to the Ordnance Office, made following a visit to Sussex. Newberry visited the Farndens' works, where it was found that water was so short that 100 tons of shot required by the office could not be delivered at Hastings or Rye before the following March. Everenden of Lewes, probably involved at Woodcock Hammer,[59] Akehurst of Warbleton, and some others, unnamed, were in similar difficulties, whereas Walter Burrell, probably at Cuckfield furnace, Stendwick (Strudwick), and Yalden of Blackdown were casting when visited.[60]

Only in a few individual cases such as the Pelham works is there anything to show how active were the furnaces and forges listed in 1653. In this decade, as before, the best-documented ironworks, that of the Brownes, is probably atypical, but it is nevertheless of interest in showing that there was still sufficient potential in the Weald for a prominent Midland family of ironmasters, the Foleys, to seek involvement there. In the early 1650s John Browne figures prominently in the State Papers, still as a supplier of ordnance, some of which was made for the navy and paid for out of receipts from the salt excise and the proceeds of confiscated church estates. In addition to iron guns Browne was still making brass pieces, some of which were cast in association with Pitt, the Houndsditch founder, others at Browne's own works. Thomas Foley took a part in the Browne operations in 1652, when he and his brother-in-law George Browne leased the forge at Frant lately held by John, father of George Browne. The Foley-Browne partnership in the Weald, which was joined by the Courthopes, covered the casting of guns at Barden and of pig iron and pots at Cowden, recorded in 1665. The guns went both to the Office of Ordnance and to the merchant market at Tower Hill. The Foleys' interest, however, was short. By 1660 their share of the partnership, and that of the Courthopes also, had been bought by the new generation of the Browne family.[61]

It is reasonable to assume that with the end of the First Dutch War the Weald looked a less favourable field for Foley investment. Government purchases of ordnance fell away, for although the Brownes managed to find outlets for their pieces right through 1656, Pitt the brassfounder had petitioned over lack of work in the previous year.[62] A comparison of the 1653 and 1667 lists speaks for itself. In the intervening decade 22 furnaces and 24 forges went out of use, even though some appear in the later record as re-stocked for the Second

Dutch War; it is with the continuing decline in the subsequent century that the next chapter is concerned.

NOTES

1. ESRO Rye 1/5/109.
2. Staffs.RO D593/S/4/28/3, 17; ESRO Danny 144.
3. 27 Eliz I, c.19.
4. PRO SP16/363/55–6.
5. APC XXV (1595–6), 453.
6. PRO LR2/299, f. 20, although see PRO SP23/254 of 1650 which shows woods ready for cutting.
7. PRO PROB11/145/217; KAO U1475/T287/1–2; ESRO ASH886, 1178.
8. ESRO Adams 126; ESRO DH 786.
9. ESRO DH 679, 692, 785–8.
10. PRO SP12/249/116.
11. PRO SP12/217/31.
12. *Ibid.* 65–6.
13. *APC* XVI (1588), 326; GMR Loseley 994/1; Staffs.RO D593/S/4/28/1.
14. Staffs.RO D593/S/4/28/3.
15. *APC* XVI (1588), 359; PRO SP12/223/16.
16. *APC* XVII (1588–9), 142–3.
17. *APC* XVIII (1589–90), 7–8; *ibid.* XIX (1590). 461–2. For copies of Lord Buckhurst's letters to justices see BL Add. MSS 5702, f.91–2.
18. *APC* XXV (1595–6), 227.
19. *APC* XIV (1587), 343; PRO SP15/30/109.
20. *APC* XX (1590–1), 5; Staffs.RO D593/S/4/28/3.
21. *APC* XXI (1591), 417–18, 431–2.
22. PRO SP12/242/34.
23. PRO SP12/266/6; 274/125.
24. *APC* XXV (1595–6), 271, 301; PRO REQ2/266/18. See also PRO SP12/240/134, 249/5, 256/38.
25. PRO SP12/264/156, 266/6.
26. *Ibid.* 244/102, 249/93; PRO C66/1452 m11, 1454 m37; PRO E351/2631–5.
27. Schubert 1948; 245, citing Sevenoaks Pub. Lib. H414; PRO E178/4143. For Browne's already excessive cutting of timber see Jack 1981: 11, citing PRO E159/408 Easter, 37 Eliz r.286.
28. PRO REQ2/32/67, 165/103; a list of those to whom Browne sold guns appears in PRO E178/4143.
29. PRO REQ2/398/13, 191/37. Reference to his debts appears in the Exchequer case brought against the Brownes in 1618 by Thomas Lusted, PRO E124/36 f.346.
30. PRO E178/4143, naming Thomas Hodgson of Pounsley, Barnabe Hodgson of Mayfield, Stephen Greensmith, without location but exporting through Lewes, Thomas Browne of Ashurst, and Peter Samyne of Cardiff.
31. East India Co., Court Book II, 6 July 1609. See also Chaudhuri 1963: 27–41.
32. E.g. PRO SP15/34/43, SP14/58/12.
33. *APC* XXXIII (1613–14), 428; XXIV (1615–16), 377–8; PRO SP14/88.
34. ESRO Glynde 1671; *APC* 1619–21, 316–17, 321–2, 340–1; 1621–3, 13–14; PRO SP14/117/51, 122/4, 180/100.
35. PRO C3/284/51, 319/23.
36. PRO SP14/118/48–9; SP15/42/66; *APC* 1619–21, 88, 90; SP16/407/70, 525/71–7.
37. PRO SP14/81, grant bk., 155; KAO TR 1295/47–8; *APC* XXXIII (1613–14), 101.
38. PRO SP14/128/109; SP15/42/66; SP14/105/92.

39. PRO SP16/12/24, 12/37; APC June–Dec, 1626, 412–13; 1627–8, 494; SP16/341/57.
40. APC 1625/6, 342–3.
41. BL Harleian 429, f.6ff., 28; PRO SP449/1, 457/1, 522/59.
42. PRO SP16/25/79; 85/91; 91/34; Blackmore 1976: 247; BL Harleian 429, e.g. f.18; PRO E351/2654, WO 49/58.
43. PRO SP16/175/97; 176/14; APC 1629–30, 135; SP16/22/87.
44. BL Harleian 429, f.121, 153; PRO SP16/273/72; 378/48; 393/13, 74; WO49/65, 75; Towes 1977: 15–20.
45. APC XXXIII (1613–14), 92; XXXV (1616–17), 138; XXXVI(1618–19), 69, 240.
46. APC 1623–5, 136–7; PRO SP14/155/11; SP16/279/37.
47. PRO SP14/103/80; APC 1619–21, 334; SP14/119/99, 120/13.
48. APC 1623–5, 104–5, 136–7; PRO SP14/182/75; APC 1628–9, 165; 1629–30, 93–4, 205; 1630–1, 297–8; SP16/148/94–5; 279/37.
49. APC Jan–Aug. 1627, 368, 379; 1627–8, 128: 1628–9, 71–2; 1629–30, 5; PRO SP16/70/103, 72/28.
50. PRO SP16/306/102.
51. PRO C3/418/106.
52. Straker 1931a: 251, ESRO Glynde 2067–8; ESRO Dunn 29/1–2.
53. ESRO Add. MSS 5699; Dunn 46/1; Fletcher 1975: 19; ESRO DH781.
54. BL Add. MSS 33154–6; Fletcher 1975; 14, 20.
55. PRO SP15/251/30.
56. SP16/449/1.
57. SP16/487/77; 491/50; PRO E178/6080; SP16/491/86; 507/130ff.
58. SP16/507/134ff; Marshall 1958: 142ff; Straker 1931a: 276.
59. ESRO SAS Gage 33/69.
60. SP18/39/31; for Strudwick see also SP18/49/112, 50/60–1, 59/114.
61. SP18/23/108; ESRO DH609; Hereford RO Foley F vi B/5312, F vi Bf/12–18.
62. SP 18/100/79.

Chapter 9   Ordnance production after the Dutch Wars: specialization and its consequences

Although Wealden iron production declined to extinction in the 150 years after the Civil War, for many years the district maintained a reputation for the excellence of its castings. Indeed, until the middle of the eighteenth century it had few serious British rivals in the production of ordnance, and it was largely upon the ironmasters of Sussex and Kent that the Office of Ordnance relied until the perfection of the Carron Company's products in 1775.

1 Changes in balance: the decline of the bar iron trade

The shift in emphasis towards the production of cast-iron objects took place in the middle and later decades of the seventeenth century. It has been shown in earlier chapters that until this time the casting of pig had exceeded that of moulded items, that furnaces and forges had been closely connected, either under common management or by an active market in pig iron, and that the wrought-iron trade had ranged far beyond the locality. Before about 1650 specialists in castings were largely gun founders, such as John Browne or Sackville Crowe.

The pattern of relationships and products appears to have changed fairly rapidly after 1650. Comparison of two major sources of information leads to this view. The first is the list of furnaces and forges extant or working in 1664 and 1667, already referred to in connection with lists of works operating in 1653. The second is a record of works obtained by John Fuller in 1717.[1] A comparison will not exaggerate changes, for particular circumstances behind each compilation combine to produce a conservative estimate of shifts in the balance between furnaces and forges. The 1664–7 lists show the results of the Dutch Wars, which led many ironmasters to equip themselves to cast ordnance, and had encouraged the survival and refurbishing of furnaces. Further, foreign competition depressed the wrought-iron trade of the Wealden forges in the 1660s and the list appears to have been intended to support petitions seeking protection for the English bar iron industry. Thus the compilers had every incentive to minimize the number of forges in their record. Conversely, the 1717 list was compiled at a time when temporary outside factors favoured the production of wrought iron. Imports were being hindered by interference with trade in the Baltic, so output in England may well have been at an enhanced level. Further, peace in 1713 had reduced government needs for ordnance.

Despite these points, comparison of the 1664–7 and 1717 lists shows that while furnace numbers were maintained, there was a significant decline in the number of forges over the period and that those which survived produced quantities small by earlier standards. Taking the forges, the 21 in use in 1667 declined to 13 by 1717. Within this decline there were a few cases of new or re-opened works, although these do not obscure the main trend. For example, Chingley, a forge which had origins in the sixteenth century, yet was not mentioned in 1653 or 1667, was converting 46 tons a year in 1717. Etchingham, similarly ignored in the earlier lists, appears in 1717.

a

b

Fig.35   Cast-iron firebacks in Anne of Cleves House, Lewes. (a) Fireback dated 1636 cast by Richard Lenard of Brede Furnace. The timber outer framing shows clearly on the representation of the blast furnace; (b) Casting probably of seventeenth-century date: 'probasti me' ('thou hast tested me). Neither the initials 'L M' nor the place or date of casting have been identified (photographs: Sussex Archaeological Society).

Two forges appear to have been newly built in 1717. Darvel seems to have been a late development, close to the furnace of that name, and Lord Montague operated a forge, perhaps sited in Battle Park.[2] To the 13 forges should be added Maresfield, not mentioned in the 1717 list, but in operation just before and leased again in that year. The 1717 list appears to be an accurate record, although three forges in Surrey are only mentioned under the names of their operators. 'Mr Dibble's' is likely to be Abinger Hammer, corresponding with an entry under Shere in 1667. 'Mr Johnson's' is Woodcock forge, also referred to in 1667, but 'Mr Gale's' is less certain, perhaps being an inaccurate reference to Tinsley, which lies within Sussex.[3]

A comparison of the lists of furnaces shows that within the similar totals there were considerable changes between 1664–7 and 1717. Nine furnaces formerly active went out of use in the half-century, whereas six which were laid up in 1664 were later revived. In addition, Barden, stated as ruined in 1664, though in fact re-leased in 1663 and absent from the 1667 list, was mentioned in 1717.[4] Three new furnaces appeared. Lamberhurst was entirely new, Heathfield may possibly have had a sixteenth-century precursor, but must have been in effect a new development, as must the 'Ashdown Forest' furnace at Pippingford.

Such comparisons between lists make the shift of emphasis clear: furnace capacity was maintained, yet in 1717 forges were converting half the quantity of pig iron worked in 1667. This change reflects the difficulties which the Wealden forge-master faced in the bar iron trade. Foreign iron, particularly from the Baltic, was being imported in increasing quantities. Continental producers had established themselves at the top of the quality range, which only the Forest of Dean forges could match;[5] they also increased their penetration of the market for the common ranges, for their low costs enabled them to

Fig.36   Cast-iron grave slabs in Wadhurst parish church. (a) David Barham 1643; the incised A B 1688 probably relates to Ann Barham (such an addition was only possible with a grey cast iron); (b) John Barham 1648; (c) Mary and Elizabeth Luck, 1707 and 1709 (photographs: Mrs P. Combes, by courtesy of the Rev T. D. M. Raven, Vicar of Wadhurst).

compete with local producers. London and the east and south coasts, traditional outlets for Wealden bar, were particularly open to these competitive imports, and contemporary comments show the extent of concern. In 1661 a Grand Jury at Lewes blamed the import of Swedish bar iron for the decay of the local industry.[6]

Drafts of further petitions were published by Parsons with the lists of 1664–7; at this time a remedy of a duty of 40s per ton on imports of iron was being suggested (Parsons 1882: 21–4). The issue remained a live one towards the end of the century, as is shown by a document of about 1690[7] which notes, again, the effect on the Wealden industry of Swedish and Spanish imports and argues against the imposition of an excise duty on home-produced iron.

In addition to imports, competition also came from the Midland forges, whose bar was cheap and of a wide range of qualities. This was sold over much of the country, and also fostered the development of the secondary trades of Warwickshire, Worcestershire and Stafford-shire (Rowlands 1975: 11–12). The products of these toolmakers, locksmiths, chainmakers, even nailers, acquired a national reputa-tion, and ironmongers such as the Crowleys were able to sell them over most of the country, undercutting the craftsmen of the south-east who had traditionally bought Wealden bar. As John Fuller noted in 1737, the water-powered slitting mills of the Midlands enabled even the Birmingham nailer to undercut smiths elsewhere.[8] This was des-pite the cost of transporting products of such low value.

In the Weald itself there were incentives to concentrate on castings. During the Dutch Wars the skills of moulding spread, indicated by the total of furnaces which adapted themselves to casting ordnance and shot. No less than 24 appear to have done so by 1667, so moulders would be available for the manufacture of peacetime goods. Their manufacture is clear from inventories of the period. For example, goods made by Peter Farnden at Conster furnace in 1671–2 for Thomas Hunt, a London ironmonger, include not only the traditional firebacks, anvils and hammer-heads, but items as diverse as plates for hearths and furnaces, paper-mill parts, cramps, box-moulds, ranges of utensils from kettles and pans to solder-pots, as well as large items, particularly sugar rolls and garden rollers. A similar range can be found in an inventory of stock of Hamsell furnace in 1708.[9]

The Farndens are a good example of the change which was affecting much of the industry. Before the Civil War their interests had taken the conventional form. Peter Farnden the elder and his brother Robert had leased Crowhurst furnace and forge from Sir Thomas Pelham in 1627, and Robert's probate inventory of 1634 shows that he also worked Hodesdale and Buckholt forges. Peter Farnden junior and

Tobias Farnden, working with the Londoner Samuel Gott, built up an operation of some size in the middle of the century. Crowhurst furnace and forge were said to make a net profit of £200 in 1648, and the furnace went on to produce guns in the Dutch Wars, as did Conster furnace, which passed with its forge from the elder Peter to Tobias Farnden in 1653. Thereafter, the shift in emphasis is clear. Four forges were run down in the 1650s; by 1664 Hodesdale was ruined, Buckholt and Crowhurst were out of use, while Conster was only mentioned as a furnace. The only forge which the younger generation of Farndens operated was Westfield, in use in 1667. This was to remain active to the middle of the eighteenth century, although the Farndens leased it to Thomas Western in 1677. However, by the terms of the agreement he had to buy 50 tons of sows each year from Conster furnace.[10]

Crowhurst and Conster furnaces were the mainstay of the Farnden-Gott business, and their capacity was greatly in excess of what could be refined at Westfield forge. Further, the partners made other excursions into casting. They made brief use of Brede furnace, property of the Sackvilles, after it was relinquished by John Browne, handing it on after 1660 to two London ironmongers, Thomas Western and Charles Harvey. The Farndens also developed their links with Thomas Collins, with whom Tobias Farnden had worked Westfield forge in 1653: in 1671 Collins leased Socknersh furnace to Peter Farnden and the founder John Roberts.[11] The Farnden business survived until the death of Peter in 1681, when the stores and tools at Conster were sold and the site disposed of.

To retain some sense of perspective, we must note the range of ways in which furnaces and forges functioned at this time. At one extreme, some furnaces relied as far as possible on casting for the ordnance trade. The Browne family, best documented in the first half of the seventeenth century, retained their position as the main suppliers of ordnance to the Crown after 1663. Between 1664 and 1678 George and subsequently John Browne supplied large quantities of guns to the Crown,[12] including a remarkable order for 1,500 pieces weighing 2,612 tons in 1665. Horsmonden, Hawkhurst, and Bedgebury furnaces produced cast-iron pieces, while a furnace in Brenchley parish, not identified on the ground, made brass guns. In 1677 they leased Hamsell furnace from John Baker to make guns and other cast wares, Baker agreeing to set up a boring mill near Birchden forge for John Browne's use. Perhaps significantly, Baker's Birchden forge was not taken by the Brownes.[13]

By contrast, there still remained a regional market for bar iron, saved for the local producer by the high cost of road transport. John

Fuller confirmed this, writing in 1735 about the bar made in Sussex for local use in the previous 40 years. The best-recorded late-seventeenth-century examples of works catering for this market were the Pelhams' forges at Bivelham and Brightling, refining pig iron from Waldron furnace.[14] Production figures are known from the Civil War to 1715, except for the years 1679–90. The two forges rarely produced anything like their full capacity. Each had been capable of refining over 100 tons of bar annually before 1650, Brightling exceeding 120 tons five times in the 1640s, while Bivelham reached 113 tons in 1640. Thereafter Brightling commonly produced 40–50 tons in a year, reaching a maximum of 88 tons in 1652 and 1662. Bivelham produced on a similarly reduced scale, but both fell even below this when Waldron switched from the casting of pig iron to shot and shells in the 1690s. The two forges only made 36 tons between them in 1694. The output was largely sold to local smiths and ironmongers. The smiths are occasionally listed in the Pelhams' accounts: they came largely from villages within a 15–20 mile radius. For example in 1704 bar went to buyers at Ashburnham, Hooe, East Hoathly, Wadhurst, Warbleton, Cranbrook, Benenden, Bexhill, Ewhurst, Greenlee, Hailsham, Catstreet, Westham and Waldron, each normally taking about 10cwt over the year. The ironmongers were more widely spread: for example, of the 40 tons dispatched from Bivelham in 1697 11 tons went to Ludd of Canterbury, 6 tons to Dane of Faversham, and 23 tons to Lewes, probably for Ambrose Galloway who was the largest and most regular purchaser, not only of bar iron from the forges but also of pig iron, hammers and anvils made at Waldron furnace. Galloway was virtually the only buyer of large consignments of pig iron after 1695, when London factors disappear from the accounts.

Despite their small output the Pelham forges do not appear to have been neglected. In 1655 Bivelham was rebuilt, and less fundamental repairs to buildings, bellows, hearths and wheels are recorded right through the accounts. There are indeed a small number of forges which contemporary sources show were worth maintaining for consistent operation well into the eighteenth century. Westfield forge remained useful by virtue of its convenient location near the tidal limit of the Brede river, which flows to Rye. It was taken on by the Midland 'Ironworks in Partnership' in conjunction with Ashburnham furnace in 1710, and was operated by Harrison and Legas in the 1740s.[15] Two other forges which appear to have been well maintained were Hawksden, for which leases and inventories survive from 1665 to 1766, and Woodcock, which was kept in operation into the early eighteenth century by lessees whose bar iron served the needs of south-east Surrey.[16]

2   Ordnance production at the beginning of the eighteenth century

From 1689 to 1713 the casting side of the industry enjoyed renewed prosperity, coinciding with the wars of those years. The demand for arms was superimposed upon the diversifying civil trade for castings, and certain founders even became short of capacity. Some rented time at a furnace normally producing pig iron. Waldron is a good example, for in 1692 William Benge paid £8 a day to have the metal from this furnace for 68 days. Later that year he took over the furnace from precisely 11 a.m. on 29 November, and by 11 p.m. on 28 February 1693 he had made 61 tons of granado shot and moulds. He was directly followed by Western who made shot and moulds through to November, and in 1694 Benge repeated his arrangement.

Two furnaces which had cast guns before or during the Dutch Wars were operating again after 1690. Peter Gott was using Coushoplea furnace, near Wadhurst, in 1691 and 1693.[17] His recorded supply of guns to the Office of Ordnance begins in 1697, so it is yet to be proved whether he actually made guns at Coushoplea. We are on firmer ground with Stream furnace, Chiddingly. Nothing is heard of this between 1664–7, when guns were cast, and 1692, but the father of John Oxley produced 210 tons 10cwt of guns there in that year and 235 tons 12cwt in 1693, all for John Fuller.[18]

The building of three new gun furnaces was made worthwhile by the armaments boom of the 1690s. The best known project was the building of Gloucester furnace, Lamberhurst, by William Benge. Benge first appeared as an armaments supplier when he sold ammunition to the Office of Ordnance in 1686 (Saville 1978: table 12–4). Where this was made is not known, but his growing involvement is indicated by his use of Waldron furnace from 1692. In 1694 he purchased Hoathly Forge, unused since 1670, and, utilizing the water supply to the forge, constructed a furnace, which is well known from Swedenborg's sketch in his *De Ferro* of 1734. He was assisted by a grant of £2,000 made by the Board of Ordnance in 1695 'for encouraging him to build a new foundry'.[19] This unusual action was the result of a complaint by the Lords of the Admiralty about shortage of mortars. In 1698 Benge was still developing his operations, acquiring land from his neighbour, Sir Robert Filmer. How long the venture continued to succeed is uncertain, for Lower writes of Benge's failure and the assignment of the works to Gott. In fact, the Ordnance Office received guns from Benge until 1700, and after a year's interval he and Peter Gott were joint suppliers of shot and guns in 1701–2. Benge was again an independent supplier from 1702 until 1705, suggesting that his problems had at least temporarily been overcome. The other major new furnace, Heathfield, was built on land leased in 1693 where 'John Fuller intended to build and set up a furnace or ironworks'. Accounts for the early years do not survive, but those for 1708–11 show a furnace casting ordnance in quantity,[20] confirmed by the supply of guns to the Office of Ordnance in all but three of the years between 1694 and 1713. The third furnace was Pippingford, built in Ashdown Forest by 1696. Here, on land disafforested in 1691, an ironworks was set up by James Hooper and Francis Diggs, both Londoners. There is archaeological evidence for two furnaces. The first was designed to produce ordnance, the second, which is likely to have superseded the first and of which there is no documentary record, cast pig iron. It is suggested that the first structure represents the venture of Hooper and Diggs, but their names do not appear among those of suppliers of guns to the Office of Ordnance. Thus they may have been subcontractors or suppliers to the merchant trade or, most likely, they may have quickly leased the furnace out. The likely lessee is Charles Manning. He supplied guns to the Ordnance Office in 1705–6, and in 1717 he is found taking a new lease of the furnace from Hooper.[21] This was for 31 years, but had his previous lease been for the more usual 21 years, his occupation would have started in 1696, the year of the first reference to the furnace.

The interest of such London investors underlines the potential seen in the Wealden iron trade in these decades. Such involvement was not, of course, limited to the last years of the seventeenth century. Thomas Western had invested in the Weald for the previous 30 years, leasing Brede furnace about 1660, and nine years later taking woodlands in Mountfield and Battle. He had also leased Ashburnham furnace and forge in 1677, the year when he took Westfield forge.[22] The Ashburnham lease was renewed for a further six years by Western in 1683: his involvement in gun casting is indicated by the use of the forge as a boring mill.[23]

Londoners were not the only outsiders who could still be persuaded to operate in the Weald. A previous case had been the entry of the Foleys into partnership with John and George Browne and Alexander Courthope between 1652 and 1660, to share in the prosperity brought to the producers of ordnance by the demands of the Dutch Wars.[24] It was to be late in the period of activity between 1690 and 1710 that such interest re-appeared. The investors were the 'Ironworks in Partnership', a consortium of ironmasters from the Midlands and the Forest of Dean, of whom the Crowleys and the Hanburys were the most prominent members. They leased Ashburnham furnace for seven years from 1709 from William Ashburnham, and Westfield Forge, also for seven years, from Peter Gott. The antecedents to the

Westfield agreement do not survive, but correspondence regarding Ashburnham furnace makes it clear that it was no easy task to negotiate an agreement with the partnership.

It is worth taking a longer look at this particular incident, beginning several years before the lease to the outsiders.[25] In the 1690s Ashburnham had been leased by Thomas and Maximilian Western, together with considerable tracts of wood on the estate. The lease terminated in 1701, and Maximilian Western did not renew. In fact he declined to take on Robertsbridge furnace in 1703, and produced for the Board of Ordnance at Moorfields foundry in London until he was killed in an explosion in 1716. William Ashburnham overestimated the value of the furnace and boring mill and lost the chance of re-letting. The correspondence with Western contains an acrimonious exchange over the condition in which the works had been left, and Ashburnham began, rather desperately, to seek a new taker. He made enquiries about the extent of Ordnance Office orders in Sussex, and on the strength of the result put repairs in hand at the furnace and the boring mill. He then set about publicizing the virtues of the works, not least to the Fullers, who had built their new furnace at Heathfield a decade before. In 1705 Ashburnham set out a useful account of the costs of running the furnace and the resources of the neighbouring woods in a letter which may well have been sent to Major Hanbury.[26] In 1706 negotiations were pursued, with Ashburnham suggesting that he should run the works in partnership with Hanbury and Crowley. Only Ashburnham's side of the correspondence is known: in it he considered the respective merits of running the furnace for castings or for pig iron. The latter could either be carried away for refining, or, it was suggested, be converted at a forge which Ashburnham was prepared to build. Ashburnham had a hard task to persuade the Midlands partnership, as one comment of 1706 shows: 'If Major Hanbury should have the ill-fortune to let slip his opportunity of taking my ironworks I am confident that he will have cause to repent it. I am not little concerned to find so ingenious a gentleman should require so much courtship in a matter so highly for his advantage.'

Ashburnham was also considering other possibilities. One was to abandon iron production and to allow the woods to be managed by a London charcoal merchant, John Kirrell. Negotiations evidently proceeded to the point of a limited use of the woods by Kirrell before his death in 1707, and the correspondence provides a source for this little-known trade. Ashburnham was also prepared to operate the furnace himself, and so kept a close watch on market prices.

By early 1708, the attempts to persuade Hanbury to take the Ashburnham works were successful. From the accounts for 1708–11 it

can be seen that a conventional, even old-fashioned business structure resulted.[27] Most pig iron was taken to Westfield forge for
conversion and the rest was sold elsewhere, carried to Pevensey
sluice for shipment or sent to Maidstone. Small castings, particularly
ships' ballast and plates of iron, were also produced in some quantity.
However, in 1711 a boring house was built, or perhaps rebuilt,
suggesting that the casting of ordnance was in prospect.

The accounts end in 1711, so it is not known if there were any
further developments in this direction. The end of the war in 1713,
and with it the need for guns for the Crown, would make the
production of small castings and pig iron more likely. It certainly
seems that Ashburnham furnace had a capacity that was impressive
by Wealden standards. William Ashburnham himself claimed in 1708
that the furnace would produce over 500 tons of pig a year under his
own management.[28] That this was not too far-fetched is shown by the
totals of 458 and 460 tons produced by his tenants in 1710 and 1711

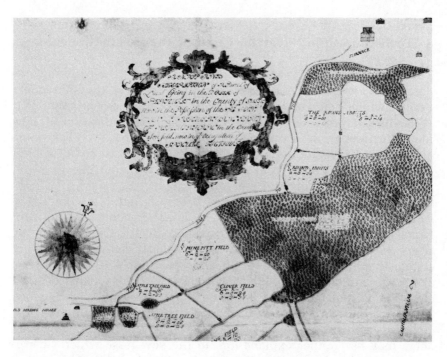

Fig.37 Ashburnham ironworks in 1717 (ESRO ASH 4385). The furnace appears to
occupy the southerly of the two working areas traced on the ground. The 'Old boreing
house' (lower left) is the site previously and subsequently used as a forge (Ashburnham
Upper forge) (photograph: East Sussex Record Office, Lewes, reproduced by permission
of the Rev J. D. Bickersteth).

respectively. The post-war market could not accommodate such output, and in the 1717 list Ashburnham is shown to produce 350 tons annually, still a very large figure for a Wealden furnace. This output contrasts with the figures for Robertsbridge and Waldron, 120 and 150 tons respectively. Even Heathfield produced considerably less: 226, 164 and 253 tons in the 1708, 1709 and 1710 campaigns.[29]

What emerges from this episode is that even in wartime one of the largest furnaces in the Weald could only be let with some difficulty. It is not surprising therefore that other landowners fared as badly, or indeed worse, in their attempts to find tenants. There is a parallel at Robertsbridge, when the furnace was in estate hands in 1703, producing guns. John Gilbert, the Countess of Leicester's steward, commented to the London agent on the possibility of a lease to Western. He appears to have had no other takers in prospect, and finally accepted that the estate had to continue with direct operation, if only to use up stocks of materials. Indeed these were virtually unsaleable, so well were the other Sussex furnaces said to be provided.[30]

3   To the Seven Years' War: the varying fortunes of the ironmasters

The Fuller list of 1717 is a useful starting point when considering how change and contraction affected the industry over the subsequent period, which may conveniently be divided at the Seven Years' War (1756–63). It provides the only comprehensive indication of how many furnaces were in action until Weale's list of 1787.[31] Forges are also covered in pamphlets of 1736 and 1750, but as some of their entries appear to derive from the list of 1717, it is not certain how far they resulted from current observation.

The ten Wealden furnaces for which output figures are entered in 1717 were all operating in the next decades. There are in addition four furnaces for which no tonnages are given in this list. One, Hawkhurst, receives no further mention and was probably a victim of the end of purchasing by the government after the peace of 1713. Coushoplea, Pounsley and Pippingford all appear on Budgen's map of 1724; Coushoplea had been referred to as a pot-house in 1712,[32] which immediately casts doubts on Budgen's accuracy, and nothing further is heard of this furnace, or of Pounsley. For Pippingford, however, there may be another explanation. In the new lease which Charles Manning took in 1717, there is an endorsement allowing him to cut timber for repairs, explaining the lack of output in that year. A puzzling part of the Pippingford story is the second furnace, making pig iron, which seems from the archaeological indications to have superseded the furnace which cast guns. Charles Manning died in 1718, and it is not known to whom the lease was assigned. Whoever it was could have abandoned ordnance production and built what Budgen named the 'New Furnace' on his map of 1724. It had a short life, for no structures appear on a map of Ashdown Forest dated 1744.[33]

Of the 13 forges in the 1717 list, Chingley, Bivelham, Burwash, Etchingham, Glaziers (Brightling), Hawksden, Westfield, Woodcock (Johnson's), Abinger (Dibble's) and Tinsley (Gale's) continued in use.[34] Etchingham is known from a Fuller account to have worked until 1729 and Chingley was tenanted in 1726.[35] For Eridge forge there is no later mention, apart from Budgen's map of 1724, and both Darvel and the unprovenanced forge of Lord Montague disappear from the record as mysteriously as they entered it.

A list of 1736 continues the story. Of the forges in production in 1717, five (Bibleham, Brightling, Burwash, Hawksden and Westfield) again appear with their tonnages. Chingley is mentioned without a figure. Barden and Maresfield were in production, having been omitted 20 years before: the latter had been leased to Ambrose Galloway, the Lewes ironmonger, in 1717.[36] It is in the Surrey entries that the 1736 list is confused. As in 1717 it included the forges of Johnson, Gale and Dibble. The first two are likely to have been Woodcock and Tinsley, the third Abinger. However, in 1736 Woodcock and 'Tenchley' are also included, with tonnages, so it is assumed that the compiler in 1736 had access to the earlier list as well as to information of his own which he failed to collate. Four other forges, omitted from both records, are otherwise known to have worked intermittently. Birchden was certainly regarded as a forge in 1719, when it was leased with Hamsell furnace.[37] Pophole, Surrey, previously heard of in 1675, is marked by Budgen on the 1724 map and appears, fleetingly, in a 1750 list. The forge at Thursley – the 'Upper Hammer' – was leased in 1720: this had also been referred to, with another local forge, by Aubrey in 1673.[38] Robertsbridge Forge was operated by Sir Thomas Webster from 1724 to 1734 (Straker 1931a: 315). These examples of intermittent use illustrate the way in which forges could be rehabilitated without undue difficulty. Finery and chafery hearths could be repaired with far less expense and trouble than was the case with a blast furnace.[39]

The 1717 list, therefore, gives a good basis for the industry. Thereafter information comes from correspondence and from accounts, and relates particularly to furnaces, over a period when the number of forges again dwindled and their output became insignificant in national terms. The major sources for the mid-eighteenth century are the letters of the Fullers, who ran Heathfield furnace, and the accounts of the executors of William Harrison.[40] Although the latter cover a mere five years, beginning in 1745, Harrison's interests had been so extensive that insight is given into the working of much of the industry. He was involved at Brede, Conster, Hamsell and Lamberhurst (Gloucester) furnaces, and his partner at Conster, John Legas, ran Waldron furnace. Just before Harrison's death an arrangement was entered whereby he took Robertsbridge furnace, as joint tenant with William and George Jewkes (Straker 1931a: 315). Harrison was also in partnership with Legas at Westfield forge, and ran the forges at Bibleham and Hawksden on his own account. As the Fullers and Harrisons subcontracted for each other, their records interlock. The Fullers' correspondence also refers frequently to the Jewkes, as it does to Ashburnham furnace, which was still part of the Crowley interest.[41]

These sources show how the ironmasters became still more reliant on castings. Production of guns for the Office of Ordnance receives particular stress, due to the rewards and the risks involved. But this aspect of the trade was largely concentrated on times of war, leaving many years when other outlets or products provided business. Indeed, wartime ordnance production was an encouraging addition to the regular trades of most of the Wealden furnaces: only a few could afford to concentrate on guns all the time, and even in wartime military orders could not be relied upon to provide consistent work. Nevertheless, casting for the Ordnance Office was an attractive gamble. There are few figures for the profitability of this business, and even less chance of any comparison with making other goods. The Fullers found that their work in 1745–6, of which much was for the Ordnance, gave a profit of £1,181 17s 6d on an outlay of £4,775. There are references in the Fuller letters which suggest that margins could even reach 30–40 per cent. However, the risks were such that results were most uneven: in 1756 Heathfield furnace was said to have gained £2,058 and in the following year to have lost £957.[42]

Despite the uncertainties, there was no lack of takers for Ordnance Office contracts, and Wealden ironmasters complained when their local rivals appeared to be receiving more than their share of work. In 1757 an outsider, Thomas Pryce of Neath, offered to cast 150 tons of guns, part of a Fuller contract, having heard of difficulties in fulfilling an order at Heathfield. A Staffordshire ironmaster, John Churchill, leased Robertsbridge in 1754, produced guns there for the Ordnance until the end of the war in 1763, and acted as sub-contractor for a Welsh ironmaster, Robert Morgan of Carmarthen, between 1761 and 1763.[43]

Crown contracts brought their difficulties, namely a combination of quality requirements which eighteenth-century technology was hard pressed to meet, and methods of administration which starved the producer of cash until orders had been met in every particular.

The control of quality took the form of inspection and proof at Woolwich. The results were anxiously awaited, and comments about proof form a recurrent theme in the Fuller correspondence.[44] The more spectacular failures were the result of rigorous tests which, as John Fuller commented to his agent, Samuel Remnant, in 1742, involved guns being fired twice with a double charge. Failure during proof was commonly caused by voids in the casting, of the kind revealed in the examination of the Pippingford gun.[45] In some cases these voids showed in the surface of the gun, and such pieces were rejected before they even reached proof. Sometimes the use of molten iron as a patching medium appears to have been tolerated; a small number of flaws repaired in this way were acceptable on the thicker parts of the casting. 'Honeycomb' guns, copiously patched, were rejected, as was any gun with weaknesses in the thin metal near the muzzle. On occasion founders attempted to repair flaws with lead, or even with screws or riveted patches (Jackson and De Beer 1973: 23–4). These pieces may have been saleable in the merchant market, but they would not pass scrutiny at Woolwich.

Founders went to great lengths to prevent unevenness in the castings, by ensuring that the furnace produced metal which would flow easily into the mould. John Fuller believed that large castings could only be made after the furnace had run for some time: 'I do generally think the guns made at first of a blast are not so good as afterwards, by reason the metal is not hot enough to run quick.'[46]

In the early stages of a blast, therefore, founders preferred to cast pig iron or small items in simple moulds. At a later stage, flaws were minimized by incorporating a large gun-head in the mould. As casting was carried out with the mould in a vertical position, poor metal of low density would float up beyond the muzzle into the head, which would be sawn off. The judgment of the founder and the moulder was important: too small a head meant the risk of a flawed muzzle, which the Fullers' correspondence shows was a common fault. Too large a head wasted metal, which was crucial when large guns required quantities of iron approaching the capacity of the furnace. The sawn-off head was disposed of for refining, and was difficult to convert into bar iron owing to its poor quality, reflected by a price lower than for pig.[47]

Great attention was paid by the Ordnance examiners to the bore of guns, made uneven by contemporary methods. Boring-mill design

had altered little since the sixteenth century and the long unsupported boring bar was free to bend as the cutter-head followed
irregularities in the interior.[48] These could result from the displacement of the central core bar (the nowell bar) during casting. Guns were
also rejected for being beyond tolerance or 'too high' in diameter.[49]
Whatever the excuses, there is a chance that over-boring may have
been done deliberately. If the founder could go to the maximum
allowable diameter there would be a greater clearance or 'windage'
between shot and bore, reducing the pressures of the proof-charge
within the gun.

Apart from faults in manufacture which affected the serviceability
of guns, the mid-eighteenth century sources record defects which
appear to have led to adverse comment rather than outright rejection.
Variations in weight occurred in guns of the same nominal length and
bore. It was, for example, commented that the Harrisons' pieces were
often heavier than those of the Fullers, whose lighter guns would be
more attractive for naval service. In addition, the outward appearance
of guns could vary, for moulds could only be used once, and each was
made using a 'draft' or 'strickle-board' to position the tapers and the
rings. Boards were often borrowed: in 1737 Fuller had a draft for a
9-pounder, 9ft 6in (2.89m) long, from Harrison, having previously lent
the latter a 6-pounder pattern.[50] Many drafts existed, because each
type of gun – 6-pounder, 9-pounder and the rest – might be ordered in
different lengths: 6-pounders, for example, were made 9ft, 8ft 6in, or
8ft long (see fig.38).

Water shortage became a critical problem when founders were
under pressure from the Ordnance Office to complete their orders. On
occasion, to finish a contract, the water wheels were used as tread-
mills: an early example appears in the accounts for Waldron furnace
in 1695–6, when five men were hired to tread the wheel for 12 days
and 11 nights.[51] This costly expedient is recorded on various occasions during the eighteenth century. In 1743 the wheels at Beckley,
Robertsbridge and Waldron were worked by foot and in 1759 payments were made at Ashburnham for treading the wheel.[52] There are
hints of more permanent means of alleviating the problem. At
Heathfield there is a series of holding ponds, although it is not known
when they were built. John Fuller wrote to Samuel Remnant in 1731
that he was 'going to erect an engine to raise water' to power his
boring mill. There is no clue as to the type of device he planned,
whether a horse gin or a Newcomen atmospheric steam engine. There
is no evidence of any actual installation, but in 1742 he built a new
boring house to re-use water from the tail-race of the furnace wheel.[53]

Difficulties in keeping furnaces in operation were compounded by

Fig.38   Eighteenth-century 24-pounder gun on the Embankment outside the Tower of London (a), with monogram of John Fuller on the trunnion (b) (both plates Crown Copyright, reproduced by permission of the Controller of Her Majesty's Stationery Office).

the problems inherent in Ordnance Office business. Orders varied greatly in their composition, sometimes comprising a range of sizes of guns, in other cases a uniform batch. The latter could raise particular difficulties if the pieces were all to be large, for a campaign was best run by starting with small guns and proceeding to the largest, as the capacity of the hearth grew with the erosion of the lining. Thus an order which consisted only of large guns forced the founder to produce other goods, even pig iron, until the furnace was in a state to make 24- or 32-pounders weighing two tons or more. Occasionally even larger pieces were required: in 1745 John Legas warned Samuel Remnant of the notice he would need to set up for the production of 42-pounders; these could weigh as much as 5,500lb, amounting to 6,000lb of metal allowing for the gun head.[54] The ideal progression from small objects to large was interrupted by the need to replace guns which failed inspection or proof. It was not always considered worthwhile to cast spares during the production of a batch, for if all passed proof the extra guns might be difficult to dispose of. Spare small guns could be sold to the merchant trade, larger pieces of common size could be kept for a future order, but those of unusual proportions risked lying at the furnace. Changing the order of casting brought much complaint, for the height at which metal was tapped from the hearth had to be altered, as had the floor level in the casting vault. As Fuller remarked in 1747, 'You do not know the difficulty of near bottoming the vault and looking out the 6-pounder tackling to make one gun'.[55]

These difficulties were linked with the problems of securing payment from the Office of Ordnance until a complete order had passed proof. There were frequent complaints about this practice, which faced the founder with the entire cost of producing a batch of guns. It could be particularly onerous if a few guns failed proof, but could not be replaced due to water shortage. There are, however, suggestions that on occasion staged payments were made, for in the Fuller correspondence in 1731 it appears that some founders, notably William Harrison, had been treated in this way.

By the middle of the eighteenth century it had become common to ease these problems by splitting orders, sub-contracting according to the casting capacity of different furnaces at a particular time. For example, in 1730 when Harrison needed extra guns Fuller undertook to produce them. He also offered to cast for Harrison 6-pounders which Sir Thomas Webster had failed to make at Beech furnace. In 1740 when Fuller was unable to complete a batch after guns had been rejected, Jewkes, who was by then operating Robertsbridge, agreed to produce the outstanding pieces, for which Fuller sent him the equipment.[56] The sub-contractor appears to have received 90 per cent of the price obtained for the guns by the founder who initially secured the order.[57] This extended outside the Weald when the Fullers corresponded with Philip Soan of Sowley, Hampshire, over the possibility of sharing contracts. In 1746 Fuller offered Soan his spare 6-pounders, and in 1746 and 1749 he offered to make any larger guns for which Soan might receive orders.[58]

Once guns were cast, the problems of transportation could further frustrate the founder anxious to secure proof and payment. The furnaces distant from the sea, notably Heathfield, were hindered by poor roads. Transport of large pieces was regarded as virtually impossible between November and March, and for the smaller items there were higher carriage charges in the winter.[59] The southern furnaces therefore sent guns by sea to London. Ashburnham products were shipped from Hastings and the Harrisons sent guns cast at Brede and Conster through Rye. The scale of William Harrison's operations required long-term hire of several ships, shown in his executors' papers as carrying iron to London in 1745–6.[60] But at times even the products of the southerly furnaces were sent overland, for long delays were encountered in embarking guns in wartime due to risks in transit. The Fullers complained in 1732 that masters of ships carrying guns would only sail if their crews could be given immunity from being pressed into naval service, and in 1748 John Legas explained to Samuel Remnant how 80 tons of guns could only leave Rye when the Hastings patrol was able to make the route secure.[61] Such problems gave added incentive for the improvement of the overland routes. Some progress had been made in the seventeenth century towards extending the navigable length of the Medway to Yalding, and in the eighteenth century barges were loaded at Brandbridge.[62] Yet in the mid-eighteenth century much iron was carried entirely by road to Maidstone, even from distant furnaces. In 1760 guns were taken from Ashburnham to Maidstone by way of Hurst Green and Marden, implying that standards of road surfacing had improved to the point where it was no longer necessary to use the upper Medway navigation.[63]

The key person at the London end of the iron trade was the ironmaster's agent. Much is heard of Samuel Remnant, who dealt not only with the Fullers but with the Harrison-Legas partnership. It was his function to negotiate Ordnance orders: he was sometimes suspected of not doing all he could to facilitate these, or of not pressing for prompt payment on completion. The Fullers feared that they were apt to be left out when orders were being shared, and for this reason they terminated Remnant's agency in 1750, taking on Jefferson Miles instead.[64] An agent also provided a link with other outlets for iron. He could sell guns which had failed proof, and Remnant even had an air furnace of his own in which he could melt unsaleable pieces.

As military orders could not provide work sufficient to keep furnaces employed, even in wartime, it is important to outline the wider market, on which ironmasters still relied. One option was to sell guns into the merchant trade, and some pieces so destined were rejects from Ordnance Office orders. The ethics of this were questionable, and in 1729 Fuller told Remnant that any gun unfit for the Crown should be destroyed. Such high-mindedness did not last, for after a disastrous inspection in 1733, in which most of a batch had been found to be over-bored, Fuller enjoined Remnant to 'look for some chap(man)' to whom the guns might be sold, in the way that founders such as Harrison disposed of rejects. Although the Fullers at times appeared to regard the merchant trade with some disdain, they did a considerable amount of such business. In the years 1708–11 merchants took about half their output, and in the 1730s John Fuller was considering setting up a commercial gun-wharf of his own. In 1738 a Mr Chatfield was selling Fuller's guns, a wharf was being actively sought, and in 1740 pieces were being proved at Heathfield for the general trade.[65]

If Fuller's approach to the wider arms trade was sometimes hesitant, the same could not be said of William Harrison. He produced quantities of guns for the East India Company, notably through the 1720s, and after his death in 1745 his executors' accounts detail stocks of merchant guns at Hamsell furnace and consignments that had been sent to Samuel Remnant from Gloucester furnace in the years 1741–4.[66]

There was also an export trade, of which much can be learned from the Fuller correspondence. An early case occurred in 1736–7, when guns in stock were offered to the King of Portugal. In the 1750s there are three instances: an order for the Queen of Hungary in 1752 comprised over 100 tons, over which Fuller hesitated: he feared that their non-standard bore would make rejected pieces difficult to sell to merchants. But an order for the King of Sardinia followed, for 130 tons of guns for cash on delivery in the Thames, and Fuller grew so accustomed to producing guns with 'French bore' that in 1754 he was only too anxious to sell to the King of Naples and Sicily.[67]

Most furnaces also cast ammunition, both for the Crown and for the wider market. Shot was useful in that it could use 'coarse' ores and be cast early in the furnace blast, before the iron was suitable for guns. Also there could be casts for shot during a campaign when ordnance orders were awaited or while patterns or other tackle were being borrowed. Some furnaces cast shot in quantity: John Legas used Waldron largely for this purpose in the 1740s, his activities being noted by John Fuller, who regarded Waldron as the furnace with the highest costs in the Weald.[68] The skills were not necessarily simple. Moulds had to be cast, as can be seen at Waldron, where about 900 pairs were made in 1744–6.[69] Shot could fail inspection by the Ordnance at Woolwich, as happened in 1744 when Waldron products were refused because of poor (presumably rough) moulds. There were many varieties of ammunition, not only shot but hollow shells. The latter were made by the Pelhams' employees when Waldron was in hand at the beginning of the century, and by works in the Harrison-Legas partnership in later decades.

Outside the arms market some vestige of the pig iron trade remained, for founders casting guns still produced pig in the early part of a campaign. Hence the Fullers' accounts show sales of pig to Ambrose Galloway at Maresfield forge between 1720 and 1737.[70] But local forges were dwindling, and their need for pig iron sank still further. Many were refining cast-iron scrap: gun-heads, despite their poor quality, were much used, and the general circulation of scrap reflected the increasing range of cast-iron goods which furnaces were making.

The production of such castings did not compare with the activities of the West Midlands founders, but it grew in diversity, as inventories and correspondence show. Ships' ballast was made at Ashburnham; cast-iron wheels were made there and at Gloucester furnace; stoves, grates and anvils were cast as well as plates for furnaces and lime-kilns.[71] Cast-iron pipes were a promising line: in 1729 an enquiry was made of John Fuller on behalf of the New River Company, and information was obtained from Robert Diamond, the Ashburnham founder, about pipes he had cast for the York Buildings Company 8ft long, 1in thick, and 15in in diameter. On the basis of this and of information about pipes cast by Sir Thomas Webster at Beech or Robertsbridge, Fuller quoted 17s per cwt in the summer, 18s in the winter, comparable with the £16–18 per ton charged for guns. Pipes, cylinders, and rollers were eminently suitable products for gun-founders, in that such objects would be cast in pits ('vaults') in the same way as ordnance. The Harrisons were casting cylinders in the years 1741–4, perhaps for steam engines or for pumps. Rollers were a considerable trade, as is to be expected in a period of agricultural improvement: the Fullers made a range, a normal roller 6ft long and 3ft in diameter selling at 16–18s a cwt, with longer examples 7ft by 4ft commanding an exceptional 21s a cwt, due, it was stated, to the problems of moulding and lifting. Sugar-crushing rollers were also made, at a time when the Fullers had interests in Jamaica plantations.[72]

The development of air furnaces was important for the production of small castings: these used draught induced by a flue, they could burn coal, and they enabled founders to remelt scrap castings. Harrison had an air furnace built at Hamsell in 1745, but he and Jewkes may have been using one as early as 1734, when they were importing cast scrap. The danger for the Weald was that air furnaces were suitable for urban use, and castings were soon made outside the traditional ironmaking areas. Fuller showed how a European trade in scrap castings was developing and how air-works in London used old guns imported from Spain, where they were plentiful enough to be found in use as street-posts. They also used pig iron imported from the colonies, from which they cast shot.[73]

4   Brief revival: the Seven Years' War and its aftermath

The last years of the Seven Years' War, before the peace of 1763, formed the final major period of activity in the Wealden industry. Despite all the problems of catering for the needs of the Ordnance Office, furnaces were well occupied by the arms trade, and there was some modest outside interest and a revival of old works. The Crowleys remained at Ashburnham, their connection strengthened by the marriage of Theodosia Crowley to William Ashburnham in 1757. John Churchill of Hints, Staffordshire, had taken Robertsbridge in 1754. There he used an air furnace and is said to have shipped in coal for its fuel. In the west John Butler appears to have revived Fernhurst: Straker (1931a: 426) notes that Butler had been described as a farmer without experience of the industry, but in fact a John Butler of Fernhurst was supplied with guns by the Fullers 25 years before. This suggests that he was at least a dealer in arms. Despite the local tradition, Butler does not appear to have supplied the Ordnance Office, but he may, of course, have operated as a subcontractor.[74]

An important revival was that of three furnaces in the East Grinstead area. One, Gravetye, was worked by William Clutton. He appears in the accounts of Ralph Knight, the carrier, who transported guns from Gravetye to Woolwich. This furnace does not appear in any seventeenth- or eighteenth-century list, so was probably an entirely new structure. However, Clutton was bankrupt in 1762 and in that year Eade and Wilton sent guns from Gravetye to London, as did Ralph Clutton and Samuel Durrant in 1763. By 1768 Raby and Rogers were operating Gravetye in conjunction with Warren furnace. This was a revival of a sixteenth-century site, but so long a period of disuse implies a total rebuilding. Alexander Master and Edward Raby appear to have leased Warren from the Evelyns about 1758, although it is not possible to say with certainty when the rebuilding took place.[75] The third furnace, Mill Place, had been worked up to 1664. In 1763 it was used by Ralph Clutton and Samuel Durrant, but it is not known what they made there. All three furnaces had been abandoned by the time Weale made his list in 1787. Of these men, a good deal is known of Jonathan Eade: with Wilton he supplied the Ordnance Office between 1756 and 1768, but earlier, in 1753, they had obtained small guns from the Fuller furnace at Heathfield, supplied to their Thames-side premises at Wapping. John Fuller claimed to make a loss on the smallest of these guns; 'Next year', he wrote wryly, 'I propose to make iron tobacco pipes.' Some of Fuller's failed 12-pounders were also sold to the partners: it is not stated whether they were re-melting the guns in an air furnace or taking them for resale.[76]

The year 1763 did indeed mark a final downturn in the fortunes of the Wealden industry. Some ironmasters, such as Edward Raby, retained a place in the merchant trade, but the general fortunes of local producers were aptly illustrated in 1777 when a friend wrote to William Burrell, the historian, 'Darvel Wood has supplied with wood a furnace for casting iron ... occupied by the owner or its tenants till the last peace with France and Spain. It is now in decay and it is feared the manufactory at Carron will prevent its revival.'[77]

The number of furnaces was to diminish, until the last cast at Ashburnham in 1813. Other disappearances, besides Darvel, were Brede, of which nothing is heard after 1766, Warren and Gravetye, about 1774, and Heathfield in 1788. At Ashburnham the level and type of activity altered in 1764. Whereas there had been six blasts over the five years 1758–63, there were only five in the next eleven years, and the proportion of guns to other products began to fall in 1764.

It was indeed before 1763 that the outside challenge to the Wealden furnaces had become clear, but the volume of work during the Seven Years' War had disguised this. The conservatism of the Office of Ordnance had been a safeguard, for there was a preference for the proven traditional suppliers. Inroads were being made into the merchant trade by founders from the Midlands and Wales: after 1763 this was to have a significant effect on the remaining market open to the south-eastern producers and few guns were cast at Heathfield thereafter. The entry of Scottish ordnance was to be even more significant. From 1764 Carron guns undercut Wealden prices, hitherto £19 per ton, owing to the use of coke, which conferred a major cost advantage.[78] Carron prices, £14 per ton, were matched only by Eade, Raby and Wilton. Their ability to do so may have stemmed from their use of newly rebuilt furnaces. It seems less likely that they were using coal for smelting, as has been tentatively suggested: the quantities recorded as brought by Robert Knight from London to the furnaces seem too small, unless there were other carriers involved. The coal was more likely to have been used by Edward Raby and his son Alexander for casting brass guns, as they were certainly doing in 1770–1.[79] It might also have been used for an air furnace, but it is not certain whether one existed at the East Grinstead works at the time.

The initial Carron success was short-lived, for the guns failed to withstand Ordnance proof, for whose rigour the Wealden founders now had reason to be thankful. For a brief interval in the 1770s some hope returned to the Weald, to disappear at the end of the decade. It was then that the Carron Company perfected naval guns, the 'Carronades', bored from the solid with an accuracy, finish and economy in weight which traditional methods could not match. The last series of Fuller letters provide eloquent comment on the changes in confidence among Wealden founders.[80] After the initial loss of orders, the failure of Carron guns in 1773 appeared to vindicate Wealden skills. The Ordnance took five pieces from Sussex to compare with five from Carron; of the latter all burst before ten firings, while all the Sussex guns survived 45. The hope of a return of the trade was seen as an opportunity to insist on improved terms for future Ordnance contacts, notably, as Rose Fuller wrote, in methods of proof and payment. But the revival was limited in scale and did not last.

Failures and closures came rapidly towards the end of the century. Churchill and Tapsell were bankrupt by 1773, leaving only three furnaces in active production by 1787; by 1800 Ashburnham was the only survivor. For Ashburnham there survives a run of accounts from 1757 to 1793, followed by more brief papers running to the closure of the furnace in 1813 and of the forge in 1826.[81] Here, the shift away from the production of guns to a wider variety of castings, apparent from 1763, continued in the 1770s. Even so, some guns were still being bored in the 1780s, for the merchant and overseas markets. Campaigns became less frequent: Weale notes that at Ashburnham and Heathfield materials were collected sufficient to run only for four to six months every two years. Output was appropriate to purely local needs, not only for castings, but for pig to be converted into bar at the surviving local forges. Heathfield made no guns at all in a six-month blast starting in December 1769, virtually all output being in pig iron.[82] Similarly, at Ashburnham the production of pig iron was significant from 1785, with 203 tons weighed in 1789 and 280 tons in 1792. Glaziers Forge was leased out in 1785 to a tenant who undertook to take pig from Ashburnham, and at some time about 1790 Ashburnham Forge, used throughout the eighteenth century as a boring mill, was restored to its former use. Nevertheless, the local wrought iron trade did not necessarily rely on the blast furnaces. Scrap as a source was increasingly plentiful, and imported pig was seen as a worthwhile possibility. For example, when Samuel Baker took the tenancy of Hawksden forge in 1766 he claimed that American pig could be economically converted in Sussex forges. The import prices appear to have been generally known, for ten years earlier Beard of Lewes had sought locally for old sows for refining, at 'American prices'.[83]

During the final half-century of the Wealden industry alternative and sometimes competing uses appeared for raw materials. Of some interest is the form in which iron ore was sold. At the end of the 1780s there are references in the Ashburnham accounts to the sale of ore, calcined in kilns. It was intended for an abrasive polish – 'Tripoli' – which was partly composed of iron ore.[84]

Of greater significance was the relationship between woodland management and the declining industry. The longer-lived furnaces and forges were still surrounded by coppiced woodlands. The Harrison papers contain useful lists of woods and their owners around Conster, Brightling and Waldron, and the Ashburnham accounts show the woods available on and around the estate. At certain times during the eighteenth century there appears to have been overprovision of wood. An early pointer is the comment by John Gilbert at Robertsbridge in 1703, when he found it impossible to sell surplus materials to his neighbours. In 1766 Samuel Baker noted the extent to which woods were grubbed out when prices were low. But at certain times, notably when wartime demand for iron was high, there were still some signs of the old overlaps in collection areas. In 1745 the Jewkes at Robertsbridge and the Harrisons at Brede and Conster were competing for wood from the intervening ground.[85]

Other uses of wood were more consistently buoyant and landowners altered their coppicing cycles to produce hop-poles and billets for use in lime-kilns. Hop-poles were said to dominate the Weald's wood trade by the middle of the century, and lime-kilns were built in many areas: the Ashburnham estate had quantities of chalk carried from the Downs to be burned with local wood. Brick-kilns, also, used quantities of wood which would previously have been cut younger for conversion to charcoal.

5   Aspects of the technology of the last Wealden furnaces

The main features of smelting technology are considered in Chapter 10. However, this brief section notes certain points of furnace practice particularly relevant to the problems of Wealden ironmasters in the eighteenth century.

It is difficult to be certain what technical changes were incorporated in Wealden furnaces over this period, for no hearths have remained for comparison with the sixteenth-century example excavated at Chingley or with survivors in other parts of the country. Furnace stacks may have grown larger in plan: Pippingford was a good deal bigger than Panningridge or Chingley, and would not be out of place beside a furnace such as Rockley (Yorkshire) or Charlcott (Shropshire). Blowing arrangements followed tradition; bellows 5m long would be little larger than their sixteenth-century forebears. Indeed, apart from hearth profiles, there were few developments in furnace design and equipment anywhere in Britain until late in the eighteenth century, and there is no sign that innovations such as cylinder blowers appeared in the Weald before its industry collapsed.

Any results of improvements might be expected in daily tonnages, in the capacity of the hearth to hold quantities of metal sufficient for large guns, in the length of campaigns, and in yields. However, tonnages must to some extent reflect the kind of work undertaken. Casting pig iron was a relatively simple procedure, with less likelihood of delay on the casting floor than when numerous small moulds had to be filled by ladling from the fore-hearth. The available figures for daily output are unfortunately scattered, and the known amounts vary widely. At one end of the scale there are some very modest figures for the production of pig iron at Waldron furnace between 1706 and 1716. Over four blasts for which records are adequate, the daily output averaged a few pounds short of 1 ton a day. This was despite the fact that the furnace was rebuilt twice within the period.[86] By contrast, Waldron's production in 1744–5 and 1754–6 was 1.4 tons a day in two campaigns when shot and shot-moulds formed virtually all the output. The furnace had again been rebuilt in 1744, suggesting that good design as well as good management was responsible for this higher rate of production. It may have been mediocre by Midlands standards, but in the Weald it was a reasonable amount.[87]

To take another early eighteenth century figure, to compare with Waldron, we can use William Ashburnham's estimate of 500 tons a year for his furnace.[88] An exaggerated claim would fit the circumstances, but if a furnace were in blast for a calender year the daily figure, 1.37 tons, would not be high by national standards. The 1717 list, of course shows a lower total, 350 tons, but we have no idea of the length of blast to which this related. There are later figures for Ashburnham, to compare with the claim of 1708. Taking six blasts, from 1757 to 1763, the average output emerges as a disappointing 1.1 tons per day. By contrast, tonnage at Heathfield does seem to have been capable of improvement. The good run of figures over the 1720s and 1730s average 1.45 tons a day over eight campaigns. This was creditable enough, but in 1770 there is an even better figure of 1.86 tons.[89] This furnace had been built as a completely new venture in 1693: its contemporary, Gloucester furnace, was also producing at a high rate by Wealden standards in the 1740s, at 1.4 tons a day. High figures could be achieved when large guns were being cast: the practice was to hold metal in the hearth, allowing accumulation over a matter of two or even three days. This technique had been developed by the middle of the seventeenth century, for in 1664 George Browne had described how he could hold four tons in the hearth. There is no sign that this was improved upon in the Weald in the subsequent century.[90]

Lengths of campaign indicate competence of operation, but all kinds of variables, hardly connected with the furnace or its operators, could curtail smelting. It was common for blasts to last for more than 200 days in the eighteenth-century Weald, and there were some which were much longer. Gloucester furnace (fig.39) seems to have had a remarkable ability to survive in blast, no doubt due to ample water provision from the River Teise. It appears that one campaign lasted from 25 September 1741 until 29 October 1744, and its successor ran from 10 January 1745 until 9 August 1746. These are really remarkable runs, particularly the first, but they do appear to be genuine, without any hint of breaks in operation.[91]

Competence of furnace design might also be reflected in the yield of iron, in terms of ore and charcoal consumption. Unfortunately, few surviving eighteenth century records are helpful in this respect. The Pelham, Fuller and Ashburnham accounts all give insufficient information about stock levels at the beginning and end of blasts: this is a problem which has bedevilled studies of furnace performance in earlier centuries; only in the cases of Robertsbridge and Panningridge has it been overcome. The only way to alleviate the problem is to average the yield for a series of years, so that uncertainties over stock assume less significance. This can be done for Ashburnham from 1761, soon after the date whence systematic blast accounts survive.[92] The figures are included in Appendix 3.

The Harrison records also suffer from insufficient information about

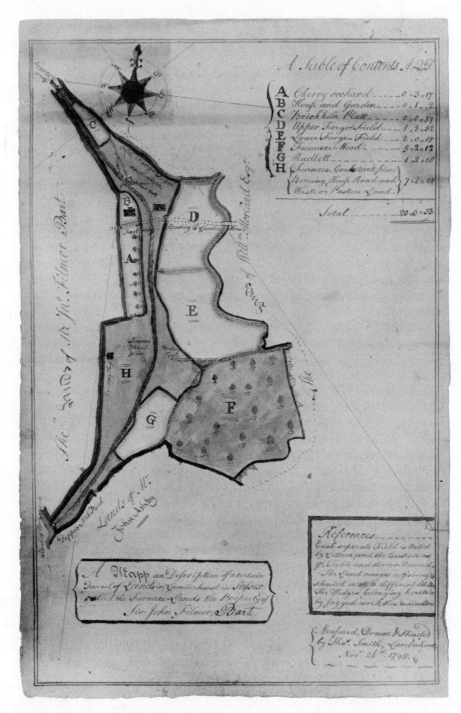

Fig.39   The site of Lamberhurst (Gloucester) furnace in 1795 (KAO U120/P15) (photograph: Kent Archives Office, Maidstone).

stock levels, although the figures for the 1744–6 blasts at Waldron, Brede and Conster are worth including in Appendix 3.

Furnace design and the competence of the founder is unlikely to be the whole answer to differences in yield. Variation in the quality of ore is as likely to be significant: in some areas, notably around Heathfield, many different kinds of ore could be extracted from one working, but the ranges did vary considerably, and it would be of great interest to sample what ore is available in the vicinity of the four furnaces referred to in the Harrison papers. A further possible complication is variation in load sizes. It is often assumed that loads were equal, by convention, across the Weald. This may indeed be so, but a note in John Fuller's Heathfield furnace book of 1745–7 does go to such lengths to define wagon loads and sack loads in terms of bushels that some local variation may be implied.[93]

6 Conclusion

With hindsight brought by the rapid decline of the Wealden industry after the Seven Years' War, it can be seen that the seeds of insecurity had been set far back in the seventeenth century, when the market for Wealden pig iron entered its long-term decline. The realities may have been disguised for some observers by the periodic revivals in the ordnance trade, and it is true that for some producers gun casting produced a good living in peace as well as in war. That this was the case is something of a tribute to their skill, encouraged by the continued patronage of the Ordnance Office, which clung to the suppliers it knew, and only slowly adopted the products of other areas. It is the closure of forges in the latter half of the seventeenth century and the small output of those which remained in 1717 which really make the contrast with the sixteenth century industry. There is no sign that Wealden ironmasters had experimented with furnace design. The incentive to innovate had been blunted rather than strengthened by the intractable problems of sparse and varied ores and unpredictable water supplies. Furnace costs were high, and could only be absorbed within the prices obtainable for ordnance. When other regions were successful in reducing their gun prices, this last bastion was broken. These points indicate how reduced a part iron production played in the eighteenth-century Wealden economy, particularly in the employment of labour and woodlands. By the mid-eighteenth century, even in time of war, furnaces were relatively uncommon, and there were many former iron-working districts where their operation and supply were but a memory, where coppices had long been used for other purposes, and where ponds had either been drained, their bays in decay, or their water used for corn mills.

It was their very rarity which drew attention to the last works, recorded by Weale when preparing his book on the iron industry of Britain in 1787. By this time even the arms trade had gone elsewhere, and works such as Ashburnham only survived to serve a vestigial local demand, itself largely supplied from outside.

NOTES

1. For published versions of this list see Lower 1866 and Parsons 1882. Insufficient stress has been given to 1667 as the most likely date of compilation (see, particularly, Straker 1931a: 61–3). Cattell 1973: 192–3, argues strongly for 1667 as the correct date. The 1717 list is in ESRO SAS RF15/25, f.9, and Hulme 1928–9.
2. As will be seen in the gazetteer, no clear indications of either a furnace or a forge site have been found in Battle Park. Straker's view that traces of ironworking have been obscured by the development of gunpowder mills remains no more than speculation.
3. The Dibble family have been located at Abinger by Mr J. Pettitt. Jeremy Johnson leased Woodcock in 1667 (ESRO SAS Gage 43/52) and lands near the forge were mortgaged by him in 1691 (*ibid.* 43/58). The Gales operated Tinsley forge in the seventeenth century, but the site lies a few yards within Sussex. Further, a 'Tenchley' forge appears in the 1736 list in addition to 'Mr Gale's'. The reliability of the Kent/Surrey entries in the 1736 list is cast in question by its own compiler, who admits that he found four forges, of which 'Mr Gale's' is one, 'in an old list'. The problem of identification is made more tantalizing by the record of the supply of pig iron, gunheads and cast items to Henry Gale by the Fullers between 1722 and 1735. ESRO SAS RE 15/7, fos.206–7, shows one delivery to Tinsley.
4. The lease is referred to in a letter to Alexander Courthope in 1663. (Courthope MSS 714–7: Mr Derek White has kindly made available copies of these papers, detached from the main collection at Lewes).
5. For example the Navy Board insisted in the 1670s and 1680s that Royal Dockyard anchor smiths use two-thirds Spanish iron (PRO ADM 106).
6. BL Add. MSS 33058, fos.81–90.
7. BL Harleian 1243, 92–3. For a review of the acceleration of iron imports in the seventeenth century see Hammersley 1972: 59.
8. ESRO SAS RF15/25: 28 Feb. 1737.
9. ESRO Dunn 47/4; Bell-Irving 1903: 177–9.
10. ESRO Dunn 27/2–6; 29/1–3, 16; 46/1–12; 47/1–11.
11. John Roberts was a noted founder, who branched out on his own. In 1677, after the end of the short joint lease of Socknersh, he took Robertsbridge works for 21 years (KAO U1500/T287/4). Although he leased the forge there, as well as the furnace, it was the latter which was more active at the end of the century (*ibid.* C173/1–10; C197/1).
12. Courthope MSS 714–7 (see n.4 above).
13. ESRO DH614, KAO U609/T3, ESRO DH611.
14. ESRO SAS RF15/25, 18 Mar. 1735, BL Add. MSS 33154, 33156. The production and destination of iron made at the Pelham works are considered in detail in Cattell 1973.
15. Hereford RO, Foley E/12/PF5/550; Sotheby lot 2282 (6 June 1966): articles of partnership between Wm Harrison and John Legas, 20 Nov. 1743; Guildhall 3736.

16. ESRO Glynde 1230, 3088, ESRO SAS Gage 43/52, 109, 148.
17. ESRO SAS Portman 538, 540; ESRO DH838.
18. This fragment of information appears in a Fuller accountant book: ESRO SAS RF15/26, f.337.
19. KAO U120/L1, C52/1, cf. Melling 1961: 97–9, PRO WO47/17 (19 Oct. 1695).
20. ESRO SAS RF4/11; RF15/1.
21. Ashdown Forest Conservators MSS; Crossley 1975c: 1–37. The 1696 document was discovered by Mr C. F. Tebbutt after the publication of the excavation report. ESRO Add. MSS 683.
22. ESRO Dunn 27/3, ESRO ASH B886, B983; Dunn 27/5.
23. ESRO ASH B1084.
24. Hereford RO Foley F/V1/B; E/12/PF5/550.
25. ESRO ASH 840–6. See also Flinn 1962: 100–1.
26. ESRO ASH 845 (5 Nov. 1705). There is no addressee, but a letter of 20 Apr. 1706 (846) shows correspondence with Hanbury in progress.
27. Hereford RO Foley (unclassified).
28. ESRO ASH 847.
29. ESRO SAS RF15/1.
30. KAO U1500/173, 6, 7, 9.
31. The list is in the Weale MSS, Science Museum Library, London; see Hodgkinson 1979.
32. WSRO PM47, ESRO SAS Portman 77.
33. ESRO Add. MSS 4084/4. The case for abandonment of ordnance production is strengthened by the Fullers' purchase of Manning's 'gun-tackle' in 1722 (ESRO SAS RF15/27).
34. Hulme 1928–9 prints the lists of 1736 and 1750.
35. ESRO SAS RF15/27; Burwash and Hawksden are among those obtaining pig from Heathfield furnace; KAO U409/T2.
36. ESRO SAS Gage 13/53.
37. BL Add. MSS 5681, f.452v.
38. Guildford Muniment Room (Surrey Arch. Soc.) LM 5/3/97; Bodleian MSS Aubrey 4: A Perambulation of Surrey (began 1673), f.138r. (Mr J. Pettitt has kindly drawn attention to this material.)
39. There is a full account for the cost of pulling down and rebuilding Heathfield furnace in 1723, amounting to £436 3s 11d (ESRO SAS RF15/26).
40. ESRO SAS RF15/25; Guildhall 3736, 6482, 6482a, 6483.
41. ESRO ASH 1815. The Crowleys worked Ashburnham and Darvel furnaces in the 1740s. ESRO SAS RF15/25 (4 Feb. 1744); see also Flinn 1962: 101.
42. ESRO SAS RF15/30, f.206r–207v. It should be noted that the word 'error' is written in by these figures. Very heavy stocking of charcoal in 1757 distorts the results, and it is not clear whether the figures for the year are complete.
43. ESRO SAS RF17/XV (8 Sept. 1757); L. J. Williams 1959: 42.
44. For proof returns see ESRO RF16/V/11, 15.
45. ESRO RF 15/25 (23 Oct. 1742); Crossley 1975c; pl. opp. p.28.
46. ESRO SAS RF15/25 (27 Jan. 1747).
47. c. £5/ton instead of £6 or more for pig.
48. See p.260. New boring houses were built at Heathfield (ESRO SAS RF15/25, 15 May 1742) and Ashburnham (ESRO ASH 1815: blast AN-1767), but there is no suggestion of anything but traditional methods being used.
49. ESRO SAS RF15/25 (15 Aug. 1751).
50. *Ibid.*, 22 Mar. 1737.
51. BL Add. MSS 33156.
52. ESRO SAS RF15/25 (15 Dec. 1743), ESRO ASH 1815 (blast AG).
53. ESRO SAS RF15/25 (27 July 1731, 15 May 1742).

54. Guildhall 6482: the maximum capacity of Ashburnham furnace in 1705 had been 5500 lb (ESRO ASH 845, 2 Apr. 1705).
55. ESRO SAS RF15/25 (27 Jan. 1747).
56. *Ibid.*, 13 Nov. 1730, 4 and 14 Oct. 1740.
57. ESRO SAS RF16/V/2. Stephen Fuller was paid 9s/cwt in 1757 by George Jewkes, who sold to the Ordnance Office at 10s/cwt.
58. *Ibid.*, 25 Aug. 1746, 18 Sept. 1846, 2 Sept. 1749.
59. *Ibid.*, 11 Sept. 1729; Guildhall 6482; ESRO ASH 1815 (blast AO).
60. Guildhall 3736.
61. ESRO SAS RF15/25 (29 June 1732); Guildhall 6482.
62. BL Egerton 2985, fos.113–14, ESRO SAS RF16/V/3.
63. ESRO ASH 1815.
64. ESRO SAS RF15/25 (11 Oct. 1750).
65. *Ibid.*, RF15/1; 8 May 1729; 16 Mar. 1733; 26 Aug. 1735; 9 May 1738; 27 Mar. 1740.
66. India Office MSS L/A9/1/5/11–12; Guildhall 3736.
67. ESRO SAS15/25 (17 Oct. 1736; 1 June 1752; 21 Dec. 1752). RF15/30; RF15/25 (30 July 1754).
68. ESRO SAS RF15/25 (11 Nov. 1749).
69. Guildhall 6482.
70. ESRO SAS RF15/27. See Saville 1982; 40 and table 1, for sales of pig iron by the Fullers, and table 2 (p.44) for names of local buyers.
71. ESRO ASH 1815; Guildhall 3736.
72. ESRO SAS RF15/25 (30 May 1729). Guildhall 3736; ESRO SAS RF15/25 (31 Oct. 1739). Also, Thomas Fuller, son of John Fuller (d.1744) was a sugar baker in London.
73. Guildhall 3736: Straker 1931a: 316, states that John Churchill used an air furnace at Robertsbridge after 1754; ESRO SAS RF15/25 (18 Mar. 1734, 19 Sept. 1735).
74. ESRO SAS RF15/25 (9 Sept. 1738).
75. PRO WO47: 52.
76. Breach 1903; Hodgkinson 1978b; ESRO SAS RF15/25, 16 Aug. 1753; 16 Jan. 1754; 5 Aug. 1754. Mr Hodgkinson has subsequently suggested to the author that the evidence for Ralph Clutton and Samuel Durrant actually casting guns at Mill Place rather than Gravetye is inconclusive.
77. BL Add. MSS 5679, f.161v.
78. Campbell 1961; 87ff.; PRO WO47/65, 66, 67.
79. PRO WO47: 76, 78; Alexander Raby gave up casting bronze ordnance at Warren and Gravetye in 1774 (*ibid.*, 47: 83).
80. ESRO RF/F/6/1; PRO WO47/81, 82.
81. ESRO ASH (nos.) 1815–1834.
82. ESRO SAS RF15/23.
83. ESRO Glynde 2771; ESRO SAS RF15/25 (3 Aug. 1754).
84. ESRO ASH 1817.
85. Guildhall 3736. For Robertsbridge see n.30 above. Guildhall 6482.
86. BL Add. MSS 33154.
87. Guildhall 3736.
88. ESRO ASH 847.
89. ESRO SAS RF15/26, RF15/23.
90. KAO TR1295/69.
91. Guildhall 3736.
92. *Ibid.*, ESRO ASH 1815.
93. ESRO SAS RF15/31.

Chapter 10

The archaeology and technology of the Wealden industry in the blast-furnace period

1 Introduction

(A) THE ORIGINS OF THE INDIRECT PROCESS

In the last 15 years fieldwork and excavations in Sussex and Kent have illuminated many aspects of the construction and use of early charcoal blast furnaces and forges. It is now possible to place results from the field alongside references in contemporary accounts, early descriptions of iron-smelting, and the details shown by Continental landscape painters of the period.

It will be necessary at the outset to show how the blast furnace operated and how it differed from the bloomery. When iron smelting is viewed on a European scale it can be seen that the blast furnace evolved from the bloomery, rather than forming a clear break in technology. In certain parts of Europe the shaft bloomery had a long history and reached a considerable size. In this type of furnace, iron ore and charcoal remained in contact at a high temperature for longer than in lower furnaces, so iron could attract carbon to a great extent. Because a high-carbon iron has a lower melting point than the normal bloom, in certain circumstances a liquid metal formed in the hearth. What might have begun as an accident was put to good use on the continent in the later Middle Ages, and cast iron became a regular product of the developing high furnace. It became possible to vary the process, making either blooms or cast iron by altering the proportions of charcoal and ore and by regulating the blast and temperature of the furnace.

Excavations have shown that these changes were taking place in Germany and Sweden in the fourteenth and fifteenth centuries. By the end of the fifteenth century many Continental ironworkers were experienced in cast iron production (Crossley 1981: 39–40).

The growth of consistent production of high-carbon iron from the blast furnace prompted secondary innovations. The founder's expertise developed as cast products grew in complexity. Mould-making for ordnance required great skill, which was developed for casting first in copper alloys and then in iron. A more fundamental innovation was the refining of the brittle cast iron into a wrought iron which the smith could forge. To do this it was necessary to remove carbon, so there evolved the finery hearth, in which a pig of iron was re-melted in oxidizing conditions where carbon was burnt out, producing a bloom. This was in turn hammered hot, using a water-powered tilt hammer, and reheated, either in the finery or in some districts in a second hearth, a chafery. In Sweden evidence has been found for the twelfth-century development of the finery, and literary references make it clear that it was in use in the middle of the fifteenth century elsewhere in Europe.

The evolution of the blast furnace on the Continent contrasts with its rapid introduction into the Weald at the end of the fifteenth century. Such archaeological evidence as there is suggests that high-shaft bloomery furnaces were not used in medieval England. In addition, the influx of foreign workers in the early sixteenth century suggests that alien skills were needed to develop a new process. Neither of these points conclusively prove that indigenous evolution did not happen, but the balance of information is at present against it (see Chapter 6, pp.113–14).

(B) CONTEMPORARY SOURCES

Literary and artistic sources for the early blast furnace and forge have long been known. We are now in a position to place these alongside the results of excavations in the Weald. Before this work began early methods were known from two Continental writers. In about 1460 an Italian, Antonio Averlino Filarète, produced a convincing account of a furnace and forge, probably in Tuscany (Crossley 1981: 39). It includes all the main elements familiar in sixteenth-century England. A good parallel is Nicholas Bourbon's description of French practice of 1517, which includes more detail, some indicating difficulties in the process which modern studies confirm (Straker 1931: 40–3). Early English descriptions come from the seventeenth century and later. Sir James Hope visited Barden furnace, Kent, in 1646, and his diary includes a valuable account of work at this guncasting establishment (Marshall 1958: 146–53). Edward Browne's description, written as part of a letter in 1660, is short, although it is accompanied by a simple sketch of the lines of a furnace.[1] In 1674 John Ray wrote a brief but useful account of furnace and forge practice, derived from information provided by Walter Burrell of Cuckfield (quoted in Straker 1931a: 44–6). To these must be added Swedenborg's description of Gloucester furnace, Lamberhurst (1734 edn: 157), which is accompanied by a sketch (Straker 1931a: 78). Of particular value are the letters of the Fullers of Brightling. Although they are not intended as formal descriptions, between them they provide numerous insights into the details of furnace operation.

Landscape paintings of the Flemish school provide a valuable assemblage of information. Henri Blès is the first and most prolific artist. He spent his youth in the Liège area, and although he moved thence, the scenes he painted early in the sixteenth century may be taken to show practice in southern Flanders in about 1500. Later in the century Patenier, Breughel, and the brothers van Valkenborch all included iron furnaces in their work and confirmed details shown by Blès (Crossley 1972: 57 n.19).

2 The field evidence: water power

In this section the physical remains of Wealden ironworks will be considered in relation to material from literary, artistic and business sources. In the Weald the oberver will see next to nothing of buildings, but considerable remaining earthworks. Thus it is particularly important to start with an explanation of how water was impounded and used by the industry, for dams ('bays'), ponds and races form the most prominent survivals.

(A) PONDS AND BAYS

These features have much in common with those used in trades such as corn milling, fulling, or secondary metalworking. Nevertheless, a detailed exploration is justified: the Weald provides a compact study area in which examples and variations of the essential features of water utilization can be found and, more particularly, it shows how the needs of the industry influenced the provision of water. The significant requirements of the blast furnace were apparent by the mid-sixteenth century. By this time furnaces used a steady flow over a longer period than any other water-powered equipment. Smelting practice and the improved choice of hearth materials were enabling furnaces to remain in blast for 25 weeks by 1550, and when Sir James Hope visited Barden furnace in 1646 he found that 45-week campaigns were considered normal (Marshall 1958: 149). If water were to run short, the furnace might have to be blown out. This would necessitate the removal and rebuilding of the hearth before smelting could be resumed. After re-lighting, a month's operation would be needed before the best-quality metal was available. It was an expensive expedient to have to use a water-wheel as a treadmill, although the Fullers' letters show this to have been eighteenth-century practice at gun-casting furnaces when the completion of an order was vital.[2] Forges, on the other hand, could be run on an intermittent basis, for their processes were essentially discontinuous. It would indeed be feasible to run a forge pond dry during the day and allow it to refill at night. The peak needs of a forge could be prodigious: some establishments had as many as four water-wheels, and even the small forges usually had two.

Wealden ironmasters were faced with problems of water supply more severe than in most other regions of Britain for the availability of water was restricted by the relatively small size and catchment areas of most of the streams. The difficulties are illustrated on the ground by the means used to impound water. It was common practice to build a dam, locally known as a bay, right across a valley, collecting the entire flow of a stream (fig.40). Surplus water was released over a spillway weir. This practice contrasts with layouts common in districts where the flow of water is both greater and more certain: in many Midland and northern valleys it was usual to set ponds parallel to a stream, diverting water into the pond when needed, but otherwise maintaining the natural flow in the stream-bed. There are indeed certain examples of this by-pass layout in the Weald (fig.42), but they are relatively rare, and seen only on the lower reaches of streams where flows are adequate and where a cross-valley bay would be impossibly long. The forges at Dedisham, Kitchenham, and Sheffield, and Ashurst furnace, are good examples, sited where water supply was

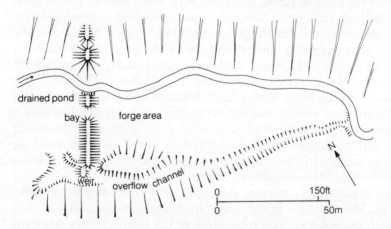

Fig.40   Woolbridge forge (TQ 571265). This small site is typical of the Weald, with the bay crossing the valley. The earthwork on the south side suggests a weir for regulating overflow from the pond, leading to a channel keeping water clear of the working area. In this example the slags and cinders found to the east of the bay suggest that the original use was as a powered bloomery, later converted to a finery forge (plan: P. Leach).

Fig.41   Scarlets furnace (TQ 443401): This aerial view shows the characteristic earthworks of an iron furnace and how they have been re-used. The pond, in water when this photograph was taken in 1952, was largely covered in weed and held by the intact bay, visible at the near end of the water. A corn mill (left-hand building) replaced the furnace, which had lain to the right of the mill, under the small central building. The tail-race ran along the left-hand edge of the vegetable garden, returning to the stream among the trees in the left foreground. The spillway weir is at the left-hand end of the bay, carrying the stream, the Kent Water, which flows eastwards through the trees. The bay was breached by a flood in 1968, but has since been reinstated. The mill, the adjacent shed, and the building on the line of the tail-race no longer stand (Cambridge University Collection: Crown Copyright reserved).

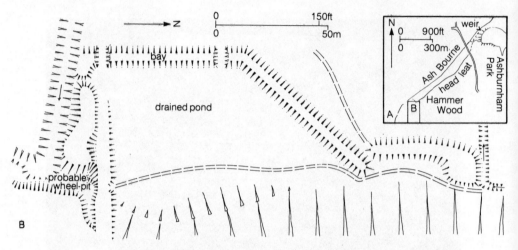

Fig. 42   Kitchenham (Ashburnham Lower) forge (TQ 679135) has a layout which is unusual in the Weald. The pond lay aside from the river, the water impounded by a long bay. It was fed by a leat which appears to have left the Ash Bourne at a weir, slight traces of which survive. The leat has been interrupted by features connected with the ornamental lake in Ashburnham Park. Modern drainage has introduced cross-dykes at either end of the pond (plan: P. Leach).

better than usual. Where this layout was used, a long leat could give an appreciable advantage, enabling the water of a pond to be maintained well above stream level. At Kitchenham the channel was about 1,000m long, at Lamberhurst the original forge had been supplied by a leat 850m in length, later employed for Gloucester furnace, and at Bibleham the leat leaves the Rother 500m upstream from the forge.

One variation of the by-pass layout is virtually absent from the Weald: in some streams in the north of England it was common for the tail-water from one site to be fed direct to a wheel downstream, without returning to the main water-course. The only suggestion of such tandem operation comes at Heathfield, where the Fullers built a boring mill in 1742 to use water from the furnace wheel, and at Freshfield, where it was agreed in 1564 that water from the corn mill should be available for the forge. In the latter case the system can be seen on the ground, although confused by the adoption of the connecting channel by the main stream, as well as by a later canal.[3]

Few Wealden bays remain intact, with ponds in water. The two in St Leonards Forest are among the finest, but examples at Cowden and Horsmonden also convey an excellent impression of how many valleys must have appeared in the sixteenth and seventeenth centuries. Later use for other purposes has often been the key to preservation, and it is to their corn mills that bays such as Sheffield, Ifield or Shillinglee owe their fine condition.

The typical Wealden pond layout (fig.43), suited though it was to the terrain, posed problems of maintenance which account for later decay. The bay and its spillways had to be sufficiently robust to withstand the force of storm water. Winter floods could break through, and there are references to considerable damage being done. In 1542, for example, the bay at Robertsbridge was breached, and the newly built furnace was partly destroyed, and in 1555 considerable repairs were needed to the dam and furnace at Panningridge.[4] This type of pond was difficult to drain for repairs and dredging, being impossible to isolate from the flow of the stream.

The method of construction of Wealden pond bays has received attention during excavations (fig.44). Sections have been cut through bays at Ardingly forge (Bedwin 1976: 42), Chingley forge (Crossley 1975b: 17), Maynards Gate furnace (Bedwin 1977–78: 167), and on the fringe of the Panningridge bay (Crossley 1972: 46). At Panningridge (fig.45) it was found that a layer of logs had been set in the marshy valley before the bay was built up, forming a base for the clay and sand of the main bank. At Maynards Gate the old topsoil had been stripped, and clay and sand were dumped without any foundation. At Ardingly and Chingley the banks were of clay, although at Chingley there was a good deal of slag and cinder in the upper levels. The only example of a core structure has been seen at Sheffield furnace, where recent pipe-laying exposed a base of sandstone blocks. The most robust bays are those where a road is taken across a valley on the crest of the bank. There are good examples at Ashburnham forge and in St Leonards Forest, although it is not always clear whether the original build or subsequent road maintenance is the more responsible for the present profile of the bank.

Bays were both strengthened and raised during the life of the ironworks they served. At Maynards Gate the excavated section has shown that slag was placed upon the original bank, probably also affording a modest increase in the depth and therefore the area of the pond. At Panningridge it was even clearer that the bay had been raised, as part of a major rebuilding. Here it was possible to estimate the original and enlarged pond areas by survey: the estimate of the first pond must be particularly accurate, for the early dam surface had been sealed by the material subsequently added. The later deposit, subject to erosion, gives a conservative estimate of the final size of the pond. Strengthening was frequently carried out on the pond side of the bay. Sometimes this was achieved by tipping slag from a track along the top, but in other cases measures were more systematic. In

a

b

Fig.43   (a) Cowden furnace pond (TQ 454400). The bay (lower right) carries a public
road. No traces of the furnace remain, but this view should be compared with the
map of 1748 (fig.68); (b) St Leonards forge pond (TQ 219289) (Cambridge University
Collection: Crown Copyright reserved).

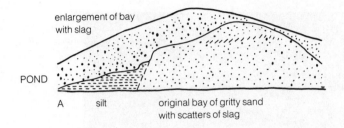

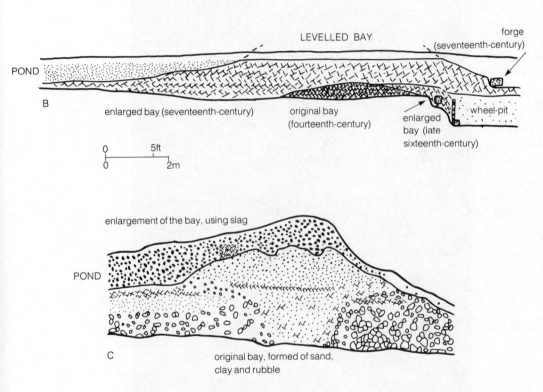

Fig.44 Excavated sections through bays (dams) in the Weald. (a) Ardingly forge (TQ 334289), showing the raising of the bay over pond-silts formed against the original, lower, bay. This enlargement may have taken place when the site was re-used for a fulling mill (after Bedwin 1976; 42); (b) Chingley forge (TQ 682335). Three deposits of clay appear in this section, the first for what was probably a hammer mill of the fourteenth century, the second for the late sixteenth-century forge, and the last, a greatly enlarged bay, for the rebuilding of the forge in the seventeenth century. This deposit was reduced in height when the field was levelled about 1800; (c) Maynards Gate furnace (TQ 539298). The section shows a significant enlargement of the bay, using slag from the furnace (after Bedwin 1977–8: opp.170).

Fig.45 Panningridge furnace (TQ 687174). The lowest level of the bay consists of logs set on the marsh when the furnace was built in 1542. (Scale in inches/cm.)

the Panningridge furnace accounts there are references to the driving of piles to strengthen weak points,[5] while at Westfield forge piles appear to have been set on both sides. Stone revetments are occasionally seen: there is a visible example at Pippingford, but it cannot be dated with certainty to the furnace period. At Scarlets a stone kerb supported courses of brick (Crossley 1979: 241), at Wassell forge sandstone blocks have been seen on the pond side of the bay, and at Huggetts furnace there appears to have been a stone wall on each side.

Piling or revetment would be most necessary near the points of weakness where water was taken over or through the bay. The number of crossings varied: there was usually one spillway and occasionally a second. Ashburnham is a case where one spillway was set in the centre of the bay, while Gosden and Socknersh have examples of a single weir set at one end. Panningridge, however, appears to have had two spillways, adjacent to the hillsides at each end of the bay.

At furnaces it would be normal to have one wheel-feed. This could form a box set in a trench across the dam, as at Chingley. With such an arrangement leakage could lead to weakening of the bay material beneath, in a position concealed from view. In cases such as the upstream site at Ashburnham furnace or Ardingly forge, a culvert through the bay could also lead to weakness if the stone or timber of the channel were inadequate. At Panningridge, in the final phase of use, there was an interesting means of reducing the number of breaks in the top of the main bay by feeding the furnace wheel from a small basin between the bay and the spillway. Forges posed a particular problem, for the larger works with multiple wheels required water in considerable volume. The double wheel at Chingley forge must have needed a wide penstock cut into the dam, and in the late seventeenth century no less than three feeds were needed. Only if wheels could be set in tandem in a single race could these risks to the dam be reduced.

There were certain establishments where two works took water from one pond. At Beckley a forge and a furnace lay at either end of the bay, and similar arrangements appear to have obtained at Langleys, Stone (East Grinstead) and Stream. At Ashburnham furnace (fig.46) the layout was rather different, with one site close to the bay and another fed by a channel some 150m long, from the same pond. In all these cases there were many points on the bays needing maintenance and, in contrast, areas of dead water in the ponds where silt would collect and reduce storage capacity if dredging were not carried out.

If the main pond could not provide sufficient water, the construction of pen-ponds was an expedient used in the steeper valleys (fig.47). Coushopley furnace had four pen ponds, at Riverhall two such bays have been found, and the Ordnance Survey of 1813 shows no less than 12 pen ponds feeding Heathfield furnace. A remarkable example of the provision of extra water has been recorded at Ashburnham (fig.48), where a channel runs for over a mile; it took water from the stream formerly used for Penhurst furnace, along a level path around spurs and over short aqueducts to reach Ashburnham furnace (Beswick and Ennever 1981). It is not known when this unique work was done. It does not appear on a map of 1717 (fig.37).[6]

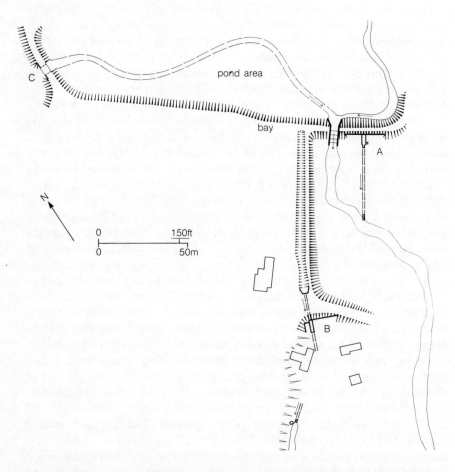

Fig.46   Ashburnham furnace (TQ 686171). This complex site had a long history, from about 1550 until 1813. There were two working areas. At (A) a wheelpit survives, its tail-race culverted and in good order. In the adjacent orchard there has been found debris suggesting a furnace, but all masonry has disappeared. At (B) a wheelpit is fed by a channel from the main bay. It is likely that a working area lay immediately to the east of this wheelpit, but no investigation has taken place. The main pond (fig.30) is dry, but a pen pond (C) on a stream flowing from the west still holds water (plan: P. Leach).

Fig.47 Eridge furnace (TQ 564350). This vertical air photograph illustrates a system of pen ponds frequently used by Wealden ironmasters. The furnace lay in the wood to the right, close to the bay. The main pond, with weed and silt diminishing its size, has a spillway at each end, one being clearly visible. Two pen ponds can be seen towards the left of the picture (Cambridge University Collection: Crown Copyright reserved).

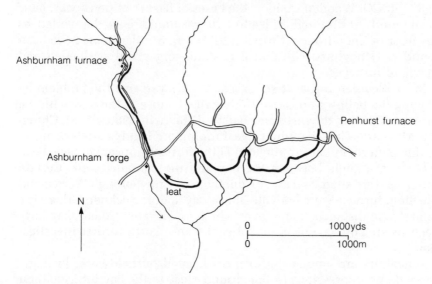

Fig.48 Ashburnham furnace had its water supply supplemented by means of a channel approximately 3.5km long. This was fed by a tributary of the Ash Bourne formerly supplying Penhurst furnace, and followed the contours of three spurs, crossing small streams by means of aqueducts. These do not survive, but the earthworks of the leat are plainly visible.

(B) WATER-WHEELS, THEIR SITING AND CONSTRUCTION

Penstocks and wheel-pits

The means of release of the impounded water to the wheels called for judgment and a degree of compromise. On the one hand, there were advantages in setting the furnace or forge buildings some small distance from the bay, to avoid leakage from the pond leading to damp in foundations or, worse, in the actual structure of a furnace. However, the further wheels lay from the bay the greater the complications of supplying and controlling the water. In the case of an overshot or pitch-back wheel, water had to be carried in an elevated trough ending in a penstock and shuttle. As Sir James Hope noted at Barden furnace in 1646 (Marshall 1958: 147): 'the water was lett in from the damme above by a slouse raised and depressed with a vectis lyke unto that of a shippe pumpe'. This had to be robust in construction, for the trough was virtually an extension of the pond. In some cases the shuttle controlling the flow of water may have been set in the bay, leaving the water to reach the wheel in a long shoot, or flash. One Flemish painting shows just this arrangement, with a man standing on the dam to operate the shuttle, remote from the founder (Schubert 1957: pl.XX). Wooden troughs, the bases of flashes or penstocks, have been found. At Pippingford I, a trough was found re-used, inverted, as the floor of the tail-race (Crossley 1975c: 8). Similar items have been found at Coneyhurst Gill and Brookland forges and at Hendall and Mayfield furnaces.

Most Wealden furnaces so far excavated overcame the problem by placing the bellows-house, with the wheel, close to the bay, with the furnace standing downstream. Batsford (Bedwin 1980: 97–8), Chingley, Maynards Gate, Panningridge, Pippingford I and Scarlets conform to this pattern, but at Pippingford II the furnace appears to have been set into the angle between the bay and the charging bank. Certain furnaces were sited well away from the bay. Crowborough Warren and Sheffield furnace were both 30–35m away, and at Socknersh there is a remarkable distance, 250m, over which an elevated trough may have been used. This layout is inexplicable, and worth further investigation.

Wheelpits are among the features located by fieldwork. In many cases damp depressions in the ground close to the bay indicate their position, which can on occasion be confirmed by the alignment of a partly silted tail-race. In some cases bays have broken at the weak point created by the leakage from a penstock, and modern streams, adopting the gap, have exposed the timbers or stonework of a wheelpit. Among several cases noted in the gazetteer, Eridge and Hodesdale forges and Markly and Verdley Wood furnaces provide good examples.

The construction of wheelpits varied, chiefly in the material used. In the sixteenth century timber-lined pits were common (fig.49): at Batsford, Chingley and Panningridge the pits were in effect timber-framed boxes with planked sides and rear end. At Chingley and Panningridge, by contrast with Batsford, the planks were set outside the vertical side members of the box, which would make them difficult to replace. A timber floor was often used, as at Panningridge II, although at Panningridge I there were no traces of planking, and the eroded hollow below the wheel would suggest that if a floor had been fitted it had not been renewed. A late-seventeenth-century example of an all-timber pit was excavated at Chingley forge. This was remarkable in having an all-timber breast, shaped to fit the circumference of the wheel. This is a feature which is often found in stone wheelpits built at eighteenth-century mills. In the Chingley example the emplacement was lightly built and set on buried sleepers. It could have been removed, leaving little trace, and the absence of a recognizable wheelpit at Pippingford II may thus be explained.

Composite wheelpits, partly of stone (fig.50), raise a number of questions. At Ardingly forge, Maynards Gate, Pippingford I and Scarlets, stone walls were set over timber floors. The planks would be difficult to replace, for in each case timber was set beneath the side walls: at Maynards Gate the problem was illustrated by a board which had resisted an attempt at removal. At Pippingford I it did seem likely that the stone walls had replaced timber sides, for mortices were present in the exposed longitudinal sleepers on which the walls were partly set. The only excavated pit constructed entirely of stone was at Chingley forge. Here a flagged floor was used, carefully laid to form a slight gradient for the escaping water.

It must not be assumed that there was a progression from timber to stone construction. The last wheelpit at Chingley forge was of timber, and this was almost certainly so at Pippingford II, whereas the earlier furnace nearby had a stone-sided pit. The length of lease was likely to be the deciding factor, for tenants would build or refurbish to a standard sufficient only to pass inspection at the end of the term.

Tail-races

The tail-race, often ignored, performed a vital function by permitting water to flow freely from the wheelpit without backing up under the wheel. At Scarlets, in its rebuilt form, there certainly does seem to

a

b

c

Fig.49 Timber wheelpits: (a) Chingley furnace (TQ 685327) (scale: 1m); (b) Panningridge furnace, c.1542 (TQ 687174) (scale: 1m); (c) Chingley forge (TQ 682335) (scale: 3ft). (a) and (b) show a form of construction found in sixteenth-century contexts, with the framework of the wheelpit exposed to the water. (c) is more sophisticated, with side-boards placed within the frame, and a curved breast set to fit closely to a pitch-back or breast-shot wheel.

have been dead water in the wheelpit, although the wheel may have been set, or re-set, high enough for rotation not to have been impeded. At Panningridge outflow became a problem in the 25 years after the furnace was built in 1542. In this period Ashburnham furnace was constructed, and the pond reached within 50m of the Panningridge wheelpit. It is significant that when Panningridge was rebuilt, the wheel was placed at a higher level to give an improved outflow (fig.51). In some cases tail-races were of prodigious length: at Etchingham forge a ditch 800m long was dug, and at Kitchenham forge the race appears to have run for about 300m. In such cases the intention may have been to secure greater head by constructing a wheelpit deeper than the adjacent river bed. To return the water a race would be required, less steep than the course of the river. As the wheelpits at these forges cannot be surveyed in relation to the adjacent rivers, this must remain conjecture, but there are instances in other parts of the country of reconciliation of levels in this way.

Tail-races were built in many forms. Some were open; indeed, at Ardingly and Chingley forges wide ditches sufficed, the banks of the latter strengthened only by large pieces of cinder taken from the finery hearth. Culverts were made necessary by the layout of certain furnaces. At Scarlets, Maynards Gate and Chingley, the casting areas were small, and necessarily extended across the lines of the tail-races. At Pippingford I the race ran between the furnace back wall and the charging bank: it was prudent to build a culvert here to prevent ore and charcoal falling from the charging bridge and choking the water-course. The culverts varied in their construction: at Chingley and Maynards Gate furnaces they were entirely of wood, at Scarlets and Pippingford I of stone and brick with wooden floors, while at the upper site at Ashburnham furnace the tunnel had a stone floor, with stone and some brick in the walls and the arched roof.

a

b

c

Fig.50 Stone and composite wheelpits: (a) Chingley forge, c.1600–1700 (TQ 682335) (scale: 2m); (b) Scarlets furnace (TQ 443401) (scale: 1m); (c) Maynards Gate furnace (TQ 539298) (photograph O. R. Bedwin) (scale: 2m). At Chingley (a) stone flags were used for the floor of the wheelpit, but in the other examples timber floors were set beneath stone side-walls. This view of Chingley forge shows the finery building, partly destroyed by a land drain of c.1800. A hearth-plate survives to the right of this intrusion. The cinder pit for the hearth can be seen against the far wall of the finery. A length of race between the original position of the hammer wheel, close to the bay, and of the finery wheel, foreground, was originally culverted, the capstones having been removed for this photograph.

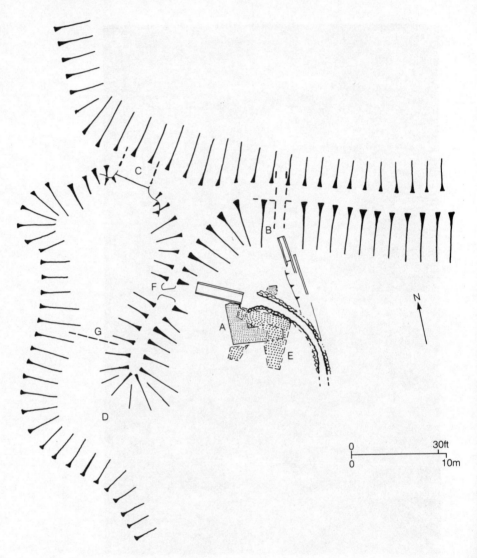

Fig.51 Panningridge furnace (TQ 687174). Near the western end of the bay and the adjacent hillside lies the site of a furnace, which was radically reconstructed in the second half of the sixteeenth century. This plan shows the early furnace (A) with its wheelpit (B). The spillway (C) took water back to the stream by a channel (D) beyond the charging bank. A second furnace (E), built on the demolition debris of the first, took water (F) from the spillway area. The latter must have been dammed by some form of weir near the southern end of the bank. As no trace survives in the most likely area (G), the barrier was probably of timber (plan: M. R. Browne).

Water-wheels

Excavations at ironworks in the Weald have provided significant additions to our information about sixteenth- and seventeenth-century water-wheels. Until recent years the wheels portrayed by the Flemish painters of the period (fig.52) were thought too fragile in appearance to have been accurately represented. But examples found at Batsford, Chingley and Panningridge show how few spokes and how small a cross-section the millwright of the period used.

Fig.52　Water-wheel at an early sixteenth-century Flemish blast furnace: detail from Henri Blès, 'Landscape with ironworks and mines' (Uffizi Gallery, Florence).

The wheel configuration normally varied with the head of water available. A high bay permitted the use of an overshot wheel. This was the most efficient type, for the buckets of the wheel were kept full of water for the greatest possible proportion of a revolution, the weight of water exercising leverage on the wheel spindle through the spokes. Batsford, Chingley, Maynards Gate and Panningridge furnaces had overshot wheels, requiring the minimum flow of water for a given power (fig.53). At Scarlets the wheel had not survived in position, so it was not certain if it had been of overshot or pitch-back type. It is surprising to find wheels with low water feeds even when fairly high bays were built. At Ashburnham the upper bay possesses a fine breast-wheel pit, with a low culvert through the dam. A deeper wheelpit and a longer tailrace would have allowed an overshot wheel

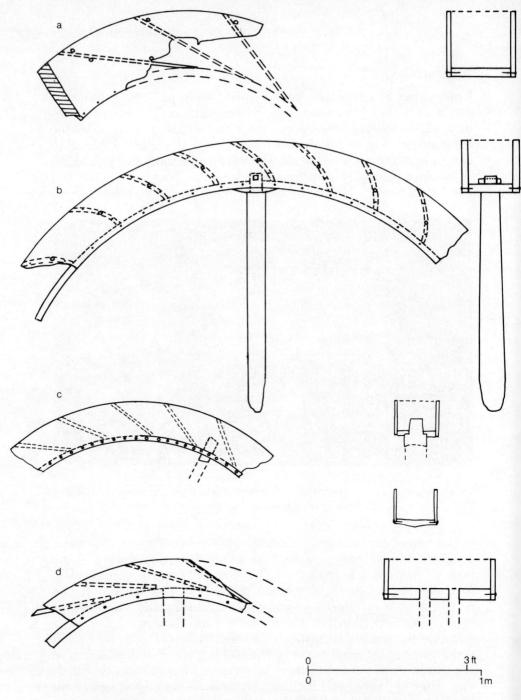

Fig.53   Water-wheels: excavated examples: (a) Chingley (fourteenth century: probably
for a hamnmer-forge); (b) Chingley furnace (sixteenth century); (c) Batsford furnace
(sixteenth century) (after Bedwin 1980: 102); (d) Chingley forge
(seventeenth/eighteenth century).

and still enabled the contents of the pond to be fully used. There are cases where it is virtually impossible to determine the type of wheel in use. At Pippingford both furnaces present such problems. In the case of the first furnace the dam has been raised and a modern brick culvert hides the back of the wheelpit. The second furnace had no surviving wheelpit: the arrangement of the tail-race suggested that the wheel had been set in a wooden trough parallel with the bay, but there were no means of establishing the direction of rotation.

The construction of the wheels so far examined has varied in detail, though not in essentials. All have been of timber. It is just possible that cast-iron parts may have appeared in the final years of the last of the Wealden ironworks, but there are neither references in accounts nor fragments recorded in the field.

The post-medieval Wealden wheelwright favoured a wheel with six to eight spokes, set either in a single row or occasionally double, as on the chafery wheel at Chingley forge. It is not known how the spokes were set into the spindles, as no wheel-centres have survived. The spokes were shouldered and tenoned at their outer ends, set through mortices in the sole-boards with a cross-tenon wedge driven through the spoke-end outside the board. Sole-boards were thick, adzed from the solid. This restricted their length, and at least six would be required to build a 3.5–4.5m diameter wheel. The segments were either scarfed or dowelled together. At the points where the spokes were taken through the sole-board, the latter was left thicker; this was particularly clear on the Chingley furnace wheel.

Side-boards were normally nailed to the sole-boards. These again were necessarily limited in length and were scarfed and nailed at the joints. The joint between sole- and side-boards would be liable to leakage of water, and a wheel at Chingley forge was caulked with calfhair. The bucket boards were set between the side-boards, at an angle to the radius which depended on whether the wheels were over- or back-shot. Most bucket boards were straight, but curved boards were used at Chingley furnace. The most effective fixing was by means of grooves in the side-boards, as at Batsford, but bucket boards could be plain butted, and nailed or pegged, as at Chingley furnace.

Only in the sixteenth-century phase at Chingley forge was there an exception to the normal form of wheel (fig.54). Here the wheelpit was divided into two chambers, side by side, and it is suggested that two wheels, probably of conventional proportions, were mounted on a common shaft. The timbers which divided the pit had been cut away, and all parts of the wheels and axle had been removed: nevertheless, the indications were sufficient for this possibility to be taken seriously.

Dimensions of water-wheels (metres)   diameter   width (overall)

	diameter	width (overall)
Batsford (overshot)	3.9	0.45
Chingley forge hammer* (breast)	less than 3.45	
Chingley forge chafery (overshot)	2.44	0.66
Chingley furnace (over-shot)	3.34	0.32
Maynards Gate (overshot)	2.5	0.32
Panningridge I (overshot)	3.66	0.38
Panningridge II (overshot)	3.05	0.48
Scarlets (overshot or pitch-back)	2.9	0.72

*No wheel survived: the diameter of pit-breast is given: an allowance must be made for working clearance.

3   The blast furnace

(A) THE MAIN STRUCTURE

Wealden blast furnaces followed a design which differed little in essentials from that illustrated by Flemish landscape painters. A tower was built, with ashlar facing, rubble core, and a stone- or

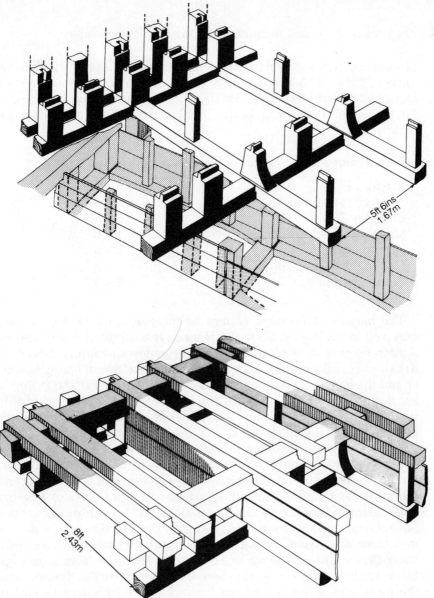

Fig.54 Double wheelpit at Chingley forge (scale in photograph: 1m). This structure dates from late in the sixteenth century. The photograph shows the surviving timbers, with those from the fourteenth-century race below and to the left of the sixteenth-century side-planks. Sleepers for the late seventeenth-century wheelpit are seen at a higher level in the foreground. The original timbers, deduced from mortices in the base-frame, are set out in the diagrams, the upper of which includes the medieval structure. The lower diagram indicates surviving upper timbers by shading. It is thought that two wheels were used on a common shaft, a compromise arising from the difficulty of building a strong wide water wheel out of wood.

brick-faced inner chamber. Most furnaces were square, with sides varying between 5.5 and 8m in length. The exception is Batsford II, whose plan measured 8m by 5.5m. Gun-casting furnaces so far examined have been larger in plan than those producing pig iron:

Plan dimensions of Wealden blast furnaces (metres)

Batsford I	5.5 × 5.5
Batsford II (ordnance)	8 × 5.5
Chingley	5.5 × 5.5
Maynards Gate (ordnance)	6.5 × 6.5
Panningridge I	5.2 × 5.2
Pippingford I (ordnance)	8 × 8
Pippingford II	5.5 × 5.5

The heights of furnaces cannot be measured, for no stacks have survived in the Weald. Sir James Hope gave a height of 20ft (6.1m) for Barden furnace in 1646, and the mid-seventeenth-century furnace at Rockley, Yorkshire, survives to a height of 5.5m. Swedenborg, however, put the height of Gloucester furnace, Lamberhurst, at 28ft (8.6m) in his description of 1734; this, if the shaft were fully charged, would produce a weight of burden which risked crushing charcoal in the lower levels of the stack.

As no excavated Wealden furnace stands more than a few courses in height, the details of elevations must be inferred. It was normal for two sides of the stack to have arches, one for blowing and the other for tapping. Surviving furnaces in other parts of England have cast-iron lintels over these entrances, and the building accounts for Robertsbridge furnace (1541) suggest the practice.[7] Here pigs of iron were purchased during construction, and examples elsewhere show that beams, of triangular section, hardly differ from large pigs. Early furnaces were strengthened by exterior timber frames, and the picture of a furnace on the fireback cast by Richard Lenard in 1636 shows how this was done (fig.35). The practice has been confirmed by the discovery of the bases of corner posts at Batsford, Chingley and Maynards Gate and by a reference in the building account for Panningridge furnace (1542–3). Such bracing was particularly important for the 'pillar' of the furnace, the corner between the two arches. This was a frequent source of trouble: the Panningridge furnace accounts show how the pillar had to be rebuilt,[8] and the excavations at Batsford and Chingley confirmed how fragile this part of the structure could be.

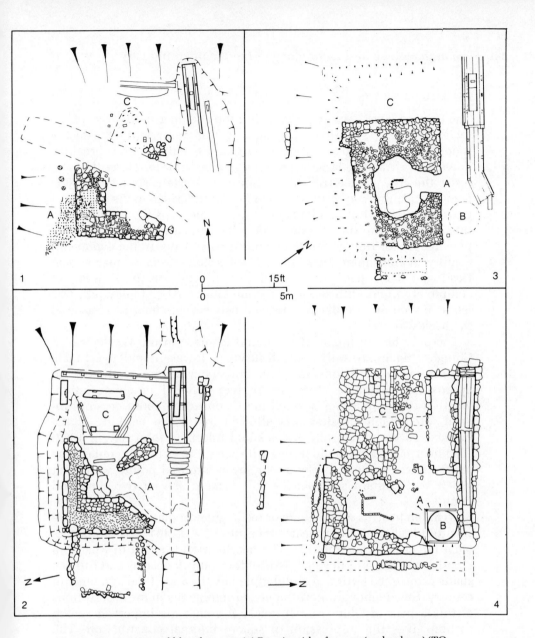

Fig.55   Four excavated blast furnaces (1) Panningridge furnace (early phase) (TQ 687174); (2) Chingley furnace (TQ 685327); (3) Batsford furnace (TQ 631153) (after Bedwin 1980: 97); (4) Maynards Gate furnace (TQ 539298) (after Bedwin 1978; opp.166). These four excavated furnaces date from the sixteenth century and show features typical of their period. Those on the left cast pig iron: Chingley had a casting area (A) over a culverted tail-race, a layout apparently originally used at Panningridge, which was later modified to cast on the opposite (west) side, where pig-beds could still be seen. The two gun-casting furnaces (right) had casting pits (B) close to wheel-races, and in the case of Batsford (3) the line of the channel has been altered to accommodate the pit. In all four cases the bellows were sited between the furnace and the bay.

(B) THE HEARTH

The furnace hearth was rebuilt within the chamber in the base of the tower for each smelting campaign. It was important to select a sandstone which would erode slowly and evenly, neither breaking down nor attracting large accretions of slag: 'Harder stone that can resist the fire', is referred to by Bourbon. Certain sources became favoured: Penhurst quarry was used for Panningridge in the middle of the sixteenth century, and a nearby source, perhaps the same quarry, interested Maximilian Western after he left Ashburnham in 1702, presumably for lining a more distant furnace. Later in the eighteenth century Ashburnham was relined with stone from a quarry near Hastings.[9] The space into which the hearth was built was not completely filled with refractory stone blocks. At Chingley part was left as a void and cinder was packed between the hearth stones and the back wall.

The only hearth fragment yet found in place in the Weald was at Chingley (fig.56). As only one half survived, it was difficult to estimate the internal dimensions in plan, but 60cm square would be an approximate estimate. This hearth had suffered much accretion, whereas contemporaries seemed more concerned about erosion. Indeed, predictable erosion was allowed for in the working of the furnace; as Walter Burrell of Cuckfield informed John Ray in 1672: 'The hearth ... grows wider and wider, so that at first it contains so much as will make a sow of six or seven hundred pound weight, at last it will contain so much as will make a sow of two thousand pound.'

Wealden hearths were square or rectangular in plan; Sir James Hope was told that the Barden hearth measured 2 × 3ft (61 × 91cm), somewhat larger than at Chingley. The hearth would be apt to wear to a circular outline, and in some parts of the country hearths and furnace shafts came to be built to a circular plan by the end of the seventeenth century. Swedenborg, unfortunately, is ambiguous in his descriptions of this aspect of Gloucester furnace, although his imperfect sketch section gives the impression of square internal construction. The hearth generally had a forward extension, the 'fore hearth', described by Hope as the 'panne' and by contemporary accounts as the 'mouth' of the furnace. This was said by Hope to allow slags to be removed, but it could also be used for ladling small quantities of molten metal into moulds. Hope describes the 'panne' at Barden as being 18ins (45cm) deep and projecting 18 ins outside the hearth.

The capacity of the hearth was of great concern, particularly to the gunfounders. The crucial requirement was to be able to hold sufficient

Fig.56 Chingley furnace hearth (TQ 685327): the only example so far found of substantial remains of a hearth in position in a blast furnace of the sixteenth century. The lining-stones are apparent, with the accretion of slag built up during the final campaign. A significant detail is the arch beneath the hearth, leaving a void to act as a drain (scale: 1m).

metal to cast a gun of the size of a culverin (2 tons) or even a demi-cannon (3 tons). In the sixteenth century such quantities were only achieved by the use of double furnaces, of which the best-known example was at Worth. No establishment of this kind has yet been excavated, so the detailed layout must be in doubt. It is assumed that a common stack was used, with a single charging bridge and a casting pit set equidistant from the hearths. It would be of particular interest to find out how the bellows were arranged, and whether two water-wheels had to be employed. By the mid-seventeenth century furnaces were considerably larger, and in the Forest of Dean capacity reached 3.7 tons per day. No Wealden furnace appears to have been able to produce this amount regularly, but in 1664 George Browne stated that it was possible to hold up to 4 tons of metal in a hearth for a single cast. Capacity of this order was reached at the end of the campaign, as a result of erosion of the lining, but there must have come a point beyond which operation carried the risk of a break-out of metal.

(c) THE STACK

Above the hearth the furnace interior flared out to form the 'bosh'. No furnace stack is known to have survived at this level in the Weald, so we rely on contemporary measurements. Barden was 5 × 6ft (1.52 × 1.82m) at the bosh, Gloucester 7ft 6ins × 8ft (2.28 × 2.43m). Above the hearth, we are told by Ray, the interior of the furnace was of brick, although in other parts of England hard stone was used. At Ashburnham the eighteenth-century accounts make it clear that high-alumina bricks ('bricks mixed with clay') were being used in the furnace. These would form the lining of the bosh, which had to be resistant to fluxing materials in the charge and would be less perme-able than a high-silica brick.[10]

A demolished hearth and shaft produce characteristic debris which often afford guidance to the position of the stack. Fieldwork (noted in the gazetteer) has located a number of mounds made up of weathered brick, refractories coated with glassy slag both on surfaces and in fractures, and accumulations of partly reduced ore with charcoal. The latter remained in the hearth and lower part of the shaft at the end of a blast. Another characteristic survival is the 'bear', a mass of cast iron, often with charcoal, ore and refractory fragments adhering. This also remained in the bottom of the hearth: when relining took place the bear would be removed, but its weight made it difficult to take far. This is illustrated by the example found at Maynards Gate, adjacent to the casting pit.

Debris from a collapsed furnace illustrates how fragile these structures became after lengthy use. Materials became porous and friable after several campaigns, and a good deal of reliance must have been placed on the external timber bracing. This was to remain a vital factor until the very end of the use of stone and brick furnaces, with wrought-iron ties replacing wood late in the eighteenth century in the Midlands and the north of England. These impressions are confirmed by the frequent references to major rebuildings found in accounts for furnaces such as Panningridge, Waldron, Heathfield and Ashburnham. They are also confirmed on the ground: at Batsford and Panningridge there had been complete rebuildings, with new furnaces constructed on rubble bases formed from the demolition of their predecessors, while at Chingley the stonework on the north side of the furnace showed that the building had been taken down to its footings before reconstruction.

(d) DRAINAGE

Beneath the furnace hearth drains were sometimes built. Wealden practice seems to have varied in this respect: at Panningridge and Batsford I there were no signs of drainage, whereas for Batsford II, Chingley, Maynards Gate and Pippingford (fig.57) the matter had been given considerable attention. In the case of Chingley a cinder-filled gully crossed the casting floor from the hearth-base to a porous filling over the culverted tail-race. The hearth base had been built as a platform supported by a vault, and the void beneath acted as part of the drain. Here there were no brick- or stone-lined channels beneath the hearth, but these were present in the other cases: at Pippingford II brick ducts connected with a stone-lined drain, which crossed the bellows area to emerge in the wall of the wheelpit. At Maynards Gate the drain vented upwards and would have linked with cavities in the hearth lining. Moisture would have been dispersed as steam at a high level, an arrangement seen in eighteenth-century hearths in other parts of the country. A peculiarity here was the presence of cast-iron plates upright between the stones lining the drain: it is uncertain whether these were placed in position or were the result of a break-out of hot metal through the base of the lining.

Drainage was also assisted by trenches dug round the outside of furnaces. There was an excellent example at Maynards Gate, where much of the stone lining and capping survived; the drain surrounded the furnace on three sides and was capped by a stone floor on the bellows side; it discharged into the wheelpit. The layout at Batsford and Chingley was similar, but the execution at the latter furnace was poor. Here the drain was unlined and had been obstructed by the

Fig.57   Pippingford first furnace (TQ 450316). Traces of a more sophisticated drainage system than at Chingley (fig.56) can be seen at this early eighteenth-century gun-casting furnace. Brick channels beneath the hearth-space led to a stone drain crossing the bellows floor to discharge into the wheelpit (left foreground). (Scale: 1m.)

building of a lean-to structure against a back-wall of the furnace, while on the bellows side the water had no clear channel through which to find its way to the wheelpit. The Batsford drains were also unlined, but followed an unobstructed route round the furnace.

(E) CHARGING THE FURNACE

The blast furnace needed a means of access to its top, into which were charged charcoal and ore. In some parts of Britain furnaces were constructed on platforms cut into steep well-drained hillsides, so that the 'high-line', the charging level, was easily formed as a terrace higher on the slope. Few Wealden locations lend themselves to such an arrangement, and in almost all cases bridges or banks had to be constructed to allow the barrowing or carrying of materials to the furnace top. Chingley is a case where a steep adjacent hillside was available, but the local drainage pattern made it necessary for the furnace to be free-standing, with a drain cut between the hill and the furnace wall. Here it would be necessary to have a short bridge to the furnace top.

It was more usual for a bank to be built, and this frequently formed a branch of the bay. At Pippingford I, for example, the materials must have been carried along the bay, on to the spur bank, and thence across a bridge to the furnace. In this instance slots survived in the top of the bank in which the beams of the bridge had rested. The bottom course of a stone bridge abutment survived at Batsford, at the base of a bank which also joined the bay. There are several sites where a bank of this kind not only served for access to the furnace but also bounded a spillway from the bay, keeping water from the working area. This layout was confirmed by excavation at Panningridge, and good examples of such earthworks can be seen at Blackfold, Iridge and Pashley. At Panningridge the bridge was exceptionally long, in effect roofing an area 5m wide which at one stage was used as a casting floor. There are references to its repair in 1548 and 1555.[11]

(F) THE BLOWING AND CASTING AREAS

The bellows

The construction of bellows is amply illustrated by Agricola (1556 [1950 edn]: 365), and there is no reason to suspect that English practice was different. Bellows boards were of massive construction, 4–4.5m long at Barden (Marshall 1958: 147), and up to 5m at Heathfield.[12] Leather was used for the sides, and references to hides are frequent in furnace accounts. Offcuts of leather and characteristic nails were found at Chingley, and staining was present on bellows-house floors at Pippingford and Panningridge. Vent boards were referred to at Panningridge. There would be flap-valves to allow the bellows to fill with air. The small wooden hinges found at Chingley may well have been fixed to these flaps.

The front ends of the bellows at Chingley and Pippingford I were mounted on sleepers, close to the outer face of the hearth masonry. No shaped stones have been found to accommodate the bellows tuyeres, and it seems that not all furnaces had iron pipes to conduct the blast into the hearth. At Barden, Sir James Hope comments: 'the bellies have no tewyron bot ther pype-ends came not within 1/2 foot of the innersyde of the fornace'. Nevertheless, the Robertsbridge and Panningridge accounts show that tuyere irons were in use in the sixteenth century.

It was common practice in the Weald for the bellows shaft to lie parallel with the dam, about 4.5m from the tuyere space in the hearth lining. Among the excavated furnaces, only Panningridge II and Pippingford II diverge from this plan. The camshaft was an extension of the water-wheel spindle: Hope named it the 'axle tree', suggesting that a single piece of timber was used. At Chingley there survived a fragment of the shaft, into which were cut two sets of mortices, each for three cams (fig.58). This confirmed the practice of having two pairs of bellows; each would operate three times per revolution of the water-wheel. As the cams were staggered, there would thus be six blasts to the revolution. At Chingley the cams had been removed: it is thus uncertain whether they were made of hardwood or cast iron. A possible profile is illustrated by Biringuccio (1540 [1558 edn]: 110). The axle-shaft would have been set in bearings; the wooden block for one of these survived on the bellows floor at Chingley, but there is no

Fig.58   Chingley furnace bellows area (TQ 685327). The trapezoid area where the bellows were set is shown (centre), containing (left) two forked posts to support the pivoted lower boards of the bellows. The furnace tuyeres lay further to the left. A fragment of the wheel-shaft has been cut at a point revealing the mortices for the three cams which actuated one pair of bellows. The cam-mortices for the further pair can be seen, offset by 60° from the nearer set. The block for the far shaft-bearing is in position. In the foreground are the remains of the wooden wall of the bellows house, built against the edge of the bay (scale: 1m).

clue as to the material used for the bearings themselves. A second support would have been built on the far side of the wheelpit.

Our knowledge of how bellows were operated is only slightly advanced by the fragments found at Chingley: no other excavation in the Weald has produced relevant material. Practice varied from the complex system of levers and counter-weights shown by Agricola to the simple direct contact between cam and bellows bottom-board in Biringuccio's *De Pirotechnia*. The Chingley system resembled the latter, for the camshaft was set at a sufficiently low level. The description of Barden shows that there the cams operated through levers, raising the bellows board 60cm, to be lowered by a lever with a counter-weight. The moving boards of the bellows were pivoted on vertical posts at Chingley. Both survived, their forked tops and pivot-pinholes intact. Fixed mountings were required for the static parts of the bellows: post-holes and beam-slots were clearly visible at Batsford I and Panningridge I, and timbers remained in position at Chingley.

Bellows areas were commonly roofed. This was clearly the case on the Continent, shown by artists of the sixteenth century. At Maynards Gate tile fragments were found on the bellows floor, and both at Panningridge I and at Chingley bases of timber walls were found at the foot of the dam, behind the line of the axle-shaft. Such buildings could be thatched rather than tiled; this is shown in the Continental illustrations and by references in the accounts for Waldron furnace.[13]

The casting area

The features of the casting floor depended upon the product. Where pig iron or small castings were produced, a flat floor was used, on which casting sand was spread. Furrows were shaped in the sand for sows and pigs: the furrows survived at Panningridge I and Pippingford II (fig.59). The indentations were parallel, without branches, confirming the impression of the written records that sows of 10cwt or 1 ton were normally cast, rather than small pigs in moulds branching from the main furrow in the sand. At Chingley only traces of sand remained, for the floor was formed of slag covering the tail-race culvert, through which the sand had percolated. The casting of small objects leaves little trace except in the case of cannon balls, for which the founder made cast-iron moulds. Half-moulds were found in excavations at Batsford, and as surface finds at Brightling and Tickeridge. Cannon balls have been found at several sites, Tickeridge being a notable case, where 4in, 5in, 6in and 7in (10cm, 12.5cm, 15cm and 17.5cm) examples are recorded. Such finds can result from the

Fig.59   Pig beds at Pippingford second furnace (TQ 451316) (scale: 1m)

proving of guns: at Beech and Heathfield furnaces it has been suggested that proving banks were used, and that shot derives from test firings. Firebacks and plates were probably cast in the sand of the floor, and it is likely that anvils and hammer heads would be cast in clay-loam moulds which were destroyed when the objects were broken out.

The casting floor would be roofed. A wooden building is recorded at Worth, the casting area at Pippingford I was littered with tiles, and fragments of a sill-beam marked the edge of the area at Chingley.

The procedure for making large castings was altogether more complex, and required fixed equipment which is immediately recognizable on the ground. To produce major items, hot metal was run along a channel in the sand, as at Pippingford I, to moulds set vertically in a timber-lined pit. Although this procedure was developed for the manufacture of guns, by the eighteenth century it was used for a variety of objects, such as agricultural rollers, sugar crushers, and water pipes.

Four casting pits have been excavated at furnace sites in the Weald (fig.60). Those at Pippingford I and Scarlets were intact, but at Maynards Gate and Batsford the linings had been largely removed. A circular hollow adjacent to the furnace debris at Langleys may be a further example.

Casting pits were constructed close to a corner of a furnace. The earliest, at Maynards Gate, was 3m in depth, but the pit at Pippingford I, dating from about 1700, measured 4.5m from the casting floor to the bottom timbers. Diameters of about 1.5m were usual. The practice was to dig a pit and to construct or insert within it a form of barrel, made of vertical staves with exterior hoops. This work must have posed great difficulty, particularly where an existing furnace was being adapted for the casting of ordnance. It is clear that at Batsford and Scarlets the original space on the casting floor had been inadequate for the insertion of a pit, and in both cases the tail-race had to be diverted. At Maynards Gate a square pit had been dug, and waterproof clay had been rammed around the timbers, giving an excellent degree of waterproofing. This was an important point, for it was vital that the pit should remain as dry as possible during casting. The problem of ensuring this was increased when the pit was close to a wheelpit or race, as at Batsford, Maynards Gate and Scarlets. At Pippingford I the furnace faced away from the tail-race, which made the problem rather less severe, although still leaving a structure well below the general water table.

The preoccupation with water-proofing can be seen in the construction of casting pits (fig.61). The staves were closely fitted and fairly

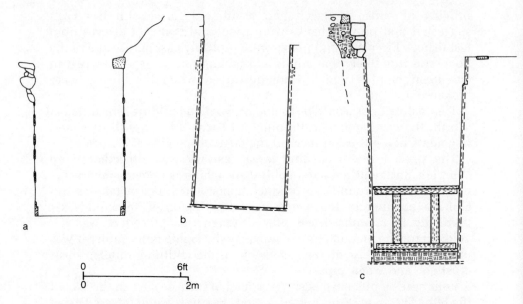

Fig.60 Gun-casting pits at Wealden furnaces: (a) Maynards Gate (TQ 539298) (after Bedwin 1977–8: 171); (b) Scarlets (TQ 443401); (c) Pippingford (TQ 450316). The method of construction was similar in each case, with vertical staves closely fitted, as in a barrel. The Maynards Gate example shows the wooden hoops which bound the staves which, in this case, had been extracted to reveal the hoops in position. The table on which moulds were set was found intact at Pippingford.

narrow, to reduce the consequences of the warping of an individual piece. At Maynards Gate fragments of 35 staves were found, at Scarlets there were 31, and at Pippingford 28 in the lower part of the pit and 25 in the upper part, which was under less pressure from surrounding water. The external hoops held the staves closely together: at Maynards Gate four double hoops and one single were overlapped, pegged, and nailed in such a way that makes it virtually certain that the pit was prefabricated and lowered into the excavation. The floor was well sealed: at Maynards Gate the boards had been driven down to a step cut on the inside of the staves; at Scarlets the staves appeared to rest on the floor, although the details of the seal could not be established; at Pippingford the methods were combined, with a layer of puddled clay between two sets of floorboards. In this last case the upper floor rested on the puddled clay rather than on stepped staves. Such constructional devices were inadequate. At Pippingford this is very clear, for lead patches cover imperfections in the staves, knot-holes had been enlarged, and both dowels and square blocks substituted. It was also standard practice to pump the pit, or

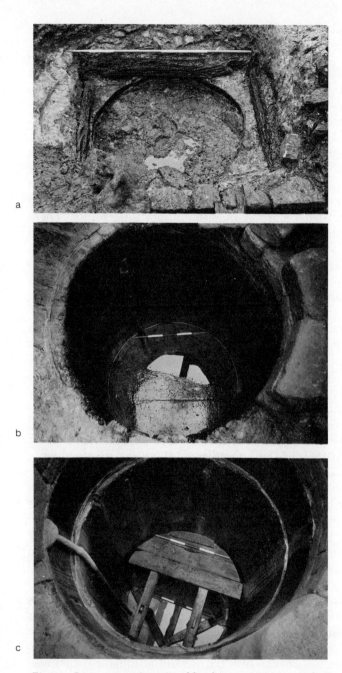

a

b

c

Fig.61   Gun-casting pits at Wealden furnaces: (a) Maynards Gate (O. R. Bedwin); (b) Scarlets; (c) Pippingford. Pipes for pumping the pits are shown at Scarlets (wooden) and Pippingford (lead). The Pippingford mould-table is shown with its top partly removed. The square timber kerb at Maynards Gate is shown in a photograph taken before removal of rubble filling the pit (scale: (a): 2m; (b) and (c): 1m).

'vault' as it was called. This is clear from the Ashburnham and Heathfield accounts.[14] Pump pipes were found at Pippingford and Scarlets, the former of lead, the latter a wooden channel nailed to the pit side in a remarkably crude way. It is not possible to say what kinds of pumps were used, for no traces have been found at any of the furnaces excavated.

The mould was set on a table in the pit. The only recorded example of a table was found at Pippingford, where it was clear that legs of differing heights could be used, according to the size of mould. When the latter was set in position it was packed around with sand, a practice which is also recorded in contemporary accounts. These refer in particular to the work involved in removing the sand, which would be necessary after every cast, and the staves at Scarlets bore the imprint of many a shovel nose, wielded in the restricted space of the pit.

A particular problem was to lift the mould and the heavy casting out of the pit. No traces of cranes or sheer-legs have yet been found, but at Pippingford and Scarlets the difficulty was to an extent alleviated by building a floor adjacent to one sector of the pit edge, at a lower level than the casting floor as a whole. In both cases these floors lay away from the furnace, and it is assumed that castings were lifted from the pits and tilted to lie in a horizontal position on the floorboards before being moved further. At Pippingford and Scarlets the pit kerbs were formed of substantial stonework, except adjacent to these floors, where the tops of the staves were exposed. The pit at Maynards Gate, by contrast, had no adjacent floor and no stone kerb, being topped by a timber edge, square in plan, with the rammed clay outside the timbers exposed. It could well be that horizontal boards had covered this clay, but had been removed when the staves of the pit had been robbed.

This is not the place for a detailed exposition of mould-making methods, important though the skill was for the reputation of the industry. The topic is covered in admirable detail in connection with eighteenth-century casting of brass cannon at Woolwich (Jackson and De Beer 1973: 80–109).[15] There are, however, certain traces of this activity which appear on the ground. The hardening of moulds was done over a fire set in a rectangular hearth: this is illustrated in the pictures of the Verbruggen foundry at Woolwich. It has been suggested that the rectangular patch of burnt sand at Batsford, enclosed by a course of stone blocks, may represent such a hearth. Mould fragments have been found in some quantity. The largest deposit is at Ashburnham furnace, but comparable material has been recorded in the excavations at Pippingford and Batsford. Surface finds of mould fragments have been made at Heathfield, Langleys, Maresfield, Mayfield, Pallingham, Robertsbridge, Stream and Waldron furnaces.

Characteristic scrap is rarely found. Reference has already been made to cast-iron shot abandoned or lost. Large castings discarded as faulty had a value as scrap, for in the sixteenth and seventeenth centuries items such as guns could be refined at forges, being treated in just the same way as pig iron. From the early eighteenth century they could be re-melted in air furnaces and further objects cast. It is thus remarkable that a faulty cannon, complete with its gun-head, should have been abandoned at Pippingford, treated virtually as hard-core by being built into the foundation of the second furnace (figs.62, 63). This is a unique find, the only unfinished cast-iron gun known to have survived in Britain.[16]

Fig.62   Cannon from Pippingford furnace: gamma-radiograph showing voids in the casting of a *falcon*. The casting-head has not been removed, as would be done prior to boring. The total length of the gun, with head, is 1945mm, without head approximately 1685mm (photograph: Ancient Monuments Laboratory, Department of the Environment).

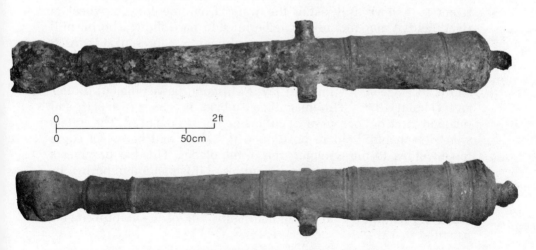

Fig.63   Gun from Pippingford furnace, complete with head: 2 views
(photograph: Ancient Monuments Laboratory, Department of the Environment).

4 Boring mills

An important adjunct to a casting furnace was a boring mill. Here the hollow-cast gun, pipe or roller was bored out to the required internal diameter, using a system which is well illustrated by Biringuccio (1540 [1558 edn]: 113). The casting was mounted on a sled or trolley and was slowly winched forward against a revolving cutter. The cutter blades were fixed to a head which formed the end of a wrought iron bar mounted in a chuck. This assembly was turned by a water-wheel or a treadmill.

There are several boring-mill sites known in the Weald, and documentary references indicate still more. At Pippingford much of the base of a mill survived (fig.64): the gun had been mounted on a trolley, whose four cast-iron wheels remained *in situ* on a track marked by two parallel beams set in slots in a clay bed. A boss-like casting lay in the middle of the track and is interpreted as some form of chuck, to hold the boring bar. A circular brick structure beyond the end of the track was probably the mounting for a windlass pulling the trolley. There was, however, no indication of how the boring bar was rotated, although the layout would have allowed either a water-wheel or a tread-wheel. A significant find here was the heap of turnings which lay alongside the mill. Deposits of this kind have since been recognized at Conster and Mayfield (fig.65).

There is ample written reference to boring mills. Ashburnham forge was converted for boring by 1677, and a new boring mill was built in the middle of the eighteenth century. The Fuller correspondence refers to a new mill using the water from the furnace-wheel at Heathfield. A map including Lamberhurst furnace shows a boring mill on the furnace tail-race, and boring equipment was present at Hamsell in 1708.[17]

A fine example of a boring bar has been found at Stream furnace, and is to be seen at Anne of Cleves Museum, Lewes (fig.66) (Butler and Tebbutt 1975). This magnificent object is 3.35m in length and retained three out of four of its cutters in place in the head. The cutters were detachable, held in position with shims, and had steel edges forge-welded to the wrought iron of the blades. This bar provides a remarkable illustration of the difficulties of this method of boring. Its unsupported length is such as to allow the head to follow any irregularities in the interior surface of the casting, and explains the search for better methods, culminating in Wilkinson's improvements patented in 1772.

Fig.64   Boring mill at Pippingford (TQ 451316). Most Wealden boring mills can be identified only by place-names, or at best by corroded heaps of turnings adjacent to streams (fig.65). At Pippingford excavation revealed beam-slots for a track on or near which the four cast-iron wheels of the boring carriage remained in place. Two of these are shown, together with what appears to be a chuck to fix a boring bar to its driving-wheel (scale: 1m).

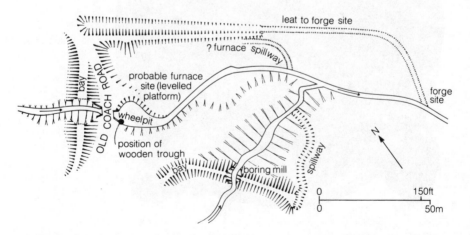

Fig.65   Mayfield ironworks: furnace, boring mill, and probable forge (TQ 593281). It is not certain whether these all worked simultaneously, although the layout would permit this. The boring mill is identifiable by deposits of corroded turnings.

a

b

Fig.66 Boring bar from Stream furnace, Chiddingly (TQ 555155). This wrought-iron bar (a) probably dates from the seventeenth century. Its head (b) had originally contained four cutters, three of which were in position when the bar was recovered (see Butler and Tebbutt 1975) (scale on bar: 1ft) (photograph: D. S. Butler).

5 Archaeological indications of raw-material supply to the furnace

(A) ORE: MINING

The extent of ore workings in the Wealden deposits is reviewed in Chapter 1. The archaeological potential for exploration of mining sites is limited by the difficulty of dating and by physical problems. So far two investigations have been undertaken (fig.67). At Herstmonceux

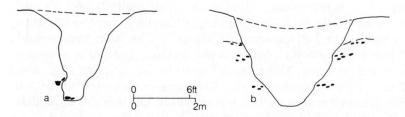

Fig.67   Orepit profiles. Re-excavated pits at (a) Herstmonceux (TQ 634143) (after Tebbutt 1978); (b) Rotherfield (TQ 521343) (after Swift 1982).

the filling of a minepit was removed, to investigate the profile of the original excavation (Tebbutt 1978). It was found that the depth was 3m and that the bottom 2m had been dug as a straight-sided pit. Near Minepit Wood, Rotherfield, two pits were sectioned by machine (Swift 1982). One was just under 3m in depth, the other slightly more. Both were basin-shaped. There are, of course, many thousand mine-pits in the Weald, and it is not yet possible to generalize on depth or form, which must depend on local conditions. It does seem, however, that miners confined themselves to shallow workings; indeed, Sir James Hope comments that around Barden the pits were 12–16ft (4–5m) deep. Nor, so far, is there any reason to suppose that 'bell-pits' were dug. These are common in the north of England, embodying a shaft which is expanded into a chamber when ore or coal is reached. In the Weald it was more usual to dig pits very close together, as indeed Hope notes in his diary, and there are places in the Weald where this practice must have led virtually to open-cast working. It is also difficult to determine the date of minepits, for few objects are likely to be found in dateable contexts within them. It has to be assumed that pits were backfilled rapidly, often a condition imposed by the owner of the ground. The date of some pits can be estimated from the documentary evidence of last working. For example, the Ashburnham accounts for the late eighteenth century indicate where mining took place, thus making it likely that the most prominent disturbances in these lands will date from this late period.

Ore fragments are frequently found on blast furnace sites, but it is unwise to draw too many conclusions from analyses. Ore in such contexts may well have been discarded, and for some reason not be typical of the material charged. Also, furnaces mixed several types of ore into the charge: John Fuller gives a detailed record of the varieties to be found in one minepit (Saville 1979), and Sir James Hope gives the impression that several types were available at Barden (Marshall 1958: 146). Of the types to be found, the most common are the nodular ores, oval lumps with a smooth surface which easily breaks up into numerous layers, and 'shelly', the purple Cyrena limestone found in many minepits and discussed in Chapter 1. The latter type would have some effect as a flux, but it is not certain what proportion of a charge it would form. There is no certainty that lime as such was added to furnace charges. In the Ashburnham accounts there are certainly references to lime being transported but it is not clear that this was mixed with the furnace charge.[18]

(B) ORE: PREPARATION

It is not clear to what extent iron ore was subjected to roasting in the Weald in the blast furnace period. In the Roman industry ores certainly were roasted, and the practice has been recognized on the medieval site at Minepit Wood. Post-medieval practice seems to have varied. In the Robertsbridge and Panningridge accounts there is no mention of roasting, and it is assumed that at these furnaces weathering was regarded as sufficient. At first sight, this is strange, for roasting can confer considerable benefits. The ore is made more permeable, thus improving reduction and increasing yields in the furnace. Roasted ore fractures, and can be sorted into the best sizes for the charge. In addition, impurities are removed, notably any excess water and sulphur. In fact it has been found that the sulphur in ores local to Panningridge is in the form of calcium sulphate, which can only be removed by heating above 1,100°C, a temperature which open-stack roasting hearths would be unlikely to achieve. It is not unreasonable to assume that it was found that Panningridge pig iron, even if smelted from roasted ore, still made a brittle bar, typical of an unroasted ore retaining sulphur. This might explain why roasting was not normally done there, even though ironworkers were, at this period, ignorant of the elements involved.

Yet there is no doubt that roasting was done elsewhere in the Weald. The field evidence is conclusive, for fragments of roasted ore were found on the charging bank at Pippingford I, on the track leading to Maynards Gate from nearby minepits, and in the vicinity of the

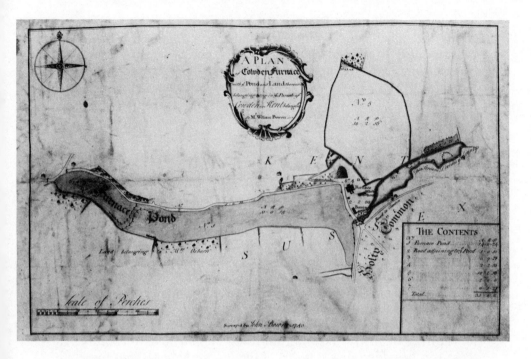

Fig.68 William Bowen's furnace at Cowden, 1748 (KAO U650/P1) (photograph: Kent Archives Office, Maidstone).

furnaces at Batsford, Horsted Keynes, Lamberhurst (Gloucester), Robertsbridge, Socknersh and Warbleton. Sir James Hope's description of Barden (1646) is illuminating, and agrees with Ray's account of 1672. Both write of ores of various kinds being burned in heaps, using charcoal, and Hope emphasizes that this practice, rather than the use of a roasting kiln, was common. Where he had seen a roasting kiln is not clear, but one has been found in a contemporary context in north-east England. In the Weald no traces have been found on the ground, and the documentary sources are far from conclusive. The kiln referred to at Ashburnham after 1757 is not certain to have been used for ore roasting, and the building marked 'kiln' on the 1748 map of Cowden furnace (fig.68) could also have been for lime rather than ore.[19]

(C) CHARCOAL

Woodland management is discussed in Chapter 7, in relation to charcoal-burning. The latter has left little trace on the ground. Many areas where cutting and burning took place are known from documents and place-names, but woodlands once coppiced for the iron industry have been used for other purposes for two centuries at least. They have grown hop-poles and wood for other forest crafts; some have been replanted, many have been grubbed up. However, ploughing can still expose areas of black soil where coaling once took place.

6   The forge

(A) THE PROCESS

In the field, the site of the finery forge is less easy to interpret than that of the blast furnace. Although the forge will possess a pond-bay and water-courses similar in layout to those of the furnace, structural remains are less readily located than the characteristic debris of a collapsed furnace stack. In addition, only two forges, Ardingly and Chingley, have been excavated in the Weald, so there is less certainty as to what constituted a typical layout. On the other hand, a number of inventories have survived (see below) listing equipment in forges leased from the early sixteenth until the mid-eighteenth century. To these can be added descriptions of the forging process, but these are less numerous or useful than those of furnace practice.

An understanding of the work carried out at the forge is necessary for the fieldworker. The process made brittle pig iron into a malleable material suitable for the smith. To do this, the pig was re-melted in an open charcoal-fired hearth, blown by water-powered bellows. The carbon was burnt out, the proportion falling from 3–4 per cent to 0.1–0.2 per cent. The only variation was at Robertsbridge where, from 1566, the process was stopped short to produce a steel, whose carbon content would remain at perhaps 0.3–0.4 per cent. A considerable quantity of slag was released from the iron, and the process of fining took place in a bath of slag in the hearth. The characteristic rusty cinders found at forge sites result from the tapping of surplus slag and from the periodic clearance of slag from the hearth as it cooled.

As the bloom formed in the base of the hearth it was kept in motion amidst the slag, and subjected to the oxidizing blast. It was eventually taken to the hammer. Here slag was expelled from the hot bloom, which was then returned to the finery for further heating and removal of impurities. Finally, the bloom was taken to the hammer to be drawn into bar. It was first drawn into a short thick bar known as an ancony and then into the section in which it would be sold. Most bars weighed about 40lb and were 2.75–4m long. The bar had to be heated during this forging, and in the Weald it was normal to use a second hearth, the chafery, for this purpose. This was also blown by water-powered bellows, but produced little or no slag. The major waste resulting from this stage of the operation was hammer-scale, which formed on surfaces around the hammer and anvil. This was particularly noticeable at Ardingly forge.

There were therefore three operations which required water power, although in the larger forges some were duplicated, as at Roberts-bridge, where there were two fineries and two chaferies. Thus the layout of wheels, with penstocks and tail-races, was more complex than at a furnace. At both Ardingly and Chingley two channels were used (fig.69). At Ardingly the re-use of the site as a fulling mill had obscured the details, but in the final phase at Chingley, one channel served the finery wheel and the other, with a divided flow, housed the hammer and chafery wheels. Both here and at Ardingly the chafery wheel was housed in an offset chamber with a separate feed, allowing a clear outflow from the hammer wheel. By contrast, in the early seventeenth century the hammer and finery wheels at Chingley appear to have been set in tandem in the same channel: this arrangement was potentially unsatisfactory, for water driving the undershot finery wheel could well be slowed to the extent of backing up under the overshot or pitch-back hammer wheel. Furthermore, independent control of the finery wheel would be impossible. The aim was, of course, to reduce the number of water-feeds through the bay to a minimum, and it is a matter for speculation whether this was ever achieved in the Weald by driving the bellows and the hammer from the same wheel. Filarète's fifteenth-century account of an Italian forge suggests just such a practice.

(B) FORGE INVENTORIES

1509	Newbridge	PRO DL29/455/7331, repr. in Schubert 1957, App.VI
1573	St Leonards	Pat.Roll 15 Eliz. pt 10, repr. in Schubert 1957, App.IX
1582	Potmans	ESRO ASH 13298
1604	Hawksden	ESRO Glynde 1227
c. 1637	Mitchell Park	Surrey Arch. Collns 18 (1903), 50–2
1651	Hawksden	ESRO Glynde 1229
1652 1655	Bayham	Sussex Arch. Collns 32 (1882), 29 ESRO DH609

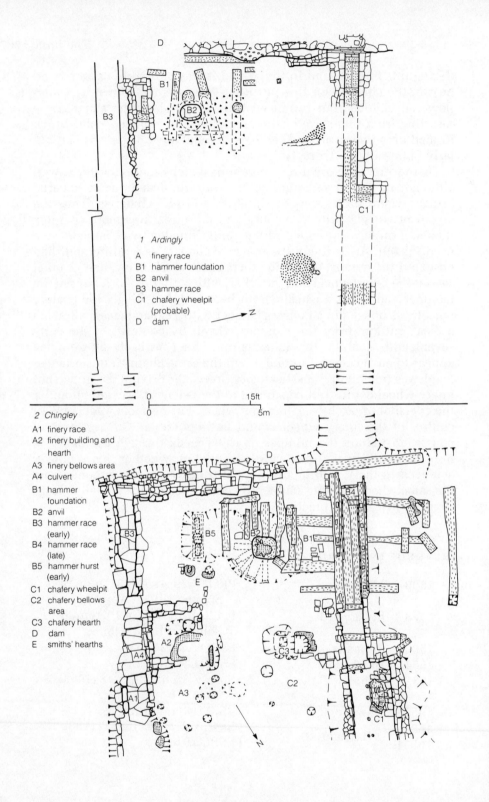

1 Ardingly

A   finery race
B1 hammer foundation
B2 anvil
B3 hammer race
C1 chafery wheelpit
    (probable)
D   dam

2 Chingley

A1 finery race
A2 finery building and
    hearth
A3 finery bellows area
A4 culvert
B1 hammer
    foundation
B2 anvil
B3 hammer race
    (early)
B4 hammer race
    (late)
B5 hammer hurst
    (early)
C1 chafery wheelpit
C2 chafery bellows
    area
C3 chafery hearth
D   dam
E   smiths' hearths

0   15ft
0   5m

Fig.69 Forges at (1) Ardingly (TQ 334289) (after Bedwin 1976: 40) and (2) Chingley (TQ 682335). The layouts were essentially similar, although at Ardingly many details had been lost due to the re-use of the site as a fulling mill. The layout at Chingley was complicated due to the removal of the hammer wheel from the east (left) channel to a new wheelpit on the west side at some time in the seventeenth century.

1664	Woodcock	SAS Gage 43/52
1665	Hawksden	ESRO Glynde 1230
1666	Horsebane	VCH Surrey II (1905), 273
1726		ESRO Glynde 3088 (i)
1727	Hawksden	ESRO Glynde 1234
1766		ESRO Glynde 3088 (ii)

(C) FORGE EQUIPMENT

Forge hearths have not survived well. It became normal by the late sixteenth century to line fineries with iron plates: eight are referred to in the inventory of St Leonards forge of 1573. Their presence is common in the seventeenth-century inventories, and they can thus be regarded as movable objects. A plate 1.3m by 0.55m found at Verredge forge is probably a side-plate. At Chingley corroded fragments of side-plates remained, but the bottom-plate had been removed. Once plates were taken out, the stone or brick surround would be subject to robbing or frost-erosion after the forge was abandoned. The chafery would be even less substantial, and it is doubtful whether many possessed iron linings. At Chingley all that remained was a hollow in the clay, reddened with heat, with fragments of a stone surround. At Ardingly the finery and chafery hearths had entirely disappeared. There are no remaining traces of finery or chafery superstructures, but eighteenth-century descriptions, amplified by references in the accounts for Robertsbridge forge constructed in 1542, show that the finery had a substantial hood, back wall and chimney. The pig of cast iron was passed through a hole in the back wall into the hearth for melting. The chimney, visible in portrayals of ironworks by Flemish landscape painters (fig.70), was a substantial structure of brick or stone; at Robertsbridge it was built of brick with clay daub and laths, a form of construction which required frequent maintenance.

The largest item of equipment at the forge was the hammer. It is possible to build up an impression of hammers used in the Weald from material excavated at Ardingly and Chingley, from references to hammer parts in local inventories and accounts, from eighteenth-century examples surviving elsewhere, and from contemporary draw-

Fig.70   Finery forge in Flemish landscape: detail from Henri Blès, 'Landscape with ironworks and mines'. The chimney is prominent; repairs to finery chimneys are frequently referred to in the sixteenth-century accounts for Robertsbridge forge (Uffizi Gallery, Florence).

ings and paintings from outside the Weald. The essential principle of the tilt-hammer was that the helve, a timber beam bound with iron hoops, was set in an iron pivot, the hurst, mounted on timber posts. At one end a cast-iron head was fitted to the helve, falling on the work placed on the anvil. A helve from Cansiron forge is now kept at Anne of Cleves Museum, Lewes. The helve was lifted by cams fixed in a drum; the shaft on which this was mounted formed the axle of the water wheel. The cams either lifted the helve mid-way between the pivot and the head (the belly-helve hammer) or forced the tail of the helve downwards, beyond the pivot (tail-helve). An additional feature was a 'rabbet', a timber positioned above the helve, forced upwards by the head as it neared the top of its travel. The rabbet, mounted only at the hurst end of the structure, acted as a spring, supplementing the weight of the head in its downward movement. The whole mechanism was supported by a heavy timber frame built into the forge structure. At Ardingly it was not certain what kind of hammer had been used, but at Chingley the layout of wheel-race and anvil suggest that a tail-helve had been in use early in the seventeenth century, being replaced by a belly-helve.

Surviving English and Continental forge hammers with parts dating back to the eighteenth century are of belly-helve design, whereas the tail-helve was more common in the lighter equipment used in secondary metal trades, notably for scythe manufacture. Contemporaries were much impressed by the size and noise of forge hammers. John Evelyn spoke of a hammer beam 'not less than seven yards and a half long and four feet square at the barrel'. By this he probably meant the overhead structural beam prominent in the surviving examples at Wortley (Yorkshire) and at Liège.

Parts of the hammer structure survived from both the seventeenth-century periods at Chingley forge. From the first came the only local example of a mounting for a hurst (fig.71). This comprised a vertical timber, its head cut as a fork to accommodate the pivot, mounted and strutted to a beam set in a pit. The second hammer was indicated by beams set on the surface between the wheelpit and the anvil; here the complete mechanism had been built above ground.

The most substantial remains, both at Ardingly and Chingley, were of the anvil-block (fig.72). In each case this was formed of a length of tree trunk. At Ardingly this timber was about 1m in length, placed in a pit and held in position by a triangle of beams set at ground level. A hollow iron cylinder with internal radial fins was placed on this base as a mounting for an anvil. At Chingley, however, the anvil base was altogether more substantial. A 1.7m length of tree trunk rested on sleepers set in the bottom of a pit. The trunk was held by radial

Fig.71   Hammer hurst at Chingley forge (TQ 682335). This construction, the base a re-used timber, related to the earlier of the seventeenth-century hammers, and was covered by working debris after the hammer and hammer-wheel were repositioned (scale: 3ft).

timbers wedged against verticals lining the pit. It is likely that anvil bases will survive at other forges, as has been found in the stream at Crowborough, providing an important guide to the layout of the works.

(D) FORGE BUILDINGS

Wealden forge buildings were usually composite structures of stone, brick and timber, with tile roofs. The Robertsbridge forge accounts record purchases of brick and tile, and tiles at Chingley confirm how the roof was covered. At Chingley stone footings remained along the pond-bay, showing how the wall served both as a revetment to the dam and as an end to the forge building. The brick chimneys for fineries and chaferies formed substantial elements in the forge walls. Parts of the forge structures, however, were formed of timber frames, perhaps open to the exterior. There was no sign of an eastern wall at Chingley, where pig iron would be brought across a culverted length of the wheel-race to the finery hearth. The west wall was marked by a

Fig. 72 Anvil blocks: (a) Chingley forge (TQ 682335). The length of tree-trunk, set vertically and braced against the edge of a pit by radial timbers, lacks its anvil, whose position could be established by traces of hammer-scale (scale 3ft); (b) Ardingly forge (TQ 334289). The anvil, or perhaps its support, rested on timber, and appeared to be a hollow casting with radial webs. It was surrounded by a thick deposit of hammer-scale (scale 20cm).

slot for a sill-beam. At Pophole there are remains of a building with one wall revetting the bay.

(E) SECONDARY WORKING AT WEALDEN FORGES

Surviving ironworks accounts suggest that most forges supplied bar iron either to local blacksmiths or to the London and south-east coast trades. So far, the evidence for secondary working at Wealden forges is slight. There are examples of repair items being made at Roberts-bridge forge for Panningridge furnace, but equally, some of the latter's requirements came from local blacksmiths. Nails were occasionally made: the Buckhurst Terrier (1597–8) shows that Sheffield forge had a building where nails were made, while at Buckholt a rusted mass of nails have been found. Such a find is necessarily unusual in the course of fieldwalking, so it is difficult to say whether the excavated evidence for late seventeenth- and early eighteenth-century metalworking at Chingley forge is typical. Here there were two small unpowered hearths, an emplacement for a hand anvil, and numerous items of iron. Many of these were probably locally collected scrap, but they must have been brought to the forge for some purpose, probably for re-use in conjunction with the new bar iron produced there. There were a number of blades which were unfinished, and it is suggested that a small edge-tool manufacture was carried on at the forge in its later years.

7 Slags and cinders from furnaces and forges

Finally, the tracing and identification of slags and cinders is a vital element in the field study of the industry. Waste materials can confirm indications given by earthworks, and stand on their own where such earthworks have disappeared or where a site has changed its use.

Blast furnace slags are readily identifiable by their glassy appearance, particularly when broken. They were usually tapped in hot liquid form from the hearth, although contemporaries tell us that it might be necessary to pull the slag out through the forehearth with hooks. It solidified as it cooled and was then broken up and discarded. The appearance of slag varies with its composition. The main constituent, silica, gives the appearance of glass, while the colour, ranging from black through green or blue to grey, depends to a large extent on the amount of iron present. In the Weald most slags were black or dark green, but in other areas in the eighteenth century the iron content was reduced by the use of limestone in the furnace charge, producing slags that were lighter in colour.

Slags and cinders were often carried from their place of origin. Blast furnace slag in particular was used for repairing roads, for making up field gateways, and for strengthening bays. This latter practice can pose a problem for the fieldworker, for slag has been found in the bays of pen ponds remote from a furnace, yet initially suggesting a works close at hand.

Most blast furnace sites have adjacent slag deposits, frequently in the valley downstream from the works. Other waste accompanies these slags, but in smaller quantities. This largely comprises materials removed from the hearth at the end of a smelting campaign. Slag can be found mixed with partly reduced ore, with charcoal, or with scraps of cast iron. On occasion sizeable pieces of cast iron have been recorded. Such 'bears' (accumulations in the hearth bottom) were sometimes left in place when a furnace was abandoned, as at Batsford, but otherwise were tipped with the slag, as at Darfold and Maynards Gate. On occasion cast-iron runners are found. Some will have solidified in a channel between the furnace hearth and a mould, others are the result of a break-out when a hearth lining has worn thin. Some such runners would be taken to the forge to be refined, but examples remained near the furnaces at Panningridge and Chingley.

Forge cinder is less easy to identify. Most characteristic are the massive rusty-brown deposits which accumulated in the bottoms of finery hearths. These were frequently removed whole and carried away. There are numerous examples on forge cinder dumps, and some forge bottoms were given a structural use, strengthening the banks of water-courses. Forge dumps also contain cinders, lighter in weight and more porous in appearance than the hearth bottoms. These cinders were raked or tapped from finery hearths during the conversion of pig to wrought iron. Also to be found is hammer-scale, a material with a rusty laminated appearance, usually forming layers on the floors of the forge around the anvil. Hammer-scale could also adhere to nearby timber and stonework, and may thus be expected in rubble from demolished forge structures. Some forge bottoms and cinders bear a resemblance to bloomery waste, but in fact only a small proportion of deposits can be so confused. Finery cinder will not contain anything with the viscous appearance of bloomery tap slag, nor can it contain ore, as do many bloomery hearth-bottoms.

8 Conclusion

This chapter has shown that many aspects of the operation of the industry have been investigated and illustrated from the archaeologist's viewpoint. A cross-section of blast furnaces, ranging in date from the mid-sixteenth to the early eighteenth centuries, have been excavated, together with two seventeenth-century forges. Not only excavation but also intensive fieldwork have provided information more comprehensive than was available to Straker. Nevertheless, outstanding questions remain: prime among these is the possibility of evolution of the finery forge from the bloomery: as indicated in Chapters 5 and 6, the end of the Middle Ages presents a blank in our knowledge of Wealden iron-smelting, and it is uncertain how many water-powered bloomeries lasted into the sixteenth century and whether they were adapted to the new process. The change would not be a difficult one, for the elements, the hammer and two hearths, were the same in number if not in size. Thus current fieldwork is directed towards the re-examination of forges known to have been at work in the mid-sixteenth century, seeking the presence of bloomery tap-slag. The results will come after the publication of this book.

NOTES

1. BL Lansdowne 5233, f.53.
2. ESRO SAS RF15/25, 4 Feb. 1744.
3. *Ibid.*, 15 May 1742; ESRO Glynde 2046.
4. KAO U1475 B6/1, B10/8.
5. KAO U1475 B10/1, B1/5.
6. ESRO ASH 4385.
7. KAO U1475 B5/1.
8. KAO U1475 B9; B3/9.
9. KAO U1475 B10/10; ESRO ASH 4465, 1815.
10. ESRO ASH 1815. Mr W. R. and Mrs M. Beswick have kindly explained the significance of this reference.
11. KAO U1475 B10/2, 2a, B10/8.
12. ESRO SAS RE15/25, 11 Sept. 1739.
13. BL Add. MSS 33156: 1691–2.
14. ESRO ASH 1815; ESRO SAS RF15/26, 13 May 1723.
15. A valuable inventory of the gun founding equipment of David Middleton of Marshalls furnace (1619) is in PRO C239/86.
16. Displayed in Anne of Cleves House Museum, Lewes.
17. ESRO ASH 3983, 1815; ESRO SAS RF15/25, 15 May 1742; Bell-Irving 1903 178; KAO U120/P15.
18. ESRO ASH 1815, 1817.
19. KAO U1650/P1.

Appendices

Appendix 1. The Wealden Iron Research Group

The Wealden Iron Research Group was founded in 1968, following a public meeting held at Brighton convened by Henry Cleere and David Crossley. Its aim was to follow up the pioneer work of Ernest Straker's *Wealden Iron*, published in 1931, 'to promote further research into the history of the Wealden iron industry, with the ultimate aim of publishing a survey and history of the industry in book form'.

A steering committee was formed, but original hopes of setting up small working parties all over the Weald proved impracticable, as only· one, the strong Buxted group led by Joseph Pettitt, became viable. This group established a pattern of regular meetings and forays, to visit sites already recorded by Straker and to explore other sites of which there was documentary evidence. Its members learned much about the nature and interpretation of field evidence to be found on ironworking sites.

In 1971 the Group was set up on a more formal basis, with a constitution, an elected chairman, executive committee, officers, and two public meetings each year. The annual general meeting, held in the summer, is traditionally preceded by a field visit and is well attended by members and others who do not normally wish to take part in routine fieldwork. The winter meeting usually consists of a lecture on some aspect of the iron industry or an allied topic. It was also decided to publish a *Bulletin*, containing short reports of work in progress or complete, and other items of general interest. Until 1981 two *Bulletins* a year were produced, but thereafter only one, owing to increasing costs. Since 1981, members have also received a newsletter. Major reports appear in national or county archaeological journals with summaries in the bulletins.

C. F. Tebbutt became the first chairman, succeeded in 1979 by Mrs D. M. Meades, and in 1981 by J. Hodgkinson. The exacting job of secretary was first filled by J. Pettitt, followed by D. Butler in 1974 and P. Willmott in 1976. After the untimely death of the latter in 1977, Mrs D. M. Meades served until 1979 and was then succeeded by Mrs S. Swift. J. Pettitt was the first editor of the *Bulletin*, followed in 1973 by D. Crossley. In 1979, in order to achieve charitable status, it was necessary for the constitution to be slightly amended. At the same time Mr Tebbutt had signified his intention to retire from the office of chairman. It was decided to create a presidency; members took the opportunity to show their appreciation of Mr Tebbutt's long and valuable service to the cause of Wealden iron research by asking him to become their first president under the amended constitution. This he agreed to do.

In 1971 a general field group was formed, with a nucleus of members from the former Buxted group. Members arranged forays to continue the work of revisiting and surveying sites recorded by Straker, their findings being used to fill standard questionnaires. Documentary and field evidence of previously unknown sites was also followed up, and many new sites were discovered, especially of the earlier periods. The results of this work formed the basis for the gazetteers in this book. The need for preservation and protection of many of the sites visited has been strongly felt, and a number have been scheduled by the Department of the Environment as Ancient Monuments at the suggestion of the Group.

Meanwhile, a number of rescue excavations had been undertaken in the Weald by the Sussex Field Unit and by teams under the leadership of David Crossley. These were funded from various sources, including the Department of the Environment. WIRG members assisted at these excavations and thereby gained valuable experience. Guided by their chairman, C. F. Tebbutt, himself an experienced amateur archaeologist, members were thus able to undertake research excavations on early bloomery sites, which yielded valuable information as to furnace types and ironmaking techniques; most proved to be of Roman date. The sole representative of the Saxon period (ninth century) was excavated and recorded as a WIRG rescue operation. Reports were published in the *Sussex Archaeological Collections*. The Group is indebted to various experts who have commented, advised, and assisted with dating their finds.

It had early become apparent that bloomery sites, represented by waste slag, were unexpectedly numerous. In an attempt to learn more about these, a study area of 182km^2 was selected to record their density, position and relationship to the geography and geology of the area. A sample number of slag heaps was then excavated for dateable pottery (see Appendix 2). In order to achieve further understanding of ironmaking in prehistoric and medieval times, one WIRG member initiated a series of experiments in which prehistoric bloomery furnace construction and assumed smelting methods were simulated; valuable insights into the skills needed were gained.

There has been considerable public interest in the Wealden iron industry. The topic has been adopted for study in schools, colleges and universities, and it has proved to be of general interest to many local societies. Members have given lectures and talks, and have arranged exhibitions, courses, and field visits for teachers and students. They have also taken part in radio and television programmes, and were successful in winning the BBC *Chronicle* Award for amateur archaeology in 1981. The Group is affiliated to the Sussex Archaeological Society, and is also a member of the UISPP Ancient Ironmaking Committee, an international body devoted to the study of the early development of the iron industry.

The Wealden Iron Research Group does not consider its work to be finished with the publication of this book, although it does believe that this is a proper stage at which to make the results of 16 years of research available to the public. Readers will appreciate that important questions remain to be answered, and there will also, no doubt, be a continuing need for rescue excavation and the corresponding opportunity to acquire new knowledge.

Appendix 2. Wealden bloomery iron-smelting furnaces*

C. F. TEBBUTT

A fieldwalking project by the Wealden Iron Research Group to assess the situation and density of bloomery furnace sites in a given study area in the Weald is described. This was followed by the simple excavation of a number of selected bloomery slag heaps in the hope of recovering dateable pottery. The majority of the sampled sites turned out to be Romano-British.

(A) INTRODUCTION

In 1976 the field study section of the Wealden Iron Research Group undertook a project concerning bloomery furnace sites in the Weald. Research was organized to answer the following questions:

1 How widespread were these sites and where did they mainly occur?
2 What was their date?

(B) DENSITY AND DISTRIBUTION

In an attempt to assess the density and situation of bloomery furnaces, a study area of 182km² was selected, comprising both high and low Weald (fig.73). Within this area a number of sites had already been

* Reprinted from *Sussex Archaeological Collections, 119* (1981), 57–64 (slightly abridged), by kind permission of the Council of the Society and the Editor (Dr Owen Bedwin).

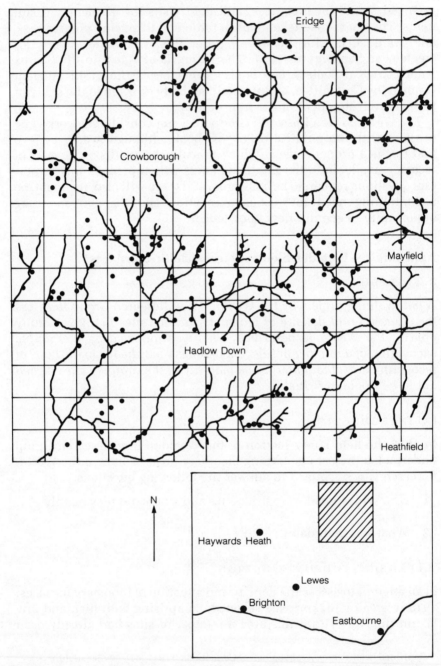

Fig.73   Sketch plan of study area showing bloomery furnace sites (grid lines are at 1km intervals).

recorded by the Group, and others by Straker (1931a), Money (1971; 1974) and Cattell (1970). Fieldwalking was based on stream valleys, where initially it was thought that most bloomeries were to be found. The majority probably are so situated, but it was soon noted that they also occur on springs, hillsides and even hilltops. The area selected has Wadhurst Clay on most of its high ground, capping Ashdown Sand, and at the junction of these strata the iron ore occurs *in situ*. Pockets of derived ore may, however, occur on pure Ashdown Sand and some bloomeries are undoubtedly based on these.

Essentials to the bloomery process are iron ore, clay and charcoal and it would have been advantageous if the first two, being difficult to transport, were to hand. A supply of water was also desirable. The surface of the Ashdown Sand itself often forms a silty clay-like substance suitable for furnace construction. It was noted that what might be called the typical bloomery site, of which many were found, was situated on the banks of a small stream which had cut a deep channel through the base of the Wadhurst Clay, thus exposing the ore to the prospecting bloomery worker. Having located this ore stratum, all that was necessary was to quarry back from the stream until the overburden became too great to make further quarrying economic, or the lens of high-grade nodular ore ran out. Numerous so-called 'bell-pits' were seen near bloomeries, but in no case could a direct link with the furnace site be shown. A probable link is, however, described by Money (1971) in the medieval period.

The finding of these stream-side sites is not difficult; some slag is inevitably washed into the stream and carried down to be deposited in shingle beds. By following the slag trail upstream the site can usually be located. It was found to be worth following even the smallest streams to their source, especially if the geological conditions were favourable.

It is probable that few sites were missed on the smaller streams, but the larger main valley streams did not prove very productive. It is possible that accumulated alluvium had covered some sites, but it is not considered likely that many furnaces were in fact situated on these large streams as sources of ore are lacking. The chances of finding sites away from streams were not very good. Present-day woodland cover over the whole of Sussex is believed to be 18 per cent, and is probably greater in the Weald. Of the cultivated ground, much is ley or permanent pasture, and the arable is only temporarily available for walking, during which time as much as possible was covered. Thus the density of bloomery sites away from the vicinity of streams remains an uncertain factor, probably significant but not great. In spite of the above limitations the results, when plotted on the map, are impressive (fig.73). When the previously recorded sites are added, the total number of bloomeries discovered in the area is 246, giving a density of 1.4 per km².

(c) DATING

Given the fact that the date of the furnaces could range over as much as 1,500 years, and that as yet no satisfactory method has been devised to distinguish medieval from prehistoric bloomery slag, dating seemed a formidable task. Even if it had been practicable to locate and excavate a significant number of actual furnaces, apart from their slag heaps, it is not possible to make definite distinction between the Wealden medieval and prehistoric furnace types. Thus the only solution was a quick method of excavation, to discover dateable artefacts, i.e. pottery. Although there is no evidence that bloomery workers lived on the sites, they had to spend long hours there, and at the few Wealden furnaces excavated (Money 1971; 1974; Cleere 1970; Tebbutt and Cleere 1973; Tebbutt 1979), pottery had been found in the slag heaps.

It was therefore determined to carry out a number of simple excavations on slag heaps in the study area, where trenches 1m wide would be unlikely to affect the furnaces themselves, which are usually to be found at some distance from the slag heap. Sites were selected on the grounds of favourable access, absence of tree roots and farm crops, and willingness of owner. In most cases this method proved successful and pottery was found in small quantities. Unsuccessful digs included those where the site had been cultivated and the slag scattered and spread by ploughing. It appears likely that some prehistoric native pottery is quickly disintegrated by weathering, but is well preserved if undisturbed.

By including the few sites where pottery sherds had previously been found on the surface it was possible to date 33 sites, and by adding to these a further seven already recorded (Straker 1931a; Money 1971; 1974; Cattell 1970), to make a total of 40. Thus a dating of 16 per cent of recorded bloomery furnaces was achieved, considered to be a significantly large sample from which to draw conclusions as to the dates of the remainder. It should be noted that the two dated by Cattell were by radiocarbon determination, which has yet to be proved a reliable method on bloomery sites. By this method, one of Cattell's sites was possibly of the pre-Roman Iron Age. In the table below, Money's Iron Age and Romano-British sites represent two phases of use of a single site. The results are as shown:

Source	Method	Iron Age	Romano-British	Medieval
Wealden Iron Research Group	Excavation and surface finds		29	4
Straker	Surface finds		2	1
Money	Excavation	1	1	
Cattell	Radiocarbon	1	1	
	Totals	2 (5%)	33 (82%)	5 (13%)

(D) CONCLUSIONS

The density of sites (fig.73) is obviously very great, especially as the numbers recorded certainly fall far short of the actual total. Slag heaps are known to have been removed for road making in both Roman (Margary 1965) and modern times (Straker 1931a: 395).

The results of dating are of the greatest interest, highlighting a large and intensive Roman industry geared, no doubt, to export from the district, in contrast to a small medieval enterprise mainly satisfying local needs. The likely organization of this Roman industry in the eastern Weald by the *Classis Britannica* has already been discussed by Cleere (1975) with the suggestion of a quite different type of organization further west in the study area. The role of regional administrative centres in this area may be much clearer when J. H. Money's unfinished excavation at Garden Hill, Hartfield, is published. At the extreme western edge of the study area, Oldlands (Straker 1931a) was almost certainly an administrative centre, and a single hypocaust tile from Morphews bloomery (TQ 509256) might indicate the presence there of a regional administrator's headquarters. The results also throw a revealing light on the occupation and exploitation of the Weald in Roman times, which must have included clearing and cultivation for food production.

Appendix 3. Development of prices and yields between the sixteenth and eighteenth centuries

[1] PRICES (a) Charcoal (load)

	s.	d.		
1539	3	0	Newbridge	PRO E32/197
1545–8	3	0		
1549	3	4		
1551–4	4	0	Panningridge and	
1555–6	5	0	Robertsbridge	
1558–60	6	0		
1562	6	8		KAO U1475
1563	8	0		(Crossley 1975a:
1564	8	0		21–2)
1565	7	8		
1566–7	8	0	Robertsbridge	
1568–70	9	0		
1571–2	8	0		
1569	6	8	Burningfold	PRO REQ2/177/32
1577	8	0	Langles	Crossley 1974; 71
1584	12	0	Panningridge	ESRO EpII/5/3
1601	12	0	Gosden	PRO REQ2/186/35
1629–30	24	6 (delivered)	Waldron	BL Add. MSS 33154
1633	24	0		
1634	26	0	Buckholt	Dunn 49/19
1657	30	0	Bedgebury	HRO Foley E/12/PF5
1677	30	0	Hamsell	ESRO DH 614
1744	17–21	0	Beckley, Brede, Brightling, Waldron, Westfield	Guildhall 3736/3
1756–7	25	6		
	30	0	Ashburnham	ESRO ASH 1815

(b) Bar iron (ton)

	£ s. d.					
1497	4 0 0 – 4 6 8		English iron	PRO E36/8
1539	5 0 0 – 6 0 0		Newbridge	E32/197
1542–3	5 6 8 – 6 0 0			
1549	8 10 0			
1554	7 0 0			
1556	8 0 0		Robertsbridge	KAO U1475: Crossley
1558	6 13 4			1975a passim
1563	11 0 0			
1568	8 6 8			
1572–3	8 0 0 – 9 0 0			
1584–8	10 0 0		Etchingham	PRO REQ2/68/50
1588	11 10 0		Weald iron sold in Nottingham	C3/243/7
1590	11 10 0		Weald iron sold in London	REQ2/201/4
1590	9 0 0 – 11 6 8		Lewes (loan)*	REQ2/129/54
1595	10 0 0		Chiddingstone	REQ2/32/67
1602	10 0 0		Worth	
	11 0 0 – 12 0 0		London	REQ/2/414/148

1627–9	14	0	0 – 16	10	0	Pelham forges	BL Add. MSS 33144
1648	18	0	0			Sussex price	Wyndham 1954, 102
1653	20	0	0			Westfield	ESRO Dunn 47/1
1654–9	16	10	0 – 18	0	0	Pelham forges	BL Add. MSS 33154
1681	12	0	0			Beckley	Dunn 47/8
1691–8	14	0	0 – 18	0	0 }	Pelham forges	BL Add. MSS 33156
1705–15	15	10	0 – 16	0	0 }		BL Add. MSS 33154
1732	18	0	0 – 19	0	0	Fuller	ESRO SAS RF15/25 (7.6.32.)
1744	14	10	0			Brightling and Westfield	Guildhall 3736/3
1795	22	0	0 – 23	0	0 }		
1796	22	0	0 – 24	0	0 }	Ashburnham	ESRO ASH 1818
1797	23	0	0 – 26	0	0 }		
1801	28	0	0			Ashburnham	ESRO ASH 1820

* Iron lent in lieu of cash: overvalued for the deal as a disguised form of interest.

(c) Pig iron prices (ton)

	£	s.	d.					
1549	1	3	4				Robertsbridge	U1475: Crossley 1975a
1550	1	13	4				Penhurst	PRO C3/73/58
1554	1	6	8					
1556	1	6	8					
1558	1	13	4					
1559	2	0	0					
1563	3	0	0				Robertsbridge	U1475: Crossley 1975a
1568	2	10	0					
1570	2	0	0					
1571	2	6	8					
1577	3	0	0				Cuckfield	PRO C3/207/25
1584	2	10	0 – 2	13	4		Panningridge	ESRO EpII/5/3
c.1590	3	0	0				Bramshott	PRO REQ2/165/34
1601	3	3	4				Gosden	REQ2/186/35
1627–9	5	0	0 – 5	10	0		Waldron	BL Add. MSS 33144
1634	5	5	0				Buckholt	ESRO Dunn 49/19
1637	5	10	0				Waldron	BL Add. MSS 33144
1657	6	10	0				Hawkhurst	HRO Foley E/12/PF5
1674	5	5	0				Socknersh	Dunn 47/7
1677	5	0	0				Beckley	Dunn 27/5
1681	5	0	0				Beckley	Dunn 46/9
1700–02	5	10	0 – 6	0	0		Waldron	BL Add. MSS 33156
1744	5	10	0				Brede	Guildhall 3736/3
1795	8	8	0 }				Ashburnham	{ ESRO ASH 1818
1813	8	8	0 }					{ ESRO ASH 1823

(d) Labour costs   Founder and filler (per 6-day founday)

	s.	d.		
1543–56	14	0	Panningridge	KAO U1475: Crossley 1975a: 23
1562	14	8	Panningridge	KAO U1475: Crossley 1975a: 23, 177
1577	14	0	Marshalls – sows and guns	Dulwich MSS: Crossley 1974: 68
	19	0	shot	
1584	20–21	0	Panningridge	ESRO EpII/5/3

1633	22 0	Waldron	BL Add. MSS 33154
1690–1	27 0	Waldron	BL Add. MSS 33156
1712–13	27 0	Waldron	BL Add. MSS 33154
1756–81	53 9*	Ashburnham	ESRO ASH 1815, 1817

* Payment to one man, perhaps for a 7-day week. It is not clear how many others were paid out of this sum.

Hammerman and finer (per ton of wrought iron)

	s. d.		
1539	13 4	Newbridge	PRO E32/197
1546–60	13 4⎫	Robertsbridge	KAO U1475; Crossley 1975a: 23–4
1569–72	13 4⎭		
1640–53	15 6⎫	Bivelham	BL Add. MSS 33154
1691	18 0⎭		BL Add. MSS 33156

(e) Guns and other castings (stated) – per ton

	£ s. d.			
1549	10 0 0		Worth	Giuseppi 1912: 300
1576	8 0 0	(shot)	Hogge	Crossley 1974: 74
1577	10 0 0		Hogge	Crossley 1974: 76
1596	16 0 0–17 0 0 (in England)		Giles de Vischer	PRO REQ2/266/18
	19 0 0–22 0 0 (in Netherlands)			
1597	9 6 8		Lewes: Rd Snelling	REQ2/165/103
1598	10 0 0		Mary Johnson to Ordnance Office	E351/2633
1600	7 6 8		Thos. Browne to Thos. Sackville	REQ2/191/37
1619	11 0 0		merchant price	BL Add. MSS 36777
	13 5 8		ordnance o. price	
1627	26 13 4	(guns in fine metal)	John Browne to Ordnance Office	BL Harl. 429, 28v
1651	18 0 0 – 20 0 0	(guns)	Horsmonden	HRO Foley F/V1/BF/8
	30 0 0	(drakes)		
1656	15 0 0	(guns)	Horsmonden	HRO Foley E/12/PF5
	20 0 0	(pots)		
1671	8 0 0	(plates)		
1674	16 0 0	(rollers)	Peter Farnden (Beckley)	ESRO Dunn 47/4
	20 0 0	(pans, stores)		ESRO Dunn 47/6
	8 0 0 – 9 0 0 (shot)			
1729	16 0 0 – 18 0 0 (pipes)		Fullers	ESRO SAS RF15/25, 30.5.29
1738	18 0 0		Fullers to Ordnance Office	ESRO SAS RF15/25, 30.8.38
1744	18 0 0 – 20 0 0			
	24 0 0	(½ pdr guns)	Harrison to Ordnance Office	Guildhall 6483
1746	14 5 0 – 17 0 0 (Gloucester furnace			Guildhall 3736/8
1749	10 0 0		merchant price	ESRO SAS RF15/25, 23.10.49
1749	16 0 0 – 20 0 0		Fullers' prices	RF15/25, 3.11.49
	24 0 0	(½ pdr guns)		
1750	13 13 0 – 16 16 0		Ordnance Office price	RF15/25, 31.3.50
	17 17 0	(½ pdr guns)		

(2) YIELDS

	Ore:Pig (loads) (ton)	Charcoal:Pig (loads) (ton)	Pig:Bar (tons)	Charcoal:Bar (loads) (ton)	Pig:Day (ton) or guns	
Newbridge 1539	7:1	5.5:1	2:1(?)*	5:1		PRO E32/197
Panningridge and Robertsbridge 1559ff.	5.8:1	4.6:1	1.5:1	5:1	.75 <1	Crossley 1975a: 17–19 PRO REQ2/125/14
Dunsfold 1583			1.5:1			ESRO EpII/5/3
Panningridge 1584	4.0–4.3:1	2.9–3.3:1			1–1.2	Marshall 1958: 149
Barden 1646					1.05 (guns)	Wyndham 1954: 102
Mitchell Park 1648		2.37:1	1.5:1			BL Add. MSS 33154
Waldron 1633	4:1	3.6:1			1.36	Saville 1982: 36–63
Heathfield	(1708–11)	(1708–11)			1.2 (1708–9) 1.2–1.57 (guns, etc. 1723–39) 1.1–1.8 (guns + pig 1769–78)	
Brede* ⎫ 1744–6	4.6	4.1			1.3 (guns)	Guildhall 3736/4
Conster* ⎬	6.2	4.3				
Waldron* ⎭	3.3	3.4				
Ashburnham 1761–74	4.3:1	5.8:1			1.4 (shot)	ESRO ASH 1815, 1817

* Uncertainties regarding these figures are referred to on pp.146 and 215.

> **Note:** except where advertised as open to the public, the sites and surroundings of the ironworks described in this book are private property, and readers are asked always to respect that privacy.

Abbreviations
BWIRG   *Bulletin of the Wealden Iron Research Group*
SAC   *Sussex Archaeological Collections*
SAS   Sussex Archaeological Society
SNQ   *Sussex Notes and Queries*
Sx Ind. Arch.   Sussex Industrial Archaeology Society

This is a checklist of all known Wealden bloomery sites. The sites are listed in alphabetical order of parishes, with National Grid references and brief bibliographical information where available. Where sites have been dated by excavation or as the result of surface finds, this information is given. More details of dated sites are given in Gazetteers B (Roman), and C (water-powered sites). References are given to first or major publications, fuller bibliographies appear for certain sites in Gazetteer B.

Ansty
 TQ 296237
Ashburnham/Warbleton
 TQ 663170   Straker 1931a: 361
Ashburnham
 TQ 670168   Straker 1931a: 362
Battle
 TQ 744131   *Roman*   Straker 1931a:
  351
 TQ 763175   *Roman*   Lemmon 1951–
  2
Battle/Westfield
 TQ 786146   *Roman*   Straker 1931a:
  330–7; *BWIRG 3*, 4–7
Beckley
 TQ 848206   *Roman*   *BWIRG 4*, 29
Benenden
 TQ 775329
Bexhill
 TQ 744092   Straker 1931a: 354
 TQ 746094
 TQ 756103   Straker 1931a: 357

Bletchingley
 TQ 333481   Straker 1931a:
  457
Brede
 TQ 813211   *Roman*   Straker 1931a:
  345–7; *SAS, OS Maps; SAC 29*
  (1879), 175–80
 TQ 846195   Straker 1931a: 344
 TQ 866195   Straker 1931a: 349
 TQ 882147   *Roman*   inf. Mrs Zoe
  Vahey
 TQ 887128   *Medieval*   inf. Mrs Zoe
  Vahey
 TQ 888149   *Medieval*   inf. Mrs Zoe
  Vahey
 TQ 889139
 TQ 892145   *Roman*   inf. Mrs Zoe
  Vahey
 TQ 895165
Buriton
 SU 738201   *Saxon (bloomforge)*
  BWIRG 17, 15

Burwash
TQ 648241
TQ 650238   *Roman?*   Straker 1931a:
300
TQ 653203
TQ 662236
TQ 674228   Group of 16 bloomeries
revealed by air photograph
Buxted/Maresfield
TQ 469251
TQ 469252
TQ 474264
Buxted
TQ 477306
TQ 482261
TQ 482302   *BWIRG 13*, 6–7
TQ 483263
TQ 483295
TQ 483300
TQ 483303   *BWIRG 13*, 6–7
TQ 484301
TQ 485253
TQ 485262   *BWIRG 15*, 6
TQ 485298   *Roman   BWIRG 13*, 6
TQ 486262
TQ 486292
TQ 490246   *Roman   BWIRG 15*, 6
TQ 490263
TQ 491249
TQ 492264
TQ 494232   *Medieval   BWIRG 6*,
21
TQ 494276
TQ 494284   *Roman   BWIRG 13*, 7
TQ 495271   *Roman   SAC 119* (1981),
57–63
TQ 495301
TQ 498225   *Medieval   SNQ 17*,
167– 8
TQ 498229
TQ 499243
TQ 499279
TQ 501226
TQ 501267
TQ 501274
Buxted/Crowborough
TQ 503279
Buxted
TQ 504229
TQ 506236
TQ 506273   *Roman   SNQ 14*, 278
TQ 507272   *Roman   BWIRG 13*, 12
TQ 509256   *Roman*   Straker 1931a:
389

TQ 509267
TQ 509271
Buxted/Crowborough
TQ 510273
Chailey
TQ 394208
TQ 417190
TQ 418191
Chiddingly
TQ 551161   *BWIRG*, 2nd ser, *1*, 22
TQ 567165   Straker 1931a: 383
Cowden
TQ 453423   Straker 1931a: 228
TQ 454414   Straker 1931a: 228
TQ 457403
TQ 458406   Straker 1931a: 228
TQ 459406   Straker 1931a: 228
TQ 476418
Cranbrook
TQ 801352   *Roman   Archaeol.*
Cantiana 71 (1957), 224; *72* (1958),
xlvii, lx–lxii; *76* (1961), xlviii
Crawley
TQ 245355   Gibson-Hill and Worssam
1976: 262
TQ 247357   Gibson-Hill and Worssam
1976: 262
TQ 249403   Gibson-Hill and Worssam
1976: 263
TQ 258353   *Roman   BWIRG 2*, 7; *4*,
25; *5*, 14; *8*, 47; Gibson-Hill 1975
etc.
TQ 263363   *Prehistoric*   Gibson-Hill
and Worssam 1976: 262
Crowborough
TQ 509284
TQ 512274
TQ 512288
TQ 529318   Straker 1931a: 263
TQ 531311
TQ 534302
Crowhurst
TQ 751130   *Roman*   Straker 1931a:
351–2; *BWIRG 8*, 10–11; *Trans.*
Newcomen Soc. 17 (1936–7), 197–
203
TQ 758110   *Roman*   Straker 1931a:
358; *SNQ 13*, 16–19
TQ 765133   *BWIRG 4*, 29
TQ 769136   *Roman*   Straker 1931a:
353; Straker and Lucas 1938
Dallington
TQ 664173   Straker 1931a: 361; *SNQ*
3, 162

Danehill

TQ 393259   *SAC 116*, 405

TQ 395258   *SAC 116*, 405

TQ 407288

East Grinstead

TQ 369355   *Roman*   Straker 1931a: 233–5

TQ 383344

TQ 392351   *Roman*   *SNQ 7*, 153; Straker 1931a: 239

TQ 395345   *Roman*   Straker 1931a: 239–40

TQ 397351

TQ 401354

East Hoathly

TQ 538176   Straker 1931a: 382

Eastwell Park

TR 001479   *Roman*   Council for Kentish Archaeology record cards

Etchingham/Ticehurst

TQ 682279   *Roman*   Straker 1931a: 297; *BWIRG 2*, 5

Etchingham

TQ 721276   Straker 1931a: 299

Ewhurst

TQ 756222   Straker 1931a: 318

TQ 773215   *Roman*   information H. F. Cleere

TQ 787241   Straker 1931a: 319

TQ 793231   Straker 1931a: 319

TQ 798214   Straker 1931a: 344

Fairlight

TQ 862131   Straker 1931a: 339

Fletching

TQ 407241   *Roman*   *BWIRG 13*, 15

TQ 426240

TQ 444209   *BWIRG, 2nd ser., 2*, 6

Forest Row

TQ 404348

TQ 407350

TQ 412349

TQ 412354

TQ 415351   *Medieval*   *BWIRG 6*, 18

TQ 416351   *Medieval*   *BWIRG 6*, 18

TQ 420358

TQ 435396   Straker 1931a: 223

TQ 440351

TQ 448383   *Roman*   *SAC 110*, 10–13

TQ 451363

TQ 451367

TQ 454362

Framfield/Little Horsted

TQ 475165   *Roman*   *BWIRG, 2nd ser., 2*, 6

Framfield

TQ 486201

TQ 487215

TQ 490216   *Roman*   *BWIRG 125*, 6

TQ 496214

TQ 498219

TQ 499207   Straker 1931a: 393

TQ 501215

TQ 502213   Straker 1931a: 392

TQ 509217

TQ 520201

TQ 529201

TQ 529219

Frant

TQ 575340   *Iron Age/Roman*   *SAC 117*, 258

TQ 577343   *Roman*   *BWIRG 13*, 13–14

TQ 578345   *Roman*   *BWIRG 13*, 13–14

Godstone

TQ 359458   Straker 1931a: 218

Guestling

TQ 839136   *SAS*, OS Maps

TQ 842160   Straker 1931a: 340

Hadlow Down

TQ 511219

TQ 517232

TQ 517249   *Roman*   Straker 1931a: 390; *SAC 111*, 115

TQ 519225   *Medieval*

TQ 520253

TQ 523239

TQ 525222   *Roman*   *BWIRG 6*, 22

TQ 526255

TQ 526260

TQ 527251

TQ 529255

TQ 532233

TQ 532256

TQ 532265

TQ 533252

TQ 536237   *BWIRG, 2nd ser., 2*, 6

TQ 538228

TQ 538237

TQ 539225

TQ 540268

Hadlow Down/Framfield

TQ 541223   Straker 1931a: 391

Hadlow Down
TQ 543228
TQ 544221
TQ 544227
TQ 544235
TQ 545222   *Roman   BWIRG 13*, 10
TQ 546221
TQ 547264
TQ 548257
TQ 548258
TQ 551231
TQ 552219
TQ 552220   *Roman   BWIRG 13,*
10–12
TQ 552231   *Roman   BWIRG 13*, 13
TQ 554231
TQ 555232
TQ 556231
Harrietsham
TQ 872514   *Roman   BWIRG 9,*
21–2
Hartfield
TQ 444319   *Iron Age/Roman*
BWIRG 15, 16–26; *Britannia 8*
(1977), 339–50
TQ 446313   *Roman   SAC 111,*
27–40
TQ 446345   *SAC 113*, 146–51
TQ 446348   *SAC 113*, 146–51
TQ 447346   *SAC 113*, 146–51
TQ 447348   *SAC 113*, 146–51
TQ 449346   *SAC 111*, 146–51
TQ 451339   *SAC 113*, 146–51
TQ 452309   *Roman   SAC 117*, 47–
56; *BWIRG 13*, 2–6
TQ 452341   *Medieval   SAC 113,*
146–51
TQ 452344   *SAC 113*, 146–51
TQ 452347   *SAC 113*, 146–51
TQ 453341   *SAC 113*, 146–51
TQ 453373
TQ 454339   *SAC 113*, 146–51
TQ 455331   *SAC 113*, 146–51
TQ 456317
TQ 457339   *SAC 113*, 146–51
TQ 458323
TQ 458343   *SAC 113*, 146–51
TQ 459333   *SAC 113*, 146–51
TQ 459336   *SAC 113*, 146–51
TQ 459337   *SAC 113*, 146–51
TQ 462389
TQ 471387   *Medieval   SNQ 17,*
167–8
TQ 474319

TQ 477385
TQ 477387
TQ 478383
TQ 478386
TQ 480384
Heathfield/Waldron
TQ 583235   *Roman*
Heathfield
TQ 586167   Straker 1931a: 383
TQ 591231   Cattell 1970
TQ 595195   *BWIRG*, 2nd ser., 1, 22
TQ 595227
TQ 600229   *Roman*   Cattell 1970
TQ 604198   Straker 1931a: 374
TQ 613205
TQ 613236   Cattell 1970
TQ 619212   Cattell 1970
TQ 623241   *Roman*   Cattell 1970;
SNQ 17, 101–3
TQ 630219   Cattell 1970
Hellingly
TQ 574159   Straker 1931a: 383
TQ 603145   Straker 1931a: 380
Herstmonceux
TQ 627123
Herstmonceux/Warbleton
TQ 628156   *BWIRG 17*, 16
Herstmonceux
TQ 632152   *Roman   BWIRG 15*, 9
TQ 633153
TQ 642129
Hever
TQ 464436   Straker 1931a: 218
Horley
TQ 300426   *Medieval   SAC 45*, 147;
BWIRG 4, 28
Horsham
TQ 206335   Straker 1931a: 442
Horsted Keynes
TQ 378323   Straker 1931a: 409
TQ 379204   Straker 1931a: 409
TQ 385262   *Roman   SAC 78*, 253
TQ 386298
Hurst Green/Salehurst
TQ 752277
Icklesham
TQ 870160   Straker 1931a: 340–1
TQ 872157   SAS, OS Maps
TQ 881166   *Roman   SNQ 6*, 247;
Straker 1931a: 458
Ifield
TQ 231371
Isfield
TQ 456205

Kirdford
  SU 978296   *?Iron Age   SAC 77, 245;*
    BWIRG 5, 11
Leigh
  TQ 533459   Straker 1931a: 219
Lenham Heath
  TQ 908503   *BWIRG 7,* 8
Lyminge
  TR 134430
Lingfield
  TQ 423410   *BWIRG 4,* 28
  TQ 423412   *BWIRG 4,* 28
  TQ 433413   Straker 1931a: 223
Lurgashall
  SU 942261   Straker 1931a: 431
Maresfield
  TQ 434275
  TQ 441296   *Middle Saxon*
    BWIRG, 2nd ser., 1, 17–20; *SAC 120,*
    19–36
  TQ 448301   *Roman   BWIRG 7,* 11
  TQ 455286
  TQ 457273
  TQ 458284
  TQ 462288   *BWIRG,* 2nd ser., 1, 21
  TQ 463234
  TQ 469240
  TQ 475267   *Roman   Straker 1931a:*
    395–7
Mayfield
  TQ 553265
  TQ 556264
  TQ 557250
  TQ 557270   *Roman   Straker 1931a:*
    386
  TQ 562239   *Iron Age/Roman*
    Cattell 1970
  TQ 565274   Straker 1931a: 284
  TQ 567250   Cattell 1970
  TQ 567268
  TQ 567269
  TQ 567278
  TQ 568247   Straker 1931a: 285
  TQ 568272
  TQ 569266
  TQ 569274
  TQ 570278   Cattell 1970
  TQ 571262
  TQ 571266   *BWIRG 11,* 5
  TQ 573263
  TQ 576268
  TQ 577260
  TQ 582293   Cattell 1970
  TQ 584280   Cattell 1970

  TQ 585303   *Roman   Cattell 1970;*
    BWIRG 13, 9–10
Mayfield/Rotherfield
  TQ 585309   Cattell 1970
Mayfield
  TQ 586298   Cattell 1970
Mayfield/Rotherfield
  TQ 586308
  TQ 586309   *Iron Age?   Cattell 1970;*
    Straker 1931a: 288
Mayfield
  TQ 587293   Cattell 1970
  TQ 589295   Cattell 1970
  TQ 590278   Cattell 1970
  TQ 593281
  TQ 593300   Cattell 1970
  TQ 596290   Cattell 1970
  TQ 597285   Cattell 1970
  TQ 597290   Cattell 1970
  TQ 598287   Cattell 1970
  TQ 599302   Cattell 1970
  TQ 602294
  TQ 605286   Cattell 1970
  TQ 611288   Cattell 1970
  TQ 625274   *BWIRG 2,* 5
Ninfield
  TQ 680124
Rotherfield
  TQ 508280
  TQ 508282
  TQ 509277   *Medieval   BWIRG 13,*
    7–9
  TQ 514278
  TQ 514279
  TQ 515277
  TQ 516279
  TQ 519267
  TQ 519325
  TQ 520327
  TQ 521266
  TQ 521324
  TQ 521337
  TQ 522326
  TQ 523277   *Roman   SAC 119,*
    57–63
  TQ 523331
  TQ 523338   *Medieval   Straker*
    1931a: 257; *Medieval Archaeol. 15*
    (1971) 86–111
  TQ 523338   *Roman   Straker 1931a:*
    257; *J. Hist. Metallurgy Soc. 8* (1974),
    1–20
  TQ 524321
  TQ 526324   *Medieval   BWIRG 15,* 3

TQ 527272
TQ 527274
TQ 527326   *Roman   BWIRG 15, 3*
TQ 528276
TQ 529277
TQ 529321
TQ 531335
TQ 532267
TQ 532332   *Roman   BWIRG 9, 2; 13,*
14
TQ 532336
TQ 538297   *?Medieval   BWIRG 12,*
4–7
TQ 540271   *Roman   Straker 1931a:*
387
TQ 541274
TQ 541294
TQ 542277
TQ 542326
TQ 543326
TQ 545323
TQ 547272
TQ 547323
TQ 548274
TQ 550302
TQ 551341
TQ 554341
TQ 555340
TQ 555343
TQ 557339
TQ 558304   Straker 1931a: 256
TQ 559280   *Roman*   Cattell 1970
TQ 561293
TQ 564321
TQ 572323
TQ 573323
TQ 574324
TQ 586321
TQ 587321
Rotherfield/Wadhurst
TQ 589322
Rotherfield
TQ 562278   Cattell 1970
TQ 562279   Cattell 1970
TQ 566288
TQ 575311
TQ 575316
TQ 576309
TQ 579314
TQ 579316
TQ 581315
TQ 581316
TQ 586319
TQ 587331   Straker 1931a: 274

Rolvenden
TQ 855303   Straker 1931a: 323
Sedlescombe
TQ 772198   *Iron Age/Roman*
Straker 1931a: 327–8
TQ 773202   *Iron Age/Roman*
Straker 1931a: 327–8
Stelling
TR 167476
Thursley
SU 902354   *BWIRG 5, 4–7; 7, 10*
Ticehurst
TQ 658271   Straker 1931a: 297
TQ 663293   *Roman*   Straker 1931a;
SAS Occ. Paper 1 (1970)
TQ 664305   *Roman   SAS Occ. Paper*
1 (1970); BWIRG 2, 4
TQ 667275
Tonbridge
TQ 601441   Straker 1931a: 220
TQ 616440   *BWIRG 15, 8*
TQ 620447   Straker 1931a: 220;
BWIRG 15, 8
Uckfield
TQ 461227
Udimore (det.)
TQ 814198   Straker 1931a: 341
TQ 860195   SAS, OS Maps
Wadhurst
TQ 590323   *Roman   SAC 119, 62*
TQ 591323
TQ 593316
TQ 594315
TQ 597319
TQ 597322
TQ 598321
TQ 598325   Straker 1931a: 273
TQ 599321
TQ 600320
TQ 606304   Cattell 1970
TQ 625273   *Roman*   Cleere 1975
TQ 645313   *BWIRG,* 2nd ser., *2, 6*
TQ 652285   *Roman*   Cleere 1975
Waldron
TQ 563175
TQ 566213
TQ 569201   Straker 1931a: 373
TQ 571211   Straker 1931a: 273
TQ 576218
TQ 582230   Cattell 1970
Warbleton
TQ 614172   *Roman   BWIRG 14,*
5
TQ 617184

TQ 642195   *Iron Age/Roman   Sx*
   Ind. Arch. Newsletter 24 (1979), 2
TQ 656184   Straker 1931a: 361
Westfield
   TQ 784186   *Roman*   SAS, OS Maps
   TQ 782165
   TQ 785175   *Roman*   Straker 1931a:
   329
   TQ 798143   Straker 1931a: 338
Westwell
   TQ 971505
   TQ 971506
Withyham
   TQ 493306
   TQ 498344
   TQ 499313
   TQ 502313
   TQ 502341

TQ 504314
TQ 504341
TQ 505339
TQ 506327   Straker 1931a: 253
TQ 507326
TQ 507340   *Roman   BWIRG* 15, 4;
   SAC 119, 61
TQ 508341
TQ 515342
TQ 516343
TQ 517335
TQ 518337
TQ 519338
Worth
   TQ 272384   Straker 1931a: 468
   TQ 359389   *Roman   BWIRG*, 2nd
   ser., 2, 4
   TQ 360390

Gazetteer B   Roman bloomeries

The entries in this section follow the alphabetical sequence of parishes given in Gazetteer A; numbers refer to fig.19.

BATTLE

1 Pepperingeye
TQ 744131
Straker 1931a: 351
Cleere 1975: 198

A 1m thick layer of slag lies beneath the garden of Pepperingeye Farm, and yielded a small sherd of samian embedded in a vitrified brick. This site could well form part of the Crowhurst Park complex (q.v.: 19).

2 Petley Wood
TQ 763175
Lemmon 1951–2
Cleere 1975: 198

This was not a site where iron was smelted, but appears to have been solely an iron ore mining and pre-treatment operation. Pits were discovered, some as large as 15–20m diameter by 15m deep, tapering towards the bottom. The spoil heaps, composed of the overburden removed during mining, produced a considerable amount of second- and early third-century pottery. There was ample evidence that the ore had been roasted and screened before being taken away to the smelting site (probably Oaklands Park), about 1.5km distant. The large amount of pottery found is rather surprising, in view of the dearth of finds at the Holbeanwood outlier of Bardown (q.v.: 57).

BATTLE/WESTFIELD

3 Beauport Park
TQ 786146
S. Arnott, *SAC* 21 (1869), 138
Rock 1879
Straker 1931a: 330–7
BWIRG 3, 4–7
VCH Sussex, III, 32

An enormous slag and refuse bank, covering nearly 1ha, was quarried away in the nineteenth century by the County Highways Surveyor, at a rate of 2,000–3,000m^3 a year for nearly ten years. Finds from the slag heap during this work and subsequently have indicated a date range from the end of the first century to the first half of the third.

The only part of the large site, covering at least 5ha, that has been excavated is a well-preserved six-room bath-house of military type. This has to date produced about 1,600 tiles with the CL BR stamp of the Classis Britannica. The bath-house was sited in the 'industrial' part of the settlement, doubtless for reasons of safety.

Considerable evidence of ore-roasting and smelting has resulted from trial excavations and from earth-moving operations during the construction of the golf course. This was situated between the slag heap and the presumed 'residential' area of the settlement.

Excavations during 1980 around the bath-house produced post-holes which seem to form part of a pre-Roman roundhouse. So far, no pottery or other finds have confirmed this indication of a pre-Roman phase at Beauport Park. (See figs.21, 22.)

BECKLEY

4 Ludley Farm
TQ 848206
W. J. Botting, *SAC* 111 (1973), 111
BWIRG 4, 29
Cleere 1975: 196

Located in Burnthouse Wood, this site is represented by a large slag and refuse bank (50 × 100m) which appears to have been disturbed, probably for road metalling. Trial excavation in the slag bank has produced a considerable amount of pottery, including samian, identified as second century, together with a coin of Hadrian. A series of small depressions in Oak Wood (TQ 852209) may be filled orepits.

BREDE
5   Chitcombe
TQ 813211
Straker 1931a: 345–7
SAS, OS Maps
Rock 1879
D'Elboux 1944: 66
Cleere 1975: 285
VCH Sussex, III, 32

This is a very large site, described by Rock as being comparable with Beauport Park (q.v.: 3). Pottery finds indicate a broadly similar date range. No excavations have been carried out on the site. However, there are remains of masonry, mentioned by Rock, still visible, and these, together with numerous finds of tiles in the vicinity, indicate the existence of substantial buildings.

6   [No site name]
TQ 882147

7   [No site name]
TQ 892145

BURWASH
8   Furnace Gill
TQ 650238
Lower 1849: 208
Straker 1931a: 300

Bloomery slag occurs along the banks of a stream running through Bough Wood. Lower refers to an 'air furnace' as having been discovered here. There is no recent dating evidence to confirm his opinion that this was a Roman bloomery.

BUXTED
9   Crabtree Farm
TQ 485298
BWIRG 13, 6–7

A trial pit dug in an area of black soil containing tap slag and cinder passed through a layer of compacted furnace lining and produced two sherds of Romano-British coarse ware. There is another small concentration of slag in the same field.

10   Front Wood, Bevingford
TQ 490246
BWIRG 15, 6
Tebbutt 1981: 61

An area of charcoal-impregnated soil and slag extends along the bank of a small stream. Along the valley above the site, are a number of quarries, possibly for iron ore. A trial trench in the refuse deposit revealed 35–40cm of tap slag, cinder, roasted ore and furnace debris. Six sherds of Romano-British coarse ware were also found.

11   Chillies Farm (Newnham Park)
TQ 494284
BWIRG 13, 7
Tebbutt 1981: 62

A thick scatter of slag and cinder on the surface of a field was tested by trial excavation and proved to be 40–50cm deep, composed of tap slag, furnace lining material, green-glazed sandstone, and a broken clay tuyere containing a plug of solid slag. One sherd of pottery was found, which appeared to be of the South-Eastern B type that was in use in this area in the first half of the first century AD: cp. Minepit Wood (q.v.: 51), Pippingford Park (q.v.: 27); this may date to just before or just after the invasion of AD 43. There was also a sherd of second-century samian.

12   Greystones Farm
TQ 495271
Tebbutt 1981: 62

Excavation of a concentration of slag and cinder produced several sherds of pottery, dated by C. M. Green to the second half of the first century AD.

13   Brook House, Burnt Oak
TQ 506273
C. F. Tebbutt, *SNQ* 14 (1954–7), 278
Cleere 1975: 192

Excavation in a large slag heap produced a number of sherds of Romano-British pottery.

14 Oaky Wood
> TQ 507272
> BWIRG 13, 12
> Tebbutt 1981: 61

Bloomery slag is scattered over a large area on both sides of a stream and in the stream bed. Ore was apparently derived from a cutting into the bank and from nearby pits. A trial excavation revealed a levelled floor of hard clay. Pottery found in the refuse is identified as Romano-British East Sussex ware.

15 Morphews
> TQ 509256
> Straker 1931a: 389
> BWIRG 6, 21
> Cleere 1975: 197
> Tebbutt 1981: 60

This is a large bloomery, from which slag and cinder have been quarried for road metalling. The finding of a single hypocaust tile, together with Romano-British pottery, indicates the possible presence of a substantial building, which Tebbutt suggests may have been an administrative headquarters.

CRANBROOK

16 Little Farningham Farm, Sissinghurst
> TQ 801352
> M. C. Lebon, *Archaeol Cantiana* 71 (1957), 224; 72 (1958), xlvii, lx–lxii; 76 (1961), xlviii
> Cleere 1975; 195–6

There is no direct evidence of ironmaking on this site. It is a substantial stone-built structure, with a hypocaust system, where a number of CL BR stamped tiles were found during excavations. There is no slag in the building itself nor in the vicinity. However, a number of tuyeres were found within the building, together with a worked iron bloom (Brown 1964). It is possible that it may have served some administrative purposes.

CRAWLEY

17 Broadfields
> TQ 262353–TQ 265355
> BWIRG 2, 7; 4, 25; 5, 14; 8, 47
> *Bull Hist Metallurgy Group 8* (1974), 51–3
> Cleere 1975: 192
> Gibson-Hill 1975; 1976

The settlement, the first to be discovered on the Weald Clay, covers about 12ha, with the main area of occupation spanning a shallow valley between a limestone ridge to the north-east and sandstone hills to the south. Rescue excavations showed that ironmaking began here in the pre-Roman Iron Age and went on continuously to the fourth century AD. No ore-roasting furnaces were found, but all the other technological features were represented, including 36 furnaces, of both domed and shaft type. Other features included a building, identified as workmen's accommodation, and an area of hard-standing metalled with iron slag.

CROWHURST

18 Forewood
> TQ 751130
> Straker 1931a: 351–2
> BWIRG 8, 10–11
> J. A. Smythe, *Trans Newcomen Soc 17* (1936–7), 197–205
> Cleere 1975: 194

A small stream enters a deep gorge after falling over a low waterfall. On the north bank, where the gorge begins to flatten out, there is a number of filled orepits, surrounded by a scatter of slag. The slag continues along the top of the gorge for nearly 100m, and there are several artificially levelled platforms. No dating material has been found. An unworked bloom of iron weighing 1.25kg was found on the site by Ernest Straker and submitted to metallurgical analysis.

19 Crowhurst Park
> TQ 769136
> Straker 1931a: 353
> Straker and Lucas 1938
> C. M. Piggot, *SAC 79* (1983), 229–32

Excavation in 1936 of the large slag and refuse heap showed it to be made up of characteristic materials – slag, cinder, furnace debris, charcoal, etc. Both single and double tuyeres were found, as well as pottery dated to the late first and second centuries. There was also an important assemblage of pre-Roman material dating from the first half of the first century AD.

The settlement probably covers at least 4ha. There are orepits along both sides of the little valley in which the settlement is located, and a deep excavation, reminiscent of the 'scowles' of the Forest of Dean, in the field above the main settlement. Several kilometres of roads in the Park are metalled with iron slag.

20   Bynes Farm
TQ 758110
Straker 1931a: 358
Lucas 1950–3
Cleere 1975: 192–3

This is a very characteristic site, on the slope of a small valley. A section cut through the slag and refuse bank in 1949 revealed the typical make-up of slag, charcoal, furnace debris, etc., along with both single and double tuyeres. The large quantity of pottery found was dated to the first and second centuries AD.

EAST GRINSTEAD

21   Ridge Hill
TQ 369355
Straker 1928
Straker 1931a: 233–5
Cleere 1975: 199

A slag heap measuring some 150 × 60m lies in swampy ground alongside the Medway. Excavation in 1927 in the heap produced the characteristic layered structure. It appears to have been deposited on the top of earlier ore-roasting or charcoal-burning hearths, 2.5–3m in diameter.

The pottery discovered on the site was identified to the period AD 100–300 by S. E. Winbolt, but the identification of the pottery from the earliest levels (by R. A. Smith) as pre-Roman needs to be treated

with some reservations, in view of his incorrect interpretation of Romano-British East Sussex ware as Iron Age at Bardown (q.v.: 57).

22   Walesbeech
TQ 395345
Straker 1931a: 239–40
Cleere 1975: 199
BWIRG 6, 18
VCH Sussex, III, 31

The large slag heap observed by Straker is now lapped by the waters of the Weir Wood reservoir, which has cut a vertical section through it, revealing the characteristic make-up. Excavations by Straker and Margary produced pottery, dated to the late first and second centuries AD. Large orepits have been identified at TQ 393341, at the edge of the Wadhurst Clay.

ETCHINGHAM

23   Shoyswell Wood
TQ 682279
Straker 1931a: 297
BWIRG 2, 5
Cleere 1975: 199

The site of this bloomery was not located by Straker, but was revealed by trenching for a gas pipeline in 1970. A stretch of c.70m of slag, ore, burnt clay, etc. was revealed in the trench running through Shoyswell Wood; the deposit was 1m thick in places. In addition, a number of depressions, probably orepits, lie to the north and south of the deposit. One sherd of East Sussex ware was found. This site is located about 2km from Bardown (q.v.: 57), of which it was probably a satellite.

EWHURST

24   Bodiam
TQ 773215

Fieldwork by the field group of the Robertsbridge and District Archaeological Society has produced evidence of iron-smelting (in the form of slag and other debris) in a field above the Roman port at Bodiam.

FLETCHING

25 Coleham

TQ 407241
BWIRG 13, 15

During the construction of the Mid-Sussex Water Company's pipeline from Ringmer to Horsted Keynes, a scatter of bloomery tap slag was found at this point, associated with six samian sherds.

FOREST ROW

26 Great Cansiron

TQ 448383
I. D. Margary, *SNQ 13* (1950–3), 100–2
C. F. Tebbutt, *SAC 110* (1972), 10–13
Cleere 1975: 194
BWIRG 16, 14

This very large site lies about 2km from the Roman London–Lewes road (Margary's Route 14). WIRG members have fieldwalked it intensively and have collected a large quantity of pottery and building materials from the surface of the 2ha 'industrial area', represented by an area of blackened soil. The coarse pottery found is largely from the late first and second centuries, the samian being largely late second-century. Two coins were found, *dupondii* of Vespasian and Trajan respectively.

FRAMFIELD

27 Crump Corner

TQ 475165
BWIRG, 2nd ser., 2, 6

A ploughed field shows two areas of black soil with a heavy scatter of slag, roasted ore and furnace lining, together with Romano-British pottery.

28 Hempstead Wood

TQ 490216
BWIRG 15, 6
Tebbutt 1981: 62

The site consists of overgrown coppice woodland at the junction of two small streams, one with fairly steep banks. There is tap slag on the slope, thinning to a scatter at the top. Small trial pits produced five sherds of Romano-British coarse ware (East Sussex ware), of first- and second-century date.

FRANT

29 Eridge Old Park

TQ 575340
TQ 577343
TQ 578345
J. H. Money, *SAC 117* (1979), 258
BWIRG 13, 13–14
Tebbutt 1981: 62

The sites of a number of small bloomeries have been found by fieldwalking in Eridge Old Park. Five are spaced out along a line about 70m long running south-west from a small pond. Two pieces of East Sussex ware were found in association with these sites.

A possible occupation site at TQ 575340 produced a substantial amount of late pre-Roman Iron Age and Romano-British pottery. Some of the earlier material is paralleled at Saxonbury, which lies 1.25km to the south.

HADLOW DOWN

30 Howbourne

TQ 517249
Straker 1931a: 390
C. F. Tebbutt, *SAC 111* (1973), 115
Cleere 1975; 195

Straker records a 'small but characteristic bloomery', with much cinder along the small stream. Ditching operations in this area in the early 1950s produced a good deal of samian, Nene Valley, and East Sussex pottery, along with window glass. A mortared stone wall was seen by N. E. S. Norris, together with much bloomery slag. It is suggested that this was the site of a substantial Roman house, the owner of which was associated with ironmaking.

31   Pounsley

TQ 525222
BWIRG 6, 22
Cleere 1975: 198
Tebbutt 1981: 62

Slag and cinder occur along the bank of a stream. The nearest orepits lie less than 1km away. Trial excavation produced two sherds, one of them second-century samian, the other East Sussex ware.

32   Bosmere Farm

TQ 545222
BWIRG 13, 10
Tebbutt 1981: 62

Bloomery slag covers part of the south side of the stream here. Trial excavation showed this to be over 30cm deep. One sherd of East Sussex ware was found.

33   Flat Farm

TQ 552220
BWIRG 13, 10–12
Tebbutt 1981: 62

Slag is scattered along the north-east side of the stream for about 100m. Trial excavation showed this to be about 30cm deep at the point where it seemed to be most concentrated. One sherd of East Sussex ware was found.

34   Scocus

TQ 552231
BWIRG 13, 13
Tebbutt 1981: 62

There is a considerable amount of slag on both sides of a stream with steeply sloping banks which runs along the fault between the Ashdown Sand and the Wadhurst Clay. Trial excavation produced the characteristic make-up – charcoal, slag and furnace debris – and a levelled clay floor. Several sherds of East Sussex ware were found in the make-up.

HARRIETSHAM

35   Runham Farm

TQ 872514
BWIRG 9, 21–2
Kent Archaeol. Rev., 1980, 28–9

Tap slag was used to metal a Roman road

running under the farm house. Considerably more slag was found during excavations of a small Roman settlement, but no furnaces have yet been identified.

HARTFIELD

36   Garden Hill

TQ 444319
BWIRG 15, 16–26
J. H. Money, *Britannia* 8 (1977), 339–50

This important site, excavated since 1973 by J. H. Money, was occupied first in the Neolithic and Bronze Age. In the late pre-Roman Iron Age (mid to late first century BC, according to recent magnetic dating), two roundhouses were built and a bank and ditch were dug for protection. Settlement was continuous into the Roman period, when several rectangular buildings, including a modest bath-house, were built to replace the earlier structures. A certain amount of ironmaking took place on the site, though most of the industrial activity was concerned with ironworking. It is possible that the Garden Hill settlement had a managerial relationship with the small early first-century bloomeries in the near vicinity, such as Pippingford Park (q.v.: 37) and Cow Park (q.v.: 38). (See fig.24.)

37   Pippingford Park

TQ 446313
Tebbutt and Cleere 1973
Cleere 1975: 198

This small bloomery, on the slope above Cinder Arch Lake, consists of a smelting furnace of the domed (Cleere's B.1.ii) type, a possible ore-roasting hearth, and a small slag heap. The sparse pottery finds are dated to the Claudian-Neronian period (somewhat at variance with the radiocarbon date of 1647 ± 60bp (BM–685)). In view of the similar discrepancy between pottery and radiocarbon dates at Minepit Wood (q.v.: 51) the pottery date, of around the invasion date of AD 43, has been preferred.

38 Cow Park
TQ 452309
BWIRG 13, 2–6
Tebbutt 1979

This site is 1.25km from Garden Hill, 750m from Pippingford bloomery, and 950m from East Wood bloomery. It is sited on Ashdown Sand, but it is postulated that the iron ore used came from pockets in the surface derived from the Wadhurst Clay which formerly overlay the Ashdown Sand. Three furnaces were found, of the domed (B.1.ii) type associated with early working at Minepit Wood (*q.v.*: 51) and Pippingford Park (*q.v.*: 37). Each of the furnaces had a reheating hearth in association with it. A smithing area was identified about 2m from one of the furnaces, with traces of an iron block supported on two substantial wooden posts. Pottery from the site was largely East Sussex ware, dated to the first half of the first century AD.
(See fig.18.)

HEATHFIELD

39 Magreed Farm
TQ 600229
Cattell 1970
Cleere 1975: 196

A bloomery site with a small (5m) refuse heap on the edge of the Wadhurst Clay, alongside a small gill. Pottery from the site is dated to the second/third century AD.

40 Knowle Farm
TQ 623241
Cattell 1970
C. S. Cattell, *SNQ 17* (1968–71), 101–3
Cleere 1975: 195

An area of blackened soil, containing tap slag, ore, furnace debris and charcoal, about 10m in diameter, near the head of a tributary of the Rother, produced second/third-century Romano-British pottery.

HERSTMONCEUX

41 [No site name]
TQ 632152

Slag is reported (by W. R. Beswick, *BWIRG 15*, 9) along a stream bank, containing Romano-British pottery.

HORSTED KEYNES

42 Freshfield Brickworks
TQ 385262
SAC 78 (1937), 253

A large quantity of pottery of first-century AD date was found in association with iron slag on this site.

ICKLESHAM

43 [No site name]
TQ 881166
Straker 1931a: 340–1
W. M. Homan, *SNQ 6* (1936–7), 247–8
Cleere 1975: 195

Straker refers to small bloomeries at Telegraph Mill and Place Farm (in the area TQ 8615). Homan found what appear to have been the bases of six shaft furnaces, with considerable bloomery slag and a denarius of Hadrian, at TQ 878165. Recent work by Zoë Vahey has revealed very considerable deposits of slag and slag-metalled road surfaces.

MARESFIELD

44 East Wood, Pippingford
TQ 448301
BWIRG 7, 11

An artificially levelled platform measuring about 10 × 6m lies on the top of a steep bank in a gill with a small stream below. A low slag heap is situated uphill, to the south, measuring c.20m across. An old trackway crossing the marshy ground at the bottom of a semicircular minepit is paved with stones where it crosses the marshy section at the bottom. Trial excavation in the slag heap produced several sherds of Romano-British coarse pottery (East Sussex ware).

45   Oldlands
> TQ 475267
> Straker 1931a: 395–7
> *BWIRG* 6, 20; 2nd ser., 2, 12–15
> Cleere 1975: 197
> *VCH Sussex*, III, 32

This appears to have been the first Roman ironmaking site to have been identified in Sussex (in 1844), and was graphically described by Lower in a classic paper (*SAC 2* (1849), 169–74). The area of the settlement covered at least 3ha and comprised working areas, refuse heaps, and inhumation burials. The coins found ranged from Nero to Diocletian, indicating a long period of occupation; the relative frequency of coins of Vespasian suggests a late first-century date for the establishment of the settlement. Tebbutt (1981: 60) describes it as 'almost certainly an administrative centre'. Little is now visible, but there is still a scatter of bloomery slag over the whole area. There are signs of extensive opencast quarrying on the east bank of the stream opposite, in Mill and Furnace Woods.

46   Little Inwoods
> TQ 562239
> Cattell 1970
> Cleere 1975: 196

A slag dump over 10m across close to a small stream provided material for radiocarbon dating. This gave a date of 130 bc–ad 70 (Hv 2985).

MAYFIELD
47   Streele Farm
> TQ 557270
> Straker 1931a: 386
> Cleere 1975: 199

Straker is very noncommittal about this site, where tap slag is to be found in the bed of a small stream. A single sherd of East Sussex ware was found by WIRG members visiting the site.

48   Stilehouse Wood
> TQ 585303
> Cattell 1970
> *BWIRG* 13, 9–10
> Tebbutt 1981: 62

Bloomery slag is scattered over an area of 1ha of woodland around a small stream at the junction of the Ashdown Sand and the Wadhurst Clay. Two trial pits dug in slag at the east end of the wood produced first-century Romano-British pottery (mostly East Sussex ware).

49   Sandyden Gill
> TQ 586309
> Straker 1931a: 288
> Cattell 1970; 1972
> *BWIRG* 8, 10

Slag occurs in a stream lying in a deep gill for a distance of at least 1km. An extensive tip on the south bank of the Tidebrook has been eroded, to reveal a good section of characteristic make-up. One sherd of possible East Sussex ware was found in the stream itself. Cattell (1972: 13) gives a date of 220 bc ± 120, presumably based on a radiocarbon date.

ROTHERFIELD
50   Scaland Wood
> TQ 523277
> Tebbutt 1981: 61

A single sherd from the slag deposit on this site is believed by C. M. Green to be 'the strongest contender for a pre-conquest date yet seen ... from an ironworking context'.

51   Minepit Wood
> TQ 523338
> Straker 1931a: 257 (as Orznash)
> Money 1974
> Cleere 1975: 196–7

This site produced on excavation a small slag and refuse dump flanking a very well-preserved specimen of a domed (B.1.ii) smelting furnace. Pottery finds were scanty and were identified as first century, spanning the conquest date of AD 43. A fourth-century date was obtained from radiocarbon analysis of charcoal from the site, but the pottery dating has been preferred. (See fig.13a.)

52 Hodges Wood, Crowborough
TQ 527326
BWIRG 15, 3
Tebbutt 1981: 62

A slag dump on the east side of a small stream produced, on sampling by excavation of a trial pit, one sherd of East Sussex ware.

53 Walnut Tree Field, Renby Grange
TQ 532332
BWIRG 9, 2; 13, 14
Tebbutt 1981: 61

A large round patch of dark-coloured soil about 50m from a small stream produced cinder, slag, furnace debris and pottery (East Sussex ware and a local copy of a 'Belgic' butt beaker – dated to the second half of the first century AD).

54 Limney Farm
TQ 540271
Straker 1931a: 387
BWIRG 6, 22
Cleere 1975: 196

Two large mounds containing bloomery slag, lying on the Burnt Oak fault at the edge of the Wadhurst Clay, produced the base of a pot, described as third-century New Forest ware by R. A. Smith.

55 Castle Hill, Home Farm
TQ 559280
Cattell 1970
Cleere 1975: 193

An extensive slag deposit (over 20m across) at the junction between the Wadhurst Clay and the Ashdown Sand. Charcoal entrapped in cinder and from the slag heap was submitted for radiocarbon determination and gave a date of ad 60–90 (Hv 2984).

SEDLESCOMBE

56 Footlands
TQ 772198
Straker 1931a: 327–8

E. Chown, *SNQ 11* (1946–7), 148–51
Cleere 1975: 194
VCH Sussex, III, 31
BWIRG, 9, 3

This is one of the largest sites in the Weald. It has slag extending along both sides of the small stream and in an area of about 2ha, which shows up black on ploughing. The pottery finds indicate occupation from before the Roman conquest down to the fourth century. Unfortunately, only the pre-Roman material deriving from the 1925 excavation by the Sussex Archaeological Society has ever been published, and so definitive evidence for fourth-century operation is lacking.

TICEHURST

57 Bardown
TQ 663293
Straker 1931a: 296
Cleere 1970
Cleere 1975: 190
VCH Sussex, III, 31

The settlement covers about 3ha, on the south bank of the River Limden. It is divided into two areas, the western half being devoted to ironmaking activities and the eastern being residential. A dump of refuse (tap slag, cinder, furnace debris, domestic waste, etc.) extends for about 100m along the south bank of the stream. There is evidence of ore-digging on the north bank of the stream and in innumerable pits within 3km radius of the settlement.

It appears to have been founded in the first half of the second century and to have continued for about 100 years. The buildings excavated (which included a standard military-style barrack block) were timber-framed. Ironmaking was carried out at the settlement itself throughout the second century but was discontinued after about AD 200, the industrial buildings being dismantled or abandoned and covered with a deep layer of domestic rubbish. Of the 28 CL BR stamped tiles found on the site, 24 were found in this layer.

After about AD 200, ironmaking appears to have been continued at a series of satellite sites, 2–3km from the main settlement and connected with it by slag-metalled roads. So far seven such sites have been tentatively identified, of which one, Holbeanwood (*q.v.*: 58) has been excavated.

The settlement appears to have been abandoned and possibly dismantled in the first half of the third century. There was no evidence for destruction by burning in the last phase, although several buildings seem to have been destroyed by fire in earlier phases. There was slight evidence of casual reoccupation in later third century.

No smelting furnaces were located during the excavations. However, two pit-type ore-roasting furnaces and a possible charcoal-burning hearth were discovered.

(See figs.10, 11, 23.)

58   Holbeanwood
  TQ 664305
  Cleere 1970
  Cleere 1975: 195

This was an outlier or 'satellite' of Bardown (see above). It is situated about 1.5km to the north connected by a slag-metalled track which runs alongside several ore pits. Excavation revealed two groups of furnaces, each consisting of six units, and a third group probably existed. These were standard Roman shaft furnaces. The scarcity of pottery and other remains associated with occupation, in sharp contrast with the main Bardown settlement, and the lack of buildings other than the timber shelters erected over the furnace groups, suggest that this was purely a work place, visited daily by ironworkers who lived in the main settlement.

(See fig. 13b.)

WADHURST

59   Frankham
  TQ 590323
  Tebbutt 1981: 62

A single sherd, which may be of third- or fourth-century colour-coated ware, was discovered on a slag deposit in this area.

60   Doozes Farm
  TQ 625273
  Cleere 1975: 194

This site was discovered during the laying of a gas pipeline. A pit containing tap slag, cinder and furnace debris, 3.5–4m in diameter, was cut through by the mechanical excavator; it was c.1m deep where sectioned. Stones enclosing an area about 30cm square on the west side of the pit seemed to form some kind of structure. Ore nodules were found a short distance away. Two sherds of East Sussex ware came from the pit. This may be a 'satellite' of Bardown (*q.v.*: 57), which lies about 4.5km away.

61   Coalpit Wood
  TQ 652285
  Cleere 1975: 193

A 'satellite' of the Bardown settlement (*q.v.*: 57), located about 1.5km to the south-west and connected with it by a clearly defined track, metalled with iron slag. There are several large orepits along the line of the track. The site is identified by a slag deposit on the side of a small gill, measuring about 15 × 10m.

WARBLETON

62   Blackman's Farm, Rushlake Green
  TQ 614172
  BWIRG 14, 5

A deposit of tap slag lies on a steep slope to the west of a stream; it measures c.15 × 20m. A test trench produced one sherd of plain samian and part of a tuyere.

63   Turners Green
  TQ 642195
  Sx Ind. Arch. Newsletter 24 (1979), 2

Romano-British pottery and radiocarbon dating showed this site to be of the early first century AD.

WESTFIELD

64   [No site name]

TQ 784186

This site is marked as Romano-British on maps held by the Sussex Archaeological Society. No further information is available.

65   Oaklands Park

TQ 785175
Straker 1931a: 329
Cleere 1975: 197

The slag and rubbish banks at this large site were quarried away for road metalling during the nineteenth century. The close dating of the settlement is very questionable, since nothing survives of the material found during these operations. It is known, however, that coins of Hadrian were found, which gives evidence of early second-century occupation. Observations in the area by Mr J. A. Paige suggest that an extensive settlement may lie beneath the modern Pestalozzi Children's Village, close to the River Brede, which would have been navigable during the Roman period. A slag-metalled road has been located at TQ 788173.

WITHYHAM

66   Bingle's Farm

TQ 507340
BWIRG 15, 4
Tebbutt 1981: 61

This site lies on the lower boundary of a small grass field running down to a small stream. Above the site are two terraces that suggest house platforms. There is an apparent ford over the stream made of stones with slag and a large 'furnace bottom'. Two trial trenches were excavated and produced thick deposits of bloomery debris and slag containing a number of sherds of East Sussex ware.

WORTH

67   Smythford

TQ 359389
BWIRG, 2nd ser., *2*, 4; 2nd ser., *5*.

A burnt clay structure (probably a smelting furnace, Cleere's Type B.1.ii) with associated bloomery slag was excavated. Archaeomagnetic tests show a first century AD date (70 ± 20).

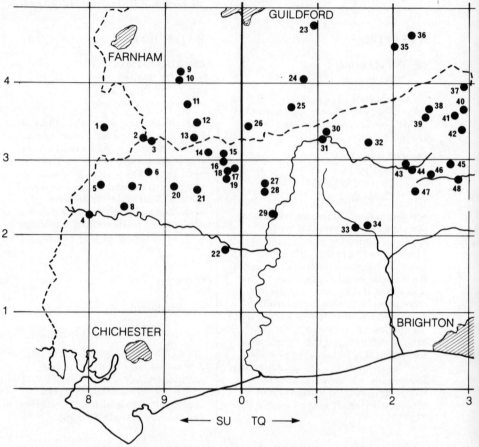

Fig.74 Distribution map of water-powered sites. Numbers refer to entries in Gazetteer
C; positions are approximate only, for exact sites see N G references in Gazetteer.

1	Standford furnace	17	Roundwick furnace	32	Warnham furnace
2	Pophole forge	18	Wassell forge	33	Shipley forge
3	Shottermill forge	19	Ebernoe furnace	34	Knepp furnace
4	Rogate forge	20	Verdley Wood furnace	35	Ewood furnace and
5	Coombe furnace	21	Lurgashall Mill furnace		forge
6	Fernhurst furnace	22	Burton forge	36	Leigh hammer
7	Inholmes Copse	23	Abinger hammer		forge
	furnace		forge	37	Tinsley forge
8	Chithurst forge	24	Coneyhurst Gill forge	38	Ifield forge
9	Thursley forges	25	Vachery furnace and	39	Bewbush furnace
10			forge	40	Blackwater Green
11	Witley Park furnace	26	Burningfold forge		forge
12	West End furnace		and furnace	41	Tilgate furnace
13	Imbhams furnace	27	Barkfold furnace	42	Worth Forest furnace
14	Frith furnace	28	Barkfold forge	43	St Leonards furnace
	(Northchapel)	29	Pallingham furnace		and forge
15	Shillinglee furnace	30	Dedisham furnace	44	St Leonards forge
16	Mitchell Park forge	31	Dedisham forge	45	Blackfold furnace

46	Slaugham furnace	54	Stone furnace and forge
47	Gosden furnace	55	Strudgate furnace
48	Holmsted forge	56	Chittingly Manor Farm
49	Woodcock forge		furnace
50	Warren furnace	57	Stumblett furnace
51	Rowfant forge	58	Ardingly forge
52	Gravetye furnace	59	Ardingly furnace
53	Mill Place furnace	60	Horsted Keynes furnace
		61	Cuckfield forge
		62	Cuckfield furnace

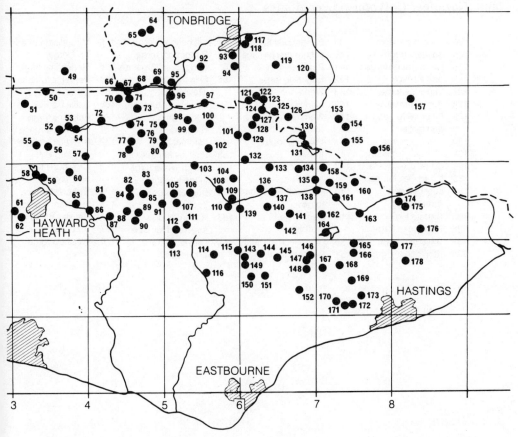

63	Freshfield forge	78	Pippingford furnace (and steel forge)
64	Bough Beech furnace 1	79	Crowborough forge
65	Bough Beech furnace 2	80	Crowborough Warren furnace
66	Scarlets furnace	81	Sheffield furnace
67	Cowden furnace	82	Boring Wheel mill
68	Cowden lower furnace	83	Oldlands furnace
69	Prinkham Farm forge	84	Old Forge furnace and forge (Marshalls)
70	Bower forge	85	Hendall furnace
71	Cansiron forge and furnace	86	Sheffield forge
72	Brambletye forge	87	Fletching forge
73	Bassetts furnace	88	Langles furnace
74	Parrock furnace and forge	89	Maresfield furnace
75	Withyham forge	90	Maresfield forge
76	Cotchford forge	91	Iron Plat furnace
77	Newbridge furnace and forge	92	Barden furnace
		93	Vauxhall furnace

94	Old Forge, Southborough
95	Ashurst forge 1
96	Ashurst forge 2 Ashurst furnace
97	High Rocks forge
98	Birchden forge
99	Hamsell furnace
100	Eridge forge and furnace
101	Henly furnaces
102	Cowford furnace
103	Maynards Gate forge and furnace
104	Mayfield forge and furnace
105	Little forge and furnace
106	Huggetts furnace
107	Howbourne forge
108	Woolbridge forge

109	Moat Mill forge
110	Old Mill furnace
111	Pounsley furnace
112	Tickerage furnace and forge
113	New Place furnace
114	Waldron furnace
115	Heathfield furnace
116	Stream furnace and forge
117	Rats Castle forge
118	Postern forge
119	Matfield furnace or forge
120	Horsmonden furnace
121	Benhall forge
122	Melhill forge
123	Breechers forge Dundle forge

124 Tollslye furnace	139 Bungehurst furnace	152 Kitchenham forge	165 Mountfield furnace
125 Bayham forge	140 Broadhurst furnace	153 Bedgebury forge	and forge
126 Lamberhurst forge	141 Burwash forge	154 Bedgebury furnace	166 Hodesdale forge
and furnace	142 Brightling forge	155 Frith furnace	167 Penhurst furnace
127 Verredge forge	143 Woodmans forge	(Hawkhurst)	168 Beech furnace
128 Brookland forge	144 Markly furnace	156 Hawkhurst furnace	169 Battle Park
129 Riverhall furnace	145 Warbleton Priory	and forge	170 Potmans forge
and forge	furnace	157 Biddenden	171 Catsfield furnace
130 Chingley forge	146 Panningridge	hammer mill	172 Buckholt furnace
131 Chingley furnace	furnace	158 Pashley furnace	and forge
132 Coushopley furnace	147 Ashburnham	159 Burgh Wood forge	173 Crowhurst furnace
133 Scrag Oak furnace	furnace	160 Iridge furnace	and forge
134 East Lymden	148 Ashburnham upper	161 Bugsell forge	174 Ewhurst furnace
furnace	forge	162 Socknersh furnace	175 Northiam furnace
135 Darfold furnace	149 Steel forge,	163 Robertsbridge	176 Beckley furnace
136 Hawksden forge	Warbleton	forge and furnace	177 Brede furnace
137 Bibleham forge	150 Cowbeech furnace	164 Darwell furnace	178 Westfield forge
138 Etchingham forge	151 Batsford furnace	and forge	

Gazetteer C   Water-powered sites

In the gazetteer of water-powered sites, the length (L) of the bay (dam) is given first, followed by the height (H). In most cases two measures of height can be given, the first as seen from the upstream side, followed by the elevation above the ground on the downstream side.

In this gazetteer, the major lists of furnaces and forges are, for brevity, referred to only by their dates. For discussion of these sources, see Chapter 6, p. 123 (1548); Chapter 7, p. 131 (1574); Chapter 8, p. 170 (1588), and Chapter 9, p. 187 (1653–7); Chapter 9, pp. 190, 198 (1717).

The locations of sites are shown in fig.74; numbers refer to that map. SM denotes site scheduled under the Ancient Monument Acts.

23   **Abinger Hammer Forge,** Abinger
     TQ 097474   Straker 1931a: 445–6

     Bay L 180m H 2.7m/3m Portion
        towards S end levelled for
        modern house and garden.
     Water system Pond level lowered
        to make watercress beds. Present
        stream flows through brick sluice
        30m from N end.
     Working area No trace, but forge
        bottoms and cinder occur near
        house.

The forge was built before 1557, when it was sold by Owen Bray to Thomas Elrington (J. Pettitt to compiler, cit. Evelyn MSS, Christchurch, Oxford), who was licensed to cut wood locally in 1560 (BL Add Ch. 44558). Edward Elrington operated the forge in 1574; there are references to leases, water, timber and cinder offences, 1579–1613, in Evelyn MSS. Listed as working in 1653 and 1664 and active c.1673 (J. Aubrey, Perambulation of Surrey (begun 1673): letter of John Evelyn to J.A.). Probably the forge of 'Mr Dibble', 1717 to 1736, James Goodyear 1766–80, James Eade 1781–2, and Edward Raby 1783–7 (Surrey RO Rates P1/5/1, 2; Land Tax Q56/7).

58   **Ardingly Forge,** Ardingly
     TQ 334289   Straker 1931a: 408–9

     Bay L 45m H 2.5m Breached by
        stream at N end.

     Re-use Fulling mill.
     [Excavated 1975–6 in advance of
        destruction and submergence
        under Ardingly reservoir
        (Bedwin 1976: 34–64)]
     See figs.44, 69, 72.

First heard of in 1571, in Ardingly Parish Registers (Sussex Record Ser. 17 (1913) passim), the forge was operated by Ninian Challenor in 1574. Between 1654 and 1685 John Spence became tenant (WSRO Add. MSS 3893–5, cit. in Bedwin 1976: 36), and operation is certain in 1653 and 1664. Ralph Drake was tenant in 1689 (ESRO SAS Abs. of private docs.: Denman 1935), Ambrose Galloway in 1695–6 (BL Add. MSS 33156).

59   **Ardingly Furnace,** Ardingly
     TQ 337287   Not included by
     Straker

     Bay L 75m H pond in water/5.25m
        Forms present road. Projection at
        N end forms protective bank and
        possible loading platform.
     Water system Spillway at N end
        takes present stream. Slight
        indication of wheelpit with
        shallow dry tail-ditch returning
        to stream.
     Working area Scatter of glassy slag
        over area, on bay and in stream.
        Plain roofing tiles and bricks in
        stream.

Francis Chalenor had lately erected a furnace at Sauceland in Ardingly in 1597 (Holgate 1927: 31).

148   Ashburnham Upper Forge,
Ashburnham (Penhurst)
TQ 687161   Straker 1931a:
364–70

> *Bay* L 140m H 3m/4m Now road, so probably raised. Downstream side revetted with forge bottoms and cinder.
>
> *Water system* At W end culvert through bay brings water along wooden trough 68cm wide × 30cm deep to wheelpit for undershot wheel. Tail-race passes under house ('Ammerbrook') to open ditch which joins main stream. At E end main stream passes under bay (road); slightly W of this a silted culvert comes from under a long low building (now cottage) built parallel to bay, and empties into stream. Local tradition of banked 4km channel following 30m contour from TQ 703170 to forge or furnace is justified on ground and in documentary evidence (*BWIRG 2*, 4–7).
>
> *Working area* Two cottages built over culverts (perhaps tail-races) appear to be part of the works. Material more characteristic of a furnace are bears on roadside W of 'Ammerbrook' and scatter of glassy slag.

Earliest reference is for 1572–3 (WSRO Lavington 830–1), to a forge of John Ashburnham, owner in 1574. He was in dispute with a creditor in 1581–2 (BL Harl. 703, f.12b, PRO STAC 5/08/36). Sold in 1611 to William Relfe (ESRO ASH B488), in 1640 to John Gyles and Benjamin Scarlett (ASH B607), via Joan Gyles to Anthony May, her son (ASH B740). Working in 1653, but ruined in 1664, the forge was known as a boring mill by 1677 when Thomas Scarlett leased it to Thomas Weston, ironmonger

of London (ASH B983) and in 1683 (ASH B1084), after the Ashburnham re-purchase of the estate (ASH A159–161). The forge site remained a boring mill through the eighteenth century (ASH map 4385 of 1717; ASH 1815, 1817) until 1789. Reinstated as a forge about 1796 (ASH 1818) and used until 1828 (ASH 1833).

147   Ashburnham Furnace,
Ashburnham (Penhurst)
TQ 686171   Straker 1931a:
364–72   SM:AM (Sx) 387

> *Bay* L 70m H 2m/4m Good condition; revetted in masonry to half height on downstream side. 23m from E end a stone and brick tunnel (now blocked) leads through bay to wheelpit; 23m from W end is a spillway with sluice gate.
>
> *Water system* Pond; now dry, supplemented by pen ponds. Wheelpit tailrace culverted to join overspill stream which passed below working area to join Upper Forge pond 160m to S. Trackway to furnace fords overspill stream; several bears revet ford banks. W of spillway a now-dry leat from pond passed through or under bay to serve second working area. For the leat from Penhurst furnace, see p. 230 and Beswick and Ennever 1981.
>
> *Working area 1* Immediately below bay, served by wheelpit (see above). Some broken cannon moulds found. (*BWIRG 12*, 7).
>
> *Working area 2* 90m S of bay. Served by dry leat which was culverted under present stone-revetted causeway near 'Pay Cottage'. Wheelpit just S of causeway. Thence race ran through culvert and along present ditch to flow into head of Upper Forge pond 75m to S. Just before this point a bank runs along E side of tail-race, turning E at right angles to join W bank of

main stream. This probably secured working area 2 from possible flooding from Upper Forge Pond. Bank contains many broken cannon moulds.
(See figs.30, 37, 46, 48.)

Built before 1554 by John Ashburnham (KAO U1475/B3/6) and owned by him in 1574. The date could be as early as 1549, when Ashburnham was employing aliens (PRO E179/190/233). For references until 1701 see under Upper Forge, as the furnace went through a similar sequence of ownerships. The furnace was recorded as working in 1653 and as discontinued but stocked in 1664. From 1701 to 1708 the works were run by William Ashburnham, who leased to the Crowley–Hanbury 'Ironworks in Partnership' (Hereford RO Foley E/12/PF5/550). Incidental references until 1757 (ESRO SAS RF 15/25/ – Fuller letterbooks) when the surviving run of yearly accounts begin (ESRO ASH 1815, 1817). The final years (1793–1813) are covered by less detailed accounts (ASH 1818, 1820, 1822–3).

95 Ashurst Forge, Withyham/ Chiddingstone   TQ 505403 Straker 1931a: 231

Bay L 140m H Irregular, 1–1.5m. Breached by Kent Water at N end and twice further S.
Working area Probably at N end where black soil occurs. Forge bottom and cinder in stream bed.

The forge was first mentioned in 1574, held by John or Thomas Stace. In 1592 (KAO U908/218) 'Pilbeams Forge' was leased by George Stace to Richard Streatfield. George Stace was involved in a dispute over delivery of iron at Tonbridge in 1597 (PRO REQ2/115/25).

96 Ashurst Forge 2, Ashurst TQ 507391   Not included by Straker

An unexplained system of ponds, banks and channels occurs for 100m along the W bank of the mill (furnace) tail-race, where large quantities of forge cinder and forge bottoms occur.

96 Ashurst Furnace, Ashurst TQ 507390   Straker 1931a: 231–2

Bay No remains, only possibility being line of present main road.
Water system No identifiable remains.
Working area No remains. Glassy slag and black soil in garden of Mill Place (site of mill). Downstream at TQ 507391 is small embanked pond (dry) with scatter of forge bottoms and cinder.
Re-use Corn mill on N side of road burnt down by 1934. Mill had dam and spillway across Medway upstream, with leat to small pond (under present railway station) and thence under road. This system possibly used for furnace.

John or Thomas Stace held the furnace as well as the forge in 1574. In 1588–90 Sir Walter Waller owned the furnace (Staffs. RO D593/3/4/28/3 and 17), which was occupied by John Phillips of London. In 1599 Thomas Browne sold cannon at Ashurst Furnace (PRO E178/4143).

92 Barden Furnace, Tonbridge TQ 548425   Straker 1931a: 219

Bay L 140m H 2m/3m by present road and probably much altered.
Water system Pond now dry. Impossible to distinguish between original system and that of later corn mill.
Working area Obscured by later mill. Plentiful glassy slag, shelly limestone and red plaintiles with square peg holes in bank of mill-race.

Possibly operated by David Willard in

1574, and certainly leased by Edmund and Abraham Willard from Thomas Smith in 1588–9, when ordnance was produced (Staffs. RO D593/S/4/28/3, 16, 17). It was in use in 1630 (KAO QSR, A82) and 1645 (PRO SP16/507/122). In 1646 it was visited and described by Sir James Hope (Marshall 1958: 146sq.). It was included in the 1653 list, but in 1664 there is a conflict between the list of that year which shows the furnace as ruined and stock accounts (KAO TR 1295/62, 68) which imply otherwise. It was in use in 1683 (KAO U458/T2/1), 1717 (100 tons p.a.), 1729 (ESRO SAS RF 15/26) and 1761 (*Sussex Weekly Advertiser* 9 Mar. 1761). It was demolished before 1787 (Sc. Mus. Weale MSS).

28   Barkfold Forge, Kirdford
TQ 029259   Straker 1931a: 425
[also known as **Idehurst**]

Bay L probably originally 90m; now almost all levelled on W of stream. On E of stream c.12m remains. H 1.2m. Contains cinder.
Water system Pond dry, deeply silted. Existing spillway with brickwork of several periods on probable site of original. Sump area and ditch to W of stream probably indicate wheelpit and tail-race.
Working area Much disturbed, probably when bay was levelled. Forge cinder in banks of stream.

Owned by the Strudwicks from 1584 (will of William Strudwick, 1584; WSRO wills 13, p.160) until at least 1614 (PRO C2 25/57). In 1634 the forge belonged to Henry Strudwick and William Westdean (BL Add. MSS 39386). See Kenyon 1952: 238, 241n.

27   Barkfold Furnace, Kirdford
TQ 030269   Straker 1931a: 424

Bay L 60m H 4m Some dressed stone visible.

Working area Depression, with bank to S, may be wheelpit; glassy slag in stream.

In use in 1602 (see Kenyon 1952: 238).

73   Bassett's Furnace, Hartfield
TQ 468374   Not included in Straker 1931a

Bay Existence uncertain; possibly on line of present road to Bassetts Manor, at TQ 467375.
Water system Possibly by long leat, but confused by that of later mill.
Working area Glassy slag occurs in S bank of stream under 0.75m of silt, and in grass field and shaws on S side.
Re-use Corn mill.

See Straker 1939: 531.

151   Batsford Furnace, Herstmonceux
TQ 631153   Straker 1931a: 360

Bay L 85m H 4m/4m breached by stream SW end.
Water system Pen pond 240m upstream (bay L 80m H 2.5m).
Working area Wheelpit at SW end in present stream. [Excavated 1978: Bedwin 1980: 89–112.] (See figs.53, 55.)

Built in 1571 by Thomas Glydd and Simon Colman on land leased from Lord Dacre. Glydd was the occupier recorded in 1574, although one version of the list does place him with Colman, another version mistakenly records Glydd as owner. Colman assigned the lease to Herbert Pelham in 1577 without Dacre's knowledge (BL Add. Ch. 30187; PRO REQ2/34/49; APC X, 176, 190). The furnace is referred to in a land transaction of 1591, not indicating whether it was in operation (ESRO Add. MSS 1981).

169   Battle Park, Battle   TQ 742146
Straker 1931a: 350–1

Bay L 160m H pond in water/4m.

Water system 'Farthing Pond'
380m to W, and small pond to
NE, supplement water supply.
Working area No evidence found.
Re-use Powder mill.

There is no firm sixteenth-century
evidence for a works here; indeed, the
only suggestion of an iron works is a
lease of 1652 from Lord Montague to
Robert Jarvis of the Park Mill with the
ironworks and all implements (Thorpe
1835: 153).

125 Bayham Forge, Lamberhurst
TQ 642366   Straker 1931a: 268

Bay L 100m H pond in water/3m
Carries road to Bayham Abbey
mansion.
Water system Spillway at S end.
Working area Converted to
ornamental gardens, now
derelict. Flowerbeds contain
much forge cinder and some
glassy slag. Cinder also occurs in
N bank of stream.

William Wybarne was the tenant of the
monastic forge in the 1520s (PRO
SC12/18/60). Owned by the Lords
Montague until 1609 (will of Anthony
Montague, 1592 – PRO PROB 11/21/22
refers only to 'my ironworks' – cf.
Imbhams furnace also), tenanted by John
Porter of Battle in 1574 and 1603 (Jack
1981: 10, citing PRO E112/127/249).
Purchased by Stephen Barnham in 1608
(KAO U840/T5), then by Walter Covert
and Samuel Gott in 1654 (Straker 1931a:
268): George Browne was tenant in that
year (KAO U840/T5), also in 1665
(Straker 1931a: 268), 1668 (co-partner
with Alexander Courthope and others –
ESRO DH 609, 611, KAO U609/T3). It is
recorded as working in 1653 and 1667.

176 Beckley (Conster) Furnace, Forge,
Beckley (Brede)   TQ 836212
Straker 1931a: 348–9

Bay L 165m H main part levelled to
70cm; N and S ends 3m. Short

projection to E along N bank of
Tillingham river.
Water system Present course of
river is that of the forge and
boring mill tail-races. Ditch S of
Mill House garden probably the
furnace tail-race.
Working area Several large
morticed timbers in river bed
probably form part of the forge
wheelpit. Much boring swarf and
forge cinder in river. At N end
(Mill House garden) is a low
circular mound behind the bay,
probably the furnace base with
cast-iron slab 1.25m × 50cm ×
15cm and much glassy slag.
Re-use Corn mill (but possibly
contemporary) served by leat
from upstream.

The forge was built by Edmund Hawes of
Robertsbridge and Richard Mullinax of
Brede in 1587 (ESRO RYE/1/5/109). The
furnace was in use by 1653, run with the
forge by Peter Farnden (ESRO Dunn
27/2). Peter Gott took a 2/7 share that
year (ESRO Add 5442/10) but the forge
was out of use by 1664, when the furnace
was listed as discontinued but re-
stocked. The Farnden involvement at the
furnace (Dunn 27/4, 27/6) ended after
the death of Peter Farnden (Dunn 46/9)
in 1681. In 1715 Samuel Gott was
operating the furnace (Dunn 46/12),
whose output in 1717 was 200 tons; Gott
left the furnace to his son in 1722. It was
marked on Budgen's map of 1724. In the
1740s the furnace was run by the
Harrison partnership (Guildhall MSS
3736; ESRO SAS RF 15/25), and in 1787
it was out of use but still standing (Sc.
Mus. Weale MSS). See also ESRO D165,
box 11, for a sketch of the furnace
buildings (1746), and a reference to the
furnace pond in water (1771).

153 Bedgebury Forge, Goudhurst
TQ 727357   Straker 1931a: 282

Bay Mainly destroyed. Possible
part survives as 22m long bank
between disused railway and
stream; faint signs of W end on

road leading to Bedgebury
Furnace. Present 'Forge Farm'
house probably occupies
remainder of bay and working
area; has pond-like meadow to S.
Remainder of bay and all cinder
probably removed to construct
nearby railway bank.

No references known; all sources
mention the furnace.

154   Bedgebury Furnace, Cranbrook
TQ 739347   Straker 1931a: 282
SM:AM(K) 291

Bay L 125m H 3m/4m. Breached
by stream at SW end. Ramps at
SW end and centre leading to
working area.
Working area At NE end a scatter of
bricks and tiles; top of 25cm ×
25cm wooden post *in situ*. At
SW end a brick floor of building
34m × 15m, perhaps of later
date. Nearby Furnace Farm
house probably contemporary.

Owned by Sir Alexander Culpepper in
1574 and 1588, the furnace was operated
by John Dunnednoll of Lamberhurst in
1590 (Staffs. RO D593/S/4/28/3, 17).
According to a note of 1843 with
Courthope MSS 715, Peter Courthope
purchased the furnace in 1613. John
Browne was casting there in 1637, when
there were complaints from Cranbrook
about his consumption of wood (PRO SP
16/363/55–6). George Browne was in
partnership with the Foleys in 1657
(Hereford RO Foley E/12/PF5/437) and
was casting guns in 1665 and 1673–7
(KAO TR1259/62; ESRO Courthope MSS
(copies) 715/7). The list of 1667 notes it
as having been discontinued before 1664
but re-stocked for the Second Dutch War.

168   Beech Furnace, Battle
TQ 728167   Straker 1931a:
325–6

Bay curved L 130m H 2m/3.5m.
Breached by present main stream
at NE end. Overspill channel W
end.

Water system Obscured by later
mill. Present main stream after
passing through bay cuts across
valley to SW to join overspill
stream. From this, near NE end
of bay, a culverted channel once
flowed SE to join main stream.
Pond dry.
Working area Furnace probably
between present main stream
and bay. Bear on bay just SW and
another just NE of stream. Large
slag heap in NE bank of stream
SE of farm road.
Re-use Corn mill.

Tentatively associated by Schubert
(1957: 367–8) with Richard Wekes,
supplier of pig to Robertsbridge forge
from 1568 (KAO U1475/B3/10), the first
firm reference is in 1574 when the
furnace was held by Thomas Hay of
Hastings. In use in 1653, it was
discontinued but re-stocked in 1664. In
1671 William Hawes held 'Beechers'
with ironworks: BL Add. Ch. 66693
(Survey of Bodiam). m.9. Production was
120 tons in 1717 and it was marked on
Budgen's map of 1724. The furnace was
leased by Richard Hay to Lord
Ashburnham and Sir Thomas Webster in
1724 (Straker 1931a: 325, cit. Battle
Abbey Charters). Webster's operations
are mentioned in a Fuller letter of 1730
(ESRO SAS RF 15/28). The furnace was
out of use by 1756 (ESRO ASH A197).

121   Benhall Forge, Frant   TQ 608376
Straker 1931a: 264–5

Bay L 90m (present road) H 4m
downstream. At NE end, bank L
35m at right angles separates
River Teise from working area.
Water system Pond dry.
Working area Obscured by later
mill. Forge cinder near mill
wheelpit.
Re-use Corn mill.

Walter Waller sold the forge to Richard
Leeche in 1574 (ESRO DH 69, 70), who
refers to it in his will of 1596 (PRO PROB
11/88/89). The forge was in Dyke hands

by 1634 (DH 72) and was leased to Foley, Courthope and others in 1655 (DH 609). Hereford RO E/12/PF5/437 gives a stock account of 1657. Although DH 961 mentions land belonging to the forge in 1678, there are no further references to operations there.

39 Bewbush Furnace, Bewbush (Ifield) TQ 239357 Straker 1931a: 458

> *Bay* L 275m H 1.5m/2.5m Forms bridle road with surface of sandstone and forge bottoms (*ex* Ifield Forge?). Downstream side revetted with brick and stone.
> *Water system* Pond dry (drained 1939–45). Spillway probably present stream. Dry channel 11m N of stream may be tail-race.
> *Working area* Glassy slag in bank S of stream.
> *Re-use* Corn mill.

There is risk of confusion with Ifield forge, less than 1km distant; both were owned in 1574 by Roger Gratwick, and there are forge and furnace slags at both sites. The first references to a furnace at Ifield are in 1567, when sows were taken to Burningfold (PRO REQ2/115/2), followed by a case in 1569 (REQ2/244/45). Four years later Roger Gratwick held the furnace (REQ2/226/4), which corresponds with the list of 1574. Wood in the forest was let to Sir Thomas Shurley in 1578, who quickly reassigned the rights to Arthur Middleton, Stephen French and John Middleton, to last until 1597. Some wood was also assigned to Roger Gratwick. Wood was made over by John Middleton to Edward Cavill, who had grant of timber elsewhere in the forest. The confusion and the waste of wood gave rise to an enquiry in 1597 (PRO E178/2313). In 1602 sows were carried from Gosden furnace to Bewbush forge, occupied by John Middleton (REQ2/166/46). Bewbush furnace, according to a Parliamentary Survey of 1649, went out of use about 1642 (PRO LR2/299, f.20), but it appears in the list of furnaces working in 1653. By 1664 it was ruined.

137 Bibleham (alt. sp. Bivelham) Forge, Mayfield TQ 641266 Straker 1931a: 295

> *Bay* L 98m H 1m/2m Breached at S end; fades out near River Rother. Probability that left bank of Rother was also raised originally to form pond on N side.
> *Water system* Pond dry. Long leat leaving Rother 500m upstream served pond; now flows through N end of bay to join ditch on S side of Newbridge Wood, flowing into Rother 600m downstream. Rother below bay may have been used for navigation.
> *Working area* Deep hollow and platform behind bay just S of leat stream, another hollow N of it. Much forge cinder and bottom near bay at this end and from nearby ditch SW side of Newbridge Wood where Tudor pewter spoon (Barbican House Museum, Lewes) found.

Possibly a Pelham forge in 1550 or before (Awty 1984: 24), and in 1567 the forge was included in a settlement by John Pelham (BL Add. Ch. 29744). The tenant in 1574 was Thomas Ellis. It was retained by Pelhams until the eighteenth century (BL Add. Ch. 29745, Add. MSS 5679–1585; Add. MSS 33144–6 – sevententh-century accounts). It was listed in 1653 and 1667. 50 tons of iron were made in 1717, 40 tons in 1736. It was marked on Budgen's map of 1724. Wm. Harrison and his partners used the forge 1741–4 (Guildhall MSS 3736). 30 tons were still produced yearly in 1787 (Sc. Mus. Weale MSS).

157 Biddenden: hammer mill (Biddenden/Sissinghurst), forge and furnace TQ 822383 Straker 1931a: 282–3

> *Bay* L 220m with possible

extension S to Hammer Wood H
(E end) 1.75mn/2.5m
Water system Pond dry.
Working area Forge site in angle of
bay at E end. Depression here
represents wheelpit, whence
channel runs to stream.
Scattered bricks, tiles, round
forge bottoms, cinder, glassy
furnace slag. Rectangular iron
slab 1.25m × 75cm.

Sir Richard Baker ran this forge from
about 1570, the pond was built then, and
had caused damage to a road bridge by
1583 (KAO P26/28/2a). Baker was owner
in 1574, and in 1590 (Staffs. RO
D593/S/4/28/13, 16), and the family
still held the forge in 1650 (KAO
U24/T279); if correctly identified as
'Horsfield in Sissinghurst' it was still
available for use in 1664. The blast
furnace slag may be explained by the
reference to a furnace in Sissinghurst in
Richard Baker's will of 1591 (PRO
PROB11/84/86). It is unlikely to have
been built long before this, for there is no
mention of a furnace in 1583, nor in
1588–90, when Baker's furnace was
clearly placed in Hawkhurst parish,
presumably at Frith. A furnace in
Biddenden or Sissinghurst was stocked
in 1653 and 1664. A forge at Horsfield
near Sissinghurst also worked in 1653
and 1667.

98　Birchden Forge, Rotherfield
TQ 533353　Straker 1931a:
260–1

Bay Road to Forge Farm L 155m H
75cm/2m Overgrown stone
tunnel at N end.
Water system Pond dry (weir is
modern).
Working area Probably now
occupied by house of later date;
garden has black soil. Behind
bay at N end is iron forge plate,
also round forge bottoms and
slag.

John Baker leased the forge by 1553
(ESRO W/A3, fos. 186–7). In 1574 it
belonged to Sir Walter Waller, but was

sold to Michael Weston in 1579 (PRO
C142/243/39). In 1595 the Earl of Dorset
bought the forge, his tenant in 1597 being
Thomas Richardson (Straker 1933: 40). It
was sold to John Baker in 1617. Richard
Maynard was tenant in 1618 (ESRO DH
1011); the forge was operating in 1653
and 1667. Baker's descendants retained
the site until the bankruptcy of Robert in
1708. John Browne built a boring mill
near the forge in 1677 (ESRO DH 614).
In 1719 trustees sold the Birchden estate,
with the forge, to Anthony Benn.
Although absent from the 1717 list, the
papers associated with the sale record
two iron mills at Birchden (the forge and
Hamsell furnace) in 1709 and 1719 (BL
Add. MSS 5681).

Bivelham Forge: *see* **Bibleham**

45　Blackfold Furnace, Cuckfield
TQ 274294　Straker 1931a:
404–5

Bay L 55m H pond in water/3m
(probably restored). At E end
widens to form furnace-charging
platform.
Water system At W end stone
stepped spillway in good
condition (probably restored).
Further spillway at E end of bay.
Pen ponds upstream said to be
modern.
Working area At E end below
charging platform low mound
represents furnace base, with
wheelpit hollow to S. Much
glassy slag and charcoal waste
nearby.

Property of Ninian Challoner in 1574.

40　Blackwater Green Forge, Worth
TQ 292363　Straker 1931a: 466

Bay L 140m H 2.75m/indeter-
minate, much altered. Forms
bridle road. Breached by stream
(bridged) 46m from N end.
Water system Pond dry. Small

existing pond at S end of bay with outlet to main stream may indicate position of spillway. *Working area* Slag-layer in N bank of stream. Forge bottoms in road surface on bay. Glassy slag in stream.

No firm references, although Blackwater might possibly be one of the two hammers in Moore (Worth) Forest in 1574 (Cattell 1979: 166).

82   **Boring Wheel Mill,** Maresfield
     TQ 456265   Straker 1931a: 398

Bay L 110m H pond in water/3m
Water system Spillway at NE end, used by later corn mill, was probably original. Corn mill took water by leat from SE corner of pond, bypassing bay.
Working area No trace now remains.

Parliamentary Survey of Ashdown Forest, 1658 (Daniel-Tyssen 1872: 191 and 206) refers to 'sluices and water courses to west end of bay', inferring working area here, i.e. not on site of later corn mill. Only evidence for connection with iron industry is in name (going back to seventeenth century) and local tradition.

64   **Bough Beech Furnace (1),** Hever
     TQ 482476   Not included by Straker

Bay L 110m H 3m/4m. Breached by stream near centre.
Water system Pond dry. Spillway probably at W end.

65   **Bough Beech Furnace (2) or Forge,** Hever   TQ 477473
     Straker 1931a: 218

Almost entirely destroyed by later construction works and diversion of stream. Glassy slag and forge cinder found.

The only references are for the years 1588–90. Thomas Willoughbie owned a furnace and forge in Chiddingstone Parish. The furnace was let to Thomas Browne who, with his founder, Ephraim Arnbold, cast ordnance (Staffs. RO D593/S/4/22/3, 16, 17). Schubert 1948: 245–6, cited Sevenoaks Public Library H414 in support of Willoughbie's sale of land and furnaces to Browne in 1589.

70   **Bower Forge,** East Grinstead
     TQ 441384   Straker 1931a: 229

Bay (Farm road) L 200m
Water system Pond dry. Leat on N side of main stream from sluice 400m upstream.
Working area Cinder only found under farm road bridge; forge bottom at TQ 442386.
No re-use, but site much altered and confused by later ornamental ponds downstream. Site confirmed by field names: Little Forge Meadow and Forge Meadow N and S of stream downstream of bay.

The forge was working in 1653, but ruined by 1664.

72   **Brambletye Forge,** East Grinstead
     TQ 414350   Straker 1931a: 241

Bay None surviving.
Water system Pond probably in dry hollow, downstream of which present stream has unnatural right angle bends.
Working area 10m downstream of junction with ditch coming in from NE are forge bottoms in stream bed and horizontal timbers in both banks at water level. Timber in N bank is large slotted baulk, possibly part of a hammer support.
Re-use Dry pond area has mound of brick kiln debris with 52mm thick (i.e. pre-mid-seventeenth century) brick wasters, perhaps

indicating early disuse of forge. Straker wrongly believed forge to be at site of later Brambletye Mill.

The forge was built by 1562, when Thomas Lutman of Balcombe, who was in debt, leased it to Henry Bowyer, who paid six years rent to enable Lutman to discharge his obligations. The details were in dispute between Bowyer and Lutman in 1572, when the former still held the lease (PRO C3/24/65). By 1574 Drewe Pickhayes owned the forge, which was leased to Robert Reynolds, who also worked Mill Place furnace (PRO SP12/95/79). Pickhayes sold Brambletye Manor to Robert Sackville in 1602, but the forge was not mentioned (PRO C3/289/8).

Auction particulars of Brambletye estate (1831) show a 2-acre enclosure named Forge Mill Mead. (Inf. from P. Wood of Turner, Rudge and Turner, East Grinstead).

177   Brede Furnace, Brede
TQ 801192   Straker 1931a: 341–4

Bay Completely destroyed by later reservoir constructioin, but probably ran across valley between reservoir dam and main road to S.

Working area In bay area is black soil, glassy slag and a bear just inside gate leading to road. In field opposite, on S side of road, is also black soil, slag and clay moulds.

Re-use Powder mill.

Built in 1578, the furnace was originally operated by David Willard, Michael Weston and Robert Woddy (*APC*, X (1587–8), 265; ESRO RYE/1/4/285). It is not known when the works became Sackville property, but a theft of an iron pot from a furnace in Brede, property of John Sackville, was recorded in 1609 (ESRO QR/E/9.108). Lawrence (d.1605) and Richard Lenard were successively tenants, and the fireback of 1636, portraying a furnace (fig.34a), is assumed

to have been made at Brede (Straker 1931a: 342). Agreements over the subsequent 25 years show how the Brede works were run by Peter Farnden and the executors of Thomas Sackville, and how Farnden, in partnership with Samuel Gott, leased the works to Thomas Weston and Charles Harvie in 1660 (ESRO Dunn 27/3, 48/2). The furnace worked in 1653 and 1664. There is no information between the lists of 1664 and 1717, in which the furnace is included, producing 200 tons in the latter years. It was marked on Budgen's map of 1724. William Harrison was casting guns at Brede in 1735 (ESRO SAS RF15/25: 26.7.35), and the operations of Harrison and his executors are well documented, 1741–7 (RF15/25: 23.6.42, 23.10.49; Guildhall MSS 3736, 6482). Weale refers to it as 'down' in 1787 (Sc. Museum: Weale MSS), while Straker's information was that abandonment took place in 1766, before conversion to a powder mill (Straker 1931a: 343).

123   Breechers Forge (Marriotts Croft), Frant   TQ 627384   Straker 1931a: 264–7

No sign of bay, water system or working area to be found. Some cinder in the path and field at TQ 627387.

This forge is apt to be confused with Benhall and Melhill (q.v.). A Mr Wybarne had ironworks with alien employees in 1544 (WAM 12261) and he is likely to be the Wybarne listed with Leeche in 1574 as holding two forges in Frant. Straker names Roger Breecher as tenant in 1557 and Galfridus May in 1576. The forge is specifically named in 1589, 1602 and 1611–12 (ESRO DH 237, 240, 242). Straker names the tenants in 1614 and 1618 as Hugh and John Muddle, and found a reference of 1634 to a place 'where the iron mill lately stood' (Straker 1931a: 265–6).

142   Brightling (Glaziers) Forge, Brightling (Burwash)

TQ 651213   Straker 1931a:
301–2

Bay (Road) L 55m H 1.25m/3m
    Revetted in stone on
    downstream side.
Water system Pond dry.
Working area Lawn between
    probable ironmaster's house and
    stream made up to some depth
    with forge cinder. Many forge
    bottoms in stream, also glassy
    furnace slag supporting Straker's
    belief in furnace here also.
    Mould for 14cm cannon balls
    preserved at Glaziers Farm.

The 1574 list is the first reference, in
which Thomas Stollyon worked the forge
for Sir John Pelham. Throughout the
seventeenth century the Pelhams
operated Brightling and Bibleham forges,
using pig iron from Waldron furnace (BL
Add. MSS 33154–6). Brightling was
listed in 1653 and 1667. 40 tons was the
output in 1717, a figure repeated for
1736. It was marked on Budgen's map of
1724. William Harrison's accounts of
1741–6 provide details of operation
during his tenancy (Guildhall MSS
3736). Although Weale shows the forge
as abandoned in 1787 (Sc. Mus. Weale
MSS), the Earl of Ashburnham had
leased it to James Bourne in 1785 for
seven years (ESRO ASH A192).

140 Broadhurst Furnace, Burwash
    (Heathfield)   TQ 631242
    Straker 1931a: 287

    Bay L 55m H 4m/4m across steep
        narrow valley.
    Water system Pond dry. Spillway
        stream from dip at E end of bay
        for 100m to stream. Pen pond
        bays (Straker) uncertain.
    Working area Much glassy slag in
        stream and E side of valley.
        Trackway on terrace to E end of
        bay.
No firm documentary references.

128 Brookland Forge, Frant
    (Wadhurst)   TQ 618349
    Straker 1931a: 278–80

Bay L 65m H 1.5m/long gentle
    slope. The length away from
    stream may be natural. Section at
    N bank of stream shows two
    periods of construction of equal
    height, turf line between.
Water system Pond dry. In shallow
    stream bed is hollowed-out
    wooden trough L 7m W 30cm,
    and further section L 4.5m (in
    line), possible trough for
    overshot wheel.
Working area Stream bed has much
    forge cinder and bottoms. On
    grass meadow downstream of
    bay molehills show black soil
    with bloomery tap slag.

The earliest reference, cited by Straker, is
to John Barham's purchase of Brookland
and Verredge forges from Humphrey
Lewknor in 1521 (KAO U840/T109).
They remained in the Barham family
until their abandonment. In 1544 aliens
were employed by John Barham (WAM
12261), and a case of 1552 shows him
operating the two forges (PRO
C1/1202/14). In 1556 he was involved in
a case regarding the supply of 92 tons of
iron to Humfrey Collett of St Saviours,
Southwark (PRO C24/41 pt 1). In 1574
John Carpenter farmed Brookland forge
from Thomas Gresham: the latter must
have in turn leased from John Barham
(1574 list), in whose will of 1583 (PRO
PROB 11/64/41) Brookland was left to
his son. Abandonment lies between a
lease to Thomas Saunders of 1610, and
1640, this being the first occasion when
the forge was described as decayed (KAO
U840/T109/5). A reference of 1636
(ESRO DH 497) does not state whether
the works was in use, although as late as
1629 sows were brought there from
Snape furnace (ESRO Q1/
EW/1:15.1.29).

172 Buckholt Furnace and Forge,
    Bexhill   TQ 746113   Straker
    1931a: 356–7

Bay L 85m H 4m/3m Breached by
    stream towards N end.
Water system Pond dry. Overspill

at extreme S end of bay from
which 220m channel (now dry)
joined stream.

Working area 3m behind bay, just S
of stream, many bricks (5cm
thick) and roof tiles (square peg-
holes) under layer of forge cinder
and bottoms. Nearby, rusted
mass of square-section nails
found. Quantities of forge waste
in and behind bay; little glassy
furnace slag.

Buckholt Farm house is
contemporary and probably for
the ironmaster.

Bartholomew Jeffrey was the tenant of
Lord Dacre for a furnace and forge at
Buckholt in 1574. He died in 1575 (ESRO
A6/321–3; PRO REQ2/84/37), and the
tenancy went to Thomas Alfrey and
others in respect of debts owed to them.
A lease to William Waters was a subject
of dispute in 1579 (PRO REQ2/80/18).
By 1634 the works, probably only the
forge, was operated by Richard Farnden
(ESRO Dunn 49/19); it was in use in
1653, but by 1664 it was infrequently
operated. The forge alone is mentioned,
as abandoned, in 1683 (ESRO RAF 9/3).

161   Bugsell Forge, Salehurst
TQ 724256   Straker 1931a:
300

Bay L 90m H 0.5m, partly levelled.
Water system Pond dry.
Working area Completely obscured
by later corn mill. Large quantity
forge cinder and bottoms in
remains of bay SW of mill.
Re-use Corn mill, which appears to
have been supplied by upstream
leat to smaller mill pond,
bypassing forge pond.

This forge was built in the lifetime of
Joan Walsh (d.1559) (ESRO A4/506),
who leased to Hugh Colyn (Vivian 1953:
114; PRO C3/13/103. George May
operated the works probably as tenant, in
1574, for in 1611 Sir Robert Walsh leased
the forge to Thomas Foxall and others,
Foxall transferring the property to John

Busbridge in the following year (ESRO
SAS RF9/63, 64). It was working in 1653,
but ruined by 1664.

139   Bungehurst Furnace, Heathfield
(Mayfield) TQ 600239   Straker
1931a:
287

Bay L 40m H 2.5m/4m Breached
by stream and 2 dry gaps.
Water system Pond dry. 200m
upstream is pen pond bay, L 25m
H 3m/3m, with signs of overspill
at E end.
Working area 22m behind bay and
1.5m from stream is apparently
circular stone foundation of
furnace with boggy hollow
suggesting wheel pit. Plentiful
scatter of glassy furnace slag.

There are no certain references, although
Straker quotes Bell-Irving 1903: 176, in
favour of its operation by the Baker
family, supported by the 1574 record of
Sir Richard Baker having two furnaces in
Heathfield and Warbleton.

159   Burgh Wood Forge, Etchingham
TQ 717276   Not included by
Straker

Bay L 100m H 2m/2.5m Breached
at E and W ends, and by stream.
Water system Pond dry. Spillway
site and deeply scoured pit at W
end. Spillway stream runs for
370m along W side of valley to
where earthworks suggest
possible mill.
Working area Black soil, forge
cinder and bottom behind and in
bay at E end where there is a
slightly raised area. Shallow pits
at W end may denote removal of
cinder heaps.

26   Burningfold Forge and Furnace,
Dunsfold   TQ 004343   Straker
1931a: 422–3

Bay L 110m H 3m/4m Breached by
stream at S end.

Water system Pond dry.
Working area Furnace site in
copse, with much charcoal dust.
Glassy slag in stream but no forge
cinder seen.

The earliest references, in 1568–9, are to
a forge (PRO REQ2/115/2, 177/32).
Thomas Gratwick ran this for Richard
Marsh in 1574, and by 1583 Simon
Bowyer was tenant (PRO REQ2/125/14).
A furnace is mentioned by Norden in
1595 (BL Add. MSS 31853). A deed of
1607 recorded the sale of the works by
William Marsh to George Duncombe and
partners (PRO C54/1924 m29). A case of
1601, however, refers to John
Middleton's forge at Burchinbridge (sic)
but if this is a garbled rendering of
Burningfold, his involvement appears to
have been more complex (PRO
REQ2/186/35). A forge at Dunsfold is
listed as working in 1653 and 1667.
Aubrey mentions an iron-mill in 1673
(Bodleian MS Aubrey 4 – A
Perambulation in Surrey – begun 1673)
while Ollard tentatively suggests use into
the rectorship of Jos. Richardson, 1680–
1742 (Ollard 1919: 1–33). This appears to
be confirmed by a mortgage of 1781,
including a furnace or forge (WSRO
Cowdray 364).

22   Burton Forge, Duncton
SU 979180   Straker 1931a:
430–1

Bay L 175m H pond in water/4m
Forms present road.
Water system Modern spillway at E
end. Spillway at W end may be
original, as spillway stream
forms parish boundary.
Working area Forge cinder behind
mill.
Re-use corn mill.

Sir William Goring's forge at Burton was
decribed by Hammond in 1635
(Wickham Legg 1936: 38). In 1653 and
1667 the forge was in operation.

141   Burwash Forge, Burwash
TQ 663231   Straker 1931a:
303–5

Bay L 65m H 1m/1.25m Breached
by stream at N end. S end now
swamp.
Water system Pond dry.
Working area Featureless.
Scattered forge cinder in and
behind bay and in stream.
Former bay visible from the air,
100m W of present one,
supporting smaller pond. Behind
this is scatter of equal quantities
forge cinder and glassy furnace
slag.

Likely, but not certain to be the fifteenth-
century Burwash forge (ESRO ASH
200a): John Collins operated here from
about 1525, in conjunction with
Socknersh furnace. His son held the
forge in 1574. Although known
throughout the seventeenth-century as
'Collins' Forge' it was in Pelham hands
by 1589 (BL Add. MSS 33142, f.22). In
1661 John Hepden of Burwash sold the
forge to Jeffrey Glyd of Dallington
(ESRO SAS RF1/1); it was not in use
in 1653 and 1667. John Fuller purchased
Burwash forge in 1700 (ESRO SAS
RF1/19) and it remained Fuller property
until production ceased in 1803. Output
was 40 tons in the 1717 list, a figure
repeated in 1736, and 30 tons in 1787
(Sc. Mus. Weale MSS). From 1719 until
1741 there are many references in
ESRO SAS RF15/26.

71   Cansiron Forge and Furnace(?),
Hartfield   TQ 453383   Straker
1931a: 229–30

Bay L 130m H 2.5/2m Breached by
stream at S end.
Water system Pond dry. Spillway
probably at present stream.
Working area Tilt hammer shaft
and wooden anvil base (now in
Anne of Cleves Museum, Lewes)
found during setting of present
electricity pylon. Forge bottoms
and cinder in stream. Much
glassy slag at N end of bay.

In spite of the finds of furnace slag, the
only references are to a forge, beginning
in 1574, with Michael Weston in

occupation. Straker notes that in 1578 it passed from William Bowyer to his daughter and in the following year Cansiron forge is referred to on the boundary of Faulkenhurst (BL Add. MSS 5681, f.220). Straker then notes Sackville Turner's acquisition of the site in 1613, the sale to the Courthopes in 1627 and their sale in 1637 (ESRO SAS Co/101). In 1639 it was acquired by Benjamin Tichborne and John Maynard, and though working in 1653 the forge was ruined by 1664. Its survival is suggested by a reference of 1700 to a road to Cansiron forge (ESRO FA 374).

Catsfield Forge: *see* **Potmans Forge**

171   Catsfield Furnace, Catsfield
TQ 732115   Not included by Straker

> *Bay* L 92m H 0.5m/0.5m Breached by stream at S end. Apparent 18m projection to W, along N bank of stream.
> *Water system* Pond dry.
> *Working area* Possibly at levelled area at S end of bay of stream. Small amount of glassy slag in stream and bank, with horizontal timbers, all below c.1m silt.
> *Re-use* Corn mill (250m downstream); the mill pond covered the furnace site.

The furnace is mentioned (Upton 1981: 16–17) as part of the manor of Bexhill in 1567. It is not otherwise known (ESRO photocopy Acc 2631 of original in KAO U269/M20). William Gardner's map of Sussex 1795 shows corn-mill pond.

130   Chingley Forge, Goudhurst
TQ 682335   Straker 1931a: 277

> [Site now flooded by Bewl Reservoir. Notes of features before excavation and inundation]
> *Bay* L 100m H barely discernible. Breached by stream at W end.

> *Water system* Pond dry.
> *Working area* Cinder seen at head of tail-race before excavation. (Report: Crossley 1975b.)
> (See figs.44, 49, 50, 53, 54, 69, 71, 72.)

Built after 1574, before 1589, when Richard Ballard was tenant of Thomas Darrell (Staffs. RO D593/S/4/28/3). About 1595 Edmund Pelham and James Thatcher bought land including the forge (Loder 1907, 52). The overflowing of the pond is referred to in 1599 (ESRO DH712). In 1628–9 pig iron was brought from Snape furnace (ESRO Q1/EW.1/15.1.1629), the wording implying that Alexander Thomas, who brought the pig from Snape, was also the lessee of Chingley. By 1637 William Darell, part-owner of Scotney and Chingley, leased the forge to Henry Darell (PRO SP23/67/811). It was not mentioned in the lists of 1653 or 1664, but was in operation in 1717, producing 46 tons. It was marked on Budgen's map of 1724. John Legas was tenant in 1726 (KAO U409/T2).

131   Chingley Furnace, Goudhurst
TQ 685327   Straker 1931a: 276

> [Site now flooded by Bewl Reservoir. Notes of features before excavation and inundation.]
> *Bay* L 50m H 2.5/2.5m Breached by stream towards S end.
> *Water system* Pond dry.
> *Working area* Waterlogged, with furnace debris seen before excavation in angle between dam and northern hill-slope. (Report as for Chingley forge.)
> (See figs.49, 53, 55, 56, 58.)

Built after 1558, the furnace supplied cast iron to Robertsbridge steelworks in 1565 (KAO U1475 B4/1). In 1574 Thomas Darrell owned Chingley furnace, with Thomas Dyke as tenant. Dyke took a new lease in 1579, but by 1588 the furnace was out of use (ESRO

DH 607; Staffs. RO
D593/S/4/28/3).

8 Chithurst Forge, Chithurst (Iping)
SU 846236 Straker 1931a: 430

Bay L 100m H pond in
water/3.25m
Water system Present spillway at E
end. Water-filled hollow near
centre of bay may be site of
wheelpit.
Working area Small quantity of
forge cinder in bank of black soil
between spillway and hollow.

56 Chittingly Manor Farm Furnace,
West Hoathly TQ 346322
Straker 1931a: 408

Bay L 90m H pond in water/3.25m
Curves away from pond.
Water system From overspill at W
end the stream flows E along
downstream side of bay to about
its centre where it turns S,
perhaps to follow original tail-
race.
Working area Near centre of W half
of bay is pear-shaped mound,
probably the furnace site.
Steeply rising ground to W may
indicate a loading platform.
Heavy scatter of glassy slag over
whole area.

Probable, but not proven that this
furnace was operated by Thomas Michell
in 1546. In that year he supplied 65 tons
of pig to Sheffield forge (Giuseppi 1912:
294), and Straker notes that he held
Chittingly manor in 1536, 1570 and
1576. He is named as having a furnace in
Hoadlye parish in 1574.

Coldharbour: *see* **Thursley**

24 Coneyhurst Gill Forge, Ewhurst
TQ 083404 Not included by
Straker

Bay L 25m H 2m/3m Breached by
stream near centre.

Water system Pond dry. Spillway
at SE of present stream where
excavations by A. J. Clark in
1961 (SyAS Ann. Rpt 1961, 6–7)
revealed wooden wheelpit and
tail-race trough 46cm wide
comprising floor and sides
supported by interior uprights.
Trough (estimated length 15.5m)
terminates in revetment
timbering at base of bay. Slag
exposed in 1982 suggests
bloomery smelting.

Conster: *see* **Beckley**

5 Coombe Furnace, Rogate
SU 815269 Not included by
Straker

Bay L 166m H pond in water/3m
Partly dug away at N end to make
level track and consolidate pond
edge. Water level now lower
than original, leaving bay back
from pond edge.
Water system Present modern
spillway at S end set to reduce
original pond level. Dry channel
just N of above probably
represents original spillway. At
N end are two semi-dry
channels, one probably tail-race.
Working area At N end where
glassy slag is concentrated.

The furnace at Harting Coombe was built
about 1589 on the site of a corn mill (PRO
E178/3119). In 1588 Francis Fortescue
the builder had part-leased the works to
his son, whereupon they had both leased
to Henry Gleed of Arlington and Michael
Martin of Rogate, finding 5,000 cords of
wood a year and sufficient ore. In 1591
enquiry was made (E178/2305) into
destruction of wood; in this it was
confirmed that the ponds for the furnace
and the forge at Habin (q.v.) were built c.
1588 (see Yates 1955: 82–5).

76 Cotchford Forge, Hartfield
TQ 470339 Straker 1931a:
251 SM:AM (Sx) 398

Bay L 55m H 1.5m/1.8m
Water system Pond dry. Probably
    at N end where forge cinder and
    bottoms occur in stream.
Working area Glassy slag in stream
    is from road surface at N end of
    bridge. Charcoal and forge cinder
    also occur in wood N of stream.

John Eversfield held the forge in 1574,
but it is not clear whether the Nicholas
Eversfield who employed aliens in 1544
(WAM 12261) had done so there. A
conveyance of 1627 refers to Sir John
Shurley making the forge over to
Nicholas Smith of London during the
lifetime of the widow of Sir Henry
Bowyer (Straker 251, citing Close Roll
2715). The Parliamentary Survey of 1656
valued the forge buildings at £35 per year
(PRO E317 (Sussex/25)) but it does not
make it clear that the works were in
operation.

132   Coushopley Furnace, Mayfield
      (Wadhurst)   TQ 604302
      Straker 1931a: 288

Bay L 100m H 2.6m/3.4m Contains
    much slag. Breached by stream
    near N end.
Water system Pond dry. First pen
    pond bay at TQ 602303 (L 140m
    H 2.5m/3m) with overspill at N
    end. Further pen pond bays
    occur at TQ 600304 and
    TQ 597305.
Working area Probably at S end,
    from where large quantities of
    glassy slag have been removed.
    An old track leads to N.
Isolated cottage (now demolished
    at TQ 599302.

The earliest reference is to John Barham
as tenant from John a lyghe for 6½ years
from 1547 (PRO C1/1202/14.) In 1556
John Barham was supplying large
quantities of iron to the London trade
(PRO C24/41 pt 1), but Barham made the
furnace over to John Baker which
suggests that Coushopley was the
furnace in Mayfield parish operated by
Baker in 1574. It was in operation in

1611, referred to in a case of that year
(ESRO QR/E.11/7a.51). In 1651 Stephen
Penkhurst and Thomas Sackville worked
the furnace in co-partnership, and in
1658 Elizabeth Penkhurst made it over to
Ferdinando and John Marsham (ESRO
DH 624–5, 781, 823, 957). It was listed as
working in 1653 and 1664, but nothing
further is known until 1692 when it was
still in Penkhurst hands, being made
over to Robert Baker in the following
year. In 1712 the site was known as a
pothouse (ESRO SAS Portman 77, 538,
540, 541, 544). Coushopley appears in
the 1717 list, without an output figure.
The inclusion on Budgen's 1724 map is
probably anachronistic.

150   Cowbeech/Cralle Furnace and
      Forge, Warbleton (Wartling)
      TQ 612151   Straker 1931a: 380

Bay L 130m (originally) H 1.5–
    3m/1.5–3m Gap between present
    N end and River Cuckmere; all of
    N end across river removed.
    Further gap at S end.
Water system Pond dry.
Working area Modern course of
    Cuckmere has been altered by
    construction of sheep dip and by
    operations of water authority, in
    course of which heavy timbers
    were found underground. Roof-
    tiles occur in disturbed ground at
    S end of bay. Glassy slag and
    forge cinder occur on bay; due to
    proximity of public road main
    slag heap would have been
    carted away.

Straker suggests that this forge belonged
to the Cheney family. Pelham Cheney
had an iron mill in the manor of
Badhurste when he died in 1559 (PRO
C142/128/80). John Manning was co-
heir in 1635 (SRS 14(1912), 149). The
furnace and the forge both operated in
1653 but were ruined by 1664. A road
leading to Cowbeech forge was
mentioned in 1655 and 1693 (ESRO SAS
RF3/89 and 4/2). There is no reference in
the 1717 list, although the forge is
marked on Budgen's map of 1724.

67 Cowden Furnace, Cowden
(Hartfield TQ 454400 Straker
1931a: 226–7

Bay L 125m H pond in water/5m
Forms public road.
Water system Present spillway at N
end, but map of 1748 (KAO
U650/P1) shows spillway at S
end, pond of 14 acres, and
sluices for two wheelpits with
tail-races.
Working area The 1748 map shows
furnace at N end and 'boring
house' at S, with 'workhouse'
between. A surviving building
may be the latter. Also depicted
is a 'kiln' to NE of furnace,
possibly where ore was roasted
or cannon moulds baked.
Re-use Cornmill.
(See figs.43, 68.)

Three furnaces, Scarlets, Cowden and
Lower Cowden lie from west to east
within Cowden parish, on or close to the
Kent Water, and are liable to confusion.
The only source which clearly shows the
three is Staffs. RO D593/S/4/28/17 of
1590, where they are described as
'Scarlets', 'the Upper furnace in
Cowden', and 'the furnace in Cowden'.
Scarlets (q.v.) can in most sources be
distinguished with some certainty, but
the other two cannot, and before the
discovery of the Lower Furnace (q.v.) on
the ground, such references were
suspected to be to one site only and the
separation in the 1590 reference to be a
scribal confusion.

In 1574 Michael Weston had a furnace
in Cowden where he had cast guns for six
or seven years; this could be any of the
sites. In 1588–90 Thomas Burre worked
the furnace specifically named 'Upper',
while one of his sureties was John
Swayseland, of the other furnace. In the
seventeenth century John Browne
worked at Cowden: in 1638–41 he was
partner of Henry Cruttenden (Hereford
RO FVIB); he is mentioned in 1651 and
1655 (*ibid.* 5307, 5312) and had
equipment there in 1664 (KAO
TR1295/62). Two Cowden furnaces,
Scarlets and 'the lower' appear in the
1664 list: Scarlets was active, but
'Cowden the Lower' was ruined, which
seems to conflict with the reference to
Browne's equipment, unless of course
the Cowden furnace ascribed to Browne
was really Scarlets and the 'lower' was
only so in relation to Scarlets, the
original lower (easternmost) furnace
having been forgotten.

Uncertainties do not end here. Leonard
Gale acquired a furnace at Cowden late
in the seventeenth century and although
the archaeological evidence extends
work at Scarlets into this period, Cowden
cannot be excluded. None of the Cowden
furnaces appear in the 1717 list, but the
map of 1748 (KAO U650/P1) shows
Cowden upper furnace complete and
apparently used by William Bowen, a
gun founder referred to in the Fuller
correspondence between 1747 and 1764
(ESRO SAS RF15/25, fos.199, 206, 211
inter alia; Sussex Weekly Advertiser
10.9.1764.).

68 Cowden Lower Furnace, Cowden
TQ 466402 Not included by
Straker

Bay None
Water system Dry leat, 350m long,
runs from weir on N side of Kent
Water along N side of 'Furnace
Mead' (Tithe Award) to disused
corn mill.
Working area All indication
destroyed by mill. Scatter of
glassy slag at E end of leat, on
allotments NE of mill, and on
adjacent road.

The only convincing reference to a
furnace in Cowden which is
distinguished from Scarlets or the Upper
furnace is in 1590, when John
Swayseland had a furnace in Cowden
(Staffs. RO D593/S/4/28/17). The 1664
reference to an abandoned 'Lower
furnace' could refer to either of the
Cowden sites (see Cowden, above).

102 Cowford Furnace, Rotherfield
TQ 559320 Straker 1931a: 256

Bay L 70m H 2.5m/3m Breached by stream at E end, and by field entrance near W end.

Water system Pond dry. Spillway and channel at W end. Wheelpit probably on site of present stream.

Working area Glassy slag in bay and stream banks.

Built in 1562, it is shown in PRO STAC 5/A2/25 that the builders William Relfe and Bartholomew Jeffrey were in dispute with Lord Abergavenny over a time-sharing agreement. The furnace does not appear in the 1574 list, and a reference of 1603 to the furnace does not suggest recent operation (Pullein 1928; 278).

79   Crowborough Forge, Withyham TQ 498326   Not included by Straker   SM:AM (Sx) 469

Bay L 120m H 2m/3m Breached by stream 35m from original W end. 6m of W end destroyed. Gap 4m from E end, on W side of which bay projects to N. Section at stream breach shows that bay has twice been raised.

Water system Pond dry. Spillway at extreme E end of bay with dry ditch towards existing stream.

Working area In locality of stream breach. Preserved in stream bed immediately downstream of the bay is the circular wooden base of an anvil block with associated planking; just downstream near right-hand bank is an apparent iron plate. Small amount of forge cinder in stream.

80   Crowborough Warren (Withyham) Furnace, Withyham   TQ 496322 Straker 1931a: 252   SM:AM (Sx) 408

[Straker places this furnace incorrectly at New Mill (TQ 489309) but admits confusion with Withyham furnace (see *Sussex Record*

Series 39 (1933), xviii, and *BWIRG 12*.]

Bay L 115m H 4.5m/5.25m Breached by stream. A 55m extension at W end is of slighter construction and was probably made after the Ashdown Forest enclosure of 1696 to divert a stream from private land on to the Forest. A dry ditch indicates the former course of the stream into the furnace pond.

Water system Pond dry. Spillway probably at W end of bay, from which runs a dry ditch banked for 65m to prevent flooding of working area.

Working area Furnace site still visible at E end, 35m downstream of bay on E side of stream, where courses of stone remain. Steep natural bank above this may have served as loading platform. The packhorse bridge at present spanning the stream where it breaches the bay is of later date, the bay being a bridleway.

Straker assumed that the ornamental lake at TQ 496350 obliterated 'Withyham' furnace: however, as there is no evidence that there was ever a furnace there, the Crowborough Warren site is at least as likely to be John Baker's furnace of 1574.

Crowham Forge: *see* **Westfield**

173   Crowhurst Furnace *and* **Forge,** Crowhurst   TQ 757122   Straker 1931a: 352

Bay L 110m H above stream level; N end 0.5m; S end, where breached by stream, 3m. Middle section levelled for houses and gardens.

Water system Pond dry.

Working area Occupied by main road, public open space and domestic property. Glassy furnace slag and forge cinder in stream with forge bottoms.

A forge is first definitely mentioned in 1574, held by John Relfe. However, the Pelhams owned Crowhurst, and as 'Mr. Pelham' employed aliens in 1544 (WAM 12661), Crowhurst must be a possible location for an early ironworks. This impression is strengthened by a reference-back in a Crowhurst Court Roll of 1591 (ESRO Acc. 2300) to an iron mill said to have been extant in 1556. Gregory Relfe rented the forge in 1588–90 (BL Add. MSS 33142, fos.13, 24), but an extent of 1588 (*ibid.*) also shows a furnace. George Martin rented the forge in 1626 (BL Add. MSS 33144), and in the following year Peter Farnden leased forge and furnace, keeping both until 1653, when Samuel Gott was named as tenant (ESRO Dunn 29/1–3; 47/1; 49/19; other refs.: BL Add. Ch. 29970, BL Add. MSS 5679). The furnace was listed in 1653 and 1664, but the forge, in use in 1653, was out of action by 1664.

61 Cuckfield Forge, Cuckfield
TQ 303235   Straker 1931a: 416

Bay L 70m H 2.5m/3.75m
Breached by stream.
Water system Pond dry. Spillway probably at E end.
Working area Dry shallow ditch-like depression at W end of bay may represent wheelpit and tail-race, and joins present stream 55m downstream. Forge cinder on bay and in stream. Cottage at W end of bay may be contemporary.

The dispute between Sir Walter Covert and Roger Gratwick in 1577 (PRO C3/207/25), over Gratwick's half-tenancy of the works, remains the only firm source, apart from the parish register entries of 1613 referred to by Straker.

62 Cuckfield Furnace, Cuckfield
TQ 304230   Straker 1931a: 416–17

Bay L 65m H 2m/3m Breached by River Adur at W end.

Water system Pond dry. Pen pond 300m upstream but bay only survives on E side of stream.
Working area Steep natural bank on E side provided charging platform; furnace site is 25m S of bay and 7m from foot of the bank. 2m W of furnace is the wheelpit from which the tail-race was culverted. Now a dry ditch from E end of the bay (overspill stream) passes along the foot of the bank and crosses valley to W to join Adur 105m below bay. Plentiful glassy slag in furnace area; charcoal on field at top of bank.

In addition to reference cited for Cuckfield forge (*q.v.*), a case of 1583 (PRO REQ2/125/14) shows Simon Bowyer sending sows to Burningfold forge from Cuckfield, presumably from this furnace. Straker noted a reference to a filler at the furnace in Cuckfield parish register, 1613.

135 Darfold (Etchingham) Furnace, Etchingham   TQ 701280
Straker 1931a: 297

Bay L 137m H 2.5m/2.5m
Breached by stream and farm track at S end.
Water system Pond dry.
Working area Disturbed by poultry houses built on slightly irregular ground near centre of bay. Scatter of glassy slag; two large lumps of slag (bears?) in stream and one E of bay.

There has been a good deal of confusion between Darfold and Darwell (Darvel) furnaces, both Straker and Schubert believing that sixteenth-century references to a furnace indiscriminately spelt in either form referred to the site now known as Darfold. The proximity of the latter to Etchingham forge, leased with the furnace, encouraged this interpretation. In fact, as indicated under Darvel, the evidence is strongly in favour of this other site, in Mountfield parish. Thus the furnace at Darfold has no recorded history.

164 Darwell (Darvel) Furnace *and* **Forge,** Mountfield   TQ 708207
Straker 1931a: 308–9

[Submerged under Darwell reservoir c.1950. Information is from notes made before submergence and when exposed by drought 1973.]

Bay L 137m H 5.5m Breached by stream near N end, and by cart track c.25m S of stream. Built of clay, either side filled in with slag. (50m at S end remained above water level in 1981.)

Water system Pond dry before 1950.

Working area Excavations by J. M. Baines 1949 revealed 'line of masonry with furnace earth and slag' between stream and cart track (notes in Hastings Museum). Also scatter of bricks 114 × 229 × 57mm. Bear and supposed sub-hearth iron plate 1219 × 610 × 127mm removed to Hastings Museum (Schubert 1957: 203 n.1); Beswick noted 'half circles of bricks 1m diameter at ground level near S end of bay', *BWIRG 7* (1974), 27.

In the sixteenth century a furnace variously spelt Darfold and Darvell was leased with Etchingham forge. A lease held by Joan Welshe, and formerly by her husband from 1540, was to be surrendered to Sir Robert Tyrwhitt c.1545 (PRO C78/1/57). In 1568 Tyrwhitt let the forge and furnace (spelt Darvell) to Thomas Glydd (ESRO Dunn 14/1, cf. Vivian 1953: 191). The contemporary Robertsbridge Survey refers to lands adjacent to Darfold or Derfold furnace, the location being unquestionably the 'Darwell' site. (D'Elboux 1944: 141–2.) One version of the 1574 list spells Tyrwhitt's furnace 'Darfold' (SP12/95/149) but another, SP12/95/175, shows Glydd as Tyrwhitt's tenant at a furnace in Mountfield parish, where Darwell lay. In 1588 Glydd was still tenant (PRO REQ2/68/50). Further confirmation of the location of Thomas Glydd's tenancy appears in WSRO

EpII/5/3, which shows that he was cutting wood in Tyrwhitt's Darvell wood in the parish of Battle in or about 1572.

31 Dedisham Forge, Rudgwick
TQ 103329   Straker 1931a: 443–5

Bay L 400m, most of which runs E to W along N side of River Arun from TQ 109330 to 105329 where it turns N for the short distance to high ground. H (near E end) 1.25m/0.75m. Much breached and levelled.

Water system Leat 475m long brought water from Arun at TQ 113331 to pond at TQ 109330. Stream from Dedisham furnace must also have been diverted into pond.

Working area Difficult to define, but much forge cinder at TQ 104329.

In 1597 Thomas French, Anthony Fowle and Thomas Middleton ran 'Detsom' forge in conjunction with Gosden furnace (PRO REQ2/166/46). The forge is mentioned in a Quarter Sessions case of 1614 (ESRO QR/E/10/72). Straker notes a Close Roll reference (2892) to the forge in 1631, and an assignment of 1650 included the forge (GMR Onslow 97/13/732).

30 Dedisham Furnace, Rudgwick
TQ 107333   Straker 1931a: 443–4

Bay L 145m H 2.25m/3.5m Breached by stream at E end. Recently much altered during restoration of pond.

Water system Pond dry until restoration. Overspill was at extreme W end, indicated by dry ditch with bank on E side.

Working area Probably at E end where much glassy slag occurs in stream, and where restoration work uncovered, at depth of

66cm, a heap of chalk lumps possibly for use as flux. Present gamekeeper's house near E end of bay is probably contemporary.

There is a Quarter Session reference in 1614 (QR/E/10/72); the last reference is an assignment of 1650 (GMR Onslow 97/13/732).

123 Dundle Forge, Pembury
TQ 629385 Straker 1931a: 267

Bay L 150m Now a public road, so probably modified.
Water system Pond dry.
Working area Orchard area mentioned by Straker is now hard tennis courts. Apparent forge cinder can still be seen beneath bridge over River Teise.

As Derondale forge, belonging to the Darrells, it was conveyed to Thomas Dyke in 1573 (ESRO DH 602–5) and listed under Dyke in 1574. There are no further references to the forge in operation, although the 'forge place' is mentioned in 1640 (DH 990) and 1678 (DH 961). In 1605 (DH 48) an iron mill 'lately decayed', formerly in occupation of John Saunders, had been occupied by William Wybarne; this may be this site, although perhaps one of the group of forges upstream.

Dunsfold: *see* **Burningfold**

134 East Lymden Furnace, Ticehurst
TQ 677291 Straker 1931a: 296

Bay L 107m H 3m/4m Breached at S end by stream and at N end by cart track.
Water system Pond dry. Spillway probably at S end in present stream.
Working area Probably at N end where mound E of bay may indicate loading platform. Small quantity of glassy slag in N bank of stream downstream from bay.

19 Ebernoe Furnace, Kirdford
SU 976277 Straker 1931a: 423

Bay L 96m, H pond in water/3m
Water system Present spillway at S end of bay may be on site of original. Apparently 3 tail-races on downstream side of bay at S end.
Working area Probably at S end of bay, where glassy slag occurs in stream banks. Forge bottom also found.

This furnace probably provided pig iron for Wassell forge (q.v.), both being the property of the Smythes of Wassell from the purchase of the estate by John Smythe in 1594 (Kenyon 1952: 235, citing WSRO Shillinglee B37/97). John Norden cited Ebernoe as an example of the use of woodlands by iron-smelters (Norden 1610: 175).

100 Eridge Forge, Frant (Rotherfield)
TQ 560350 Straker 1931a: 257–8

Bay L 145m H 2m/2.4m Breached by stream and farm track.
Water system Pond dry.
Working area Lying along stream bed immediately downstream of bay is 5m length of timber, c.30cm square, with mortice slots near each end. Timber of similar width can be seen in bank section, protruding at right angles; above it is layer of roof-tiles. These probably indicate the site of the wheelpit. Much forge cinder visible in stream and banks. 'Forge Cottage' may be contemporary.

Although included in the 1574 list under Lord Abergavenny, there is no further dependable reference until 1653 and 1667, when the forge was continued in hope of work, although it is possible but not certain that this was Thomas Luck's 'new forge' of 1636 (ESRO QR/E/35/91) and 1644 (ESRO Add. MSS 5699) near 'Park Place'. The forge appears on Budgen's map of 1724. In 1717 the output was 30 tons, and it is possible that the tenancy was successively in the hands of Henry and Robert Weller of Frant. The former took pig iron from Waldron in 1700–1 (BL Add. MSS 33156), the latter from Heathfield in 1723 (ESRO SAS RF15/27). The Wellers are not known at any other local forge.

100   Eridge Furnace, Frant
(Rotherfield)   TQ 564350
Straker 1931a: 257–8

Bay (present) L 210m H pond in water/7.5m Believed to have been raised and extended in nineteenth century.
Water system Overspill, previously at centre of bay, was moved to present position at S end in nineteenth century. Several pen ponds upstream.
Working area No evidence, but small quantity of glassy slag on lower slope of bay.
(See fig.47.)

Lord Abergavenny owned this furnace in 1574, but a much earlier origin is possible. French workers appear in the Rotherfield parish registers in 1538, and Schubert suggested that they worked here. The agreement with Relfe and Jeffrey on the sharing of Cowford furnace (q.v.) has been taken to indicate that Lord Abergavenny had his own workers and thus his own furnaces in 1562 (Schubert 1951: 241 and PRO STAC5/A2/25). In 1603 there was a furnace in Eridge Park (Pullein 1928: 278).

138   Etchingham Forge, Etchingham
TQ 701266   Straker 1931a: 298

Bay Impossible to determine whether bay ever existed (railway passes through site).
Water system Pond (if any) dry. Water was conveyed by long leat from upstream and returned to main stream by tail-race 800m long.

Working area Some incomprehensible banks between the railway and 'Forge Cottages'. Forge cinder in leat banks and on both sides of railway.

A reference, of 1521, to John Ongerfield, hammersmith, of Etchingham may be a pointer to an early forge here (PRO KB9/486). This site was certainly in operation by 1540 (PRO C78/1/57); Sir Robert Tyrwhitt employed alien workers, probably here in 1544 (WAM 12261). It was included in the complaint by coastal towns about timber shortage in 1548, and in 1568 was let by Sir Robert Tyrwhitt to Thomas Glydd with Darvell furnace (q.v.) [ESRO Dunn 14/1, Vivian 1953: 191]. Tyrwhitt and Glydd were named owner and tenant in 1574. The forge is referred to in a rental of 1584 (Dunn 37/3). The last sixteenth-century references are to a case involving Glydd in 1588 (PRO REQ2/68/50, 72/21). The forge had been used in 1653 but was laid aside in 1664; however in 1693–4 hammers and anvils were bought from the Pelhams' Waldron furnace (BL Add. MSS 33156). It produced 50 tons in 1717. It was marked on Budgen's map of 1724.

174   Ewhurst Furnace, Ewhurst
TQ 810248   Not included by Straker

Bay L 175m H 2m/2.5m Breached by stream. 30m levelled at N end.
Water system Pond dry.
Working area Main scatter of glassy slag is at S end, together with bricks and roof-tiles.

Probably built by 1580 (ESRO RYE 47/26/22), little more is known. If this was 'Mr Lynitt's furnace', the sows in Thomas Glydd's will of 1590 (PRO PROB 11/77/1) may have lain here although Darvell (q.v.) is also a possibility. An isolated seventeenth-century reference is in the Tufton MSS, a list of tools at Ewhurst furnace (KAO U455/E1) in about 1664. It was listed as working in 1653, discontinued but re-stocked in

1664. (See also Northiam furnace); Lower's list (Lower 1866: 15–16) cited two furnaces, Ewhurst and Northiam, while Parsons (Parsons 1882; 21–2) prints 'Ewhurst at Norjam'. Lower's version was considered faulty by Straker, who did not know of this furnace.

35   Ewood Furnace and Forge,
        Newdigate   TQ 201447
        Straker 1931a: 451–4

Bay L 190m H 2.75m/3m Centre
        section has limestone revetment.
Water system Pond dry. Spillway
        at W end. There are now two
        culverts through the centre of the
        bay. The western culvert, in
        ashlar sandstone is now dry, the
        eastern culvert leads to a pool
        (mill wheelpit) and tail-race.
Working area Obscured by later
        corn mill. Glassy slag near
        wheelpit and in tail-race stream.
        There is forge-bottom cinder
        between the timber-framed mill
        house and the bay.

The ironworks had been built by 1553, when the Nevills' manor of Ewood was sold to the Londoners George and Christopher Darrell. In 1554 they leased the manor, including the ironworks (as well as Leigh forge, *q.v.*) to John Stapley of Framfield and Gregory Newman, grocer of London, and in the same year sold their interests in the property (a share being bought by Anthony Pelham of Buxted). Nevertheless, some Darrell involvement appears to have continued, for a Frenchman, Robert le Jean, worked for George Darrell in 1557 (PRO E179/185/275) and in 1563 Darrell was licensed to cut wood notwithstanding statute regulations (*Cal. Pat. Rolls 5 Eliz.*,478). Christopher Darrell bought his way back into the property in 1574, when the ironworks were operated by Robert Reynolds (see Mill Place furnace and Brambletye forge). Darrell was suggested by Straker (1931: 146–7) to have had assistance from the Crown in this purchase; the ironworks were

exempted from the 1581 Act restricting wood cutting in the Weald (23 Eliz. c.5), and in 1582 the Crown was in possession of the wood, leasing to Henry Darrell. A survey of 1575, printed in Giuseppi 1902 (PRO E178/2242), shows a furnace and a forge. See also Close Rolls (PRO C54) 486, 506, 777, 934.

6   Fernhurst Furnace, Fernhurst
        (Linchmere)   SU 878283
        Straker 1931a: 426–7

Bay L 90m H pond in water/4m S
        end revetted with sandstone.
Water system Pond restored.
        Disused spillway at S end
        rebuilt, but recent flood damage
        showed older timber
        construction. Flood damage to
        modern spillway at N end
        revealed stone and brickwork,
        possibly remains of wheelpit and
        tail-race.
Working area Probably at N end
        where there is much glassy slag.
        (See fig. 34.)

A furnace known as North Park was operating in 1653, but ruined by 1664. There is a map of 1660 which gives a sketch of the furnace (WSRO Cowdray 1640). In the eighteenth century, John Butler began casting ordnance at Fernhurst about 1762 (Swanton and Woods 1914: 152). However, the claim by the authors of the latter that Butler was a stranger to the business is incorrect: John Butler of Bramshott had bought 18-pounder guns from Heathfield furnace in 1738 (ESRO SAS RF15/25, f.91).

87   Fletching Forge, Fletching
        TQ 424229   Straker 1931a: 415

Completely destroyed by later corn
        mill. Iron slab (1m × 1m × 5cm)
        used as well cover at Mill Farm
        house may have come from
        forge.
Re-use Corn mill.

In 1574 the forge was owned by Lord

Buckhurst and worked by Richard
Leeche.

63   Freshfield Forge, Horsted Keynes
TQ 386245   Straker 1931a: 411

Bay None
Water system Used water from tail-
race of contemporary (sixteenth-
century) corn mill. This
watercourse is now the main
river.
Working area 90m E of existing
remains of corn mill
foundations, timbers can be seen
lying lengthwise in stream bed.
Downstream the S bank is
revetted with forge bottoms and
cinder. Mill House (c.1550) has
charcoal in garden.

In 1564 and 1565 Drewe Barantyne
owned a forge at Freshfield (ESRO
Glynde 2046, 2048), confirmed in the
1574 list. Nevertheless, one version of
the list mentions Anthony Morley as
owner of a forge here, confirmed by a
reference of 1602 (PRO C3/284/51) to
John Cowper, who had bought the forge
from Morley. Either there were two
forges on the Ouse (Cattell 1979: 168) or a
change of ownership in or about 1574
confused the compilers of the list. No
second site has been found. Cowper
conveyed the forge to Stephen
Penkhurst, the above Chancery case
arising from encumbrances to the
property involving William Cowper (son
of John), William Crowe and David
Middleton (see also ESRO DH 780). The
forge was extant in 1633 (ESRO
QR/E/33/2), 1652 (DH 957), 1653 (list)
and 1656, when sold by Stephen
Penkhurst to the Knight family of
Cowden (DH 783) with all equipment.
The list of 1664 shows the forge to be
ruined.

155   Frith Furnace, Hawkhurst
TQ 736325   Straker 1931a:
320–1

Bay L 100m H 3m/3.5m Used as
farm road. Near S end a bank
projecting E was probably a
loading platform, and separates
the working area from a deep pit.
Water system Pond dry. Small
stream passes through stone
culvert under bay to the former
wheelpit. Here a timber baulk,
30cm × 30cm with mortice
holes, lies across the stream and
just E of this are 2 vertical posts
18cm × 18cm, all below water
level.
Working area At furnace site,
below loading platform, many
bricks lie just below the surface.

Frith is the most likely site of Sir Richard
Baker's furnace of 1574 and 1588, for
Hawkhurst Mill furnace was owned from
1579 by the Culpeppers and Baker's forge
at Sissinghurst is specifically stated
(Staffs. RO D593/S/4/28/3) to have no
furnace. This document states that
Baker's furnace was about 6.5km from
his home (in Cranbrook). Frith furnace
lies 5.65km away from Cranbrook. Even
so, Baker's will of 1591 (PRO
PROB11/84/86) is worded in a way
which does not exclude Sissinghurst as a
site for his furnace.

14   Frith Furnace, Northchapel
SU955309   Straker 1931a: 428
SM:AM (Sx) 405

Bay L 100m H 4m Slightly curved.
Breached by stream at W end.
Water system Pond dry. Spillway
was probably at W end.
Working area Probably at E end of
bay where a bear remains and a
small stream (tail-race) joins the
main stream. In this area are
roof-tiles and Tudor-type bricks.
A farm track, from Eastland Farm
to N, leads here and a short way
to the SE is the site of a now-
demolished house, probably
contemporary.

This furnace is easily confused with
Shillinglee; Cattell (1979: 165) argues
convincingly that 'Frith' belonged to the
Earl of Northumberland in 1574, leased

to Margaret Blackwell, occupied by William Walpole. Schubert had thought (1957: 375) that the 1574 'double furnace' was Frith, but Cattell considered Shillinglee a more likely identification. William Yalden rented the furnace with Mitchell Park Forge in 1636 and 1645 (Kenyon 1952; 237). It is included among the furnaces listed in 1653 and 1664. The furnace operated during the eighteenth century, closing in 1776 (Schubert 1957: 375). See Wyndham 1954: 93–103, for details of the seventeenth-century history of the furnace. It is included in Budgen's map of 1724.

Glaziers Forge: *see* **Brightling**

Gloucester Furnace: *see* **Lamberhurst Furnace**

47 **Gosden Furnace,** Lower Beeding
TQ 229251   Straker 1931a: 417, 436

Bay L 95m H pond in water/4.75m Projection at E end protected working area from spillway stream.
Water system Spillway at E end is stonebuilt and may be original. Modern pipe through bay at W end leads to swampy hollow and ditch which may indicate wheelpit. At pipe exit are two collapsed stone slabs 1.5m × 30cm × 8cm.
Working area Small heaps of black glassy slag containing sandstone occur near E end. Most of the area is swamp due to leakage from spillway stream. An old track leads to W end of bay.

Probably erected in 1580 by Roger Gratwick, it is likely that the furnace was supplied with wood granted under a patent of 1578 to Sir Thomas Sherley and assigned to Gratwick among others (PRO E178/2313). In 1595 a lease was taken by William and Neville Cheeseman from

John Middleton, who was also an assignee of Sherley's rights in the forest. Disputes centred on quantities of wood to be delivered to the furnace and of sows to be furnished for the lessor (PRO REQ2/186/35, 166/46). The case still proceeded in 1602.

52 **Gravetye Furnace,** West Hoathly
TQ 366342   Straker 1931a: 236

Bay L 110m H 1.25m Much damaged: breached by stream at E end. Modern pond bay with pond in water, 45m to S.
Water system Pond dry. Possible wheelpit at E end of bay, N of which Straker's 'sump hole' may be part of the tail-race.
Working area Probably at E end, N of which is a small amount of glassy slag. (The bear at E garden entrance to Gravetye Manor is from Mill Place furnace.)

This was a late furnace, belonging to Clutton and Co., William Clutton being bankrupt in 1762 (Hodgkinson 1978: 24, citing *Sussex Weekly Advertiser* 13.12.1762). Guns were carried from Gravetye for Eade and Wilton in 1762, but in the following year Ralph Clutton and Samuel Durrant were the consignors. It was demolished by 1787 (Sc. Mus. Weale MSS). Straker's ascription to John Blacket in 1574 has not been substantiated.

Habin Forge: *see* **Rogate Forge**

Hammer Mill: *see* **Biddenden**

99 **Hamsell Furnace,** Rotherfield
TQ 538344   Straker 1931a: 262

Bay L 73m H pond in water/2.4m
Water system Spillway at NE end.
Working area Probably near NE end where glassy slag occurs in spillway stream. Obscured by modern landscaping.

Ralph Hogge's complaint of 1573 shows Alexander Fermor to have been casting ordnance at Hamsell within the previous six or seven years (PRO SP12/95/15, 16). There is no earlier source. Fermor owned the furnace in 1574. Robert Baker held Hamsell in 1583, John Baker in 1639 (Attree 1912). The furnace appears in the lists of 1653 and 1667; in 1664 John Baker sold metal made for shot at Hamsell to George Browne (KAO TR1295/73). John Baker leased the furnace to John Browne in 1677, for the casting of ordnance (ESRO DH 614). Robert Baker was bankrupt in 1708. Straker cites an inventory of that year mentioned by Bell-Irving (1903: 177–9). The furnace does not appear in the 1717 list, although references to Birchden forge, 1709–37 (BL Add. MSS 5681, f.452) include mention of a furnace, perhaps Hamsell. William Harrison used Hamsell for casting ordnance between 1744 and 1750 (ESRO SAS RF15/25, 28.3.44; Guildhall 3736, 6482, 6482a). An air furnace was built there in 1745 (6483). It was demolished by 1787 (Sc. Mus. Weale MSS).

Harting Furnace *see* **Coombe Furnace**

156   Hawkhurst Furnace and Forge,
Hawkhurst   TQ 774313
Straker 1931a: 321–3

Bay L 95m plus an unknown length at N end destroyed in building Furnace Farm. H 1.5m/nil (completely silted up by later corn mill pond).
Water system Pond dry.
Working area Furnace: probably on site of present Furnace Farm, where there is a scatter of glassy slag.
Forge: probably at S end where large quantities of forge cinder and bottoms occur near present Forge Mill House (converted from later corn mill).
Re-use Corn mill at S end, working up to 1914; this had 500m long leat from upstream, along S side

of furnace pond, to mill pond contained on its W side by furnace pond bay.
(See Ellenden and Furnace Farm map 1779, KAO U814/P14.)

Straker's view that this site belonged to Richard Baker in 1574 is hard to support, his furnace probably being at Frith (q.v.).

In 1579 Stephen and Agnes Atkyns conveyed Wenebridge Forge, Hawkhurst to Francis Culpepper (ESRO Danny 1550). 'The Wents' is a name still in use c.2km to the north of this site. The Danny collection (nos. 1551–2, 1560, 144, 146) contains references through to 1667: a new channel to the forge pond was dug from Hooke Farm in 1607, and in 1615 the works were bought by Peter Courthope. The first reference to a furnace is in 1644 (Danny 144), and by 1657 it was being used by the Foley/Courthope/Browne partnership (Hereford RO Foley E/12/PF5/437). In 1660 the Foley share was sold to George Browne and Alexander Courthope, and in 1664 there is an inventory of Browne's goods at the furnace and the forge (KAO TR1295/62). The 1664 list confirms that the furnace was stocked, though it had been out of use. In 1668 John Browne entered the partnership (KAO U609/T3, ESRO DH 611). The Courthopes were using the forge in 1701 (KAO U1500/A17/9); the furnace is included in the 1717 list without an output figure, while a map of 1729 shows the forge (KAO U78/P7). The corn mill is shown in a map of 1779 (KAO U814/P14).

136   Hawksden Forge, Mayfield
TQ 623266   Straker 1931a: 294–5

Bay L 88m H 2.3m/1.5m Breached by stream near N end.
(Recent cutting into bay N of stream has revealed successive additions to height; the first of blast furnace slag, then clay, and finally of forge cinder)
Water system Pond dry. Wheelpit and tail-race probably on site of present stream. Long marshy

pond at S end, probably site of spillway, has culvert leading to it under S end of bay.

Working area At N end, where is much forge cinder. Area has been raised by metalled farm road. Associated timber-framed house is probably contemporary.

Hawksden forge was Morley property in the sixteenth century (ESRO Glynde MSS; BL. MSS 5679, 5682), the date of the first reference being 1559 (Glynde 184 and PRO C142/124/160). In the 1574 list no Morley is mentioned, and of the two occupiers of forges at Mayfield Richard Greene is more likely to have been leasing Hawksden, for the other, Isted, is said in one version of the 1574 list to have worked his own forge. Nevertheless, a Thomas Isted held land near Hawksden in 1590 (Glynde 1224). By 1593 the site included a furnace (1225), which is also mentioned in 1598 (1267), but not in 1603 (1277) or in successive leases (some with inventories), in 1651 (1229) and 1727 (1234). It is, however, listed as working in 1653 and 1667. Thomas Sands, tenant, obtained pig iron from Waldron furnace between 1699 and 1704 (BL Add. MSS 33156) and from Heathfield in the years 1720–5 (ESRO SAS RF15/27). He was tenant between 1702 and 1719 (Glynde 2784), making 40 tons of bar in 1717, a figure repeated in 1736. It was marked on Budgen's map of 1724. The forge was operated by William Harrison and his executors between 1741 and 1746 (Guildhall 3736). There was difficulty in securing a tenant in 1765–6 (Glynde 2770–1, 3088). The forge was demolished before 1787 (Sc. Mus. Weale MSS).

115   Heathfield Furnace, Heathfield
TQ 599187   Straker 1931a:
374–6   SM:AM (Sx) 385

Bay L 150m on S side of stream; possibly a further 75m on N side (now destroyed). H 2.3m/3.3m Gap in centre recently enlarged.
Water system Pond dry. Furnace

wheelpit probably at S end, where semicircular bank surrounds low area. E of this, possible culverted tail-race emerges to feed ditch along valley edge. Main pond is small, but tributary streams have pen ponds, and estate map of 1795 shows in addition 12 pen ponds on main stream. Existing pond at TQ 594196 has a brick spillway of exceptionally fine workmanship.

Working area Furnace almost certainly at S end, where high ground provides loading platform served by hollow way. Burnt stones and clay occur just below turf in this area. Boring mill probably located to N, towards stream, where occurs rusted swarf and scraps of cannon mould. No evidence found of boring mill further downstream. At TQ 597186 small wooded quarry was traditionally a gun-proving site; part of cannon said to have been found here.

Although there are references to a furnace in Heathfield parish in the sixteenth and early seventeenth centuries (Cattell 1979: 167 and ESRO SAS RF4/73), there is no link with this site. So far as is known, Heathfield furnace was a new development, built by the Fullers in 1693 (RF4/11). In the 1717 list it is shown producing 200 tons a year and it was marked on Budgen's map of 1724. The furnace lies at the centre of the Fuller operations in the production of ordnance in the eighteenth century (in particular RF15/1, 15/25–27). In 1787 it was recorded as casting 100 tons (Sc. Mus. Weale MSS). The furnace was last used in 1793.

Hedgecourt: *see* **Warren Furnace**

85   Hendall Furnace, Buxted
(Maresfield)   TQ 471259
Straker 1931a: 397   SM:AM
(Sx) 419

Bay L 70m H 3m/4m
Water system Pond dry.
Working area Glassy slag and
    charcoal on steep left bank of
    stream S of bay, where sloping
    track leads to site. Partially
    buried in stream S of bay is a
    wooden trough, possibly a flash
    for overshot wheel.

Schubert (1957: 377) suggests that the
Pelhams employed French workers here
in 1544, but there is nothing to confirm
such an early start. Hendall was owned
by Nicholas Pope in 1574, but a 'Pope's
furnace' is referred to c.1560 as being
within 3 miles (5km) of wood in
Framfield manor (ESRO Searle 13/1). It
was occupied (1576–81) by Ralph Hogge
(Dulwich MSS). A Ralph Pope kept sows
at Buxted in 1618–20 (ESRO DH 1011:
Inventory of Richard Maynard of
Birchden Forge); this might suggest that
Hendall was still in use.

101   Henly Furnace (Upper), Frant
        TQ 601338   Straker 1931a:
        275

Bay L 40m H 3m/4.5m Breached
    by stream.
Water system Pond dry.
Working area Flat area W of stream
    may be furnace site, with much
    glassy slag and no sign of forge
    cinder; alternatively this may be
    that of a pen pond for the lower
    site, the slag brought thence.

**101   Henly (Brinklaw or Bunklaw)
        Furnace (Lower),** Frant
        TQ 602336   Straker 1931a:
        275   SM:AM (Sx) 388

Bay L 50m, plus probable 20m
    washed away by stream at N end.
    H 2m/3m
Water system Pond dry.
Working area Probably at S end
    where is large bear and much
    glassy slag. Hollow may indicate
    wheelpit. Square metal plate
    from site is preserved at Earlye
    Farm. No sign of forge cinder.

Straker assumed this to be John
Carpenter's forge, recorded as at
Brinklaw in 1574. There is no written
evidence to dispute this, but the absence
of forge cinder must make the
identification tentative.

97   High Rocks Forge, Frant/
        Speldhurst   TQ 557382   Not
        included by Straker (but see below)

Bay L 80m H 2m/2.5m Breached
    by streams S of centre, by gap 8m
    N of stream, and by slight gap
    just S of stream. Projecting bank
    at S end protecting working area
    from spillway stream.
Water system Pond dry. Possible
    wheelpit at present stream;
    another possibly indicated by
    dry shallow ditch leading from
    low bay gap. Spillway and
    stream at S end. Pen pond (dry)
    120m upstream, with bay L 60m
    H 2.5m/2.5m with spillway at N
    end.
Working area Probably in S part,
    where forge bottoms and cinder
    occur. Few pieces of cinder also
    at pen pond bay.

Straker discovered this site after
completing *Wealden Iron*, but no
documentary material is known (Straker
1939: 206).

Hoadly or Hoathly Forge: *see*
Lamberhurst Forge

166   Hodesdale Forge, Mountfield
        TQ 748183   Straker 1931a:
        328–9

Bay L 250m H 2m/2.75m 'S'-
    shaped. Large breach by stream
    at S end.
Water system Pond dry. Heavy
    timbers with mortice slots, in
    stream bed, may indicate
    wheelpit.
Working area At S end where there
    are forge bottoms and cinder.
    Charcoal in Eastland Wood. Iron

plate (70 × 24 × 5cm) in stream. House at Woodsdale may be contemporary.

The identification of Hodesdale with the 'forge in Netherfield' in 1574 has not been challenged: the forge was in use in 1634 (ESRO Dunn 49/19) and 1653, and although listed as ruined in 1644 is named in 1669 and 1678 (ESRO ASH B886 and 1027), but in neither year is there any reference to it operating.

48 Holmsted Forge, Cuckfield
TQ 282274 Straker 1931a: 405–6

Bay Destroyed 1928.
Water system Pond dry.
Working area Forge cinder in stream and adjacent field.

Straker's assumption that Ninian Challoner operated this forge in 1574 is acceptable, although this may have been a joint arrangement with Walter Covert (Cattell 1979: 168). The interests of these two men in Slaugham and Cuckfield have not been satisfactorily resolved. Straker showed that the forge became Burrell property in 1605, and it appears in Ninian Burrell's will of 1615 (PRO PROB11/125/50). Pig came from the Burrell furnace at Tilgate between 1636 and 1656. It was listed as working in 1653, but ruined by 1664.

Horsebane: *see* **Thursley**

120 Horsmonden Furnace, Brenchley (Horsmonden) TQ 695412 Straker 1931a: 280–1

Bay L 135m H pond in water/4m
Water system Spillway at S end.
Working area Probably indicated by irregular ground and glassy slag at middle to S end. Bear in spillway stream.

This was a gun-casting furnace through most of its existence. The date of construction is not known, but in 1574 it

was owned by Thomas Bartell or Brattle and worked by Mr Ashburnham. In 1579 it was leased by Thomas and Henry Darrell to Thomas Dyke, Brattle retaining an interest (ESRO DH 606). In 1588 Brattle's lessee is referred to as William Ashburnham, who in turn sub-let to the gun founder Thomas Johnson of Hartfield (Staffs. RO D593/S/4/28/3, 16). Brattle was a scythe-smith (DH 606), and is not heard of again. Johnson was gunstone maker to the king (PRO E351/2629), but his use of the furnace was short-lived, as in about 1596 John Iden and Robert Pothill worked the furnace for Sir Thomas Waller (E178/4143); in 1604 Thomas Browne had taken over operations (BL Add. MSS 34218). The Brownes' involvement lasted at least until 1668; during their use of the furnace it was as important as any ordnance works in the Weald, casting brass as well as iron ordnance (BL Harl. 429/153, ESRO DH 611). John Browne's work there is thoroughly documented (see Chapter 8). The furnace is listed as working in 1667. The only later reference is to the Harrisons' boring mill at Horsmonden in 1744 (Guildhall 3738), but it is uncertain whether this was at the former furnace pond or somewhere else in the parish.

60 Horsted Keynes Furnace, Horsted Keynes TQ 379287 Straker 1931a: 410–11

Bay L 155m H pond in water/3m
Water system Modern spillway 45m from NW end probably lies on the original site. At SE end tail-race from adjacent corn mill is culverted under bay into banked channel (now breached) to bypass furnace area (which it now floods). Water-filled hollow 60m from SE end probably indicates wheelpit.
Working area Glassy slag in area of wheelpit. Farm track from NW along base of bay mounts to its top opposite furnace site to form probable loading platform, on

which occurs roasted ore and burnt clay.

Sir William Barrantyne employed Frenchmen in Danehill Horsted in 1544 (WAM 12261, cf. Awty 1978: 18; 1979: 7), thus it is presumed that the furnace was in use by this time. It remained Barrantyne property in 1574, worked by Anthony Morley. A series of references in ESRO Glynde MSS (2067–8, 2087–8, 2094, 2119) cover the years 1643–75. Operation at this period is confirmed by the lists of 1653 and 1667. See also Giles Moore's diary for reference to purchases from the furnace of iron pots and plates in 1656–9 (Bird 1971: 24–5).

107   Howbourne Forge, Buxted
TQ 515250   Straker 1931a: 389–90

Bay Completely destroyed. Possibly ran NW from Howbourne Farm along present farm track to where forge cinder and bottoms occur in stream.
Water system Pond dry.

The forge was mentioned as being within 3 miles (5km) of woods in Framfield manor in a survey of c.1560 (ESRO Searle 13/1). In 1574 it was worked by John Paler of Rotherfield. It was still in use in 1653, but ruined by 1664.

106   Huggetts Furnace, Hadlow Down (formerly Buxted)   TQ 534260
Straker 1931a: 387–8

Bay L 100m Levelled except at NW end. At SE end ran slightly N of present farm road with which it converged at NW end. Had stone revetment on both sides.
Water system Pond dry. Spillway was at SE end. Wheelpit and tail-race are probably indicated by remains of ashlar wall in SE bank of later corn mill tail-race, but not aligned with mill wall.
Working area Covered by later corn mill and farm buildings. Present

farm road probably acted as ramp to loading platform on bay. Plentiful glassy slag. Tudor-type bricks occur in stream; cannon balls have been found.
Re-use Corn mill and sawmill. Timber-framed house at TQ 532261 probably contemporary.

In 1573 Ralph Hogge claimed that Arthur Middleton, who had Huggett's furnace, had begun to cast guns in William Levett's time (PRO SP12/95/16); it was mentioned in the survey of Framfield manor woodlands of c.1560 (ESRO Searle 13/1). Arthur Middleton was the owner in 1574.

Idehurst: *see* **Barkfold Forge**

38   Ifield Forge, Ifield   TQ 245365
Straker 1931a: 460

Bay L 140m H pond in water/5m
Working area Obliterated by later corn mill. Glassy slag and forge cinder on bay.
Re-use Corn mill.

The confusion with Bewbush (q.v.) has been noted. Roger Gratwick's forge, in the 1574 list, is assumed to have been at Ifield, but as both forge and furnace slags can be found at Ifield and Bewbush, this attribution is open to question. Thomas Fenner had an iron mill in Ifield before · 1569 (PRO REQ2/226/4). The reference to sows carried to Bewbush Forge in 1602 (REQ2/166/46) could also perhaps relate to Ifield. The forge was burnt by Waller's forces in 1643 and appears not to have been rebuilt.

13   Imbhams Furnace, Chiddingfold
SU 932329   Straker 1931a: 420

Bay L 90m H no access/4m. Forms present road to Furnace Place.
Water system Pond dry. Bridge over present stream probably indicates original spillway.
Working area Level area at S end of

bay, opposite house 'Furness', where charcoal and roasted ore are scattered, is probably furnace site. 'Furness' may be the ironmaster's house or built on its site.
Boring mill pond to the NW at SU 929355 is still in water.

None of the late sixteenth-century references are entirely certain. Straker 1931a: 420 suggested construction c.1570; Cooper (1900: 40–50) thought a water-course in Thomas Quennell's will (1571) related to the furnace; the furnace as yet unused in 1574 may well have been Imbhams, leased by Lord Montague (Cattell 1979: 164). It may, therefore, have been one of the unnamed ironworks in Anthony Viscount Montague's will of 1592 (PRO PROB11/81/22).

The furnace operated in 1653, and was listed as equipped to cast guns in 1664: in the latter year George Browne and Alexander Courthope had indeed leased it from John Yalden (KAO TR1295/43) and stocked it; in 1666 the problems of carrying heavy guns from Imbhams through Guildford are mentioned in a letter to Browne from his agent or manager (*ibid*, 92). The 1667 list shows Imbhams as laid aside by Browne.

7   Inholmes Copse Furnace,
      Stedham   SU 855263

Bay L 88m H pond in water/3m
Working area Extensively damaged during 1968 floods. Much glassy slag carted away.

160   Iridge Furnace, Salehurst
       TQ 749277   Straker 1931a: 320

Bay L 80m H 2.25m/3.25m
    Breached by stream at N end where it curves to W. Near S end a right-angled projection served as a loading platform and protected the working area from flooding by the spillway stream.
Water system Pond dry. S of loading platform shallow gap in

bay opposite dry ditch indicates spillway.
Working area Furnace site located by burnt clay and bricks protruding from base of N side of loading platform. Much glassy slag.

This furnace was projected in 1575 (Vivian 1953: 115) when Thomas Walsh sold to John Wilgose a strip of land in Bexhurst, which Wilgose intended to use for water supply for his proposed furnace, but it is not clear when the furnace was constructed. The furnace and a water-course are referred to in 1607 (PRO C142/292/162). In 1654 a furnace in Salehurst was included in a settlement made by Sir Annesley Wildgos on his marriage (ESRO Add. MSS 521). It does not appear in the lists of 1653, 1664 or 1717, although Straker found it marked on eighteenth-century maps.

91   Iron Plat Furnace, Buxted
      TQ 499242   Straker 1931a: 390
      SM:AM (Sx) 389

Bay L 100m H 1.25m/1.25m
    Breached by stream at W end and by farm gateway near E end.
Water system Pond dry.
    Depression at W end 20m from stream probably indicates spillway. Near E end, 25m downstream of bay, shallow circular pit with dry ditch-like depression to S may represent tail-race. Series of pen ponds upstream to TQ 498249.
Working area Probably at E end, where natural bank with much charcoal could have served as loading platform. Some glassy slag on bay.

It has not been satisfactorily established whether this was one of Ralph Hogge's works: in the years 1576–81 (Crossley 1974: 52) he had a furnace in Buxted: Iron Plat is one possible site.

152   Kitchenham (Ashburnham Lower)
       Forge, Ashburnham TQ 679135
       Straker 1931a: 371–2

Bay L 280m H 0.75m/9.75m Does
not span Ashburn valley but
encloses part of SE side against
high ground.

Water system Pond dry. Probably
filled by leat (1,000m long) from
River Ashburn, now indicated by
shallow ditch along NW side of
Hammer Wood. Tail-race
probably indicated by E ditch of
meadow on S side of site. Deep
ditch running NW to River
Ashburn may have been used for
navigation.

Working area At SE end of bay
where erosion has exposed large
quantities of forge bottoms and
cinder.

(See fig.42.)

This was one of the two forges of John
Ashburnham occupied by John Gardner
in 1574. By 1578 Thomas Glydd and
Thomas Hayes worked Kitchenham in
conjunction with Panningridge furnace
(PRO STAC5/G4/28). In 1590 the
Commissioners of Sewers threatened
unsuccessfully to demolish the forge as
an obstacle to drainage (Jack 1982: 25,
citing PRO E123/4, p.270). The forge was
sold to Edward Broomfield in 1611 and
by him in 1634 to Laurence Somers and
others, whose tenants were a group
including Richard Relfe. After 1640 it
was owned by John Fogge and William
Hay (ESRO ASH B489, 546, 605). It had
been in use in 1653, but was said to be
ruined by 1664, although a marriage
settlement of 1667 (ASH 776) makes no
mention of this.

34   Knepp Furnace, Shipley
    TQ 163211   Straker 1931a: 418

Pond still in water, but original bay
thought to have been destroyed
by widening of A24 road.

Straker notes that the Carylls worked the
furnace for the Duke of Norfolk from
1568 until 1604, but no further
references have been found, and the
works appear not to have been recorded
in 1574.

126   Lamberhurst (Hoadly or
    Hoathly) Forge, Lamberhurst
    TQ 661361   Straker 1931a:
    269–73

No bay

Water system 800m leat, W half of
which is present course of River
Teise and remainder is dry, fed
small pond from which culvert
led to forge site (present disused
corn mill). Tail-race, culverted
under road to present stream,
utilized by later corn mill built
subsequent to 1794 map.

Hoadly Forge was newly built by
Alexander Collins in 1548 (Tawney and
Power 1924: I, 237–8). It is referred to in
the Inquisition into Collins property
(PRO C142/142/75). In 1574 it was
owned by Stephen Collins, but in 1584
he sold the forge to Robert Filmer (KAO
U120/T99). It is listed as working in
1653 and 1667. It remained Filmer
property until 1694 (*ibid.*, L1, C52/1),
when it was bought by William Benge
before the construction of Lamberhurst
(Gloucester) furnace. The corn mill is
shown on a map of 1795 (KAO
U120/P15) (fig. 39).

126   Lamberhurst (Gloucester)
    Furnace, Lamberhurst
    TQ 662360   Straker 1931a: 269

No bay

Water system Leat from forge site,
indicated by dry channel in
Cherry Orchard Field (S of
Furnace Mill House and W of
road leading to it), ends at
furnace site. Plentiful supply of
water could have been made
available for both forge and
furnace by diverting the whole
flow of River Teise if necessary.

Working area Furnace site
probably indicated by glassy slag
and roasted ore just inside
gateway S of Cherry Orchard
Field. Adjoining high ground
would be convenient as loading
platform and probably

determined furnace position. No sigof wheelpit; tail-race was probably culverted under road to join nearby forge tail-race stream. No trace remains of boring house site and its curious linear feature shown on 1795 map. Boring wheel may have been on forge and furnace tail-race stream. Present Furnace Mill House believed to date from c.1722.

Re-use Corn mill built c.1812. (See fig.39.)

The furnace was built by William Benge in 1695 on land purchased the previous year (KAO U120/L1, P14, 15). Samuel Gott was owner from soon after 1700. In 1717 it produced 200 tons, and its design was noted by Swedenborg in 1734. It was marked by Budgen on his map of 1724. In 1743, John Legas brought the furnace into the group of works run in partnership with William Harrison (Guildhall 3736, 6482; ESRO SAS RF15/25f 213v–214; Sotheby documents – sale catalogue 6.6.1966). It remained Harrison property in 1787, when Weale noted it as standing and able to work (Sc. Mus. Weale MSS). It is marked on a map of 1795 (KAO U120/P15): fig.39.

88   Langles Furnace and Forge, Maresfield   TQ 451239   Straker 1931a: 400

Bay L 100m H 2m/2m Projection at W end to protect working area. E end widened to form loading platform. Gap at E end.
Water system Pond dry. Original spillway probably at W end on site of present stream. Modern (disused) spillway at W end probably replaced wheelpit and tail-race for forge. Furnace wheelpit at E end has dry channel to main stream.
Working area Forge at W end where forge cinder predominates. At E end, W of wheelpit, low bank consisting of collapsed wall of burnt stones

and clay surrounds probable furnace area. Immediately to W, circular hollow may be site of casting pit. Large scatter of glassy slag with one piece of cannon mould. On line of bay, on high ground to E, level platform with charcoal may be site of charcoal store.

The furnace was used by Ralph Hogge in the 1570s and 1580s (Crossley 1974: 48–79), but there is no other firm information. A map of 1653 shows a forge at the west end of the bay, with no sign of a furnace at the east, except for a channel, perhaps the disused tail-race (ESRO SAS E/9).

36   Leigh Hammer Forge, Leigh TQ 222461   Straker 1931a: 455–6

No features remain, but forge cinder found in stream.

In 1551 lands named Burghett and Grovelands were leased by Henry Lechford to Richard Wheler and William Hawthorne (Straker 1931a: 146–7). By 1554, when the lease was transferred to George and Christopher Darrell, ironworks were in operation. Subsequently the forge was transferred and used with Ewood (*q.v.*); it was included in the right given to the Darrells to cut wood in 1563 (PRO C66/982 m.9).

105   Little Forge and Furnace, Buxted TQ 513260   Straker 1931a: 388 SM:AM (Sx) 395

Bay L 85m H 0.75m/1.75m Breached by stream at both ends.
Water system Pond dry. Spillway probably at E end, on course of present tributary stream. Wheelpit and tail-race at W end.
Working area Almost certainly at W end, to which hollow-way leads. This site appears to be of three periods: (1) indicated by bloomery slag and forge or

furnace bottoms, stratified below silt of later pond, in left bank of W stream 20m N of bay; (2) glassy furnace slag and sixteenth-century pottery (including Raeren stoneware) occurs in lowest layers of filled-in pit being eroded by E stream as it turns sharply W, S of bay; (3) indicated by forge cinder as main filling of pit.

'Little Buxted Hammer' was within 3 miles (5km) of woods in Framfield manor c.1560 (ESRO Searle 13/1). It was owned by Arthur Middleton in 1574 and by Anthony Fowle in 1611 (ESRO SAS Portman 109, 110). Iron was carried to the forge in 1636 to be made into dripping pans by Hugh Pray (ESRO R/E/35.91). Straker notes (without source) a possible conveyance of 1652 including a furnace as well as a forge. A forge at Buxted was working in 1653 and 1667 and certainly retained equipment in 1667 (ESRO AB193).

21   Lurgashall Mill Furnace,
Lurgashall   SU 940258
Straker 1931a: 431

Lurgashall corn mill has recently been dismantled for re-erection at Singleton Open Air Museum. Observation revealed no signs of an earlier ironworks on this site. Glassy slag does however occur in the area, with the possibility of a furnace near S end of bay.

Before 1585 Peter Younge of Midhurst made a pond and built a furnace here, and in that year sold the three acres to Anthony Viscount Montague (WSRO/SAS BA54, 62, 1584–5). Straker found that the furnace appears to have been operated by William Yalden for the Montagues in the next century; his reference to Yalden's 'bloomery' has not been explained.

90   Maresfield Forge, Maresfield
TQ 460228   Straker 1931a: 400–3

Bay L 175m H pond in water/4m Probably altered by later use and landscaping.
Water system Apparently much altered.
Working area Probably in area of present spillway at SW end of pond, where forge bottoms and cinder are concentrated. Wheelpit and tail-race N of spillway may be of later date.
Re-use Powder mill, early nineteenth century

Built before 1574, the forge was then recorded as Gage property, leased to John Faukenor. It remained in Gage ownership throughout, being referred to in 1589 and 1594 in ESRO SAS Gage 13/45 and 6/3. It was leased by William Crowe in 1619 (Gage Addnl. 918, PRO C3/319/23), by Anthony Fowle in 1654 (Gage 13/49) and by John Newnham in 1669 (13/50). It was listed as working in 1653 and 1667. The forge was not entered in the 1717 list, despite the lease (with inventory) to Ambrose Galloway in that year (Gage 13/53). In 1736 the output was listed as 60 tons, and 30 tons in 1787. Galloway used the forge for much of the century, although in 1772 Benjamin Molyneux announced that he had taken it (*Sussex Weekly Advertiser* 6.1.72) while in the following year Elias Standon was advertising thence (*ibid.* 26.4.73). In 1787 the tenancy was held by Willis (Sc. Mus. Weale MSS).

The forge is shown on Budgen's map of 1724. The Dawson map, claimed to be of that year and reproduced by Straker (p. 401) has been shown to be a fake (Pettitt 1976: 20).

89   Maresfield Furnace, Maresfield
TQ 462232   Straker 1931a: 400–3

Bay L 75m H 1.25m/1.75m
Water system Pond dry. The present stream seems inadequate to fill this pond.
Working area From high ground on W side of bay a short bank, running E parallel to bay, may

have been loading platform. Much glassy slag with pieces of cannon mould S of bay.

The furnace was closely associated with the forge (*q.v.*). In 1614–19 the furnace was operated by David Middleton and William Crowe, between whom were disputed the costs of equipment (PRO C3/319/23). The furnace was used by Sackville Crowe during his monopoly of the casting of merchant guns (PRO SP14/118/48–9).

144 Markly (Rushlake Green) Furnace, Warbleton   TQ 624183
Straker 1931a: 379

Bay L 85m H 5m/4.5m Breached by stream.
Water system Pond dry. Wheelpit and tail-race probably in present stream, where are timbers and a bear. Ponds further upstream fed leat to the corn mill downstream at TQ 622180.
Working area Probably on E side of stream close to bay where are furnace lining, bricks and glassy slag.

It is uncertain whether this furnace existed in the sixteenth century, for none of those listed in Warbleton parish in 1574 satisfactorily fit this site. Nevertheless, the works in the parish in 1548 could well include Markly. In 1617 Thomas Stolion mortgaged 'Rushlake furnace' to Sir Thomas Pelham (BL Add. Ch. 30920), the first convincing reference. Straker noted purchases of pig iron from this furnace in 1645 and 1655, but it was not included in the 1653 or 1664–7 lists.

Marriotts Croft: *see* **Breechers Forge**

Marshalls Furnace: *see* **Old Forge**

119 Matfield Furnace(?) or Forge(?), Brenchley   TQ 649430
Straker 1931a: 281

Bay L 110m H 2.75m Breached by streams at both ends.
Water system The W stream has two bays for pen ponds (dry):
(1) TQ 647429 L 35m H 0.75m
(2) TQ 645427 L 80m H 3m/3m breached by stream near centre. Probably Straker's site. His 'casting sand' located 1.5m W of stream, 3m downstream of bay.
The E stream had bay for pen pond at TQ 647424 L 60m, now levelled.
Working area Only evidence for any ironworkings comes from place names – large Cinder Field occupies much of area between two streams; there is also Cinderhill Wood (TQ 650427).

There are no convincing grounds for accepting this as an iron furnace, for seventeenth-century references to founding in Brenchley fit better with Horsmonden furnace, on the boundary of the two parishes. Matfield could, perhaps, have been the Brownes' brass foundry, although brass pieces were cast at Horsmonden. The place-names could refer to bloomery cinder.

104 Mayfield Forge, Mayfield
TQ 594281   Not included by Straker

Bay Dual use with Mayfield furnace.
Water system Leat, now dry, originating from the extreme N end of the furnace pond bay runs in partly banked channel for c.170m before joining stream. Just before stream is reached, and N of public footpath, another dry channel loops round to join stream 45m further downstream. Wheelpit may be in this area.
Working area Probably within loop. Forge-type cinder and forge bottoms occur in stream at this point, but not immediately upstream. Section exposed in N bank shows filled-in hollow with charcoal, slag and roof tiles at

base. 150m downstream on N bank are Great and Little Forge Fields (Mayfield Tithe Award). (See figs.32, 65.)

104   Mayfield Furnace, Mayfield
TQ 593282   Straker 1931a:
292–3   SM:AM (Sx) 401

Bay L 110m H 2m/2.5m Breached by stream near SW end. Disused Mayfield–Tunbridge Wells road (old coach road) runs along SE side of bay and cuts through its NE end, displaced soil being banked on SE side of road.
Water system Pond dry. Prominent banked dry channel, originally from extreme NE end of bay, probably leat to forge site downstream. Remains of lesser channel to S may be furnace spillway. Wheelpit probably on site of present stream. Pen pond with bay at TQ 588284 and another with bay on line of present road at TQ 590283. Further pen ponds in side-stream with bays at TQ 590282 and TQ 588281.
Working area Partly destroyed by old road. Levelled platform just downstream of bay, above left bank of stream, from which bricks and stones are being eroded. Scatter of glassy slag all over area, especially at SW end. Partly submerged bear just downstream of present bridge, and part of wooden trough near right bank.
Boring mill Tributary on SW side joins main stream 110m downstream of bay. On this tributary is secondary bay (L 60m) with spillway at SE end, breached by present stream. Immediately downstream of breach, on right bank, is small level platform and in stream are large stone blocks apparently part of a structure. Downstream, the banks have scatter of broken

cannon mould and boring swarf. Pen pond at TQ 591280. (See fig.32, 65.)

Schubert 1957: 381 refers without citation to iron works on the Archbishops of Canterbury's lands at Mayfield in 1545, but these were not necessarily this furnace. Thomas Gresham acquired the furnace by 1570, is referred to in Hogge's petition of 1573 as casting guns, was licensed to export cannon in 1574 (PRO S P 12/95/62) and 1578 (HMC *Hatfield*, V, pt 2: 216; Bell-Irving 1903: 59, 175–6). He was listed as owner in 1574. In 1598 Thomas May bought the furnace (which was being operated by Barnabe Hodgson between about 1599 and 1609 (PRO E178/4143); the Bakers were the next purchasers in 1617. The furnace is listed as working in 1653, and repaired in 1664. (See ESRO AMS 5831, reproduced as fig.32.)

103   Maynards Gate Forge, Rotherfield
TQ 540298   Not included by Straker

Bay As Maynards Gate furnace, with dual use of pond
Water system High above stream, on N side, a possible leat banked on stream side runs from near the level of the furnace bay downstream for 125m; the 35m nearest the bay have been destroyed. Leat ends abruptly above levelled area towards the stream, with indications of wheelpit and tail-race.
Working area Forge-type cinder occurs in stream, adjacent to and downstream from the levelled area; upstream of this point only furnace slag was found.

103   Maynards Gate Furnace,
Rotherfield   TQ 539298
Straker 1931a: 254–5

Bay L 70m H 1m/3.75m Breached by stream. Gap at N end.
Water system Pond dry. Wheelpit

at S end. Pen pond at TQ 533302.
Working area At S end, where
furnace and gun-casting pit were
revealed by rescue excavation in
1976 (Bedwin 1977–8: 163–78).

Probable but not certain that Anthony
Fowle operated at Maynards Gate by
1562 (PRO STAC5 A2/25, cited in
Schubert 1957: 381). In 1574 Maynards
Gate was a gun-founding furnace, owned
by Lord Buckhurst and operated by
Arthur Middleton. In 1576 Middleton
supplied charcoal to Edward Fyltness
and the furnace was noted in 1603
(Pullein 1928: 278). It was operating in
1653, but ruined by 1664.
(See figs.44, 50, 55, 60, 61.)

122 **Melhill Forge,** Pembury
      TQ 615381   Straker 1931a:
      264–7

      Slight undulations may represent
      silted-up pond and bay. Forge
      cinder scattered in main and side
      streams, but no clear nucleus.

Straker was cautious over ascribing
references to forges in this valley to
Melhill rather than Benhall (*q.v.*).
However, references in 1630 and 1633
(ESRO DH 97, 100) show that
Whittingham Fogge had an iron mill and
forge at Melhill, sold to William Dyke in
the latter year. As Straker's succession of
sixteenth-century references to a forge
culminate in its possession by the Fogges
at the beginning of the seventeenth
century, it is likely but not certain that
the site's existence can be taken back to
1567, when a forge was first mentioned
(manor rolls of Frant, cited by Straker).

53   **Mill Place Furnace,** East
      Grinstead   TQ 374349   Straker
      1931a: 236–7

      Bay L c.100m H 0.5m/0.75m
      Destroyed except for small
      portions at N and S ends.
      Breached by stream at S end.
      Signs of stone revetment along

base of middle destroyed
section.
Water system Pond dry. Silted
ditch from near centre of bay to
main stream may indicate
spillway or tail-race.
Working area Much glassy slag in
present stream and on farm roads
in vicinity. Apparent bear
protrudes from road surface 75m
E of bay. Large bear at E garden
entrance to Gravetye Manor is
from this site. Mill Place farm
house may be contemporary.

An owner of this land, Richard Amill
had allowed ore to be dug in 1565 (ESRO
A6/380). In 1574 Mills is described as
owner of a furnace, leasing to Robert
Reynolds (PRO SP12/95/79), who
worked Brambletye forge. The furnace
was in use in 1653, discontinued by
1664, but then restocked. It does not
appear in the 1717 list, but in 1763
Robert Knight carried 100 guns for
Clutton and Durrant, who then owned
Mill Place and operated Gravetye. It has
not been established that Mill Place was
in blast at this time (Hodgkinson 1978b:
18 and subsequent research).

16   **Mitchell Park Forge,** Northchapel
      SU 977297   Straker 1931a:
      429

      Bay Much altered.
      Water system Pond dry.
      Working area Only visible remains
      are in stream, downstream of
      Hammer Bridge. 20m away is a
      short section of rough
      stonework, below a cinder layer,
      and at 50m two cinder layers.

Straker thought of this as Thomas
Smith's forge of 1574 at Shillinglee, but
Cattell favoured a pairing with Frith
furnace, making Mitchell Park
Blackwell's forge. If this were so,
Mitchell Park could be the forge of
Thomas Blackwell where pig was taken
from Ifield in 1569 (PRO REQ2/244/25).
There is an inventory for the forge
(Giuseppi 1903), probably made in 1637.
The long-term connection between Frith

and Mitchell Park is strengthened by this joint lease to the Parliamentary supporter William Yalden of Blackdown in 1645 (Kenyon 1952: 235). See also Wyndham 1954: 93–103.

109   Moat Mill Forge, Mayfield
TQ 592251   Straker 1931a: 286

> *Bay* (possible) L 50m H 0.5m/0.75m Follows line of public footpath N from the above NGR, with possible extension S along right bank of main stream.
> *Water system* Pond dry.
> *Working area* Only evidence is forge bottom lying in main stream at footpath bridge. No cinder found where indicated by Straker.

This may be one of the un-named Mayfield forges in the 1574 list. The only firm references are later, in Mayfield parish register (burial) entries: the death of a boy at the moat forge (19 Jan. 1588) and J. Gayn of moat forge buried on 3 May 1616.

165   Mountfield Furnace and Forge,
Mountfield   TQ 749196 Straker 1931a: 326

> *Bay* L 125m H 3.5m/3m Breached by stream at W end and farm track at E end.
> *Water system* Pond dry.
> *Working area* Probably at far E end where hollow, surrounded by low circular bank, may indicate furnace site. Nearby is scatter of furnace lining, bricks, roof tiles and glassy slag. Forge possibly at W end where stream contains possible forge cinder.

This was a forge in 1548. That it was Richard Weekes' furnace in the 1574 list is shown by the Robertsbridge survey of 1567–70 (D'Elboux 1944: 159). There are no later references to operation, though deeds of 1668, 1669 and 1676 (ESRO ASH 870, 886, 951) mention an 'old' furnace.

77   Newbridge Furnace and Forge,
Hartfield   TQ 456325   Straker 1931a: 248–50   SM:AM (Sx) 399

> *Bay* L 180m H 2m/3m Breached by road and Newbridge Mill leat; partly removed W of road. W end forms a semicircle, part of which was probably designed to protect the working area from spillway flooding. Two gaps in the semi-circular portion may indicate inlets to wheelpits.
> *Water system* Pond dry. Present restored spillway probably on original site. Two dry hollows within the semi-circular part of the bay, with dry ditches to main stream, may indicate wheelpits and tail-races.
> *Working area* The semi-circular portion of the bay contains forge cinder and bloomery-type tap slag. N of destroyed length of bay, next to the road, is a scatter of glassy slag and charcoal. Large quantities of glassy slag are known to have been removed from small field to N.
> (See fig.28.)

Built in 1496, the early details of operation are referred to in Chapter 6, pp. 111–13. Two-part cannon are included in an inventory of 1509 (PRO DL29/455/7331). The furnace was leased to Thomas Boleyn in 1525 (DL29/445/7160). An account (PRO E32/197), probably of 1539, records costs and yields in an unsatisfactory form (Chapter 7, p. 146). It shows the furnace and forge to have been some distance apart. It also indicates that this furnace was very small, with only 160 tons' annual production. In 1574 Henry Bowyer had a royal furnace and forge in Ashdown forest; in one version of the list this is identified as a double furnace at Newbridge. The last reference is in 1603 (DL29/451/7250, 459/7420).

113   New Place Furnace, Framfield
TQ 509195   Straker 1931a: 393

Bay L 110m H pond in
water/1.75m
Water system and *working area*
Extensively altered and
landscaped. Glassy slag in S
tributary stream near main road.

No firm references, apart from the
possibility that this is one of the furnaces
noted as within 3 miles (5km) of woods
on Framfield manor c.1560 (ESRO Searle
13/1).

175 Northiam Furnace, Northiam
TQ 817245   Straker 1931a: 320

Bay L c.55m H 2m Destroyed
except for 9m at SW end.
Water system Pond dry (Straker
records restoration). Modern
spillway at SW end.
Water area Glassy slag on bay and
in stream banks.

ESRO QR/E/38.105 (Apr. 1637) refers to
a lodge built on the top of Northiam
furnace, and to a theft of iron. It worked
in 1653, but in 1664 it had been out of
use but subsequently restocked. (see
Ewhurst furnace).

North Park Furnace: *see* **Fernhurst**

**84 Old Forge Furnace and Forge
(Marshalls),** Maresfield
TQ 459258   Straker 1931a:
398–9

[Three houses, 'Burnside', 'Forge
Cottage' and 'Green Ford' and
their gardens, occupy this site,
making identification of features
difficult.]
Bay L 130m H 3m/3m with a
projection towards the pond at S
end, which forms N bank of
probable spillway stream.
Breached by stream 100m from N
end, and by 'Green Ford' garage
driveway.
Water system Dry channel
(unusually narrow) at extreme S
end is probably spillway stream.

Part of this is still culverted
under the garden of 'Burnside'
and the main road before joining
the main stream. Present stream
may indicate the site of one
wheelpit.
Working area Levelled for houses
and gardens. Much glassy slag in
all gardens; forge cinder and
bottoms in stream bed.

In 1574 there was a furnace and a forge at
Marshalls, the furnace being one of those
referred to in Ralph Hogge's accounts of
1576–81 (Dulwich MSS). Hogge built the
house (Marshalls) about a mile away. A
new furnace was built by David
Middleton and William Crowe between
1614 and 1619 (PRO C3/319/23,
E190/755/20); an inventory of
Middleton's gun-founding equipment is
in PRO C239/86.

94 Old Forge Southborough,
Tonbridge   TQ 594428
Straker 1931a: 222

Scatter of forge cinder; all other
traces obliterated during
construction of railway viaduct.

David Willard built this forge in 1553
(PRO C66/874 m.27). Ten years later he
was challenged by the copyholders of
Southfrith for use of timber, and for
building one more iron mill than
permitted (PRO REQ2/285/39). This was
one of the two forges worked by Willard
in 1574 (Sir Thomas Fane was the
owner). Between 1623 and 1679 the forge
worked with Vauxhall furnace (KAO
U38/T1/1–15). There is a risk of
confusing this forge with those at Postern
and Rats Castle.

83 Oldlands Furnace, Buxted
TQ 477272   Straker 1931a:
394–5   SM:AM (Sx) 430

Bay L 70m H pond in water/4m
Projecting bank at W end to
provide loading platform and
protect working area.
Water system Original spillway at

W end, now dry. Present
spillway stream cuts through
probable working area.
Working area Destroyed by modern
spillway. Glassy slag in stream.

It is as yet unproven that William Levett
cast ordnance here in the 1540s,
although he owned land at Oldlands
PRO PROB11/37/39). There is no proof
that Ralph Hogge had a furnace here.
(ESRO Searle 13/1; Dulwich MSS). Later
there is a clear reference to a furnace at
Oldlands, leased by William Crowe and
David Middleton between 1614 and 1617
(PRO C3/319/23).

110   Old Mill Furnace, Mayfield
TQ 588245   Straker 1931a: 285–6

Bay Almost certainly the present
main road.
Water system Pond dry.
Working area Much glassy slag in
swampy ground E of road. House
at N end of bay probably
contemporary; name suggests re-
use as corn mill.

Information on the ownership of this
furnace is circumstantial, involving a
presumption that it belonged to the
Bakers through the sixteenth century. In
1543 John Baker of Isenhurst employed
aliens, and Old Mill is close to Isenhurst.
In 1574 John Baker had a furnace in
Mayfield, but this is as likely to be
Coushoplea. However, there is no doubt
that in 1618 John Baker owned Old Mill
(ESRO Drake 131). Richard Maynard had
been tenant, and his inventory (ESRO DH
1011) includes items at an unnamed
furnace, assumed to be Old Mill. It
appears that Maynard had been in arrears
with rent before his death (PRO
C78/311/11). This case confuses the
issue by referring to Richard Heath as
owner in 1616.

29   Pallingham Furnace, Wisborough
Green   TQ 041227   Straker
1931a: 425

Bay L 147m H 3.7m/5m Forms

present road. Low berm 4m wide
on pond side. Contains large
quantities of slag.
Water system Pond dry. At extreme
N end a dry spillway and
channel, with protective bank,
lead to the natural stream course.
Adjacent, to S, is a smaller
channel which may be the
wheelpit and tail-race of boring
mill. Present stream, banked
along the S side of the dry pond
and running close to the bay on
its downstream side, is almost
certainly artificial.
Working area At S end artificial
level-topped mound is probably
loading platform. N of this,
irregular ground may indicate
site of furnace, wheelpit and tail-
race. Flat area near N end may be
the site of a boring mill. There
are large quantities of glassy slag
all over site. One piece of clay
mould has been found.

Built in 1586–7 by Edward Caryll, this
furnace was listed as working in 1653
and 1664. In addition to Straker's
reference to Walter Bartlett carrying ore
to the furnace in 1630, Bartlett also
shipped pig iron from Rye to Arundel in
1633 and 1636, suggesting that he was
short of pig with which to supply forge
customers (PRO E190/764/9, 766/19).

146   Panningridge Furnace, Dallington
TQ 687174   Straker 1931a:
362–4   SM:AM (Sx) 386

Bay L 100m H 1.5/2.5m Broken in
centre by present stream.
Water system Pond dry. Spillways
originally at each end of bay,
with banks to maintain dry
working area.
Working area See excavation
report in *Post-Medieval
Archaeology 6* (1972), 42–68.
Two periods of operation found:
radical revision of wheelpit and
race layout.

The best-documented furnace in the
Weald, with accounts from 1542 to 1563

(KAO U1475, see Crossley 1975a). The tenancy of Relfe and Jeffrey (1563 onwards) is ill-documented, apart from their supply of pig iron to Robertsbridge forge; it must have ended in or before 1572, when John Ashburnham is said (WSRO EpII/5/3 f.48r) to have occupied the furnace, as he did in 1574. In 1584–6 it was run by Thomas Glydd (*ibid.*, PRO STAC5/G4/28). James Caigheym, who worked at Panningridge, appears in Dallington parish registers in 1582 and 1586. By 1611 the furnace was no longer standing (ESRO ASH A126). (See figs.30, 45, 49, 51, 55.)

74   Parrock Furnace and Forge,
Hartfield   TQ 458357   Straker 1931a: 241–4

Bay L 70m H 1.5m/1.5m Probably originally extended a further 80m to N and 120m to S.
Water system Pond dry. Spillway probably at present River Medway. One wheelpit may be indicated by a hollow 30m N of present S end of bay (between bay and farm road) with ditch (tail-race?) under road to join River Medway. Ponds in valley to S may be pen ponds.
Working area Much forge cinder and bottoms occur near right bank of Medway in field immediately E of farm road, with small scatter of glassy slag. Excavation of the nearby sixteenth-century pottery kiln in 1977 revealed an area where iron artefacts were manufactured (Freke 1979: 87).

Straker's outline begins with Robert Scorer as lessee, supplying shot in 1513, with the Warner family as owners until the sale to William Saunders in 1547. There were aliens at Parrock in 1544 (WAM 12261). Disputes between Saunders and the current lessee, Bowyer, are recorded in PRO STAC2/24/422, 25/107, 27/30 and STAC3/8/38. Details of tenancies are contained in ESRO Searle 7/3 (1571) and PRO REQ2/272/1

(1579). In 1574 the furnace and forge were worked by George Bullen for Lord Buckhurst. In 1595 Thomas Johnson, the Crown gunfounder, was involved in a dispute over iron at Parrock (REQ2/228/13). By this time Parrock was the property of William Garway and, by 1600, of John Garway. No references have been found subsequent to this, Straker's final date.

158   Pashley Furnace, Ticehurst
TQ 710295   Straker 1931a: 298–9

Bay L 80m H 3m/3m Complete, as present stream follows course of spillway stream at W end. Spurs from W half form probable loading platform and protective bank.
Water system Pond dry. Indications of wheelpit and tail-race near W end. Two pen ponds (dry): TQ 711299 Bay L 120m H 2m/3m. Breached by main stream at E end and tributary at W end. TQ 710297 Bay L 90m H irregular. Breached by stream near centre. Spillway at W end.
Working area At W end, enclosed on three sides by bay, loading platform and protective bank. Level platform in bank may be furnace site. Thick scatter of glassy slag; also on bay and in stream bank.

The furnace was the property of Sir James Boleyn until 1543, when it was sold to Thomas May. It remained May property throughout the sixteenth century (1574 list), the last reference being to Anthony May in 1614 (Vivian 1953: 135; Straker, citing Hodson and Odell 1925, 133–4, 154). In 1544 May employed aliens (WAM 12261).

167   Penhurst Furnace, Penhurst
TQ 705163   Not included by Straker

Bay L 100m H 2m/2.5m Only 50m of E end now remains.

Water system Pond dry. After
disuse, part of water source for
pond was diverted via Ashburnham aqueduct to Ashburnham
forge or furnace ponds.
Working area Tree-topped mound
near W end of surviving bay,
surrounded by glassy slag, may
indicate furnace.

This is probably the furnace referred to
in PRO C3/73/58: c.1545: Ninian Burrell
leased part of his manor of Penhurst to
Sir Nicholas Pelham to build a furnace.
This was constructed by 1550 and was
the subject of a disputed sub-leasing to
John Glazier of Penhurst. There is a
useful reference to the roasting of ore in
this case.

78   Pippingford Furnace, Hartfield
TQ 450316   Straker 1931a:
247–8   SM:AM (Sx) 394

Bay L 125m H 3.5m/3.5m
Breached by stream at E end.
Water system Pond dry.
Working areas (two furnaces). See
excavation report in *Post-Medi-
eval Archaeology 9* (1975), 1–37.
(See figs.57, 59, 60, 61, 64.)

The first furnace was built very close to
the site of the Steel Forge, on Steel Forge
River. The Steel Forge pond, marked on a
map of 1692 (SAS Map Cat p.7 accn 1398
stack 2/f) appears to be slightly upstream
(north) of the furnace bay. No furnace is
mentioned in a survey of 1693 (ESRO
Add. MSS 4084/4) but in 1696, when
this part of Ashdown Forest was
enclosed, a furnace had been built
(Tebbutt 1977: 12–13). In 1717 Charles
Hooper leased a furnace here to Charles
Manning of Dartford (ESRO Add. MSS
683), but whether Manning had the
previous tenancy is not known. He was
allowed timber to repair the furnace. In
1723 some of Manning's gun tackle was
sold (ESRO SAS RF15/27, f. 207). On
Budgen's map of 1724 'New Furnace' is
marked, but it is not known whether this
had been 'new' in 1696, or whether the
later furnace found on the site was thus

known, and whether this was built in
1717. No ironworking is indicated on a
map of 1738 (SAS, *ibid.*).

In the 1717 list a furnace in Ashdown
Forest is mentioned, but without an
output figure.

2   Pophole Forge, Linchmere
(Shottermill)   SU 874326
Straker 1931a: 449–50

Bay L 51m H 2m/2m Breached by
sluices for the two modern
streams.
Water system Pond dry. 3m wide
stone sluice at N end in working
order. Smaller ruined sluice near
S end, below which shallow
trough-like stone may be from
sluice cill. Smaller sluice
probably formed wheelpit.
Working area Cinder heap and
scatter on bay and in stream.
Ruined walls of stone building
c.10 × 5m beside smaller sluice
stream, with one short side
revetting bay. 'Hammer Lane'
leads to site.

As part of the site lies in Bramshott
parish, the 'forge in Bramshott' run by
Henry Campion in 1592 and 1594 (PRO
REQ2/186/6, 165/34) could be Pophole.
In 1574, however, Pophole was listed as
a furnace. Disputes over rent are
recorded in 1601 (PRO REQ1/21, pp.263,
289, 304, 630, 637). In 1653 and in 1667
Pophole was a working forge. Although
not named in the 1717 list, there can be
little doubt that this is 'Lord Montague's
forge', there recorded as making 50 tons.
It appears as a forge on Budgen's map of
1724. Sows are recorded as being carried
to Pophole forge in 1683–6 (WSRO
Cowdray 96). In 1769 and 1774 there are
clear references to a furnace as well as a
forge (WSRO Cowdray 1443–5), while in
1777 it was described as a foundry
(*Sussex Weekly Advertiser* 13.1.1777).

118   Postern Forge, Tonbridge
TQ 606462   Not included by
Straker

Bay L 140m H 1.5m to 2.75m
Forms 'Postern Lane'.
Water system Pond dry. Spillway
at W end.
Working area Forge bottoms and
cinder, and cannon balls found
by owner of Postern Forge house
which is timber-framed and
probably contemporary.

Liable to confusion with Rats Castle
Forge and Old Forge. Probably among the
five ironworks operated by David
Willard (PRO REQ2/285/39), Postern
was constructed after the right to build a
forge was leased to Sir George Harper
and Thomas Culpepper in 1553 (PRO
E178/1093; C66/874 m.27). Sows were
carried to the forge from Riverhall
furnace in 1600 (*Calendar of Assize
Records, Eliz. 1, Sussex*, no. 1934).

170 Potmans (Catsfield) Forge,
Catsfield   TQ 725117   Straker
1931a: 354–6

Bay L 112m H 3m/3.25m Breached
by stream and also near W end.
Curves to S at E end.
Water system Pond dry. Probably
spillway at W end.
Working area Destroyed by large
quarry behind bay. General scatter
of forge cinder on and behind bay;
apparent bloomery tap slag on bay
just W of stream.

Straker's early sixteenth-century
references relating to Potmans do not
confirm the existence of a forge, which is
more likely to have been built by William
Waters after 1579, for in 1582 it was
'lately erected' (ESRO ASH B298).
Waters sold the forge to Thomas Alfraye
in 1588 (ASH B333); Richard Alfraye's
lease in 1637 is the last known reference
(ASH B573).

111 Pounsley Furnace, Framfield
TQ 529219   Straker 1931a:
391   SM:AM (Sx) 407

Bay L 140m H 2m/3.75m Two gaps
in NW half. Breached by stream
at SE end.

Water system Pond dry. Tail-race
may be indicated by culvert
emerging at NW end of site.
Working area Levelled area at NW
end, under which culvert stream
flows, and on which a bear
remains with much glassy slag.
At SE end are large heaps of
apparent bloomery slag under
thin layers of glassy slag.

The iron mill in Framfield, included in
the complaint of the coastal towns in
1548, can safely be named as Pounsley.
The furnace is mentioned in the survey
of woods in Framfield (ESRO Searle
13/1) dating from c.1560. In 1574 it was
held by Robert Hodson, in 1580 by
Lawrence Levit (Attree 1912: 141). In
1586 Levit still owned the lands (PRO
C142/211/192). It was held by 1608 by
Mary Eversfield (Attree 1912: 84) and
worked by Thomas Hodgson in 1609
(PRO E178/4143). The founder at
Pounsley was brought before the Quarter
Sessions in 1629 (ESRO QR/E, 29/63).
The notorious Stephen Aynscombe,
founder and illegal exporter of ordnance,
worked the furnace in 1619–21 (ESRO
Glynde 1671; *APC 1619–21*, 321–2,
1621–3, 13–14). It worked in 1653 and in
1664, though discontinued, was
restocked. In 1671 ordnance was
transported to South Malling from
Framfield, most likely originating at
Pounsley (ESRO QO/EW 6.54). In 1693
land is mentioned near Pounsley
furnace, without any hint of its
continuing operation (ESRO SAS
Portman 310).

In the 1717 list 'Mr Pounsley' appears,
with no output figure. It was marked on
Budgen's map of 1724. A 'Pounslow'
forge is listed as working in 1653, but
ruined in 1664.

69 Prinkham Farm Forge, Cowden
TQ 494409   Not included by
Straker

Bay L 185m H 2m/2.6m Only the
portion S of Kent Water survives,
with 3 gaps.
Water system Pond dry. N gap in

bay may indicate spillway; remaining 2 possibly wheelpits. *Working area* Small amount of forge cinder.

117   Rats Castle Forge, Tonbridge TQ 612468   Straker 1931a: 222

Bay Completely destroyed, but position may be indicated by hedge line to W of an area containing heaps of forge cinder and bottoms. *Water system* pond dry.

Not positively associated with any documentary source, but likely to be another of David Willard's 1553 forges, as Old Forge and Postern (*q.v.*).

129   Riverhall Furnace and Forge, Frant (Wadhurst)   TQ 608335 Straker 1931a: 275–6

Bay L 60m H 0.6m/2m Traces of an extension across present road, curving N to divert tributary stream into pond. Near the centre a spur, probably the loading platform, protrudes N at right angles. *Water system* Pond now dry. Difficult to determine owing to re-use as corn mill. Upstream are pen pond bays at TQ 605333 and TQ 606344. *Working area* No signs of forge or furnace working at two pen ponds (cf. Straker). At lowest bay, however, was much glassy slag, also forge bottoms and cinder.

Operated by Nicholas Fowle in 1562 (Schubert 1951: 242) 1573 (PRO SP12/95/15, 16) and 1574; sows were carried to Postern forge in 1600 (*Calendar of Assize Records Eliz. I*, no. 1934). In 1648 Riverhall had a forge (ESRO QR/E 78.104). By 1664 the furnace and the forge were ruined, having been working in 1653.

163   Robertsbridge Abbey Forge, Salehurst   TQ 756236 Straker 1931a: 310–8

Bay No bay at site of forge *Water system* Pond dry. Water supply was from distant pond by way of a leat c.280m long deeply cut through rising ground. Possibility of small pond at forge site indicated by higher ground (silting?) on W side of present access road. *Working area* On E side of access road, where there is a scatter of forge cinder and roofing tiles.

Built by Sir William Sidney in 1541–2 (KAO U1475 B5/1–2). The accounts for the forge are virtually complete until 1574 (U1475 *passim*; ESRO Shepherd deposit A1745) when it was leased to Michael Weston and partners. Steel was made from 1566 (U1475/B4/1–2) and the buildings so used were described in 1609 (BL Add. MSS 5680, 91r). Henry English was tenant in 1628 (KAO U1500/T287/1, 28), William and Robert Hawes in 1651 (T287/2–3) and John Roberts in 1677 (T287/4). Stock is listed for 1703 (U1500/C2/17). The forge was listed as working in 1653 and 1667. Thomas Snepp, sr and jr, worked the forge from 1707. Sir Thomas Webster bought the estate in 1721, and although his operations are referred to in the Fuller correspondence (ESRO SAS RF15/25), less is heard of the forge than of the furnace. In 1768 James Bourne and partners leased the forge and furnace, in 1787 Bourne making 50 tons a year (Sc. Mus. Weale MSS). It is not known to have worked after ceasing to be rated in 1793 or after a bankruptcy sale in 1801.

163   Robertsbridge Abbey Furnace, Ewhurst (Salehurst) TQ 751231   Straker 1931a: 310–18

Bay L c.200m Recently levelled except at W end where it forms part of farm road. Levelled portion appears to have glassy slag forming part of its foundation.

Water system Pond dry.
Working area At W end, where low
mound indicates site of furnace.
Around it are scattered pieces of
furnace lining, roasted ore,
cannon mould, and roof tiles
with square peg holes. An
existing ditch, running N, is
presumably the tail-race. Glassy
slag is scattered nearby. House
immediately W of bay has bear in
garden.

The furnace was built, with the forge, in
1541–2, by Sir William Sidney (KAO
U1475 B5/1–2). It was abandoned in
1546 and not re-used until 1574 when
the Sidney ironworks were leased to
Michael Weston and partners. It is
referred to in a survey of 1567 (D'Elboux
1944). The furnace appears in the 1653
and 1667 lists. The seventeenth-century
tenancies follow those of the forge (q.v.).
The furnace was run by the estate at the
beginning of the eighteenth century
(KAO U1500/C2/20–2) and is listed in
1717 as making 120 tons p.a. After the
sale to Sir Thomas Webster the furnace
was run by the estate for 10 years from
1724, but was then leased to Harrison
and Jewkes. Reference to Jewkes'
activities between 1742 and 1749 appear
in Fuller letters (ESRO SAS RF15/25).
The lease of 1754 to John Churchill the
Staffordshire ironmaster, shows a late
interest in the Weald by a Midland
founder. In 1787 the furnace was still
standing, capable of operation (Sc. Mus.
Weale MSS). The last rating was in 1793.

4   Rogate (Habin) Forge, Harting
     (Rogate)   SU 800224   Straker
     1931a: 432

> *Bay* L 100m H 2m. Silting on both
> sides.
> *Water system* Two marshy hollows
> at N end may indicate wheelpit
> and spillway. Two possible pen
> ponds.
> *Working area* Buried under silt.

Two Exchequer commissions of 1589
(PRO E178/3119) and 1591 (E178/2305)

confirm that this forge operated with
Coombe furnace (q.v.). They were
established c.1587–8 on the lands of
Francis Fortescue of Harting. The site of
the forge had formerly been that of a corn
mill. In 1588 the works were leased to
Henry Gleed of Arlington and to Michael
Martin of Rogate. The enquiry of 1591
enumerated the felling of timber trees in
1590–1. In 1632 it was recorded in the
ledger book of Harting Manor that
'Harting Coombe' was formerly a great
wood, being cut down and the soil
cleared to the benefit of herbage and
feeding (Yates 1955: 82–5; Jack 1982:
26–7).

17   Roundwick Furnace, Kirdford
      SU 992287   Straker 1931a:
      423–4

> *Bay* L 130m H 5m Breached by
> stream at N end.
> *Water system* Pond dry. Marshy
> hollow at S end probably
> indicates spillway and another
> opposite bay centre may be
> wheelpit.
> *Working area* Probably opposite
> centre of bay, where there is a
> bear. Glassy slag in stream. At E
> side of site an old track running
> NW–SE has incline to top of bay,
> possibly used for loading.

No satisfactory evidence is available for
this furnace, supposed by Straker from a
passage in *The High Stream of Arundel*
(c.1636–7) to have operated at that time.

51   Rowfant Forge, Worth
      TQ 316378   Straker 1931a:
      467

> *Bay* L 100m H pond in water/high
> (inaccessible) Forms present
> road.
> *Water system* Modern spillway at
> W end, probably site of original.
> *Working area* Occupied by houses
> and gardens. Forge bottom in
> garden of 'Studio'.
> The site of Rowfant Supra may
> have been under the present Fish

Pond (in water) at TQ 321372, where there are signs of a broken bay. A scatter of forge slag appears on the arable field to the north of this spot.

In use in 1574 by Roger Whitfield of Worth, and by Thomas Whitfield in 1600–3 (PRO REQ2/414/143). The forge was in use in 1653, but out of use in 1664; however an annuity had been paid on a *furnace* at Rowfant c.1660 (ESRO Wadhurst United Charities deeds).

44   St Leonards Forge, Lower Beeding   TQ 219289   Straker 1931a: 433–40

Bay L 100m H pond in water/4m Carries present main road. Stone revetting wall can be seen opposite wheelpit.

Water system Many pen ponds. Shallow circular pit near centre of bay indicates wheelpit. Tail-race ditch recently filled in. Present spillway at SE end is probably on original site and has a bank protecting the working area.

Working area Much disturbed by landscaping by golf club. House near N end of bay probably contemporary.

(See entry for St Leonards furnace and forge; also fig. 43b.)

43   St Leonards Furnace and Forge, Lower Beeding (Nuthurst)   TQ 213291   Straker 1931a: 433–40

Bay L 95m H 1m/2.5m Mainly straight, but appears irregular on account of quarrying from each side and gap cut for cart-track. Starts at Hawkins Pond stream at E end; breached by Goldings stream 30m from W end. Projection near W end for loading platform.

Water system Pond dry. Supplied by water from Hawkins pond (in water), Goldings stream, and St Leonards forge pond which has pen ponds at TQ 232302, 247298, 248299.

Working area Forge area was to the E next to Hawkins stream where forge bottoms and cinder occur.

Furnace site is on W side, 2m from bay and 4m from Goldings stream. In a deep hollow are many large displaced stones and 5cm thick bricks, with some upright remains of furnace lining still in situ.

The works were in operation in 1561, leased until 1568: Schubert 1957: 386, speculated that a 21-year lease could thus have begun in 1547. In 1574 Roger Gratwick held both the forges, on a sub-lease from William Dix and John Blennerhasset, who took the forest lease in 1573 (PRO STAC5/G3/6, G3/32; C66/1103/448). In 1575 Gratwick obtained sows from Walter Covert at Cuckfield furnace, which Gratwick leased in 1577 (PRO C3/207/25). St Leonards furnace was built in 1584 and was the subject of dispute between Gratwick and the lessees of Gosden furnace. In 1601 the works were granted to Sir John Caryll for 60 years (BL Add. MSS 5705, fos.10r, 17v); they were in use in 1653. In the Parliamentary Surveys of the Forest in 1655 (PRO E317/Sussex/35) the upper and lower forges were valued at £27 and £32, but the furnace had been out of use for about 40 years. Both forges were ruined by 1664. They were derelict in 1676 (BL Add. MSS 5705).

66   Scarlets Furnace, Cowden   TQ 443401   Straker 1931a: 224–5

Bay L 70m H 1.5m/3m When breached by flood in 1968 section showed original bank of clay, raised by soil containing glassy slag. Pond side was revetted by wall 0.6m thick with lower courses of stone and upper of brick.

Water system Pond now in water
(restored in 1977). Modern
spillway at S end with bank
protecting working area. The
flood breach revealed two
wooden tunnels through bay,
with control gates, which may
refer to later corn mill as may
the wheelpit which they serve.
Working area Excavations near N
end revealed furnace site,
wheelpit and gun casting pit. No
evidence for *forge* operation has
been found (cf. Straker) (*BWIRG*
9 (1976), 23; Crossley 1979: 239–
49).
Re-use Corn mill.
(See figs.41, 50, 60, 61.)

Problems of identification are less severe
than with the Cowden furnaces (*q.v.*), for
Scarlets is identified on several
occasions. In 1590 Francis Knight
occupied Scarlets (Staffs. RO
D593/S/4/28/17). In 1646 the furnace
and a water mill worked at Scarlets
(Attree 1912: 137). Stock was listed there
in 1655–7 (Hereford RO 5312), and the
furnace was in operation in 1664, making
guns or shot in the Dutch wars. The later
history cannot be isolated from that of
Cowden.

133 Scrag Oak (Snape) Furnace,
Wadhurst   TQ 637297   Straker
1931a: 289–90

Bay L 100m H 0.3m/1m Most has
been levelled but its line can still
be traced. Breached by stream
near E end.
Water system Pond dry.
Working area Probably at W end,
from which hollow way leads to
Scrag Oak farm house
(contemporary).

The date of construction is not known. In
Quarter Sessions records of 1629 Snape
pig iron is recorded as delivered to
Brookland, Chingley, Hoadly and
Verredge forge (ESRO Q1/EW/1). In
1634 sows were delivered by Alexander

Thomas at the furnace (ESRO DH 1086),
and in 1640 sows were carried to
Burwash forge (ESRO QR/E.48.11). The
furnace was working in 1653 but ruined
by 1664. Land 'formerly a furnace pond'
was referred to in 1703 (ESRO SAS
Courthope 296).

86 Sheffield Forge, Fletching
TQ 404238   Straker 1931a:
412–14

Bay Much altered or destroyed by
canalization of River Ouse, and
by a railway bridge. Originally it
partially surrounded a pond
against high ground on the E
flood plain of the river.
Remaining is a bank L 170m, H
1m/1.5m running parallel to
present river for 100m before
turning E at right angles to reach
the high ground.
Water system Pond dry. Original
leat from Ouse destroyed by
railway. E boundary ditch of
meadow, known as Hammer
Ditch, is almost certainly the tail-
race. Old meanders of Ouse can
be seen S of the site.
Working area Almost certainly at E
end, where occur many forge
bottoms and cinder. Traces of
buildings in plough-soil at
406240.

Built before 1546 (Giuseppi 1912: 278)
probably by 1544, when the Duke of
Norfolk employed aliens (WAM 12261).
The forge was mentioned in the
complaint of the coastal ports in 1548. Its
condition was noted in 1550, when it
was leased for 21 years to Thomas Hogan
(PRO E315/221/f.119). In 1574 the forge
belonged to Lord Buckhurst whose
family sold it to Christopher Nevil in
1623 (BL Add. MSS 5682, f.158r). The
building and implements are noted in
1597–8 in the Buckhurst Terrier (Straker
1933: 72). In 1633 it was referred to in a
case of disorder in Quarter Sessions
(ESRO QR/E/33/2). The forge operated
in 1653, was laid aside in 1664, yet was

leased in 1670 (MSS Radford Deeds Misc., in private hands, Cal. in ESRO).

81   Sheffield Furnace, Fletching
TQ 416257   Straker 1931a: 412–14

Bay L 85m H pond in water/3.5m Recent pipe-laying through E end revealed core wall of sandstone blocks.
Water system Spillway at W end probably original. Wheelpit and tail-race obscured by later mill.
Working area 30m S of bay and 2m E of mill tail-race are foundations of building 6m × 6m. Large heap of glassy slag between present house and overspill stream. N end of house is probably contemporary, but S half was built later on slag foundations.
Re-use Corn mill, ceased work in 1928.
(See fig.31.)

Like the forge, the furnace was in operation by 1546, and subject of accounts while in Crown hands (Giuseppi 1912: 278). Thomas Hogan's lease of 1550 (PRO E315/221), if maintained after the restoration of Norfolk property in 1553, would have run to 1571. No furnace is mentioned in 1574. A corn mill had been built on the furnace site by 1597–8 and nail-making was carried out in the brewhouse: Straker 1933: 72.

15   Shillinglee Furnace, Kirdford
SU 972308   Straker 1931a: 429

Bay L 220m H pond in water/5.5m Forms present road; brick wall on pond side. Local information suggests former height 1m below present.
Water system Three existing sluices. (1) Main sluice at N end has brickwork similar to bay wall, and stone dated 1703

(1708?). (2) Corn mill sluice, adapted c.1900 to provide electricity for Shillinglee House, has similar brickwork to (1). (3) Overspill sluice at S end in brick and concrete with 1779 datestone.
Pen ponds at SU 963324, SU 963321, SU 962315.
Working area Occupied by present farm house and buildings. Scatter of glassy slag.
Re-use Corn mill.

Built by 1574, sows for Burningfold forge were weighed at Shillinglee in 1583 (PRO REQ2/125/14). The works had closed by 1620, when it was used as a mill (Kenyon 1952: 236).

33   Shipley Forge, Shipley
TQ 149208   Straker 1931a: 418–19

Bay L 110m H 2.5m/3m Curves round pond at S end; breached by stream near centre.
Water system Pond dry. Spillway at N end where some stonework remains and dry channel leads to main stream. One wheelpit is almost certainly at the site of a deep pool through which the present stream passes downstream of the bay. Possibly another wheelpit was at S end, from which another dry channel converges on present stream.
Working area No obvious signs, but forge cinder and bottoms occur near S end and in present farm track W of bay. Part of nearby Hammer Farm house probably contemporary.

3   Shottermill Forge, Haslemere (Thursley)   SU 883324   Straker 1931a: 448

This site was later used as a corn mill; pond now dry. Main road crosses site, possibly following line of bay. Railway embankment runs along N side.

Probable working area now occupied by house where charcoal and cinder occur in garden. Cinder also occurs in two streams passing under road.

Marked as a forge on Budgen's map of 1724, the works, Straker notes, is said to have stopped in 1776 (Capes 1901: 179).

46 Slaugham Furnace, Slaugham
TQ 249285 Straker 1931a: 404

> *Bay* L 185m H pond in water/5.5m Forms present road. Low projection at E end protected working area from spillway stream.
> *Water system* Spillway at E end (modernized); spillway stream recently diverted. Possible wheelpit and tail-race indicated by dry hollow and ditch c.30m W of spillway stream. One pen pond.
> *Working area* Glassy slag at E end.

Worked in 1574 by Chaloner and Covert, the furnace was occupied by William Cheeseman of Rotherfield in 1597 and 1601 (PRO REQ2/166/46, 186/35).

Snape Furnace: *see* **Scrag Oak Furnace**

162 Socknersh Furnace, Brightling
TQ 705233 Straker 1931a: 306–7

> *Bay* TQ 703233 L 100m H 1m/2m Breached by stream at S end; has right-angled projection at N end to contain spillway stream.
> *Water system* Pond dry. Spillway channel at N end turns abruptly round bay projection to join main stream, and continues for 250m to furnace site.
> *Working area* Unusual position, on present main stream 250m downstream from pond bay. Furnace site indicated by mound on N bank from which protrudes

glassy slag and furnace-lining material. Pair of stone-built cottages c.80m to NE may be contemporary; gardens contain much charcoal. Roasted ore dump, disclosed by uprooted trees, occurs to N (in same field) where footpath to site leaves old cart-track.

Likely to have been one of the earliest furnaces, Socknersh appears in John Collins' will of 1535. Evidence in the Star Chamber case of 1594 (below) refers to Alexander Collins having built the furnace; he had secured rights of flooding on neighbouring land in 1537, but this must have been after the furnace was built. As he had employed aliens in 1525 and rented Burwash forge from 1526, a similar starting date could be sought from the furnace. The Collins were involved in the building and early operation of the nearby Panningridge and Robertsbridge works for Sir William Sidney (KAO U1475/B9, B2/3). Socknersh furnace is referred to in Alexander Collins' inquisition in 1553 (Holgate 1927: 10). In 1574 it belonged to a further Alexander Collins, leased to Thomas Collins. A dispute over water rights in 1594 (PRO STAC5/C1/7, C25/10) outlines the operation of the furnace as far back as 1537. Thomas Collins' will of 1612 (PRO PROB11/120/75) refers to the furnace, stocks and woods. It worked in 1653, then went out of use but was re-stocked in 1664 for wartime operation; in 1671 it was leased by Thomas Collins for four years to Peter Farnden and John Roberts (ESRO Dunn 27/16; see also 47/4, 5, 7, 36; BL Add. MSS 5680, 117r). Although marked on Budgen's map of 1724 it does not appear in the 1717 list.

1 Standford Furnace, Bramshott
SU 819344 Straker 1931a: 450

> All features now covered by modern industrial development but glassy slag can be found in stream banks.

It is not yet possible to separate sources for this furnace from those for Pophole (*q.v.*).

78   Steel Forge, Hartfield
c.TQ 450316   Straker 1931a: 247–8

No surface indications have yet been recognized, but the position of the forge can be estimated from a map of 1692 (see under Pippingford) which shows the Steel Forge pond downstream from the confluence of the streams at TQ 449312, and less precisely from a survey of the forest of 1539 (copy in possession of Ashdown Forest Conservators, differing from PRO E32/197) describing the forge as 'standing on the brook at Newbridge in distance from the said iron mills [Newbridge] a space of two flight shots or more'.
No sign of the Steel Forge or its dam were found when silt was removed in 1980 from the dry pond of Pippingford furnace; it is possible that the latter may overlie the forge, although no such indications were found during excavation of the furnace.

The Steel Forge was built c.1505 (PRO DL 42/21 p.185) and is presumed to have used a variant of the bloomery process. References to lessees appear in Duchy of Lancaster accounts (DL 29/445–7/7153 sq); in 1549 it was granted with 'Stumlet' furnace to Thomas Gaveller and Francis Challenor (DL29 447/7187), reverting to John Gage in 1554 (ESRO SAS Gage 19/6); he re-transferred it to the Crown in 1554 (19/8). The forge and furnace in Ashdown marked as held by Henry Bowyer in 1574 are more likely to be Newbridge, as the Steel Forge may have been abandoned by then. The site was certainly waste by 1634 (KAO U269/E171). The reference to the Steel Forge in the 1658 Parliamentary Survey (PRO E317/26) does not show if it was operating.

149   Steel Forge, Warbleton
TQ 604170   Straker 1931a: 378

Bay L 140m H 1.5m/2m Very irregular and broken. Breached by stream at E end.
Water system Pond dry. Hollow at E end, from which dry ditch leads to stream, probably represents wheelpit and tail-race. Pond for Woodmans furnace 550m upstream may have been used as pen pond (*see* Woodmans furnace, Warbleton).
Working area At E end, where occur forge bottoms, cinder and charcoal.

This is a strong contender for inclusion among the four iron mills and furnaces in Warbleton of which the coastal towns complained in 1548. The identification with the 'Warbleton Forge' of 1574 and 1610 (ESRO SAS RF4/73) is probable but not certain. The forge was in use in 1653, but was listed as ruined in 1664. The name Steel Forge was used about 1719, when charcoal was carried thence to Heathfield furnace (ESRO SAS RF15/26), but there is no reference in the 1717 list.

54   Stone Furnace and Forge, East Grinstead   TQ 382343
Straker 1931a: 238

Site is now under W end of Weir Wood reservoir. Drought in 1973 permitted access.
Bay L 135m H 1m/1m (reservoir silting). Breached by stream near centre.
Working area Evidence for both furnace and forge. Heaps of glassy slag occur at N end; forge cinder and bottoms near centre.

The 1574 reference to a furnace owned by Payne and operated by Duffield fits this site; as there is forge cinder,

Duffield's forge is also likely to have been here.

116 Stream Furnace and Forge,
Chiddingly   TQ 555155
Straker 1931a: 384

Bay L 155m H 1.6m/3m Carries bridle road. A ramp leads down towards working area.
Water system Pond reduced to swamp. Modern spillway at W end. Position of forge and furnace wheelpit and tail-race probably obscured by those of later corn mill at E end.
Working area Probably in present mill house garden, where much charcoal occurs, and where was found the cannon boring bar now in Anne of Cleves Museum, Lewes (Butler and Tebbutt 1975: 38–41). Recent excavations of crashed German aircraft in field immediately S of bay revealed much glassy slag and fragments of cannon mould. 100m down the mill tail-race the bank is revetted with forge bottoms.

This site began as a forge, the hammer at Chiddingly being included in the complaint of the coastal towns in 1548. John French had a hammer, c.1560, within three miles (5km) of woods in Framfield (ESRO Searle 13/1), and in 1574. The building of a furnace is suggested by the lease by Stephen French, 'forgemaster' in 1597 of the 'Lower furnace, called the New Furnace' for 21 years to Edward Montagu (BL Add. Ch. 30132). In 1648 the pond was still called the 'Forge Pond' (ESRO SAS RF5/26), yet a forge and a furnace are mentioned in 1653 and 1667. Guns were cast at 'Stream Furnace' in 1692–3 (ESRO SAS RF15/26). The furnace is marked on Budgen's map of 1724 but had not been listed in 1717.

55 Strudgate Furnace, Ardingly
(Balcombe)   TQ 329323
Straker 1931a: 407

Bay L 100m, has been restored and raised.
Water system Pond in water.
Working area Glassy slag in stream.

This furnace is only known from the 1574 list, in which it was operated by Henry Bowyer, and from a lease of 1584, in which Lord Abergavenny let it to Ralph Valey (PRO C154/1308).

57 Stumbletts Furnace, Maresfield/
West Hoathly   TQ 399306
SM:AM (Sx) 443 Not included in Straker 1931a:, but see Straker 1936–7: 217–18.

Bay L 70m H 3m/3.5m Breached by stream in S half; gap due to soil removal in N half. Right-angle projection 45m long at centre to protect working area from flooding.
Water system Pond dry. Overspill at extreme N end of bay joins main stream to W.
Working area Furnace site just S of main stream close to bay. Glassy slag in the stream.
Re-use Probably the site of Vinolds Mill (Buckhurst Terrier 1597–8, Straker 1933: 53).
(See fig.29.)

Built in 1534 on Duchy of Lancaster lands, it was at first let to John Levett, who died in 1535. It was managed by William Levett, the Buxted ordnance-maker (PRO DL446/7168–76). The furnace was leased with the Steel Forge in 1549 to Thomas Gaveller and Francis Challenor (DL447/7187 but reverted to John Gage in 1554 (ESRO SAS Gage 19/6) and transferred by him to the Crown in 1554 (19/8); the last reference is in 1570 (DL458/7386), for it does not appear in the 1574 list.

[Witley and] Thursley 3 Forges,
Witley and Thursley   Straker 1931a: 447–8

10a Upper Hammer   SU 916403

Bay L 100m H silted pond/3m

Water system The hammer pond, now bisected by the A3 road, is fed by a chain of ponds on a stream which flows north from Gibbet Hill. From the bay the stream flows to the Lower Hammer pond; a second channel bypasses the lower pond, flowing to the Forked Pond, now named Warren Mere. The latter post-dates the 1874 O.S. map, which shows the channel, which does not appear on the Tithe map of 1840, so post-dates the ironworks.
Working area Forge cinder present.

10b Lower Hammer   SU 916408

Bay L 100m – restored, pond in water.
Water system Pond fed from the Upper Hammer pond.
Working area Re-used for silk ('Crape') mill.

9   Coldharbour Hammer (Horsebane)   SU 920406

Bay and Water system New Pond: possibly the ironworks pond.
Working area Forge cinder in stream below New Pond.

There are three forge sites which, with Witley Park furnace, are hard to distinguish within the documentary sources. The Upper and Lower Hammers lie on the westerly stream flowing into the Forked Pond, within Witley parish, whereas Coldharbour, on the eastern stream, is partly in Witley, partly in Thursley. The first mention is in 1608 (GMR LM/349/53) when ironworks, newly erected, were leased by the Mores of Loseley to Henry Bell. They were mortgaged to him in 1617 (Close Roll, 15 Jas. I, 24,1) and purchased by him in 1623 (doc. in private hands cit. Giuseppi 1903: 27–52). The property, including the manor, purchased in 1614–15 (GMR LM/349/100), was settled on Bell's great-nephew Anthony Smith in 1629 (PRO C142/526/54). The Smiths leased the works to William Yalden in 1666 and there is an inventory of the period (Godalming P. Lib. GD/WC16, 151). The Hammer Pond and the 'New Pond in Witley' were leased to Henry Roper in 1671 (Godalming P. Lib. SL72, 78), and Aubrey refers to iron ore and to two forges in Witley Park in 1673 and two great hammer mills in Thursley or Witley parish (Bodleian MS, Aubrey 4 – Perambulation of Surrey). The works and ponds, including Coldharbour, were leased in 1681 (GMR LM5/2/9), the Upper Hammer again being leased in 1720 (GMR LM5/3/97). Roque's map of 1762 (GMR G9025/5) shows an 'iron mill' at the lower site, merely marking the upper as 'hammer pond' and ignoring Coldharbour. Pig iron was carried to the remaining forge in 1767 (GMR LM/1064/9). The 'Crape Mill' was referred to in 1805 (Malcolm 1805: I, 103).

112   Tickerage Furnace and Forge, Framfield   TQ 515211
Straker 1931a: 392

Bay L 73m H pond in water/2.75m Carries bridle road.
Water system Existing spillway at S end and wheelpit at N end likely to be original.
Working area Part levelled, remainder occupied by corn mill. Furnace and forge unlikely to have been contemporary owing to restricted space. Forge cinder in stream below bay; forge bottom in mill house garden. Glassy slag on road surface, and much, with charcoal, in mill house garden extending at leat 80m from road. Found on site (now in Tickerage House garden) are cannon balls of 4, 5, 6 and 7in diameter (102, 127, 152, 178mm), also one half of iron single mould for 7in ball and some part-spheres, probably mould cores.
Re-use Corn mill (locally known as 'Striking Mill').

The first reference is to a cottage near the

hammer in 1617 (ESRO Adams 137, f.117). The forge, working in 1653, was ruined by 1664.

41   Tilgate Furnace, Worth
TQ 284355   Straker 1931a: 465

> *Bay* has been levelled and almost all traces removed by Furnace Green housing estate, Crawley New Town. Tithe Award map shows pond near Furnace Farm, supplied by channel from main stream at TQ 281351.
> Existing (dry) channel returns to main stream at TQ 287361.

There is no evidence to support the view that this was Henry Bowyer's furnace in Moore Forest in 1574: Strudgate is as likely. A furnace and forge in Worth, apparently Tilgate and Tinsley, were leased by John Middleton and John Needler in 1617 (WSRO Lytton 127). In 1653 Walter Burrell was recorded as having set his furnace to work for casting shot (PRO SP18/39/31) and it is most likely that this relates to Tilgate. In the 1653 list the furnace was in use, then discontinued but re-stocked in 1664. Roads to and from the furnace are referred to in 1685 (WSRO Lytton 202–3). When in 1690 Leonard Gale and Henry Johnson, owners of Tilgate farm, enjoined their tenant Thomas Budgen to maintain the upper and lower ponds, there was no indication that these were kept in water other than for fish (PRO C5/79/84).

37   Tinsley Forge, Worth
TQ 291395   Straker 1931a: 468

> Little remains to be seen. The bay was levelled some years ago. Only a small quantity of forge cinder can be found.

This was Henry Bowyer's forge in 1574; when he died in 1589 he had *two* iron mills at Tinsley (Holgate 1927: 26), and stock at works unnamed, of which

Tinsley forge would be one (PRO PROB11/74/74). Sir Henry Bowyer owned the forge in 1607 and 1608 (WSRO Lytton 125, GMR Loseley 1084/19). Tinsley appears to have been held by John Middleton and John Needler in 1617 (WSRO Lytton 127). In 1656 the forge was bought by Leonard Gale, who worked there in partnership with Walter Burrell. It was in use in 1653 and 1667. The reference to a Mr Gale's forge in the 1717 list fits Tinsley, despite the list's placing of the forge in Surrey, for the Fullers supplied Henry Gale with sows between 1721 and 1736, one delivery to Tinsley (ESRO SAS RF15/27, f.207).

124   Tollslye Furnace, Frant (Lamberhurst)   TQ 632371
Straker 1931a: 268

> *Bay* L. c.120m H not recorded/c.3m Breached by stream at SW end.
> *Water system* Pond dry. Tail-race may be indicated by line of ponds leading from NE end of bay to join stream.
> *Working area* Probably at NE end where is concentration of glassy slag and charcoal.

There are only slight indications of a short life in the early part of the seventeenth century. The name 'Furnace Wood' appears to have replaced 'Kingswood', the latter appearing on a Bayham estate map of 1640, copying an original of 1599 (Eales 1947: 134).

In 1634 Alexander Thomas was to deliver 10 tons of sows at 'Tedye' furnace (ESRO DH 1086). There are no references in the 1653 or 1664 lists.

25   Vachery Forge, Cranleigh
TQ 062370   Straker 1931a: 446–7

> *Bay* L c.140m H much eroded. Breached by present stream. W end curves towards S. Forms public footpath with footbridge over stream. Hammer Lane, with

ford, cuts through bay and runs parallel to upstream side.
Water system Pond dry, crossed by railway embankment. Thornhurst and Cobblers Brooks join within pond area. Wheelpit probably at site of present stream. Spillway indicated by dry channel W of stream.
Working area Forge cinder in stream bed and W bank; much charcoal at field edge. At Hammer Farm house (part possibly contemporary) are many forge bottoms and an iron plate 46 × 30 × 5cm with fused slag on one face.

This forge only operated in the sixteenth century: Straker states (no ref.) that it was built by the Brays before 1557, operated for them in 1574 by John Lambard, or Gardener, who was summoned for illegal use of wood in 1573 and 1581. The hammer pond and the furnace pond were leased to Lambard in 1587 (Surrey RO 85/13/205) suggesting that he was still operating the works (see Straker 1941: 48–51).

25   Vachery Furnace, Cranleigh
TQ 071375?   Not included by Straker

Only evidence for this furnace is documentary, suggesting (see below) a furnace upstream of the forge in 1587. Fieldwork has failed to locate it on either Thornhurst or Cobblers Brooks; the site is probably covered by the later (1814) Vachery Pond.

This furnace pond was leased to John Lambard, or Gardener, in 1587 (Surrey RO 85/13/205). Whether this means that a furnace had by then gone out of use, and its pond was used as storage for the forge, or whether Lambard, described as 'forgeman', had extended his operation to a newly-built furnace is not clear.

93   Vauxhall Furnace, Tonbridge
TQ 593440   Straker 1931a: 222

Bay L 60m H 2.5m/2.5m Breached by stream at W end where section shows height had been raised by slag.
Water system Pond dry. Spillway probably at W end. At E end dry tail-race joins stream.
Working area At E end is a levelled area 4m from bay and near tail-race.

The furnace was in operation by 1552, when the Duke of Northumberland contracted with Robert True, ironfounder, to blow '13 foundays and 2 days'. This arrangement was disputed by True (PRO C1/1387/53). At the end of 1552 the Duke leased Southfrith, with furnace and forge, for 40 years, to Sir George Harper and Thomas Culpepper, who were allowed to build another furnace and forge (BL Harl. 77G18). The works were sub-let to David Willard (PRO REQ2/285/39; BL Harl. 85 H6; PRO C66/874 m.27). In 1571 Culpepper took the option of relinquishing the lease, the wood virtually exhausted (PRO E178/1093). In 1574 David Willard worked for Sir Thomas Fane, at a furnace which appears to be Vauxhall: in 1588 Edmund and Abraham Willard worked a furnace in Tonbridge parish, near Southfrith, called Borne Mill furnace, which can hardly be other than Vauxhall (Staffs. RO D593/S/4/28/3, 16). Leases from 1622 to 1679 include the ironworks (KAO U38/T1–15), but for how much of this period they were capable of working is not clear, particularly as they do not appear in the lists of 1653 and 1664.

20   Verdley Wood Furnace, Fernhurst
SU 906265   Not included by Straker

Bay L 65m H 9m/9m Breached near centre, by present stream.
Water system Pond dry. Sandstone blocks of wheelpit and tail-races remain in present stream.

Working area Furnace foundations remain above ground level just W of stream.

127 Verredge Forge, Frant
(Wadhurst)   TQ 621352
Straker 1931a: 278

Bay L 120m H 3m/3m Forms present road.
Water system Pond dry. Present stream passes under bay (road) at S end before turning sharply N parallel to bay. Near N end it again turns E and is joined by tributary culverted under road.
Working area At N end, where stream turns E, is a mass of forge bottoms and cinder in stream bank and bed. In left bank are roofing tiles and 6cm thick bricks; in right bank are courses of laid stonework at water level. In stream bed is iron plate 1.3 × 0.55m.

The sources for Verredge correspond closely with those for Brookland (*q.v.*). They are first mentioned in 1521, at a time when both are more likely to have been bloomery than finery forges. They were still Barham property when they went out of use in the mid-seventeenth century (KAO U840/T109). They were not, however, leased out as a pair. In 1573–4 Christopher Darrell rented Verredge from John Barham (ESRO DH603; also 1574 list), in contrast with Brookland which was held by John Carpenter via Thomas Gresham. In 1610, however, Thomas Saunders was tenant of both forges (KAO U840/T109/7). The final reference to this forge is in 1642 (*ibid.* T109/1).

114 Waldron Furnace, Waldron
TQ 566181   Straker 1931a: 381–2

Bay L 75m H 2.5m/2.5m Downstream height may have been increased by recent removal of soil from recent pond to S. Breached by main stream at

E and small stream at W ends.
Water system Pond dry.
Working area Channel through E end bay stops short, suggesting wheelpit and culverted tail-race. Black soil in this area. At W end where stream cuts through bay are bricks (5cm thick), roof tiles, fragments of cannon mould and glassy slag.

This furnace was in existence by c.1560, the tentative date given to the survey of woodlands in Framfield parish, which includes Waldron in the list of works within 3 miles (5km) (ESRO Searle 13/1). In 1574 it belonged to Sir John Pelham, leased to Thomas Stollyan. Straker notes their carriage of iron to Pevensey. The furnace and its woods are mentioned in Sir Thomas Pelham's will of 1620 (ESRO SAS Pelham A106; PRO PROB11/145/217). The operation of the furnace by the Pelhams is well documented from 1639 to 1715 apart from the years 1678–92 (BL Add. MSS 33154–6), and the major source is supplemented by reference in the Fuller collection between 1625 and 1703 (ESRO SAS RF2/49, 57, 58, 109, 154). It is included in the 1653 and 1664/7 lists, and in 1717 cast 150 tons. It was marked on Budgen's map of 1724. In the seventeenth century pig iron and shot, rather than ordnance were cast, but from 1747 guns were made. The furnace was by this time run within the partnership which included Legas and Harrison (Guildhall 3736, 6482; RF15/25). The last date of operation is not known, but the furnace had been demolished by 1787 (Sc. Mus. Weale MSS).

145 Warbleton Priory Furnace,
Warbleton   TQ 644174   Straker 1931a: 359

Bay L 65m H c.8m (inaccessible due to dense undergrowth) Breached by stream near W end. Projecting bank at E end, to protect working area from spillway flooding, widens to form loading platform.

Water system Spillway at E end.
Spillway channel turns abruptly
W behind bay, to avoid hollow
way leading to site, and has
sandstone blocks and a bear set
to protect corner from erosion.
Wheelpit probably on line of
present stream. Two pen ponds
50m and 100m upstream.
Working area On E side of stream
are glassy slag, charcoal, roasted
ore, roof tiles and Tudor-type
bricks. Levelled area on E side of
spillway channel has high
charcoal content. No evidence
for forge (or at pen ponds).

The only firm reference to operation is
for 1574, when Thomas Stollion held the
furnace from John Baker, although an
entry in the Dallington parish register for
January 1599 refers to a person resident
at the Priory furnace.

32   Warnham Furnace, Horsham
(Warnham)   TQ 168323
Straker 1931a: 441

Bay L 180m H pond in water/4m
Water system Relates to later use.
Working area Much glassy slag
found during road widening over
area; small amounts E of present
mill buildings.
Re-use Corn mill.

In existence by 1609 (Straker, citing deed
in private hands), when operated by Sir
John Caryll. Horsham churchwardens
(Straker) borrowed the furnace weigh-
beam in 1621 and 1645. It was working
in 1653 but ruined by 1664.

50   Warren Furnace (Hedgecourt),
Worth   TQ 348393   Straker
1931a: 214–16   SM:AM (Sx) 471

Bay L 80m H pond in water/5m
Recently restored.
Water system Spillway (restored)
at W end. Stonework at E end,
from which leads a culverted
channel, probably indicates
wheelpit and tail-race.

Working area Scatter of glassy slag,
together with small amounts of
coal and bronze slag. On E bank
of spillway stream, c.30m from
bay, flat metallic area may be
remains of boring swarf.

There are two distinct periods of use. For
the first, from before 1567 until about
1627, the furnace was Gage property, let
to John Fawkner and John French in
1567 and operated by John Thorpe in
1574 (ESRO SAS Gage 13/97, 35/15,
43/32, 45/16). Edward Raby cast iron
and probably brass ordnance here from
c.1762 until 1774 (Hodgkinson 1978a:
24–5, 1978b: 11–24). In 1787 Weale
noted its abandonment (Sc. Mus. Weale
MSS.

18   Wassell Forge, Kirdford
SU 981281   Not included by
Straker

Bay L 80m H 1.5m/3m Forms
present road. Pond side faced
with unmortared sandstone
blocks. Projection at W end to
protect working area from
spillway stream.
Water system Pond dry. Stone-
built spillway at W end may be
original. Present sluice and
wheelpit for mill are of later
origin; 20m W of mill sluice is
shallow ditch leading from pond
to face of bay, which may
indicate site of forge
sluice.
Working area Levelled for modern
use. Forge bottoms in boundary
wall; cinder in stream banks and
bed below spillway.
Re-use Corn mill.

Probably newly built in 1574, for Cattell
argues (1979: 165) that this is listed as
the forge of Thomas Smith in Shillinglee
park as yet unused (Kenyon 1958: 45). In
1582–3 sows were sent from Shillinglee
furnace to Wassell forge by Simon
Bowyer (PRO REQ2/125/14). It was
working in 1621 and 1641 (Kenyon 1952:
235).

12 West End Furnace, Chiddingfold
SU 939345 Straker 1931a:
421

Bay L 64m H 2.5m/3m Breached
by stream. Concave towards
pond. S end covered by public
road.
Water system Pond dry. Course of
overspill channel (dry) survives
from N end of bay. Present
stream probable site of wheelpit
and tail-race.
Working area Loading ramp
protruding from S end of bay
indicates probable furnace site.
Scatter of black glassy slag.

178 Westfield (Crowham) Forge,
Westfield   TQ 814172   Straker
1931a: 338–9

Bay (pre-1980) L 110m H
1.90m/1.90m Confused at N end,
with possible right-angle
projection. Wide breaches by
stream at centre and near S end.
(1980) All levelled SE of stream
by Southern Water Authority,
and spoil used to make up right
bank of stream.
Water system Pond dry. Dry ditch
running NE from near SE end of
bay may indicate spillway or old
stream course. Squared timbers
(140 × 140mm to 225 × 225mm)
occur lying horizontally in
stream on either side of bay line.
Possible pen pond SW of road at
TQ 812169.
Working area Probably was
indicated by irregular ground
27m SE of stream, where was
scatter of forge cinder and roof
tiles. Spread of charcoal near SE
end of bay. Levelling of bay
revealed stone wall foundation
62cm wide, starting 34m from
stream on downstream side of
bay line, extending 7.8m. Spoil
from bay included complete sow
3.4m long, many forge bottoms,
and scrap metal (casting risers,
sheet lead etc.). Fragment of

cannon previously dredged from
stream. The cannon is in Anne of
Cleves Museum, Lewes.
'Forge Cottage', now destroyed, at
TQ 815171.

Straker notes the complaint from Rye
about the use of water by this forge in
1580: although it was not included in the
1574 list it had in fact been planned in
1573 (ESRO RYE 60/9/13). In the
seventeenth century it was operated by
Peter Farnden (ESRO Dunn 27/2, 5, 6;
46/2, 4. It was listed as working in 1653
and 1667. At the beginning of the
eighteenth century it formed an outlying
part of the Midlands 'Ironworks in
Partnership' on a 7-year lease from 1710
(Hereford RO Foley E/12/PF5/550). In
1717 it produced 50 tons, probably in
Samuel Gott's ownership, for it was he
who left the forge to his sons in 1722
(ESRO DE 22). It was marked on
Budgen's map of 1724. In November
1743 the forge was included in the
partnership between John Legas and
William Harrison, with Beckley and
Lamberhurst furnaces (Sotheby's sale
catalogue 6/6/1966), the operations of
which are detailed in the Harrison
accounts (Guildhall 3736). The forge was
out of use by 1787 (Sc. Mus. Weale
MSS).

75 Withyham Forge, Withyham
TQ 500353   Straker 1931a:
253

Bay L 85m H 2m/2.75m Breached
by stream near NE end.
Water system Pond dry. Remains of
stone and brick wheelpit at NE
end probably relate to later use.
Working area Small amount of
forge cinder downstream.
Present house at SW end of bay
named as 'Forge Cottage' in early
deeds.
Re-use Corn mill.

Nothing has been discovered to add to
the 1574 reference to John Baker's forge
at Withyham.

Withyham Furnace: *see* **Crowborough Warren Furnace**

11   Witley Park Furnace, Witley
        SU 927374   Not included by
        Straker

> *Bay* L 65m H 4m/5m Breached by
> stream at E end; approached by
> ramp at W end. At E end
> projection to S is probably
> loading platform.
> *Water system* Pond dry. Dry
> channel from c. centre of bay
> widens, indicating wheelpit.
> Tail-race was probably culverted
> but reappears when about to
> enter tributary to main stream.
> Main stream probably site of
> spillway.
> *Working area* Hollow, 4m
> diameter, to E of wheelpit,
> probably indicates furnace site.
> Cart track to S leads over
> culverted tail-race to ramp and
> bay top.

Witley Forges: *see* under **Thursley**

**49   Woodcock Hammer (Wire Mill)
        Forge,** Godstone   TQ 369419
        Straker 1931a: 217

> *Bay* L 165m H pond in water/3m
> *Water system* Existing spillway at
> E end, wheelpit and tail-race all
> appear to relate to re-use of site.
> *Working area* Scatter of forge
> cinder on bay.
> *Re-use* Wire mill and corn mill.

Lingfield parish register refers to
'Swanne of the Hammer Mills' in 1561.
The forge was worked by John Thorpe in
1574, with Warren furnace. It appears in
Gage leases between 1629 and 1738
(ESRO SAS Gage 33/69, 43/52 (with
inventory), 54, 58, 109, 123, 144, 148). It
is listed as working in 1653 and 1664; it
is most likely to be 'Mr Johnson's' forge
in 1717, the output then and in 1736
being 40 tons. Thomas Stanford

converted sows from Heathfield between
1729 and 1732 (ESRO SAS RF15/27).
The forge is included in a survey of land
belonging to Edward Evelyn in 1748
(SAS Map Catalogue, p. 7). From 1758 to
1774 it was used by Edward Raby
(Hodgkinson 1978: 11). It was out of use
by 1787 (Sc. Mus. Weale MSS).

143   Woodmans Forge or Furnace,
         Warbleton   TQ 603176
         Straker 1931a: 377–8

> *Bay* L 170m H 3m/3.6m Breached
> by stream at E end.
> *Water system* Pond dry. Spillway
> at W end, from which leads
> deep, now dry, channel 75m
> long which does not rejoin main
> stream. Slightly E of centre of
> bay a slight depression may
> indicate wheelpit.
> *Working area* On E side, where
> ploughed field has black area
> with much forge cinder and
> bottoms, which also occur on
> bay and in stream. No evidence
> for furnace on site apart from
> some small pieces of glassy slag
> in stream on either side of bay,
> probably washed here from
> Heathfield Furnace (less than
> 1.5km upstream).
> Stream bank section shows deep
> silt layer overlying working area.
> This, together with short
> spillway stream, suggests later
> use as pen pond for the Steel
> Forge downstream.

Firm facts are short for this site. Straker,
followed by Schubert, regarded it as a
furnace, under Sir Richard Baker's name
in 1574, but the lack of slag should be
noted. As a forge it seems likely, by
process of elimination, to be one of those
in Warbleton in 1548, subject of
complaint from the Sussex coastal
towns. The Woodman ascription is
unproven: he was active at this time, for
immigrants made charcoal for him in
1549 and 1550 (PRO E190/233, 239, 244,
247), but it is not known for certain
where he worked.

108 Woolbridge Forge, Mayfield
TQ 571265   Not included by
Straker

Bay L 65m H 2m Breached by River
Rother near centre. At W end
small projecting bank to N and
larger one to S protected working
area from flooding by overspill
channel.
Water system Pond dry. Overspill
channel beyond W end of bay
joins Rother downstream.
Working area Scatter of forge and
bloomery-type slag occurs
behind bay and in stream.
(See fig.40.)

Suggested by Cattell (1979: 171) as one of
the Mayfield forges of 1574: 'Hammer
Wood' is adjacent.

42 Worth Forest Furnace, Worth
TQ 290335   Straker 1931a:
460–4   SM:AM (Sx) 471

Bay L 60m H E side of stream
3m/2m W side 2m/3m Breached
at centre by stream and probably
at W end by railway. Just W of
stream, projection to N probably
served as charging platform and
protected working area from
flooding.
Water system Pond dry. Present
stream probably site of overspill.
Working area Wet area behind bay
5m W of stream may indicate
wheelpit, and slight depression

running N from it, the tail-race.
Sow (now in Haxted Mill,
Edenbridge) found in stream
18m below bay and bear 15m
further downstream. Scatter of
glassy slag. On E side of stream
the high ground level compared
with the W side suggests a silted
up pond. This ends 25m below
the bay in a slight bank and a 1m
drop, possibly site of an earlier
furnace. The bear and glassy slag
on the bank nearby may be
connected. Also here on W side
of stream is N–S bank 55m long.

This was a double furnace, built for the
Crown in 1546 under the supervision of
William Levett, on the confiscated lands
of the Duke of Norfolk (Giuseppi 1912:
276–311). Guns were cast under Levett's
control from 1547, and when the works
were leased to Clement Throckmorton in
1550 (PRO E315/221, fos.119–20), the
condition of the works was noted, and an
option was given to pay rent in the form
of guns and ammunition. The property
was restored to the Duke of Norfolk in
1553. In 1574 it was leased by John
Eversfield, but Lord Abergavenny was
stated as owner. In 1580 and 1582,
indeed, Eversfield was paying rent on the
ironworks, but as this was at a mere £10
p.a., compared with the £90 paid in
1550, their potential must have been
seen as poor. This is the last reference,
unless Thomas Whitfield's ironworks in
Worth parish in 1603 was this furnace
(PRO REQ2/414/148).

Bibliography

Note: Abbreviations of titles follow the Council for British Archaeology recommendations.

Acts of the Privy Council, vols.X (1577–8)–XXXIV (1615–16) (1895–1925); vols. for 1616–1630 (unnumbered) (1927–60)

Georgius Agricola, De Re Metallica (Basle 1556; 1950 edn ed. H. C. and L. H. Hoover)

R. J. Adams, 'Bloomery furnace experiments', Bull Wealden Iron Res Group 15 (1979), 11–15

D. F. Allen, 'Iron currency bars in Britain', Proc Prehist Soc 33 (1967), 307–35

P. Allen, 'Pursuit of Wealden models', J Geol Soc London 138 (1981), 375–405

N. S. Angus, G. T. Brown and H. F. Cleere, 'The iron nails from the legionary fortress at Inchtuthil, Perthshire', J Iron Steel Inst 200 (1962), 956–68

F. W. T. Attree, 'Notes of post-mortem inquisitions taken in Sussex', Sussex Rec Soc 14 (1912)

J. Aubrey, Perambulation of Surrey (1673)

B. G. Awty, 'Denization returns and lay subsidy rolls as sources for French ironworkers in the Weald', Bull Wealden Iron Res Group 13 (1978), 17–19

B. G. Awty, 'Provisional identifications of ironworkers among French immigrants listed in the Denization Rolls of 1541 and 1544', ibid. 16 (1979), 2–11

B. G. Awty, 'Identification of places of origin of French ironworkers', ibid. 17 (1980), 2–6

B. G. Awty, 'The continental origins of Wealden ironworkers, 1451–1544', Econ Hist Rev, 2 ser, 34 (1981), 524–39

B. G. Awty, 'Aliens in the ironworking areas of the Weald: the Subsidy Rolls 1524–1603, Bull Wealden Iron Res Group, 2 ser, 4 (1984), 13–78

O. R. Bedwin, 'The excavation of Ardingly fulling mill and forge', Post-Medieval Archaeol 10 (1976), 34–64

O. R. Bedwin, 'The excavation of a late sixteenth/early seventeenth century gun-casting furnace at Maynard's Gate', Sussex Archaeol Collect 116 (1977–8), 163–78

O. R. Bedwin, 'The excavation of a late 16th century blast furnace at Batsford, Herstmonceux, East Sussex, 1978', Post-Medieval Archaeol 14 (1980), 89–112

E. M. Bell-Irving, Mayfield, an Old Wealden Village (1903)

W. R. Beswick and C. C. Ennever, 'The Penhurst-Ashburnham leat', Bull Wealden Iron Res Group, 2 ser, 1 (1981), 4–7

T. Bevan, 'Sussex ironmasters in Glamorgan', Trans Cardiff Naturalists Soc 86 (1965–7), 5–12

K. Bielenin, 'Schmelzversuche in halbeingetieften Rennöfen in Polen', in Guyan et al. 1973: 62–71

K. Bielenin, Starozytne Górnictwo i Hutnictwo Zelaza w Górach Swiętokryzyskich (1974, Krakow)

W. de G. Birch, Cartularium Saxonicum, I (1885)

R. Bird, 'The journal of Giles Moore', Sussex Rec Soc 68 (1971)

V. Biringuccio, De Pirotechnia (1540; 1558 edn, Venice)

H. L. Blackmore, The Armouries of the Tower of London, I: Ordnance (1976)

P. F. Brandon, 'The common lands and wastes of Sussex' (Ph.D. thesis, University of London, 1963)

P. F. Brandon, The Sussex Landscape (1974)

W. P. Breach, 'Extracts relating to Sussex ordnance from a carrier's account book', *Sussex Archaeol Collect 46* (1903), 63–8

C. E. Brent, 'Employment, land tenure and population in eastern Sussex, 1540–1640' (D.Phil. thesis, University of Sussex, 1974)

C. E. Brent, 'Rural employment and population in Sussex between 1550 and 1640, part 1', *Sussex Archaeol Collect 114* (1976), 27–48

C. E. Brent, 'Rural employment and population in Sussex between 1550 and 1640, part 2', *ibid. 116* (1977–8), 41–55

C. R. Bristow and R. A. Bazley, 'Geology of the country round Royal Tunbridge Wells', *Mem Geol Surv Great Britain* (1972)

G. Brodribb, 'Stamped tiles of the Classis Britannica', *Sussex Archaeol Collect 107* (1969), 102–25

G. T. Brown, 'A Roman bloom of iron from Cranbrook, Kent', *J Iron Steel Inst 202* (1964), 502–4

D. S. Butler and C. F. Tebbutt, 'A Wealden cannon-boring bar', *Post-Medieval Archaeol 9* (1975), 38–41

Calendar of Liberate Rolls, 2 (1930); 4–6 (1959–64)

Calendar of Memoranda Rolls (Exchequer), 1326–7 (1968)

Calendar of Patent Rolls, Edward III, 11 (1358–61) (1911)

R. H. Campbell, *Carron Company* (1961)

W. W. Capes, *Scenes of Rural Life in Hampshire* (1901)

C. S. Cattell, 'Preliminary research findings relating to the bloomery period of the iron industry in the upper basin of the eastern Rother (East Sussex), *Bull Hist Metall Group 4.1* (1970), 18–20

C. S. Cattell, 'A note on the dating of bloomeries in the upper basin of the eastern Rother', *ibid. 5.2* (1971a), 76

C. S. Cattell, 'An evaluation of the Loseley list of ironworks within the Weald in the year 1588', *Archaeol Cantiana 86* (1971b), 85–92

C. S. Cattell, 'Bloomeries in the upper (east) Rother basin', *Bull Wealden Iron Res Group 3* (1972), 13

C. S. Cattell, 'The historical geography of the Wealden iron industry' (MA thesis, University of London, 1973)

C. S. Cattell, 'The 1574 lists of Wealden ironworks', *Sussex Archaeol Collect 117* (1979), 161–72

J. A. Charles, 'The coming of copper and copper-base alloys and iron: a metallurgical sequence', in Wertime and Muhly 1980: 151–82

K. Chaudhuri, 'The East India Company and the organisation of its shipping in the early 17the century', *Mariners Mirror 49* (1963), 27–41

A. J. Clark, Note on Coneyhurst Forge, in *Ann rep Surrey Archaeol Soc* (1961), 6–7

H. F. Cleere, 'A note on Roman bloomery tuyeres', *Sussex Archaeol Collect 101* (1963a), 48–53

H. F. Cleere, 'Primitive Indian ironmaking furnaces', *Brit Steelmaker* (Apr. 1963b), 154–8

H. F. Cleere, *The Romano-British industrial site at Bardown, Wadhurst* (Sussex Archaeol Soc Occ Paper 1, 1970)

H. F. Cleere, 'Ironmaking in a Roman furnace', *Britannia 1* (1971a), 203–17

H. F. Cleere, 'Cyclical operations at Roman bloomeries', *Bull Hist Metall Group 5.2* (1971b), 74–5

H. F. Cleere, 'The classification of early iron-smelting furnaces', *Antiq J 52* (1972), 8–23

H. F. Cleere, 'The Roman iron industry of the Weald and its connexions with the Classis Britannica', *Archaeol J 131* (1975), 171–99

H. F. Cleere, 'Some operating parameters for Roman ironworks', *Inst Archaeol Bull 13* (1976), 233–46

H. F. Cleere, 'The Classis Britannica', in Johnstone 1977: 16–19

H. F. Cleere, 'Roman harbours south of Hadrian's Wall', in *Roman Shipping and Trade: Britain and the Rhine provinces*, ed. H. F. Cleere and J. du Plat Taylor (CBA Research Report no. 25, 1978), 36–40

H. H. Coghlan, *Notes on Prehistoric and Early Iron in the Old World* (Pitt Rivers Museum Occ Papers Techn 8, 1956)

D. C. Coleman, 'The economy of Kent under the later Stuarts' (Ph.D thesis, University of London, 1951)

T. S. Cooper, 'The will of Thomas Quennell, of Lythe Hill, Chiddingfold, yeoman, 1571', *Surrey Archaeol Collect 15* (1900), 40–50

J Cornwall, 'Lay Subsidy Rolls, 1524–5', *Sussex Rec Soc 56* (1956)

E. J. Courthope and B. E. R. Fermoy (eds.), 'Lathe Court Rolls and Views of Frankpledge in the Rape of Hastings', *ibid. 37* (1931)

D. W. Crossley, 'A sixteenth-century Wealden blast furnace: a report on excavations at Panningridge, Sussex, 1964–1970', *Post-Medieval Archaeol 6* (1972), 42–68

D. W. Crossley, 'Ralph Hogge's ironworks accounts, 1576–1581', *Sussex Archaeol Collect 112* (1974), 48–79

D. W. Crossley, *Sidney ironworks accounts 1541–1573*, Royal Historical Society: Camden Fourth Series 15 (1975a)

D. W. Crossley, *The Bewl Valley Ironworks* (1975b)

D. W. Crossley, 'Cannon-manufacture at Pippingford, Sussex: the excavation of two iron furnaces of c.1717', *Post-Medieval Archaeol 9* (1975c), 1–37

D. W. Crossley, 'A gun-casting furnace at Scarlets, Cowden, Kent', *ibid. 13* (1979), 239–49

D. W. Crossley, 'Medieval iron smelting', in D. W. Crossley (ed.), *Medieval Industry* (CBA Res Rep 40, 1981), 29–41

B. W. Cunliffe, *Fifth Report of the Excavations of the Roman Fort at Richborough, Kent* (Society of Antiquaries Research Report no.23, 1968)

B. W. Cunliffe, *Excavations at Fishbourne 1961–1969 – Vol 1: The Site* (Society of Antiquaries Research Report no.26, 1971)

B. W. Cunliffe, *The Regni* (1973)

C. D. Curtis, M. J. Pearson and V. A. Somogyi, 'Mineralogy, chemistry, and origin of a concretionary siderite sheet (clay-ironstone band) in the Westphalian of Yorkshire', *Mineralogical Mag 40* (1975), 385–93

C. D. Curtis, C. Petrowski and G. Oertel, 'Stable carbon isotope ratios in carbonate concretions: a clue to place and time of formation', *Nature 235* (1972), 98–100

J. R. Daniel-Tyssen, 'The Parliamentary Surveys of the County of Sussex, 1649–53, part 2', *Sussex Archaeol Collect 24* (1872), 189–287

H. C. Darby and E. M. J. Campbell, *The Domesday Geography of South-East England* (1962)

O. Davies, *Roman Mines in Europe* (1935)

R. H. D'Elboux, 'Surveys of the Manor of Robertsbridge', *Sussex Rec Soc 47* (1944)

H. G. Dines and F. H. Edmunds, 'The geology of the country round Reigate', *Mem Geol Surv Great Britain* (1933)

G. Duby, *Rural Economy and Country Life in the Medieval West* (1968)

H. S. Eales, *Frant, a Parish History* (1947)

H. Ellis, 'Inventories of goods etc.', *Sussex Archaeol Collect 13* (1861), 127–31

J. Evelyn, *Silva, or a discourse of forest trees* (2 vols, 1664)

A. Everitt, 'The marketing of agricultural produce', in J. Thirsk (ed.), *The Agrarian History of England and Wales*, IV (1967), 466–592

M. L. Faull and S. A. Moorhouse (eds.), *West Yorkshire: an Archaeological Survey to AD 1500* (1981)

A. J. Fletcher, *A County Community in Peace and War: Sussex, 1600–1660* (1975)

M. W. Flinn, *Men of Iron* (1962)

P. J. Fowler, 'Agriculture and rural settlement', in Wilson 1976: 23–48

A. Fox, 'Excavations at Kestor', Trans Devon Assoc 86 (1954), 21–62

D. J. Freke, 'The excavation of a 16th-century pottery kiln at Lower Parrock, Hartfield, East Sussex, 1977', Post-Medieval Archaeol 13 (1979), 79–126

S. Frere, Britannia (2nd edn, 1974)

J. Gibson-Hill, 'The excavation of a Romano-British iron working site at Broadfields, Crawley, West Sussex', Bull Inst Archaeol 12 (1975), 35–42

J. Gibson-Hill, 'Further excavations at the Romano-British iron-working site at Broadfields, Crawley', ibid. 13 (1976), 79–88

J. Gibson-Hill and B. C. Worssam, 'Analyses of Wealden iron ores and their archaeological significance', ibid., 13 (1976), 247–63

J. W. Gilles, 'Die Grabungen auf vorgeschichtlichen Eisenhüttenplätzen des Siegerlandes. Ihre Bedeutung und die hüttentechnischen Erfahrungen', Stahl Eisen 56 (1936), 252–63

J. W. Gilles, 'Versuchsschmelze in einem vorgeschichtlichen Rennofen', ibid. 78 (1958), 1690–5

J. W. Gilles, 'Rennfeuer in der römerzeitlichen Siedlung in Ahrweiler Wald', ibid. 80 (1960), 943–8

M. S. Giuseppi, 'The Manor of Ewood and the ironworks there in 1575', Surrey Archaeol Collect 17 (1902), 28–40

M. S. Giuseppi, 'Rake in Witley with notes on the ironworks on Witley and Thursley heaths', ibid. 18 (1903), 11–60

M. S. Giuseppi, 'The accounts of the iron-works at Sheffield and Worth in Sussex, 1546–1549', Archaeol J 69 (1912), 276–311

M. S. Giuseppi, 'Ironworks at Tudeley, Kent', Archaeologia 64 (1912–13), 145–64

E. S. Godfrey, The Development of English Glassmaking (1975)

J. J. Goring, 'Wealden ironmasters in the age of Elizabeth', in E. W. Ives et al. (eds.), Wealth and Power in Tudor England (1978), 204–27

J. L. M. Gulley, 'The Wealden landscape in the early 17th century and its antecedents' (PhD thesis, University of London, 1960)

W. U. Guyan, R. Pleiner and R. Fabešova (eds.), Die Versuchsschmelzen und ihre Bedeutung für die Metallurgie des Eisens und dessen Geschichte (1973)

A. F. Hallimond, 'Iron ores: bedded ores of England and Wales. Petrography and chemistry', Spec Rep Min Res Great Britain (Mem Geol Surv) 29 (1925)

G. F. Hammersley, 'The history of the iron industry in the Forest of Dean region, 1562–1660' (PhD thesis, University of London, 1972)

G. F. Hammersley, 'The charcoal iron industry and the fuel, 1540–1750', Econ Hist Rev, 2 ser, 26 (1973), 593–613

T. M. Harris, 'Burnt ferns from the English Wealden', Proc Geol Ass 92 (1981), 47–58

E. Hart and S. E. Winbolt, 'Thundersfield Castle, Horley: a medieval bloomery', Surrey Archaeol Collect 45 (1937), 147–8

J. Haslam, L. Biek and R. F. Tylecote, 'A Middle Saxon iron smelting site at Ramsbury, Wiltshire', Medieval Archaeol 24 (1980), 1–68

H. Hingst, 'Die vorgeschichtliche Eisengewinnung in Schleswig-Holstein', Offa 11 (1952), 28–37

Historical Manuscripts Commission, Report on the MSS of Lord De L'Isle and Dudley at Penshurst Place, I (1925)

C. Ho and J. M. Coleman, 'Consolidation and cementation of recent sediments in the Atchafalaya Basin', Bull Geol Soc Amer 80 (1969), 183–92

J. S. Hodgkinson, 'The carrier's accounts of Robert Knight, Part 1', Bull Wealden Iron Res Group 13 (1978a), 24–5

J. S. Hodgkinson, 'The carrier's accounts of Robert Knight, Part 2', ibid. 14 (1978b), 11–24

J. S. Hodgkinson, 'The Weale manuscripts', ibid. 16 (1979), 11–14

L. J. Hodson and J. A. Odell, Ticehurst (1925)

M. S. Holgate, 'Sussex Inquisitions', *Sussex Rec Soc 35* (1927)

R. Holinshed, *Chronicles of England* (1586)

W. Hudson, 'The three earliest subsidies for the County of Sussex, 1296, 1327, 1332', *Sussex Rec Soc, 10* (1909)

E. W. Hulme, 'Statistical history of the iron trade of England and Wales, 1717–1750', *Trans Newcomen Soc 9* (1928–9), 12–35

S. Jack, 'Sources for the history of the Wealden iron industry in the Public Record Office. Part 1: Inquisitions', *Bull Wealden Iron Res Group 17* (1980), 12–14

S. Jack, 'Sources in the Public Record Office for the history of the Wealden iron industry. Part 2', *ibid. 18* (1981), 7–11

S. Jack, 'Sources in the Public Record Office for the history of the Wealden iron industry. Part 3', *ibid. 19* (1982), 21–30

D. A. Jackson and T. Ambrose, 'Excavations at Wakerley, Northants, 1972–75', *Britannia 9* (1978), 151–66

M. A. Jackson and C. De Beer, *Eighteenth-century Gunfounding* (1973)

R. Jenkins, 'The rise and fall of the Sussex iron industry', *Trans Newcomen Soc 1* (1920–1), 16–33

R. Jenkins, 'Ironfounding in England, 1490–1603', *ibid. 19* (1938–9), 35–49

D. Johnstone (ed.), *The Saxon Shore* (CBA Res Rep 18, 1977)

D. K. C. Jones (ed.), *The Shaping of Southern England* (1980)

G. H. Kenyon, 'Wealden iron', *Sussex Notes Queries 13* (1952), 234–41, 321–2

G. H. Kenyon, 'Petworth town and trades', *Sussex Archaeol Collect 96* (1958), 35–107

L. L. Ketteringham, *Alsted: Excavation of a 13th–14th century sub-manor house with its ironworks in Netherne Wood, Merstham, Surrey* (Surrey Archaeol Soc Res Vol 2, 1976)

G. W. Lamplugh, C. B. Wedd and J. Pringle, 'Iron ores [contd] – Bedded areas of the Lias, Oolites and later formations in England', *Spec Rep Min Res Great Britain* (*Mem Geol Surv*) *12* (1920)

G. T. Lapsley, 'The account-roll of a fifteenth-century ironmaster', *Engl Hist Rev 14* (1899), 509–29

C. H. Lemmon, 'Fieldwork during the season 1952', *Trans Battle Dist Hist Soc* (1951–2), 27–9

Letters and Papers, Foreign and Domestic, Henry VIII, I–XXI.1 (1864–1908)

W. Llewellin, 'Sussex ironmasters in Glamorgan', *Archaeol Cambrensis*, 3 ser, 9 (1863), 81–119

G. W. E. Loder, *Wakehurst Place* (1907)

C. Lorenz (ed.), *Géologie des pays européens – France, Belgique, Luxembourg* (1980, Paris)

M. A. Lower, 'Iron works of the county of Sussex', *Sussex Archaeol Collect 2* (1849), 169–220

M. A. Lower, 'Iron works of the county of Sussex', *ibid. 3* (1850), 240–8

M. A. Lower, 'Sussex iron works and iron masters', *ibid. 18* (1866), 10–16

B. H. Lucas, 'The Bynes Farm Romano-British bloomery', *Sussex Notes Queries 13* (1950–3), 16–19

J. Malcolm, *A Compendium of Modern Husbandry* (1805)

I. D. Margary, 'Roman communications between Kent and the East Sussex ironworks', *Sussex Archaeol Collect 86* (1947), 22–41

I. D. Margary, *Roman Ways in the Weald* (1965)

P. Marsden, 'The County Hall ship, London', *Int J Naut Archaeol Underwater Explor 3* (1974), 55–65

P. Marshall (ed.), 'The diary of Sir James Hope, 1646', *Miscellany IX, Scot Hist Soc*, 3 ser, *50* (1958), 127–97

I. Martens, 'Some reflections on the classification of prehistoric and medieval iron-smelting furnaces', *Norwegian Archaeol Rev 11* (1978), 27–47

D. Mathew and G. Mathew, 'Iron furnaces in south-east England and English ports and landing-places', *Engl Hist Rev 48* (1933), 91–9

T. May, *Warrington's Roman Remains* (1904)

E. Melling, *Kentish Sources*, III (1961)

A. Miles, 'Bloomery slag at Lenham Heath, Kent', *Bull Wealden Iron Res Group 7* (1974), 8

J. H. Money, 'Medieval iron-workings in Minepit Wood, Rotherfield, Sussex', *Medieval Archaeol 15* (1971), 86–111

J. H. Money, 'Iron Age and Romano-British ironworking site at Minepit Wood, Rotherfield, Sussex', *J Hist Metallurgy Soc 8.1* (1974), 1–19

R. A. Mott, 'English bloomeries (1329–1589)', *J Iron Steel Inst 198* (1961), 149–61

J. E. Mousley, 'Sussex county gentry in the reign of Elizabeth' (PhD thesis, University of London, 1955)

J. E. Mousley, 'The fortunes of some gentry families of Elizabethan Sussex', *Econ Hist Rev*, 2 ser, 11 (1958–9), 467–83

J. Norden, *The Surveyor's Dialogue* (1610 edn)

A. Ohrenberger and K. Kaus (eds.), *Archäologische Eisenforschung in Europa* (1977, Eisenstadt)

S. L. Ollard, 'Dunsfold and its rectors', *Surrey Archaeol Collect 32* (1919), 1–33

P. J. Ovenden, *Bull Wealden Iron Res Group 5* (1973), 4

J. L. Parsons, 'The Sussex ironworks', *Sussex Archaeol Collect 32* (1882), 19–32

D. P. S. Peacock, 'Bricks and tiles of the Classis Britannica', *Britannia 8* (1977), 235–48

P. L. Pelet, 'L'architecture des fourneaux à fer primitifs, évolutions autonomes et tendances générales', in Ohrenberger and Kaus 1977: 173–80

R. A. Pelham, 'Studies in the historical geography of medieval Sussex', *Sussex Archaeol Collect 72* (1931), 154–84

J. Pettitt, 'Pushing back the frontier', *Bull Wealden Iron Res Group 6* (1973), 3

J. Pettitt, 'Maresfield powder mills, furnace and forge', *ibid.* 9 (1976), 19–21

H.-G. Pflaum, *Carrières procuratoriennes équestres sous le Haut-Empire* (1960–1, Paris)

B. J. Philp, *The excavation of the Roman forts of the Classis Britannica at Dover 1970–1977* (Kent Monograph Series no.3, 1981)

R. Pleiner, *Die Eisenverhüttung in der 'Germania Magna' zur römischen Kaiserzeit* (1965, Berlin)

R. Pleiner, 'Early iron metallurgy in Europe', in Wertime and Muhly 1980: 375–416

M. Prestwich, *Cranfield: Politics and Profit under the Early Stuarts* (1966)

C. Pullein, *Rotherfield: the Story of some Wealden Manors* (1928)

O. Rackham, *Ancient Woodland: its History, Vegetation and Uses in England* (1980)

E. J. B. Rathery, *Des Relations sociales et intellectuelles entre la France et l'Angleterre* (1856, Paris)

J. Ray, *A Collection of English Words not generally used . . .* (1674)

RIB: R. G. Collingwood and R. P. Wright, *Roman Inscriptions of Britain* (1965)

M. Richards, 'The Wealden iron industry' (PhD thesis, University of London, 1924)

A. L. F. Rivet, *Town and Country in Roman Britain* (2nd edn, 1964)

J. Rock, *Sussex Archaeol Collect 29* (1879), 168–74

M. Rostovtzeff, *The Social and Economic History of the Roman Empire* (2nd edn, rev. P. M. Fraser, 1957)

M. B. Rowlands, *Masters and Men in the West Midlands Metalware Trades before the Industrial Revolution* (1975)

L. F. Salzman (ed.), 'Post-mortem inquisitions relating to the county of Sussex, 1–25 Elizabeth', *Sussex Rec Soc 3* (1904)

L. F. Salzman, *English Trade in the Middle Ages* (1931)

L. F. Salzman (ed.), 'Ministers' accounts of the Manor of Petworth, 1347–53', *Sussex Rec Soc 55* (1955)

R. V. Saville, 'Some aspects of the role of government in the industrial development of England 1686–1720' (PhD thesis, University of Sheffield, 1978)

R. V. Saville, 'The missing half of a letter by John Fuller on the iron mines in the County of Sussex', *Bull Wealden Iron Res Group 16* (1979), 17–20

R. V. Saville, 'Income and production at Heathfield ironworks, 1693–1788', *ibid.*, 2 ser, *2* (1982), 36–62

H. R. Schubert, 'The northern extension of the Wealden iron industry', *J Iron Steel Inst 161* (1948), 245–6

H. R. Schubert, 'The superiority of English cast-iron cannon at the close of the sixteenth century', *ibid. 162* (1949), 85–6

H. R. Schubert, 'The economic aspect of Sir Henry Sidney's steelworks at Robertsbridge, in Sussex, and Boxhurst, in Kent', *ibid. 164* (1950), 278–80

H. R. Schubert, 'A Tudor furnace in Waterdown Forest', *ibid. 169* (1951), 241–2

H. R. Schubert, 'Early refining of pig iron in England', *Trans Newcomen Soc 28* (1951–3), 59–75

H. R. Schubert, 'The first English blast-furnace', *J Iron Steel Inst 170* (1952), 108–10

H. R. Schubert, *History of the British Iron and Steel Industry from c.450 BC to AD 1775* (1957)

W. Lindsay Scott, 'Excavation at Rudh' an Dunain cave, Skye', *Proc Soc Antiq Scotland 68* (1933–4), 200–23

R. B. Sharpe, *Calendar of Letter Books of the City of London* (1899)

E. R. Shephard-Thorn, J. G. O. Smart, G. Bisson and E. A. Edmonds, 'Geology of the country around Tenterden', *Mem Geol Surv Great Britain* (1966)

W. P. D. Stebbing, 'Subsoils in farming: the farmer and his mentors before William Smith', *Proc Geol Assoc 52* (1941), 257–72

E. Straker, 'Roman ironworks near East Grinstead', *Sussex Archaeol Collect 69* (1928), 183–5

E. Straker, *Wealden Iron* (1931a)

E. Straker, 'Leigh hammer', *Surrey Archaeol Collect 39* (1931b), 146–7

E. Straker, 'Westall's Book of Panningridge', *Sussex Archaeol Collect 72* (1931c), 253–60

E. Straker, 'The Buckhurst terrier', *Sussex Rec Soc 39* (1933)

E. Straker, 'A lost Tudor blast-furnace found', *Sussex Notes Queries 6* (1936–7), 217–18

E. Straker, 'Lost mills of the Medway', *Sussex County Mag* (1939), 531

E. Straker, 'The Vachery ironworks', *Surrey Archaeol Collect 47* (1941), 48–51

E. Straker and B. H. Lucas, 'A Roman-British bloomery in East Sussex', *Sussex Archaeol Collect 79* (1938), 224–32

E. W. Swanton and P. Woods, *Bygone Haslemere* (1914)

E. Swedenborg, *De Ferro* (1734, Dresden and Leipzig)

G. S. Sweeting, 'Geology of the country around Crowhurst', *Proc Geol Assoc 36* (1925), 410–18

G. Swift, 'Minepit surveys', *Bull Wealden Iron Res Group*, 2 ser, *2* (1982), 15–21

G. Swift and C. F. Tebbutt, *WIRG Newsletter*, no. 4 (1983)

R. H. Tawney and E. Power, *Tudor Economic Documents* (3 vols., 1924)

A. J. Taylor, 'Records of the Barony and Honour of the Rape of Lewes', *Sussex Rec Soc 44* (1939)

H. Taylor, 'Third report on Rowberrow Cavern', *Proc Spelaeol Soc 2* (1922–3), 40

J. H. Taylor, 'Sedimentary ores of iron and manganese and their origin', in *Sedimentary Ores Ancient and Modern (revised): Proc 15th Inter-Univ Geol Congr* (1969), 171–86

C. F. Tebbutt, *Bull Wealden Iron Res Group 5* (1973), 11

C. F. Tebbutt, 'The prehistoric occupation of the Ashdown Forest area of the Weald', *Sussex Archaeol Collect 112* (1974), 34–43

C. F. Tebbutt, 'An abandoned medieval industrial site at Parrock, Hartfield', *ibid. 113* (1975), 146–50

C. F. Tebbutt, 'Iron sites on Ashdown Forest', *Bull Wealden Iron Res Group 11* (1977), 9–13

C. F. Tebbutt, 'The excavation of a 'bell-pit' in Benzells Wood, Herstmonceux, Sussex', *ibid. 14* (1978), 6–7

C. F. Tebbutt, 'The excavation of three bloomery furnaces at Hartfield, Sussex', *Sussex Archaeol Collect 117* (1979), 47–56

C. F. Tebbutt, 'Wealden bloomery iron smelting furnaces', *ibid. 119* (1981), 57–64

C. F. Tebbutt, 'A Middle Saxon iron-smelting site at Millbrook, Ashdown Forest, Sussex', *ibid. 120* (1982), 19–36

C. F. Tebbutt and H. F. Cleere, 'A Romano-British bloomery at Pippingford, Hartfield', *ibid. 111* (1973), 27–40

J. Thirsk (ed.), *The Agrarian History of England and Wales, IV, 1500–1640* (1967)

T. Thorpe, *Battle Charters* (1835)

R. G. Thurrell, G. A. Sergeant and B. R. Young, 'Chamosite in Weald Clay from Horsham, Sussex', *Rep Inst Geol Sci no.70/7* (1970)

H. C. Tomlinson, 'Wealden gunfounding: an analysis of its demise in the eighteenth century', *Econ Hist Rev, 2 ser, 29* (1976), 383–400

H. C. Tomlinson, *Guns and Government: the Ordnance Office under the Later Stuarts* (1979)

W. Topley, 'The geology of the Weald', *Mem Geol Surv Great Britain* (1875)

R. M. Towes, 'The casting of bronze guns in the Weald in the seventeenth century', *Bull Wealden Iron Res Group 11* (1977), 15–20

R. F. Tylecote, *Metallurgy in Archaeology* (1962)

R. F. Tylecote, 'Ores, slags and metals from Panningridge', in Crossley 1972: 66–8

R. F. Tylecote, *A History of Metallurgy* (1976)

R. F. Tylecote, J. N. Austin and A. E. Wraith, 'The mechanism of the bloomery process in shaft furnaces', *J Iron Steel Inst 209* (1971), 342–63

R. F. Tylecote and E. Owles, 'A second-century iron-smelting site at Ashwicken, Norfolk', *Norfolk Archaeol 32* (1960), 142–62

J. Upton, 'Catsfield furnace: a new discovery', *Bull Wealden Iron Res Group, 2 ser, 1* (1981), 16–17

Victoria County History: Kent, III (1932), 384–9

Victoria County History: Surrey, II (1905), 263–76

Victoria County History: Sussex, II (1907), 241–9

S. P. Vivian (ed.), 'The manor of Etchingham cum Salehurst', *Sussex Rec Soc 53* (1953)

L. E. Webster and J. Cherry, 'Medieval Britain in 1974', *Medieval Archaeol 19* (1975), 259–60

T. A. Wertime and J. D Muhly (eds.), *The Coming of the Age of Iron* (1980)

H. J. O. White, 'The geology of the country near Lewes', *Mem Geol Surv Great Britain* (1926)

L. G. Wickham Legg, 'A relation of a short survey of the Western Counties', *Camden Third Series, 52* (1936): *Miscellany 16*, 1–128

T. S. Willan, *The English Coasting Trade, 1600–1750* (1938)

T. S. Willan, *The Muscovy Merchants of 1555* (1953)

J. H. Williams, *St Peter's Street, Northampton: Excavations 1973–1976* (1979)

L. J. Williams, 'A Carmarthenshire ironmaster and the Seven Years War', *Business Hist 2* (1959), 32–43

D. M. Wilson (ed.), *The Archaeology of Anglo-Saxon England* (1976)

S. E. Winbolt, 'Excavations at Saxonbury Camp', *Sussex Archaeol Collect 71* (1930), 222–36

S. W. Wooldridge and D. L. Linton, *Structure, Surface and Drainage in South-East England* (1955)

B. C. Worssam, 'Iron ore workings in the Weald Clay of the western Weald', *Proc Geol Assoc* 75 (1964), 529–46

B. C. Worssam, 'Iron ore workings near Horsham, Sussex, and the sedimentology of the Wealden Clay ironstone', *ibid.* 83 (1972), 37–56

B. C. Worssam, 'A new look at river capture and at the denudation history of the Weald', *Rep Inst Geol Sci* no.73/17 (1973)

B. C. Worssam and J. Gibson-Hill, 'Analyses of Wealden iron ores', *J Hist Metallurgy Soc* 10 (1976) 76–82

H. A. Wyndham (4th Baron Leconfield), *Petworth Manor in the Seventeenth Century* (1954)

A. Yarranton, *England's Improvement by Land and Sea* (1677)

E. M. Yates, 'The iron furnace and forge in Rogate', *Sussex Notes Queries* 14 (1955), 82–5

Index

Index compiled by Lyn Greenwood

All place-names have been indexed as most locations are mentioned in the text as well as in the Gazetteers. For a resumé of the site and its location, readers should go directly to the Gazetteers: the content of the entries in the Gazetteers has not been indexed.